Preserving Summer's Bounty

Preserving Summer's Bounty

A Quick and Easy Guide to Freezing, Canning,
Preserving and Drying What You Grow

EDITED BY SUSAN MCCLURE
AND THE STAFF OF THE RODALE FOOD CENTER

Rodale Press
Emmaus, Pennsylvania

Parts of this book have been adapted from *Stocking Up III, Rodale's Garden-Fresh Cooking, The Healing Foods Cookbook, Prevention's Quick and Healthy Low-Fat Cooking,* and *New Vegetarian Cuisine,* all published by Rodale Press, and from *Cooking with Herb Scents,* published by Western Reserve Herb Society.

Library of Congress Cataloging-in-Publication Data

Preserving summer's bounty : a quick and easy guide to
    freezing, canning, preserving, and drying what you grow /
    edited by Susan McClure and the staff of the Rodale Food
    Center.
          p. cm.
    Includes bibliographical references (p.   ) and index.
    ISBN 0–87596–648–9 (hardcover)
    1. Vegetables—Preservation. 2. Fruit—Preservation.
3. Cookery (Vegetables) 4. Cookery (Fruit)
I. McClure, Susan. II. Rodale Food Center
TX612.V4P74 1995   94–45012
641.4—dc20   CIP

ISBN 0–87596–979–8 paperback

Distributed in the book trade by Macmillan

12   14   16   18   20   19   17   15   13   paperback

RODALE
LIVE YOUR WHOLE LIFE™

We inspire and enable people to improve their lives and the world around them
For more of our products visit **rodalestore.com** or call 800-848-4735

To everyone who loves
garden-fresh food.
We hope this book inspires you to
enjoy the pleasures of summer's bounty
throughout the year.

Contents

Part One: Using What You Grow

Part Two: Recipes from the Garden

Acknowledgments

W HAT FUN it's been to organize *Preserving Summer's Bounty*! I've enjoyed working with these great recipes and hustling up these helpful harvest hints. Part of the fun has been working with the talented people who've contributed to this book. I want to thank Ellen Phillips, Rodale Garden Books editor; JoAnn Brader, Rodale Test Kitchen manager; Nancy Zelko, food researcher for the Rodale Test Kitchen; Anita Hirsch, Rodale Food Center nutritionist; Dr. Kenneth Hall, professor of Nutritional Sciences and extension food scientist for the University of Connecticut; Sharron Coplin, food and nutrition specialist with the Ohio State University Extension Service; and Dr. Judy Harrison, Cooperative Extension food agent at the University of Georgia. I'm also extending a special thanks to Donna Agan, editor of *Cooking with Herb Scents*, and to all of the members of the Western Reserve Herb Society who contributed herb tea recipes. Thank you one and all!

—Susan McClure

How to Use
This Book

WHEN YOUR HARVEST comes in, turn to *Preserving Summer's Bounty* for all the answers about what to do with all those ripe, delicious fruits and vegetables. Look in Part 1, "Using What You Grow," for easy-to-follow explanations of preserving processes and techniques. We will take you step-by-step through the more complex projects, such as canning, with no-fail details. For simpler jobs, such as making dried zucchini chips, you'll learn how and why different methods work, along with plenty of time-saving tips.

In Chapter 1, you'll find each vegetable and fruit listed alphabetically for easy reference. Each entry provides keys to ripeness, how to harvest, how to store produce until you're ready to use it, plus at-a-glance guides to how to preserve it. There are also harvest hints, recommended cultivars, creative cooking ideas—even safety tips.

Chapters 2 through 8 tell you how to freeze, can, preserve, pickle, dry, juice, and store crops in a root cellar. Each chapter works this way: First, it explains how a particular preservation process like canning works. Then it lists the supplies and equipment you'll need so you can gather everything together before you dive headlong into a task. Next, you'll find information on general procedures—the kind of background details that often are missing in recipes but are essential for success. Finally, you'll get the specifics, such as step-by-step instructions, timetables, and conversion charts.

Part 2, "Recipes from the Garden," presents over 200 health-conscious recipes to help you use what you've grown and stored away. Refer to it for ideas about how to make wholesome, delicious vegetable and fruit dishes or fast, crowd-pleasing salads, casseroles, herb mixes, desserts, and teas. You may be surprised by all the delicious ways you can use homegrown produce.

Preserving Your Garden's Bounty

IF THERE'S ANYTHING BETTER than growing harvest-fresh produce, it's storing some away for a cold or rainy day. The delicious flavors of sun-ripened fruits and additive-free vegetables will delight you while the garden is in full production—and much, much later, when it is safely put to bed. While others are settling for store-bought, you'll be savoring your garden's bounty.

Storing what you harvest takes a little time while the garden is producing heavily, but it saves you time later. Then your jars, freezer containers, and dried mixes will be right where you need them—at your fingertips. And putting up your harvest isn't complicated—not with the clear, step-by-step instructions in this book. Freezing, canning, preserving, pickling, drying, juicing, and root cellaring—it's all here in *Preserving Summer's Bounty*, along with hundreds of wholesome, mouthwatering recipes featuring your stored fruits and vegetables.

If you don't have the leisure time to linger in the kitchen—don't worry. We've made *Preserving Summer's Bounty* user-friendly. We have plenty of quick recipes (along with a few that take a little longer but are really delicious for those days when you have a little extra time). Look for new, faster, and better ways to deal with old cumbersome jobs like making tomato sauce and cooking down fruit butter plus convenient methods for pickling and root cellaring.

Many recipes are tailored for smaller families, who may not have the room to stockpile mountains of canned goods but would like to enjoy the full flavor of homegrown herbal mixes or the savory pungency of herb mustard. And throughout the book, we use surefire procedures, natural ingredients, and delightful recipes, all approved by the Rodale Food Center.

With *Preserving Summer's Bounty*, you also can use extras from your garden to produce gourmet combinations, convenience foods, extra-nutritious dishes, money-saving staples, and special diet options—with just a whirr of your food processor and hum of a microwave. You'll find that your homemade sauces, soups, and salads are so tempting that you won't have any trouble eating the minimum five servings of fruits and vegetables a day recommended by the U.S. Department of Agriculture (USDA). It's a great way to eat well without worrying about extra pounds.

So, don't wonder what to do with the bushels of beans, towers of tomatoes, and zillions of zucchini your garden produces one minute longer. Save it and savor it—with help from *Preserving Summer's Bounty*.

PART ONE

USING WHAT YOU GROW

CHAPTER ONE

A Guide to Harvesting Vegetables, Fruits, and Herbs

YOU'VE GOT your own garden, and that's great! Gardening provides fun, exercise, and, best of all, produce that you can use in hundreds of ways. You no longer need to be captive to the whims of the market—you can grow what you like best and eat it harvest-fresh, chemical-free, and untouched by additives. You can enjoy your favorite kinds of corn or beans as well as unusual things, such as Japanese pears or heirloom 'Moon and Stars' watermelons.

Growing your own produce lets you take charge of the harvesting process. Pick fruits and vegetables when their quality is at its very best and they have reached the right stage of maturity for eating, canning, freezing, or drying. Then, you don't have to lose any time getting the food from the ground into safekeeping.

Sometimes you can organize the garden so that produce will ripen when it is convenient for your use—and sometimes you can't. Most people can't control when their apples, berries, peaches, and pears will be mature. Once planted, fruit trees and berry plants will bear their fruit year after year when the time is right. You're at their mercy and must be prepared to harvest just when the pickings are ready if you want to get the fruit at its best.

Growing for Harvest

Vegetables are a different story. Because most are annuals and bear a certain number of weeks after they are planted, you can plan your garden to allow for succession plantings that extend the harvesting season and furnish you with a continuous supply of fresh food. This means that you can eat fresh vegetables over several smaller harvests if you wish (and the weather cooperates) and be able to preserve small batches as different waves of vegetables ripen.

By planting three smaller crops of tomatoes instead of one large crop, you won't be deluged with more tomatoes than you can possibly eat and process at one time. Or you can space your three pea plantings ten days apart in early spring, and you'll have three harvests of peas and plenty of time to plant a later crop of something else in the same plots after you pick all the peas.

Plant vegetables that don't keep well, like salad greens, at least twice. Start with early lettuce about a month before the last frost and follow it with cauliflower. After the onions are out of the ground, put some fall lettuce in their place for September salads. If corn is one of your favorites and you've been waiting out the long winter for the first ears to come in, by all means, eat all the early-maturing corn you want. But make sure that you plant enough late corn for freezing later on.

Harvest as late as possible in fall when you grow vegetables that keep well in underground storage—crops like cabbage, potatoes, root crops, and squash. You won't have to worry about keeping vegetables cool during warm September and early October weather. Green and yellow beans, planted in early May, can be followed by cabbage in mid-July for a fall harvest. You can leave some vegetables, like parsnips and Jerusalem artichokes, right in the ground over the winter. So plant some late crops of these vegetables specifically for this purpose.

Time your harvests so you pick each fruit and vegetable at perfection. Zucchini (top) that has been left on the vine too long is unfit for anything but puree. Tender young zucchini are perfect for fresh eating sliced in salads or stir-fries and make delicious pickles. Beets (bottom) left in the ground too long become tough and woody, but baby beets are at the ideal stage for canning, freezing, or pickling.

AN HEIRLOOM HARVEST

When you are looking for new crops for your garden or orchard, don't overlook heirloom fruits and vegetables. These are plants that have been passed down for generations by families and cultures around the world. Many have special qualities like different flavors, unique colors, or extra-long storage capacity. Most are open-pollinated, which means that the harvest time will vary somewhat and you will have fresh produce over a longer period of time. Browse through the small sampling of cultivars that follows to get a brief taste of what heirlooms are all about.

Heirloom Vegetables

- Beans, green: 'Blue Coco' snap bean, which originated in pre–1775 France, has purple pods and grows well in hot, dry weather.

- Beans, lima: 'Cliff Dweller' lima bean, from the ancient Apache culture, tolerates heat and drought and produces light-colored seeds splashed with dark highlights.

- Beets: 'Chioggia', an early Italian beet, is striped with alternating rings of red and white flesh.

- Carrots: 'Oxheart' carrot, introduced in 1884, grows short and thick, which makes it good for heavy soils and root-cellar storage.

- Eggplant: 'Turkish Italian Orange' eggplant, from Turkey, produces small, round, red-orange fruit that is mild and prolific.

- Lettuce: 'Oakleaf' lettuce, which originated in the 1800s, has handsome oak-shaped leaves with wavy margins. 'Rouge D'Hiver', a romaine lettuce from nineteenth-century France, has bronze leaves and solid heads. It thrives in cool and warm weather.

- Pumpkins: 'Small Sugar' pumpkin, a favorite of American pioneers from 1860, is sweet, firm, and tender, perfect for pies or any kind of cooking.

- Tomatoes: 'Big Rainbow' tomato, a mammoth-fruited plant from Minnesota, has green, yellow, and red skin and red-and-yellow-streaked flesh.

Heirloom Fruits

- Apples: 'Black Gilliflower', discovered in eighteenth-century Connecticut, ripens so dark red that it looks black. It's excellent for drying and cooking. 'Grosse Mignonne', sold as early as the mid-1600s, has greenish white, extra-juicy fruit. 'Sauvignac', introduced in the mid-1800s near Quebec City, Canada, is hardy to –50°F.

- Currants: 'White Imperial', brought to America in the late 1800s, has transparent white fruit and is more flavorful than any other currant.

- Pears: 'Seckel', grown in Europe since 1790, has small brown fruit with exceptional sweetness.

- Watermelons: 'Moon and Stars' watermelon, grown by the Amish for over 80 years, has red flesh and a green rind speckled with yellow stars and a large golden moon. ❖ ❖ ❖

 # Handling the Harvest

One of the biggest advantages of growing your own produce—or picking it garden-fresh in a friend's yard—is that you can handle it with care. Then everything you pick at the moment of ideal ripeness will be perfect for preserving. You'll understand how important harvest treatment is when you know a little about what happens to fruits and vegetables after harvesting.

Once plucked from the plant, fruits and vegetables stop growing, but respiration and enzyme activities (which add up to

WHERE TO FIND HEIRLOOM VEGETABLES AND FRUITS

To locate the long-lost tomato your grandmother used to grow or to browse for something different to try, check out the *Garden Seed Inventory,* published by the Seed Saver's Exchange. This 500-page volume lists thousands of different plants and gives brief descriptions and sources for each. A good resource for finding heirloom fruit cultivars is the *Fruit, Berry and Nut Inventory,* which lists all cultivars of fruiting trees and bushes available today, along with where to buy them. This 500-page book is also available through the Seed Saver's Exchange.

If you want to sample heirloom apples so you can decide which cultivars to grow, you can order a boxful from Applesource, 1716 Apple Road, Chapin, IL 62628 (applesource.com).

Catalogs That Specialize in Heirlooms

You may not be able to find heirloom vegetable seeds in garden centers, but these days they are showing up in large seed and nursery catalogs. You'll find an even bigger selection of cultivars in specialized heirloom catalogs such as the ones in the following list. Some of these companies charge a fee for their catalogs, so write first.

Abundant Life Seeds
P.O. Box 279
Cottage Grove, OR 97424
abundantlifeseeds.com

Hidden Springs Nursery
170 Hidden Springs Lane
Cookville, TN 38501
hiddenspringsnursery.com

Native Seeds/SEARCH
526 N. 4th Avenue
Tucson, AZ 85705
nativeseeds.org

One Green World
28696 S. Cramer Road
Molalla, OR 97038
onegreenworld.com

Redwood City Seed Company
P.O. Box 361
Redwood City, CA 94064
ecoseeds.com

Seed Saver's Exchange
3094 North Winn Road
Decorah, IA 52101
seedsavers.com

Seeds of Change
P.O. Box 15700
Santa Fe, NM 87506-5700
seedsofchange.com

Sonoma Antique Apple Nursery
4395 Westside Road
Healdsburg, CA 95448
applenursery.com

Southern Exposure Seed Exchange
P.O. Box 460
Mineral, VA 23117
southernexposure.com

Southmeadow Fruit Farms
P.O. Box 211
Baroda, MI 49101
southmeadowfruitgardens.com

RIPE CHERRIES

UNRIPE CHERRIES

Ripe fruits like these cherries (top) are best for canning, while unripe fruits (bottom) have more pectin and make better jellies.

aging) continue. The physical and chemical qualities deteriorate rapidly. As a result, appearance and flavor fade, and the nutrient content decreases, particularly fragile vitamin C.

Keeping Fruits and Vegetables Fresh

Fruits and vegetables should be prepared and canned or put into the freezer, dryer, or cold storage as soon as humanly possible after harvest. But despite our best intentions, distractions and delays are a part of life. If you find some of them getting in the way of your garden-to-storage routine, at least take precautions: Cool your food right after you pick it. Move foods into the refrigerator, except for tomatoes and basil.

Tomatoes and basil actually lose flavor or quality in low refrigerator temperatures. If you have more of these items than you can eat right away, process them immediately, while all the other vegetables and fruits are chilling. Or put the basil in a glass of water like cut flowers, and leave the tomatoes out of the sun on the kitchen counter for a few hours until you have time to deal with them.

Fruits and vegetables are at their best when you first pick them. And no storage technique, no matter how good it is, will make a great food out of so-so fruits or vegetables. The most that you can expect is to preserve most of the goodness that the food first started with. If you've taken the effort to grow good food, you owe it to yourself to make the extra effort to harvest it at the right time and get it into proper storage as soon as you can.

SOURCES OF MODERN GARDEN SEEDS

There are so many seed catalogs out there, it's hard to choose. You'll develop your own favorites after a few seasons, but these will get you off to a good start.

W. Atlee Burpee & Co.
300 Park Avenue
Warminster, PA 18974
burpee.com

The Cook's Garden
P.O. Box C5030
Warminster, PA 18974
cooksgarden.com

Irish Eyes Garden City Seeds
5045 Robinson Canyon Road
Ellensburg, WA 98926
irish-eyes.com

Johnny's Selected Seeds
955 Benton Avenue
Winslow, ME 04901
johnnyseeds.com

Nichols Garden Nursery
1190 Old Salem Road NE
Albany, OR 97321
nicholsgardennursery.com

Park Seed Company
Parkton Avenue
Greenwood, SC 29647
parkseed.com

Renee's Garden Seeds
6116 Highway G
Felton, CA 95018
reneesgarden.com

A Crop-by-Crop Guide to Harvesting Vegetables, Fruits, and Herbs

Here are tips on when to harvest many of your favorite crops and highlights about some of the best cultivars you might want to grow. You'll find handy long-term preservation ideas listed as symbols beside each entry as follows:

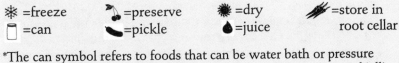

❋ =freeze   🍒 =preserve   🌼 =dry   ⚡ =store in

⬚ =can   🥒 =pickle   💧 =juice   root cellar

*The can symbol refers to foods that can be water bath or pressure canned. The preserve symbol refers to food made into jams and jellies.

Vegetable and Herb Harvesting Guide

Artichokes ❋ ⬚ 🥒

Harvest artichokes when the buds are tender and full but the bracts are still closed. You've waited too long once the bracts turn purple and the flowers begin to form. Use pruning shears or a sharp knife to cut off the bud and 4 to 6 inches of the stem, which can be edible, too. You'll harvest the large central bud on each stem first. It will be followed by side buds if your growing season is long enough. Don't be surprised if your artichokes don't bloom the first year—they're perennials, so it takes them a while to get going. Even if they do, don't harvest until the second year to allow the plants time to establish themselves.

You can grow artichokes even if you live in a cold climate where perennial cultivars aren't hardy. Try 'Imperial Star', a high-yielding annual.

Asparagus ❋ ⬚ 🥒 🌼

In cool climates, wait until the third year after planting to begin harvesting asparagus. But in warmer areas, you can harvest lightly the second year after planting. When tight-headed spears reach 6 to 10 inches tall, twist or cut them off just below soil level. On mature plantings, you can harvest for six to eight weeks in spring.

For high yields, grow 'Jersey Knight' and 'SYN 4-56' (formerly 'Jersey Giant'). Because these cultivars seldom include female plants, they can produce several times the number of spears of older cultivars. For warm climates, try 'UC 157'.

Basil ❋ 🌼

Keep basil flower heads pinched off for the most flavorful leaves. Pinch off shoot tips when you need a little basil. Or cut stems back by one-half their total length if you want to preserve some of this spicy herb.

Sources of Fresh Produce

If you don't have your own garden, or if you need to supplement what your garden grows, here are other ways to get ultrafresh produce.

- Place a special order with a local farm market. Have them pick a blend of fully or partly ripe items—as you request—early in the morning and you'll still have the day to preserve the food.

- Harvest at a pick-your-own organic orchard or garden. If you have several cultivars to choose from, ask which is best for the type of preserving you have in mind.

- Subscribe to Community-Supported Agriculture. For a fee, you'll get a regular supply of fresh produce and, maybe, rights to harvest produce.

- Ask gardening friends, relatives, and neighbors to call you if they anticipate overabundant harvests. Then you can pick what you need before it gets overgrown or aged.

- Support your local farmers' market. Find out which stalls actually grow what they sell and establish a good relationship with them. You might persuade them to let you know what produce they expect to have the following week so you are able to make plans for preserving accordingly.

- Put an ad in a school, church, or organization bulletin asking to share the costs and work of a garden for harvesting privileges. ❖ ❖ ❖

Grow 'Dark Opal' basil for making red herb vinegars. With its showy purple leaves, it's attractive in your flower beds, too.

Beans, Dried ❄ ▯ ☀ ✺

If you plan to dry beans and store them, delay harvest until the seeds are so dry you can't dent them with your thumbnail. But if the weather turns wet, pick them all, and let them finish drying outdoors. Experiment with the many interesting heirloom dried bean cultivars such as 'Vermont Cranberry', 'Jacob's Cattle', 'Logan Giant', and 'Rattlesnake'. Or try ethnic favorites such as 'Mexican Black Turtle' and Japanese 'Adzuki Express'.

Beans, Fava ❄ ▯ ➴ ☀

Harvest plump, unblemished pods of fava beans when very young and eat them like snap beans. Freeze or can them like snap beans, too. Or, wait until the bean seeds start to swell in the pods. Harvest and eat as is, or wait until they reach full size, but remove the outer skin that surrounds the mature seed. You also can let the mature beans dry in the pod or indoors in a dehydrator.

Beans, Green and Yellow ❄ ▯ ➴ ☀

Harvest most snap beans when the seeds are barely visible and the pods are as wide as a pencil, about one to two weeks after the blos-

Creative Cooking

DRIED BEANS

Spice up dried beans when you've almost finished cooking them by adding garlic, ginger, and low-sodium soy sauce. Or try rosemary and finely grated orange rind. Another good combination for beans is caraway seeds, dry mustard, and paprika. ❖ ❖ ❖

soms appear. The length of the pod—and occasionally the width—will vary according to the cultivar. Check the seed packet or catalog description for details. Snap off pole beans just below the stem and you'll be able to pick again from the same spot later in the season. Bush beans yield only one harvest, so it doesn't matter where you snap the pod from the bush.

You also can wait to harvest beans until the bean seeds mature and the pod begins to thin. Shell the beans, and cook or freeze them to enjoy a rich buttery flavor.

When preparing to freeze or dry snap beans, you need to blanch them in boiling water first. You'll know you've blanched long enough when 'Royal Burgundy Purple Pod' and 'Royalty Purple Pod' turn from purple to green.

Beans, Lima ❄ ▯ ✹

Harvest lima beans when the seeds are green and tender, just before they reach full size and plumpness. If you plan to dry the beans and store them, delay harvest until they are so dry that you can't dent them with your thumbnail. But if the weather turns wet, pick them all, and let them finish drying indoors.

Bush Beans

For a regular supply of bush beans all summer, stagger your plantings. Plant some seeds every couple of weeks through the first half of the growing season.

Pole Beans

By harvesting young pole beans promptly, you'll encourage bean plants to continue to produce. If you let the beans mature, productivity will decline.

Lima Beans

For an early start in cool-season areas, grow bush lima beans, such as 'Geneva' and 'Packer DM'. These cultivars are tolerant of cool soils. ❖ ❖ ❖

Beets

For most uses, harvest when the beets are 1½ to 2 inches in diameter. You can allow them to get a bit larger for root cellaring. To avoid damaging the roots, pull by hand rather than digging with a tool.

Beet greens are good for salads or steaming. Harvest them anytime throughout the season by taking a few outer leaves from each plant.

For pickling, try baby beets such as 'Little Ball'. For slicing, choose long (up to 8 inches) and slender 'Cylindra' or 'Formanova'. For root cellaring, grow 'Lutz Green Leaf' (also known as 'Winter Keeper'), 'Long Season', or 'Sweetheart'.

Broccoli

Harvest broccoli florets before the dark green blossom clusters begin to open and display yellow flowers. Side heads will continue to develop after you remove the central head until cold kills the plant.

For a big first harvest of broccoli, look for cultivars like 'Emperor' and 'Premium Crop' that bear a large central head. For a bountiful harvest of side shoots, try cultivars such as 'Green Valiant' and 'Saga'.

Brussels Sprouts

Harvest brussels sprouts when the sprouts reach full size and are firm but before they grow loose, yellow, and tough. Start at the bottom of the stem and work your way up as the sprouts mature. You can pick brussels sprouts for many months, even if temperatures go below freezing.

One of the most interesting brussels sprouts cultivars is 'Rubine', an heirloom with beautiful red sprouts and bluish leaves.

Cabbage

Use a sharp knife to cut off cabbage heads once they have formed and are firm but before they split open. If you leave a stub of stem on the plant, it may resprout for a second, small harvest. You'll have to be prompt about harvesting early cultivars, which pass peak maturity quickly, but you'll have more flexibility when picking some later cultivars. You can help prevent cabbage heads from splitting after a rain by using a spade to cut off roots on one side of the plant. Split heads won't keep long, so use them within a few days or make them into sauerkraut. (See "Sauerkraut Grandma's Way" on page 123.)

For winter root cellaring, grow late-maturing storage cultivars of cabbage such as 'Lasso', 'Perfect Ball', and 'Storage No. 4'.

Cabbage, Chinese

Harvest individual outer leaves of Chinese cabbage as you need them or cut off the entire plant after the head forms. Pull the plant up with the roots attached if you plan to store it in a root cellar.

Carrots

Carrots vary from 2 to 8 inches long, depending on the cultivar, so check the seed packet or catalog to see at what size yours mature. Then pull a sample root—one of the big ones with dark green leaves. The best carrot will be approaching its mature size and width and will have developed a rich orange color. To get carrots out easily, grab the greens near the ground and pull. If the soil is heavy, moisten it and loosen around the carrots with a trowel.

Baby carrots ideal for pickling or canning include 'Baby Spike', 'Lady Finger', 'Kinko', 'Planet', and 'Thumbelina'. For freezing or fresh use, try extra-sweet 'A-Plus Hybrid', 'Ingot', or 'Lindoro'.

Cauliflower and Broccoflower

Before you can harvest white-headed types of cauliflower, you'll have to give them a special blanching, or whitening, treatment. (Some cultivars are self-blanching, so check the catalog before ordering.) When these cauliflowers develop curds that are 2 to 3 inches in diameter, tie the outer leaves above the head to keep it creamy and mild-flavored. Heads will be ready to cut off the stalk 4 to 12 days after tying. Check them often. They

---

Creative Cooking

GREEN BEANS

For a delicious, easy vegetable, toss cooked green beans with dill seeds and a little butter.

LIMA BEANS

Puree cooked lima beans with garlic and spices for a quick sandwich spread or party dip.

BEETS

Shred beets and combine them with a small amount of lemon juice. Microwave for two or three minutes, stirring every minute. When just tender, rinse the beets, toss with vinaigrette, and refrigerate until ready to serve. ❖ ❖ ❖

should be full but not ricey, discolored, or blemished.

To avoid blanching cauliflower, grow self-blanching cultivars such as 'Amazing' and 'Ravella Hybrid'. Another option is to choose sweet, green-headed broccoflowers such as 'Alverda' and 'Cauli-Broc Hybrid' or a purple-headed cauliflower like 'Violet Queen', none of which need blanching.

Celery

To make celery stem bases cream-colored and mild-flavored, cover them with soil to blanch them for two to three weeks before harvesting. To harvest, slice off the stems at their base. Or lift the plants, roots and all, to encourage long keeping in a root cellar.

Chives ❋

Cut the leaves back to the base when you harvest chives. Take just a few leaves, or cut the entire plant back and let it resprout. Use the flowers to make a pretty lavender-colored herb vinegar.

GARLIC CHIVES

There's more to chives than purple pompon flowers—you can also grow garlic chives (*Allium tuberosum*). Garlic chives are very nice ornamental plants for the herb or perennial garden.

They have rich green, straplike leaves, clusters of rose-scented starry white flowers, and attractive black seedheads. (Don't leave the seedheads on the plant until they shatter, though, unless you want lots of volunteer seedlings.) As the name implies, garlic chives also have a delicious garlic flavor. ❖ ❖ ❖

Cilantro ❋

Harvest pungent-flavored cilantro leaves promptly, before the plants flower. For a longer growing season, plant a dozen cilantro seeds every couple weeks during cool weather.

Collard Greens

See "Kale and Collard Greens" on page 15.

Corn ❋

Snap corn ears off the stalk when the silks are dry and brown and the tips of the ears are full. If you pull back the husks, you'll see that the kernels are fully filled out. Then test to see if the kernels are in the milk stage, a time of maximum sweetness. In the milk stage, if you break a kernel open, whitish corn "milk" will flow out. Once corn gets past this stage, the kernels become doughy.

Harvest Hints

CORN

For an extended harvest of fresh corn, plant early, midseason, and late-maturing cultivars. ❖ ❖ ❖

Cook or preserve ordinary sweet corn immediately because the sugars break down quickly. If you want more time between picking and preserving and you enjoy very sweet corn, grow sugar-enhanced cultivars, which will stay sweet in the refrigerator for about a week because their sugar breaks down more slowly. Some sugar-enhanced corn cultivars are 'Bodacious' (yellow), 'Stardust' (white), 'Super Elite 181' (white), and 'Tuxedo' (yellow). Another new type of corn, the super-sweet cultivars, have twice as much sugar as regular sweet corn, so harvested ears keep even longer. But they can be difficult to germinate and must be separated from other kinds of corn. Super-sweet cultivars include 'Honey 'n Pearl' (bicolor) and 'How Sweet It Is' (white).

If you grow popcorn, let the corn mature on the ears until the husks become brown and dry. Unfortunately, getting the moisture content just right for popping can be tricky. So grow interesting ears with colored kernels, such as 'Baby Blue', 'Calico Popcorn', 'Little Jewels', 'Miniature Colored', or 'Pretty Pops', so you can enjoy them as decorations. Or you can grind them for cornmeal if they won't pop.

Cucumbers

Check your cucumber vines daily during the peak of the growing season so you can find fruit at the perfect stage of maturity. You want slicing cucumbers that are slender and dark green. Once they begin to turn a lighter color, they are past prime and can be watery and seedy. If you let them get to this stage, the vines will stop producing new cucumbers.

Judge when to harvest pickling cucumbers according to their size. You'll probably want to pick them when they're from 1 to 4 inches long, depending on the pickling recipe you're using. If they get bigger, you can still enjoy them as a salad cucumber. When you cut any kind of cucumbers off the stem, leave a little bit of stem on the fruit.

For a small garden, try bush cucumbers like 'Bush Pickle' or 'Salad Bush Hybrid'.

For unique and crunchy pickles, grow heirloom 'Lemon' cucumbers or tiny, 1- to 2-inch-long 'Cornichon' or 'Vert De Massy'.

Creative Cooking

CUKES

For quick appetizers, top cucumber slices with smoked salmon, cream cheese, and a sprig of dill. Or try a topping of cottage cheese, chopped toasted walnuts, and a sprig of fennel. ❖ ❖ ❖

Dill ❊ ☀

Grow dill for its fragrant leaves or seeds. Harvest the leaves one at a time, or cut the entire plant back. For seeds, wait until the heads are mature but not so ripe that the seeds scatter free.

Eggplant ❊ 🥒 ☀

You can pick eggplant from the time the fruits are small to when they near mature size, which varies according to cultivar. But don't wait until the fruits develop seeds and lose the gloss on the skin. Cut eggplant off the plant using a sharp knife or pruning shears. Leave a little bit of stem on the fruit.

In addition to the common, pear-shaped eggplant, you can grow cylindrical oriental types such as 'Ichiban Hybrid', 'Orient Express', and 'Pingtung Long', which are good for slicing. For pickling, look for baby eggplant like 'Little Fingers' and 'Pirouette'.

Endive

For the mildest flavor, blanch endive before harvesting. If you have some of the larger, slower-growing cultivars, such as 'Broad Leaf Batavian', tie the outer leaves together when the plants are 12 to 15 inches in diameter and the leaves are completely dry. Harvest the entire head in about three weeks. For smaller, quicker-growing endive cultivars, such as 'Neos', cover the plant with an upside-down pot for two to three days, then harvest. For root-cellar storage, pull the plant up, roots and all, before a hard freeze.

Garlic ❊ 🥒 ☀ ✏

Pull up garlic bulbs when the tops are dry and bent to the ground. Inside the bulbs, the cloves should still be inside their papery sheaths. Cure garlic bulbs like onions.

Herbs ❊ ☀

Ideally, you should harvest most herbs just before they are ready to blossom when their essential oils are at their peak. This is true of basil, lemon balm, marjoram, mint, oregano, rosemary, sage, savory, and thyme. But don't let this tip stop you from harvesting at other times of the year. You'll still get great flavor early or late in the season if you pick fresh, healthy-looking leaves. This is especially true of parsley (which doesn't flower the first year you grow it) and French tarragon (which never flowers). Harvest them whenever you need them. Herbs such as anise, caraway, and dill must flower to produce their flavorful seeds. Cut these seedheads when mature but before they dry and scatter to the ground. (For more details, see the individual herbs by name.)

Horseradish

Dig horseradish roots in spring or fall. Break or cut off what you need and replant the rest.

Jerusalem Artichokes

Dig Jerusalem artichoke tubers from the end of the summer through the winter; they'll taste sweetest if you wait until after a heavy frost. Cover the planting with a bale of hay if you want winter access in cold climates. Just harvest a few tubers at a time. Or, dig all the tubers in the fall, replant a few for next year, and store the rest in a root cellar.

Kale and Collard Greens

Pick leafy kale and collard greens individually for a small harvest, or cut back the entire plant for a big harvest. Both kinds of greens taste best after a light frost in fall. Harvest them early in the day when they are cool and crisp.

Kohlrabi

Harvest the swollen stem of kohlrabi when it becomes 2 to 3 inches wide. Pull the roots out or cut the ball off the roots if you don't want to disturb plants growing nearby.

Leeks

For a mild flavor and cream-colored base, hill soil up around the growing leek plant to cover the bottom 4 to 6 inches of the stem. You can harvest leeks young or let them grow a foot tall with stem bases from 1 to 2½ inches in diameter. Then dig or pull up the entire plant.

Creative Cooking

GARLIC

Use a little of your homegrown garlic to make this versatile vinaigrette. Mix 1 clove of minced garlic, 3 to 4 tablespoons red wine vinegar, ½ teaspoon Dijon mustard, and freshly ground pepper. Stir well, then slowly dribble in ½ cup olive oil, whisking all the while. Serve over salads or steamed vegetables. ❖ ❖ ❖

Lettuce

Harvest lettuce leaf by leaf as you need it, or cut off the entire head. Let leaf lettuce grow full and bushy, but harvest it before it stretches up to bolt. If the weather is cool and the soil is rich, it may sprout again. Harvest iceberg lettuce cultivars when they develop a round, firm head. Other kinds, such as 'Boston' and 'Butterhead', will have smaller and looser heads when they're full size.

Pick any lettuce early in the day when it is crisp and mild. Wash it thoroughly but briefly right after harvesting, then towel or spin dry to prevent vitamin loss.

Most of us think of lettuce as highly perishable, but some lettuce cultivars, such as 'Winter Density', can linger in a garden or cold frame deep into winter.

Marjoram, Sweet

Harvest sweet marjoram when in bud to add a slight spiciness and a lovely sweet fragrance to salad dressings and sauces.

Melons

See "Melons" on page 26.

Mesclun

Grow any greens that you like to combine in salads to harvest young as mesclun. Some favorites are arugula, chicory, cress, endive, lettuce, and parsley. When they are several inches tall, clip the leaves back to about ¾ inch above the ground. With a little fertilizer, they may sprout again.

Creative Cooking

BAKED ONIONS

Wrap large, unpeeled onions in foil and bake at 350°F for one hour. Serve with fish, meat, or poultry. ❖ ❖ ❖

Okra

Young okra pods are ready for harvesting just a few days after the flowers fall. At this stage, they will still be tender, but if you let them grow, they quickly become woody. Depending on the cultivar, prime pods will be 1 to 3 inches long.

For areas with short seasons, try an early okra cultivar like 'Annie Oakley II'. For a pretty change of pace, try red-fruited 'Burgundy' okra. It's handsome on the bush and will turn green when cooked.

Onions ❊ ▯ ➴ ☀ ⫽

You can thin young onions to serve as scallions, or let them mature to form bulbs large enough for slicing or cooking. The bulbs will be full size when the tops brown and fall over. Pull up the bulbs and spread them out separately to cure out of direct sunlight in a warm, dry place with good air circulation. After about two weeks of curing, they'll be ready for storage.

For winter root cellaring, grow firm, pungent storage onions like 'California Wonder Red', 'Copra', and 'Sweet Sandwich'. Sweet onions that don't keep a long time include 'Granex' and 'Walla Walla'—don't grow more than your family can eat in a month.

For pickling or canning, try small-bulbing onions such as 'Crystal Wax Pickling', 'Italian Button Onion', and 'Snow Baby'. Pull these bulbs when they are no bigger than 1 inch in diameter.

Oregano, Greek ❊ ☀

Trim off individual branches of this spreading herb, or trim the entire plant back by several inches. You can harvest super-spicy Greek oregano, the plant to buy for the "real" oregano flavor, before, during, or after flowering.

Parsley ❊ ☀ ⫽

Harvest outer leaves of parsley as needed, pinching or cutting the stems off at the base. You can continue to harvest parsley through the spring of its second year, before it bolts to seed.

Parsnips ❊ ☀ ⫽

Wait to harvest parsnips roots until after a heavy frost, which will give them a sweeter flavor. As long as the garden soil is well drained, you can leave parsnips in the ground all winter. Mulch with straw or a floating row cover for extra protection. Harvest parsnips early in the spring, before they start growing again.

Peas, Black-Eyed, Cow, Field, and Southern ❊ ▯ ☀

If you like peas you can freeze, can, or dry, and use in southern dishes, grow these relatives of the garden pea. The pods grow from

Creative Cooking

PEAS

Top cooked peas with minced, roasted red peppers. Or choose an herb topping like minced dill, marjoram, or mint. Another option is toasted sesame seeds.

PEPPERS

Puree ripe bell peppers to make a flavorful, low-calorie thickener for thin sauces.

POTATOES

Make flavorful, low-fat baked potato stuffings out of stir-fried sweet red peppers, sliced mushrooms, snow peas, minced ginger, and garlic. Or fill potatoes with chopped, steamed asparagus, toasted pinenuts, and minced garlic sautéed in olive oil and topped with grated Parmesan cheese. ❖ ❖ ❖

6 to 12 inches long, producing ten or more peas per pod. Harvest the pods when very young and eat like green beans. Let the seeds reach full size and eat them green like shelled peas. Or let them dry on the vine until the pods shrivel and the peas won't dent under your thumbnail. If the weather turns wet before the peas are entirely dry, finish drying them in a dehydrator or the oven.

Peas, Garden, Snap, and Snow ❄ ▯ ☀

Cut off garden peas or snap peas when the pods are firm and well filled. But don't wait until the seeds reach their fullest size or they won't be as sweet.

Pick snow peas earlier, before the pods fill out and get tough. If you harvest a little late, you can shell snow peas just like garden peas. Use or process peas immediately, before the sugars break down.

Peppers ❄ ▯ ⬥ ☀

You can pick peppers when they're young or when they're full size but still green. This encourages the plant to produce more young peppers. But you also can let peppers ripen completely and turn red, yellow, orange, or purple, their sweetest stage. But be careful—peppers can overripen quickly, so watch them closely.

For rainbow-colored pickled peppers, grow the cultivar 'Sweet Pickle'. It produces 2-inch-long red, orange, yellow, and purple peppers.

For hot peppers that dry easily, grow thin-fleshed 'Caliente', 'Cayenne', and 'Super Cayenne Hybrid'. For pickling, grow 'Early Jalapeño', 'Hungarian Wax', 'Jalapeño', 'Pepperoncini', and 'Serrano'.

Potatoes ❄ ▯ ☀ ⬥

If you want thin-skinned new potatoes, harvest small tubers when the potato vines begin to flower. But for storage, let the potatoes mature and the protective skin toughen after the vines die back. If the weather is warm and dry, you can let the tubers cure in the soil for two weeks after the vines die. If not, move them into a warm, dark, dry place indoors. (Always keep potatoes in total darkness. They develop toxic alkaloids, stored in green-colored flesh, when exposed to sunlight.)

Search seed and nursery catalogs for cultivars of red, pink, purple, blue, and golden potatoes. These flavorful small potatoes taste great, even without a lot of butter and sour cream.

Pumpkins and Winter Squash ❄ ▯ ☀ 🗡

Let all pumpkins and winter squash ripen fully on the vine. Their skin should be hard, not easy to puncture with your thumbnail. When you cut the fruit off the vine, leave a couple of inches of stem attached. Be sure you bring all winter squash and pumpkins indoors before a heavy frost, which could damage the skin and limit storage time.

Radicchio 🗡

Harvest radicchio heads when they are full and firm. With cultivars such as 'Giulio', you'll find the head growing down under the taller outer leaves (look closely). But with some cultivars, you'll have to coax the plants into heading up. Cut off all the leaves, and then the plant will resprout into a head.

Creative Cooking

PUMPKINS

Small- to medium-size pumpkins are more tender and better for baking.

WINTER SQUASH

Bake apples or pears along with winter squash. Then puree the fruit and use it in addition to the squash for a flavorful filling. ❖ ❖ ❖

Radishes

Harvest radishes according to bulb size. Pull quick-growing, globe-shaped or cylindrical radishes as soon as they produce a small bulb up to 1 inch in diameter. If you let them go longer, they'll get pithy inside. Or plant Japanese 'Daikon' radishes in summer, and harvest them in fall when they reach about 1 foot long and 3 inches wide. Heirloom winter storage types, such as 'Black Spanish' and 'China Rose', can get larger than quick-growing radishes and still stay firm. They also tolerate some frost, so you can harvest them in late fall and store them in the root cellar.

Rhubarb

See "Rhubarb" on page 29.

Rutabagas ❄ 🌿

Harvest rutabagas when the fleshy ball gets to be 4 inches wide. If possible, wait until it has been exposed to several light frosts, which makes the flavor sweeter, but avoid heavy frost. To harvest, pull up the plant and cut the leaves back to 1 inch long.

Sorrel, French ❄

Harvest the young tender leaves of French sorrel for using in salads in spring. Or pick slightly more mature leaves for sautéing into a flavorful lemony sauce in summer.

Soybeans, Green ❄ 🗋 ☀

Pick green soybeans when the pods are almost mature but still green. Keep an eye on the plants when they near this stage because they quickly pass prime. You also can let the beans dry on the vines. But be sure to harvest them before the stems turn brown and the beans fall out of the pods. It helps to lay a sheet of newspaper under the plants to catch any beans that come loose.

Spinach ❄ 🗋 💧

Pluck off individual outer leaves of spinach as you need them, or cut off the entire plant when it forms a full rosette. Harvest promptly—spinach bolts fast, especially as the weather warms up.

Squash

See "Pumpkins and Winter Squash" on page 19 and "Zucchini and Summer Squash" on page 22.

Creative Cooking

SORREL

Sauté 2 cups of sorrel leaves in a little butter over low heat. The leaves will melt into a lemony sauce for vegetables, pasta, fish, or poultry. ❖ ❖ ❖

Sweet Potatoes ❄ 🗋 ☀ 🌿

Harvest sweet potatoes in the fall near the time of the first frost but before the soil temperature drops to 55°F. Dig the tubers gently, using care not to damage the thin skins, and move promptly into a shady area to prevent sunburn. Cure for a week or two to help the skins toughen. When curing, keep sweet potatoes out of direct sun, but in 85° to 90°F temperatures and 80 to 90 percent humidity. One way to create this much warmth is by using solar energy. Lay the potatoes on a layer of black plastic and cover them with a second sheet of black plastic. But move them indoors if night temperatures get below 55°F.

Swiss Chard ❋

When the outer leaves reach 4 to 8 inches high, remove them as you need them, or cut the entire plant back and let it resprout.

Thyme ❋ ✺

Cut back shoot tips to harvest a little thyme. Or uproot whole sections of the plant to get larger harvests and prevent aggressive spreading.

Tomatillos ❋ ◻ ➘ ⫽

Harvest tomatillos when the fruits become sweet but pungent and turn yellow or purple, depending on the cultivar, but remain enclosed inside the husks.

Tomatoes ❋ ◻ ✺ ◆ ⫽

Let tomatoes ripen on the vine for best flavor. To use them for slicing or canning, harvest tomatoes when they're firm and red. When soft and extra ripe, the acidity levels can drop, making it risky to can them. You can make pickles and preserves out of green tomatoes. Or if they have streaks of pink among the green, you can let them ripen gradually on your kitchen counter. You can encourage them to ripen quickly by enclosing them in a paper bag with an apple.

For an extended season of fresh tomatoes, plant early, midseason, and late-ripening tomato cultivars. To encourage extra-early ripening, prune a tomato plant back to only one or two stems and tie the stems up to one or two stakes.

To save time when making tomato sauce, use dry-fleshed paste tomatoes such as 'Bell Star', 'Milano', 'Roma VF', and 'Viva Italia'.

Creative Cooking

TOMATOES

When fall frost is nearing and it's apparent that new tomato fruit won't have enough time to mature, pinch off all flower clusters and new fruits. By doing this, you allow the plant to direct all its energy to maturing existing fruit. Also, remove any leaves that are shading this ripening fruit. ❖ ❖ ❖

Creative Cooking

ZUCCHINI AND SUMMER SQUASH

Cut off the large golden male flowers of zucchini and summer squash to stuff or use in salads. (Leave one male flower per plant.)

Later in the season when you have an abundance of fruit, you can puree zucchini in a food processor and use the puree to replace milk in soups, stews, and casseroles. ❖ ❖ ❖

Turnips ✳ ☀ ⚚

Harvest turnips when they are young and tender, about 2 or 3 inches in diameter, or before the weather gets hot in late spring or early summer. In hot or dry weather, or at larger sizes, they'll get woody and bitter.

Watermelons

See "Watermelons" on page 30.

Zucchini and Summer Squash ✳ ▯ ➴

Harvest zucchini or summer squash when they're young, tender, soft-skinned, and without seeds. The size will vary according to the cultivar and what you intend to do with them. For salads and pickles, pick the fruit when it's 2 to 4 inches long. For sautéeing or stuffing, you can let squash get 5 to 6 inches long.

Summer squash come in an assortment of round, oval, cylindrical, long-necked, and scalloped shapes in many tints of green, gold, and cream. Grow a variety of cultivars for a little adventure.

Squash are favorites for preserving. Winter squash is a natural for root cellaring, while zucchini and summer squash are good frozen, canned, or pickled.

Fruit Harvesting Guide

Apples

Apples are ripe when they change to their mature red, yellow, or green color and remain firm. The taste should have the appropriate blend of sweetness and tartness typical of the cultivar you grow. Gently tug the apple free from the branch with the stem attached, which helps the apples keep longer. When ripe, the fruit should pull free without breaking the tree's fruiting spur.

Early-maturing apples may not store well. Use them promptly for freezing, canning, preserving, or juicing. Later apples such as 'Granny Smith', 'McIntosh', 'Northern Spy', and 'Winter Banana' (an heirloom variety) can be good candidates for root cellaring or storing anywhere that's humid and has temperatures around 33°F.

Apricots

Apricots develop full flavor if you let them ripen fully on the tree. They will turn dark gold or orange when ripe and should be soft but firm.

For a change of pace, try growing hybrid plumcots, which combine the flavors of apricots and plums.

Blackberries and Boysenberries

These berries need to ripen fully on the vine to become sweet and succulent. Wait to pick until they are easy to pull off the bush, usually a day or two after they turn black. Or harvest slightly underripe, reddish blackberries for preserves. Harvest in the cool of the morning and process as soon as possible to preserve fresh-picked flavor.

Blueberries

Wait several days to a week after berries turn a ripe shade of purplish blue, then sample one to see if it is soft and sweet enough. If so, harvest all the others that have the same color and texture. Leave the more immature berries until they're ripe.

Cherries

For freezing, canning, drying, or juicing, let cherries ripen fully, so they'll be sweet and juicy. You'll know the time is right if they

---

Harvest Hints

BLACKBERRIES

To save harvesting time and trouble, grow thornless blackberry cultivars like 'Navaho' and 'Thornfree'.

BLUEBERRIES

Enjoy fresh blueberries for as long as possible by planting early, midseason, and late-ripening cultivars. ❖ ❖ ❖

begin falling off the tree and the birds won't leave them alone. In fact, you may need to cover the tree with bird netting to get to this stage. If the cherries begin to split, you've waited too long.

For baking or preserving, you can harvest sour cherries before they are fully ripe. Pull cherries gently off the tree, stem and all, if possible; they'll store longer. If you can't get the stems loose without damaging the fruiting twigs, then pull the cherries off and leave the stems behind. Process the fruit right away.

Crabapples

If you happen to have a large-fruited crabapple on your property, you can harvest the fruits and use them for preserves. Pick them when the fruit turns its mature red, yellow, or pink color. (Check the catalog if you're not sure what color fruit your cultivar bears.)

Currants

For fresh eating or freezing, let currants grow very ripe and sweet. They will change to the mature red, black, or translucent white to yellow color that is typical of the cultivar. If you want them to have a higher pectin content for jelly, harvest slightly underripe.

Creative Cooking

GRAPES

- If you are canning grapes and don't want to mess around with seeds, you'll save a lot of time if you use seedless grapes such as 'Concord Seedless' (purple), 'Himrod Seedless' (white), 'Reliance Seedless' (red), or 'Remaily Seedless' (white).

- If you don't spray your grapevines, you can use the grape leaves for stuffing or pickling. ❖ ❖ ❖

Dates

As long as the weather is dry, you can let dates ripen on the tree. When ready, the skin will turn yellow-red or brown and the flesh will be sticky and sweet. But if the weather becomes wet, harvest nearly ripe dates promptly to keep them from spoiling.

Figs

Pick fruit that's not quite ripe daily. Ripen at room temperature for a day or two. Ripe figs are soft, and their skin may begin to split. Figs spoil easily but will keep for a week in the refrigerator. Store them in brown paper bags in closed containers.

Gooseberries

Gooseberries are ripe when they change to their mature color, which varies from pink to green depending on the cultivar. Let them

Creative Cooking

LEMONS

- Freeze lemon wedges in ice cubes to add to iced tea.
- Thin-skinned lemons are best for juice and lemon zest. Firm, thick-skinned fruits are best for marmalade. ❖ ❖ ❖

ripen on the bush for eating fresh, or harvest when slightly immature for preserves. Wear heavy gloves to avoid the spines.

Grapes ❋ ⬜ 🍒 ☀ 💧 ⚡

Grapes are ripe when the fruits become aromatic and sweet. Taste a few to be sure. Pick grapes in the morning, when they're cool. Cut off entire bunches with sharp shears. Handle the bunches of grapes by the stem so you won't damage the fruit.

Guavas ❋ 🍒 💧

Let guavas ripen on the tree for best flavor, or pick them slightly underripe for jellies. When mature, the skin will be white, yellow, or green; the flesh will be juicy and yellow, white, pink, or red, depending on the cultivar. Check the tree frequently for ripe fruit.

Kiwis ❋ 🍒

Hardy kiwis mature in late summer and ripen in autumn, becoming about 1 inch long and bright green. You'll know they are ripe because they'll be soft, juicy, and falling off the vine.

The less hardy fuzzy kiwi or Chinese gooseberry ripens to have firm, juicy green flesh wrapped in furry brown skin. Both kinds will store in the refrigerator for weeks.

If you only have room for one hardy kiwi vine, make sure you buy a cultivar like 'Issai' that is self-pollinating.

Lemons ❋ 🍒 🥒 ☀ 💧

Harvest lemons when they are juicy and mature. In subtropical areas, you can harvest lemons year-round. Those you pick in fall and winter usually keep better than those harvested in spring and summer.

The 'Spanish Pink' lemon, which has green-and-yellow-striped fruit and pink flesh, is the source of the original pink lemonade. It's also a lovely tree with variegated foliage and pink flowers.

Limes ❋ 🍒 ☀ 💧

Pick limes straight from the tree when the skin turns yellow-green to dark green, depending on the cultivar, and the flesh is juicy. You'll harvest acid (sour) lime cultivars primarily in winter, but watch the tree in other seasons for an occasional ripe lime. Sweet limes mature only in winter.

Melons ❄ 💧

Let melons ripen on the vine to become sweet and flavorful. Use one or several different tests to tell you when a melon is ripe. For muskmelons or cantaloupes, smell the fruit near the stem to see if it has a sweet odor. Look for a yellow tinge underneath the skin netting. Put pressure on the stem. When ripe, the stem will separate easily from the fruit.

To determine the ripeness of honeydew and most French Charentais melons, feel the blossom end. It should be springy. The stem end should smell sweet. On a honeydew, the skin color will change from green to cream, and it will lose its waxy look when ripe. Cut these types of melons off the vine since they don't slip free like muskmelons.

Mulberries ❄ 🍒 💧

For fresh eating, freezing, or juicing, let mulberries ripen fully on the tree until they turn succulent and sweet. They will mature to black, deep red, pink, or white, depending on the cultivar. Harvest mulberries slightly underripe for preserves.

If you look through catalogs from fruit tree nurseries, you'll find mulberry cultivars with extra-large, extra-abundant, or extra-flavorful fruit. It's worth the extra time and money to buy these cultivars—seedling mulberries can bear dry, flavorless berries.

Nectarines

See "Peaches and Nectarines" on the opposite page.

Oranges ❄ 🥫 🍒 ☀ 💧 🌿

Let oranges ripen fully on the tree for maximum sweetness. To tell when the fruit is ripe, you need to consider the cultivar and the season of the year. If you look at an orange's skin color, you'll see it is a mixture of green, orange, and yellow. In fall, the green predominates until the weather turns cool

---

Creative Cooking

ORANGES

Choose thin-skinned oranges for juicing and thick-skinned oranges for marmalade.

PEACHES

- To peel peaches fast, dip the fruit in boiling water for 20 seconds to loosen the skin.

- Freestone peaches tend to be juicier. When pureed, they make a great sweetener or sauce. Combine 1 cup peach puree with $1/2$ to 1 teaspoon citrus juice, and serve. ❖ ❖ ❖

enough to slow tree growth. Then the green fades and other pigments take over. In the spring, when growth begins, green pigments will appear again in perfectly ripe fruit. So don't let skin color fool you; cut a promising-looking fruit open and taste it to be sure the crop is ready.

When harvesting, you can pull off the fruit of 'Navel', 'Valencia', and other cultivars with tight skins. But you'll have to cut off loose-skinned types such as 'Mandarin', 'Temple', and tangerines. Use clippers, and leave the fruit with about ½ inch of stem. Trim the stub remaining on the tree back close to the parent branch.

Peaches and Nectarines ❄ ▯ 🍒 ☀ ◆

Let peaches and nectarines ripen on the tree to develop full flavor. You'll know the time is right when the skin changes to yellow or red, depending on the cultivar. The fruit should be soft (but still firm) and aromatic. For preserves, harvest these fruits slightly underripe. To keep from bruising the fruit, remove it from the stem by cupping the fruit in your hand, tipping it up, and twisting it sideways.

Extend your peach harvest season by growing cultivars that ripen early, midseason, and late (from July through September). An early cultivar is 'Sweethaven'; midseason includes 'Redhaven' (freestone) and 'Reliance'; and late cultivars include 'Belle of Georgia', 'Elberta' (freestone), and 'Encore'.

For white-fleshed peaches, try 'Champion White' or 'Early White Giant Peach'. For white-fleshed nectarines, choose 'Goldmine', 'Heavenly White', or 'Nectacrest'.

Pears ❄ ▯ 🍒 ☀ ◆ ✐

A European pear is one fruit that shouldn't ripen completely on the tree. If you wait until the last few weeks of ripening, stony granules form in the flesh, making it mealy and brown. Instead, pick the fruit when it reaches full size and the skin turns light green. The stems will separate easily from the tree. If you cut one pear open, you'll see the seeds are starting to turn brown. You can store pears at just above freezing, then bring them to room temperature to finish ripening.

'Bartlett' pears are good for canning. 'Colette' produces for an extended period, from the end of August through fall. Good keepers for the root cellar include 'Beurre d'Anjou', 'Bosc', and 'Red Anjou'.

Asian pears, such as 'Hosui', which have different ancestors than European types, should ripen fully on the tree. The skin will turn yellow or golden brown, and the flesh will be sweet and juicy.

Persimmons ❋ 🍒

Snip persimmons off the tree when they are ripe and firm. If you have an astringent cultivar, let the fruit become very soft and sweet before you eat it. You can use non-astringent types when they are a little firmer. You can even leave persimmons on the tree during the winter; they retain good flavor through freezing and thawing.

Plums ❋ ⬜ 🍒 ☀ 💧

For fresh eating or drying, let plums ripen completely until they are soft and sweet. For canning and preserves, harvest plums before they ripen fully. Pick them as soon as the skin develops a grayish bloom and while the fruit is only slightly soft and tart. Handle gently, and leave the stem attached.

Leave European plums on the tree until they are ready to eat. Pick Japanese cultivars such as 'Shiro' and 'Superior' a little earlier and let them ripen indoors. You can leave prune plums such as 'Stanley' and 'Earliblue' on the tree long after they are ripe.

Pomegranates ❋

Let pomegranates ripen on the tree into autumn, as long as the fruit doesn't split. You'll know they are ready when the fruit becomes red-tinted or yellow.

Quinces ❋ 🍒 🌾

Let quinces ripen fully on the bush until the skin changes from green to yellow. For freezing or preserves, you can wait to harvest until after the first fall frost. For refrigerator or root-cellar storage, pick them a few weeks earlier.

Raspberries ❋ ⬜ 🍒 ☀ 💧

To develop full flavor, let raspberries become completely ripe before you harvest them. They will become soft, succulent, sweet, and easy to pull off the stem. They will have changed to the mature color—bright to burgundy red, dark purple, golden, or black—

depending on the cultivar. For preserves, you can pick the berries when they are slightly immature.

When the first berries begin to ripen, make a point to check the planting at least every other day. If the berries get too soft, they could crumble when you pick them. You'll also want to pick all ripe berries right after any rain. Moisture can spread mold through ripe and unripe berries.

Since raspberries are delicate, handle them gently. Process them immediately to preserve their flavor.

Rhubarb ❄ 🫙 🍒 ☀

Give a new rhubarb planting time to become established before harvesting—don't harvest the first year. The second year you can harvest lightly, picking only the thickest stalks. Once the plant is growing strongly, harvest for up to eight weeks in the spring. You want to pick tender stalks between 12 and 24 inches long before the leaves are fully grown. Cut or twist them off at the base. Discard any roots and leaves that may have come along with the stalks— unlike the stalks, they're toxic.

Rose Hips 🍒 ☀

Rose hips, the autumn fruit of shrub roses, are great for preserves or teas. When ripe, they turn deep red and develop a mellow, nutlike taste and high vitamin C content. Wear gloves to keep from getting scratched by rose thorns, and clip rose hip clusters off the bush with pruning shears.

Strawberries ❄ 🫙 🍒 ☀ 💧

If you're freezing or drying, let strawberries ripen fully on the plant to develop maximum flavor. When the fruit turns from green to red, softens, and becomes fragrant and sweet, it's ready. Check the planting daily while the berries are ripening and remove all that are ready so they won't become moldy. It's best to harvest early in the morning when the fruit is cool. Gently twist it off its stem. Or cut the fruit free with a short stem attached, which helps the fruit retain its juices. Don't pull on the berry or you could bruise it. If you want strawberries for preserves, harvest them slightly underripe. Use or preserve strawberries promptly.

To extend the strawberry harvest season, grow early-fruiting June bearers, everbearers that produce smaller crops in early and late summer, and day-neutral cultivars that fruit off and on all summer and fall.

Watermelons

You should let watermelons ripen completely on the vine for best flavor and color. But determining when they are ready can be a little tricky. Look at the light-colored spot underneath the fruit, where it rests on the ground. It should have changed to a golden color. Then see if the tendril closest to the fruit is dead—a good sign of ripeness for many, but not all, cultivars. Try knocking on the melon. If it sounds hollow, it's probably ripe—or overripe. If it sounds metallic, it's probably green.

CHAPTER TWO

Freezing

*I*n this age of microwaves and convenience foods, many of us rely on our freezers more than ever before. We stock them with commercial frozen dinners, vegetables, and fruits so we're never caught short. These foods are easy to use, fast to cook—especially with a microwave—and will keep for a long time with very little effort on our part. But their quality sometimes leaves a little—or even a lot—to be desired.

That's why it pays to freeze your own foods. With this book, it's easy to make delicious, convenient-to-use foods that are better than those you're buying at the grocery store. Frozen homemade pizza will taste extra delicious with a sweet sauce made from garden-ripened tomatoes. Muffins will be super-rich and moist with fresh shredded zucchini. Prepare your favorite foods—pasta toppings, vegetable casseroles, fruit cocktails, pureed sauces. Use some for dinner now, and freeze the rest for later. It will be less expensive than buying commercial frozen foods, and your home-frozen foods will be free of additives and low in salt, sugar, or fat, if you wish.

Keeping That Garden-Fresh Taste

Freezing is an excellent option when you want to preserve your garden extras, keeping them as delicious as when you picked them. By quickly freezing produce right out of the garden, you'll capture vegetables with a higher nutrient content than if you ate them when they were fresh but several days old. For example, frozen beans contain more vitamin C than fresh beans stored in the refrigerator for two days. Many other vegetables lose two-thirds of their nutrients by the time you purchase them in the grocery store. Broccoli is the exception. Fresh broccoli stays more

HOW TO SAVE VITAMINS

For the most nutritious frozen produce, follow these simple guidelines when you harvest and prepare to freeze vegetables and fruits from your garden.

- Prepare your foods as soon after you've harvested them as possible, preferably within minutes but no more than six hours later. Chill foods that can withstand refrigerator temperatures if you can't freeze right away. (See page 6.)

- Blanch your vegetables in steam rather than boiling water so fewer nutrients leach out into the water. (For details, see page 48.)

- Work efficiently when blanching and cooling your foods before you freeze them: The faster you work, the less time your food has to combine with the oxygen in the air. This causes a process called oxidation, which results in some nutrient loss.

- Abide by the old inventory rule: first in, first out. Eat foods that went into the freezer before the others so nothing sits in there longer than need be. Most fruits and vegetables are good for 8 to 12 months, some even longer.

- Keep frozen produce at a steady 0°F. ❖ ❖ ❖

nutrient-rich up to nine days after harvesting than when it's promptly frozen. Despite this exception, freezing will preserve more vitamin C than canning or drying, although no method will save it all.

Freezing Pros and Cons

One disadvantage of freezing is the cost. A new freezer can be expensive, plus the electricity to keep it running. But nothing will preserve most foods the way freezing does. When you consider flavor, color, texture, and nutrients, the flexibility you have in freezing food combinations, and the time you save by freezing rather than canning or drying produce, the money is well spent.

How Freezing Works

Freezing puts your produce into a state that resembles suspended animation. But freezing isn't a method of sterilization, like heat processing in canning. You'll destroy many microorganisms by blanching, but some, most notably the molds, continue to live even though their growth is retarded and their activity rate is slowed down by freezing. As a result, most produce will stay good for a year or more in the freezer.

You have to freeze your food carefully to avoid side effects of freezing temperatures. If not carefully sealed, produce can dry out or develop freezer burn. If fruits and vegetables contain a high percentage of water or if they freeze slowly, ice crystals can develop in the tissues, making the thawed produce soft, even mushy. Fortunately, these problems are easy to avoid if you follow the steps on page 48.

 ## Supplies for Freezing

Stock up on all the equipment you'll need before the peak harvest season. Sometimes good freezer containers can be hard to find when tomatoes are coming in fast and furious. By planning ahead, you can shop for bargains—even on your freezer—and save a bundle. Then you'll have everything you need to move ultrafresh produce quickly into freezer storage.

Choosing Vegetables, Fruits, and Herbs for Freezing

Use fresh vegetables, fruits, and herbs right after they're harvested to capture the sun-ripened taste and nutrition. Use vegetables that are sweet and tender. Fruits should be ripe and of prime eating quality. Immature fruits are usually higher in tannins and other compounds that cause darkening. Some compounds also become bitter during freezer storage and thawing. You usually don't have to blanch fruits.

In general, the vegetables best suited for freezing are those you usually cook before serving. These include asparagus, beets, beet greens, broccoli, brussels sprouts, carrots, cauliflower, kohlrabi, lima beans, peas, rhubarb, spinach, squash, and sweet corn.

Quality Conscious

WHAT WENT WRONG?

If your frozen foods aren't as good as you'd hoped they would be, there may be a simple explanation. Run down this list and see if anything sounds familiar.

- If your frozen vegetables are mushy, you may have blanched them too long.

- If they have big ice crystals on them, they froze too slowly. Check to see if your freezer is cold enough—it should be hovering at 0°F. ❖ ❖ ❖

Some vegetables freeze best after they've been cooked. These include beets, pumpkins, sweet potatoes, waxy potatoes (for home fries), winter squash, and zucchini.

Vegetables that you usually eat raw, such as avocados, celery, cucumbers, lettuce, onions, and radishes, are least suited for freezing, at least by themselves, though they can be cooked into a sauce with other vegetables and frozen that way.

Almost all fruits, especially berries, freeze very well, but they can grow softer when frozen, as they do when they are cooked. Mangoes, papayas, pears, and watermelons lose more texture than others, so they don't freeze well. See "A Crop-by-Crop Guide to Freezing Vegetables and Fruits" on page 49 for the freezing potential—and limitations—of specific foods.

Before choosing herbs to freeze, read about freezing herbs on page 46. You can freeze most herbs, but basil, chervil, chives, cilantro, dill, lovage, mint, oregano, parsley, sorrel, sweet marjoram, tarragon, and thyme lend themselves well to freezing.

Other Options

If your freezer space is limited or if you want to do as little slicing and blanching as possible, think about alternative methods of storage. Root cellaring or in-the-garden storage works well for carrots and other root crops. Potatoes, for the most part, don't freeze well, but they keep fine in a root cellar if you cure them properly first. The same is true of onions and garlic. Canning is a better option than freezing for beets, pears, sauerkraut, and pickled vegetables. You can keep dried beans in a cool, dry place if you wrap them so they're airtight. When you have a small freezer and a big garden, check out all the methods listed for a particular vegetable or fruit in the index before you assume freezing will be best for you.

Freezer Containers

Freezer containers do more than hold produce. They also seal out air, which causes deterioration of the food and creates tough, bleached-out freezer-burn spots. You can prevent these common problems from the start by freezing produce only in freezer-safe packaging that's moisture- and vapor-proof. You can choose from square, rectangular, or round plastic freezer containers as well as canning jars and plastic freezer bags. Here's the scoop on each.

Rectangular or square plastic containers. These boxy containers fit efficiently into a freezer, and you can buy them in bulk inexpensively. They are reusable, but if you plan to reuse them, you might want to line them with freezer-proof plastic wrap so the food won't stain or leave odors in the interior. Also, be careful about putting them in the dishwasher. Heat may make the top warp so it won't snap on cleanly and seal well. To double-check the seal, fill the container with water, close the lid, then turn it upside down and see if water leaks out. To be sure of the seal on packed containers, encircle the seal with freezer tape to make it airtight.

Round or cylindrical containers. These containers are for general-purpose storage, but you can find types that are freezer- and microwave-safe, which means you don't need to dirty other dishes when warming the frozen food. The tops screw on, which give them a more reliable seal than snap-on containers. But the round shape doesn't make for efficient packing. And they're more expensive than square freezer boxes, so they may not be economical for a person with a large garden, warns Dr. Judy Harrison, cooperative extension food specialist at the University of Georgia.

Canning jars. Canning jars or other recycled jars, especially those with a wide mouth and straight sides, are suitable for the freezer. Jars can get jostled around in the freezer when you're hunting for something; those with straight sides are more stable and less likely to tip over and break. Leave at least 1 inch of open headspace, so frozen food can expand during freezing without breaking the glass. And chill the food well before freezing so the jar won't break with the rapid temperature change.

Freezer bags and wrap. Freezer bags are the ultimate in convenience, but they're not reusable, so they're not as cost-effective or environmentally friendly as the other containers. Available in pint through 2-gallon sizes, there's one for every purpose. Pack produce in single-serving packages or in bulk in large resealable bags that you can open to pull out food and then reseal.

Or save some money by getting the bags that you seal yourself. Fill them with vegetables or fruits packed without syrup. Then close tightly with a twist-tie, tying the bag as close to the contents as possible so there's little air in the package. Don't use the thin plastic bags that you get at the supermarket produce counter. They aren't strong enough and are likely to rip or tear.

You can also buy freezer wrap or foil; they are useful for covering casseroles and other foods you want to freeze for future use.

Choosing a Freezer

If you're going shopping for a freezer, look for one that meets standards for energy efficiency and you will save plenty of money in electric costs over the next couple of decades. But you can still plan to spend up to $100 annually in electricity.

You can use plastic boxes, glass jars, or plastic bags to store frozen food. Just make sure they're approved for freezer use.

Meals in minutes: That's what you'll have if you freeze your vegetables in freezer- and microwave-safe containers. They'll go straight from the freezer to the microwave, then to your table—in minutes!

Safety Stop

PICKING PLASTIC BAGS

You've seen the many different kinds of plastic bags in the grocery store—and you may have been tempted to use more than one kind for freezing or reheating produce. But there are big differences between the kinds of plastics used, which can affect the quality of frozen foods and the safety of foods cooked in plastic bags.

According to Dr. Judy Harrison, cooperative extension food agent for the University of Georgia, microwaving frozen food in plastic bags raises concerns about food safety. If you don't use plastic that's appropriate for the microwave, it might melt and leak food out or leach chemicals into your food. "If products say they're okay for boiling or microwaving, they should be fine," says Harrison. "But if it says it's for the freezer, you could get into trouble by boiling it."

For example, Dow Foods has several different brands of Ziploc bags that are suitable for different uses. All are made of polyethylene, but freezer bags are thickest, storage bags are less thick, and sandwich bags are the thinnest. Ziploc also carries vegetable bags, with hundreds of tiny vents in the side to let out excess moisture. But they're strictly for refrigerator storage. Dow doesn't recommend any Ziploc bags for boiling;

they begin softening at 195°F. Read the package labels on any plastic storage bags closely so you'll know how they're safe to use. Here are some guidelines.

Freezer bags. You can fill freezer bags with solids and liquids, put them in the refrigerator or freezer, and microwave on the defrost setting—not high power. You can't boil in them.

Storage bags. These will keep solids and liquids fresh in the refrigerator. They can be used for freezing but will keep food in good condition for no more than a month in the freezer. You can microwave them on the defrost setting but can't boil in them.

Sandwich bags. Don't fill them with liquids, and don't freeze, microwave, or boil in them. However, you can put them in the refrigerator.

Plastic bread bags. One kind of plastic bag to avoid altogether is a plastic bread bag. The exterior of these bags is printed with lead-contaminated ink, which doesn't hurt the bread inside. But if you turn the bag inside out and fill it with any slightly acidic food like an orange, you'll leach the lead out into the food within minutes. This can be a big problem for children, who can suffer from lead toxicity at low levels of exposure. ❖ ❖ ❖

Quick Tip

Labeling Freezer Containers

Before you put freezer containers into the freezer, note the type of food inside and the date you're freezing it. Write directly on freezer bags with a freezer or permanent ink marker. These won't fade or smudge, unlike felt-tip or ballpoint pens. To label containers, write the information on freezer tape (which won't lose its stickiness in cold temperatures) and attach it to the box or jar. Put the label in a conspicuous spot on the front or top of the container so it's easy to see. Then you can pick out the fruit or vegetable you want at a glance and use up the oldest produce first. If you are freezing different cultivars of the same fruit or vegetable, mark the cultivar on the label as well, so you'll learn which kind freezes best. ❖ ❖ ❖

Label your freezer bags or boxes with the type of produce and cultivar name, date frozen, and number of servings. If you'd like, you can list additional information about thawing and cooking the food.

As long as you are buying a new freezer, be sure it has all the features you'll be needing now and in the future. They include the following:

Upright freezers. Upright freezers resemble refrigerators. They have shelves that are easy to organize, fill, and empty. You can find everything from small upright freezers with 1½ cubic feet of space to large freezers with 30 cubic feet of space. As compared to chest freezers, upright models take less floor space, but they're more expensive to buy and operate than chest freezers.

Chest freezers. Chest freezers are longer than high and open from the top. They take up more floor space than upright freezers but cost less. You'll have to stack your produce in them, organizing it in containers so you can find what you need. Chest freezers are available in sizes ranging from 5 cubic feet to 28 cubic feet.

Freezer options. To encourage fast freezing, look for freezers with temperature controls. You can turn the temperature down when you add new freezer foods and return it to 0°F once they are solidly frozen. Or get a freezer with fast-freezing areas, which stay extra cold to freeze produce fast. For convenience, look for models with automatic defrosting, but be prepared to spend more to buy and operate them.

Freezer Organization

The organizational skills of many of us meet their match when it comes to the freezer, especially the chest freezer. Even a well-marked bag of snow peas can get buried under a frozen quiche and rest in peace there well after next year's harvest is blanched and frozen away.

One solution to this all-too-common problem is to conduct a quarterly inventory of your freezer's contents. Another, probably more rational, strategy is to keep an inventory log. A big blackboard on the wall next to your freezer is nice, but a clipboard is almost as good.

Start by listing each food category. Then add specific foods to each category as you store them away, and subtract them as you take them out. If you're like most people, you'll forget to put some foods on your log, so you may have to verify your lists by doing an inventory occasionally. But at least you'll have a pretty good idea of what's there at all times, making it easy to plan meals ahead and replenish the freezer periodically.

> Quick Tip
>
> ### FAST FREEZING
>
> To help your newly prepared foods freeze fast, add no more than 3 pounds of freshly prepared food per cubic foot of freezer space every 24 hours. ❖ ❖ ❖

Upright freezers look like refrigerators, but they're all freezer. It's much easier to find what you need in an upright freezer than in a chest freezer, where you may have to dig through layers of frozen produce to find the package you're looking for.

Knowing what's in your freezer is one thing; knowing where it is is another matter. To lick that problem, draw yourself a freezer map and keep that nearby, too. Assign one section of your freezer to each food category. Since frozen packages tend to slip and slide around a lot in chest freezers, especially when you're hunting for something in a hurry, you may want to formalize assigned areas with wire baskets or big plastic milk crates (which are sold all over the place for everything but milk these days) or even cardboard boxes. If you've got an upright freezer, it might be easiest to give each type of food its own shelf, and mark it as such.

Freezing Methods

These techniques will make your projects run smooth as ice before, during, and after freezing. Most foods need to be blanched before they're frozen, but blanching techniques differ depending on the type of produce you plan to freeze. (You will find specific blanching times for crops, starting on page 49.) Sometimes you can skip blanching entirely; see "Alternatives to Blanching" on page 44 for some good ideas.

Blanching Vegetables

If you have ever tried to freeze vegetables without first blanching them, you may have discovered the horrible cardboard flavor they acquire after a few months in the freezer. They bear no relation to the succulence of the tender beans and corn you so hopefully packed away last summer. This is the work of enzymes. Vegetables, as they come from the garden, have enzymes working in them. These break down vitamin C in a short time and turn sugar into starch. They are all slowed down (not stopped) by cold temperatures, but they are inactivated by heat through blanching.

The blanching idea isn't new. Methods for scalding or steaming fresh produce in preparation for freezing were introduced over 50 years ago. Since then, however, researchers have been discovering more about the effects of using this pre–cold-storage process. They have found that blanched vegetables are somewhat softened so that they can be packed more easily and solidly into freezer containers. But more important, they've discovered that blanching inactivates the enzymes that age food and cause unnatural colors and disagreeable flavors and odors to develop while the foods remain frozen.

To Blanch or Not to Blanch?

The Rodale Food Center's taste tests of blanched versus un-blanched freezer vegetables confirmed the fact that blanching is worth the effort. Taste-testers sampled blanched and unblanched broccoli, corn, and green beans after three months in the freezer. The vote was unanimous: All the testers chose the blanched vegetables because their colors were brighter, they tasted fresher, and they had more crunch. The unblanched broccoli was the big loser; it had developed an unpleasant smell and an aftertaste.

Some of the best research done on the blanching issue comes from the University of Illinois. Researchers there froze a variety of vegetables, blanched and unblanched, and tested batches of each several times over the course of a year. Those that had been blanched rated good to very good on taste, texture, and looks, even after nine months in the freezer. On the other hand, un-blanched samples that had been stored for only one month received general acceptability scores between poor and fair. Unblanched products developed strong off-flavors and lost color during the first month in the freezer.

Over even longer storage periods, the vegetables that were not blanched deteriorated still further, some of them so much that they were considered inedible. Most became faded, dull, or gray; all became tough or fibrous; and some, broccoli especially, developed an objectionable haylike flavor.

Blanching produce before freezing preserves food color, stops continued ripening, and prevents changes in flavor. Steam-blanch vegetables in a steamer basket set over boiling water. You can also blanch produce by plunging it into boiling water.

More Benefits of Blanching

There is another benefit to blanching besides taste, texture, and looks. Experiments have shown that nutrients are retained in greater amounts in many vegetables that are blanched before freezing. Studies published by the North Dakota Cooperative Extension Service show that if foods are prepared and frozen properly, they retain much of their original food value. For example, consider the following:

• The only carbohydrate that changes after blanching is sugar (sucrose), which is reduced to simple sugars (glucose and fructose) during long storage. This is of no importance.

• Minerals might leach into water during the blanching and cooking of vegetables, but this loss is usually no greater than when cooking fresh vegetables.

• Vitamin A is lost only when vegetables are not blanched.

ICE WATER METHOD

ICE CUBE METHOD

There are two ways to cool blanched vegetables before freezing them. You can plunge the blanched produce into ice water until it's cool. But to save the most nutrients, you should set the produce in a pan that's set in a larger container full of ice cubes and ice water. Then cover the produce with a bag of ice cubes until the vegetables are cool to the touch.

After blanching and cooling vegetables, gently roll them in a towel to dry them off before freezing.

• B vitamins, such as thiamine and riboflavin, are lost when you leave the produce in the freezer too long and when you cool and blanch the produce in water, since B vitamins are water-soluble. But the loss is greater if the vegetables are not blanched. Some thiamine is also lost by heat in cooking.

• Vitamin C is easily lost through submersion or cooking in water as well as through oxidation. Vegetables lose some of their vitamin C through blanching, but without this process, the loss would be much greater. The same amount of vitamin C is lost in cooking fresh vegetables.

Another study conducted by the University of Illinois shows that blanching makes a dramatic difference in the vitamin C content of frozen foods. The study found that blanched vegetables kept more of their vitamin C, and the longer they were stored, the bigger the difference in vitamin retention. After only one month,

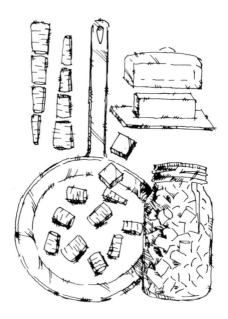

Sauté-blanch carrots before freezing them by sautéing sliced carrots in a little butter to seal in flavor and nutrients.

blanched peas kept 11 percent more vitamin C than unblanched peas. By three months, the blanched samples had 36 percent more, and after nine months in the freezer, 89 percent more. Time was even more of a factor with green beans. After nine months, the blanched beans had 1,300 percent more vitamin C than the unblanched ones!

• When comparing steam blanching vegetables to boiling-water blanching, researchers have found that steam is more gentle on flavor, color, and water-soluble nutrients such as vitamins B and C. The differences range from 9 to 23 percent more vitamins in those vegetables that were steam-blanched, with the biggest savings in vitamin C.

Microwave Blanching

Using a microwave to blanch your vegetables before you freeze them doesn't reduce the blanching time, and it may not be as thorough as boiling. But microwaving doesn't heat up your kitchen—a definite benefit in the heat of summer. For best results with microwave blanching, follow these guidelines.

• Limit the amount of your vegetable to 4 cups of leafy green vegetables or 2 cups of all other prepared vegetables.

• Use a 1-quart, round, glass casserole or similar microwave-safe container.

• Add ¼ cup of water to the container before adding the vegetables.

• Cover the container with microwave-safe plastic film.

• If your microwave is a 650- or 700-watt model, is larger than 1 cubic foot, and has a mode mixer or a revolving table, use the recommended blanching times for high-wattage ovens, given in the table on the opposite page. Otherwise,

A no-fuss, no-muss way to blanch vegetables is in a microwave. Cut 2 cups of produce into small pieces, put them into a microwave-safe dish with ¼ cup water, and microwave according to the table on the opposite page.

Microwave Blanching Timetable

Vegetable	Preparation	Minutes at High Wattage	Minutes at Low Wattage
Asparagus	Wash, cut off tough ends, cut into 2" pieces	3–5	–
Beans, snap	Wash, snap ends, remove strings, cut into 1"– 2" pieces	3	4–5
Broccoli	Wash, trim, cut into 1"– 2" pieces	5	8
Cauliflower	Wash, trim, cut into 1"– 2" pieces	5	7
Corn, sweet	Cut off kernels; for cream-style corn, scrape tips and juice to combine with kernels	4	6
Peas, sweet or black-eyed	Wash pods, shell, and rinse	4	6
Peas, edible pod	Wash pods, snap ends, remove strings	4	6

SOURCE: These guidelines are recommended by Dr. Gerald Kuhn of the Department of Food Science at the Pennsylvania State University.

Quality Conscious

USE SOFT WATER

Use soft water to blanch vegetables. Hard water can make vegetables tough. If you have hard water, use distilled water to do your blanching. ❖ ❖ ❖

use the times recommended for low-wattage ovens.

• Air-cool your blanched vegetables by spreading them in a single layer on a large tray. You can package and freeze them after five minutes of cooling time.

Blanching Fruits

With the exception of rhubarb and quinces, you won't need to blanch fruits. But you can give them a quick dip in boiling water to loosen the skin and make them easier to peel.

Creative Cooking

ALTERNATIVES TO BLANCHING

If blanching in water or steam gets boring, use alternative methods such as the following:

- Sauté root vegetables such as carrots and turnips in a little butter or oil until they begin to soften. Then freeze them.

- Roast root vegetables. Start with small whole beets or 2- to 3-inch-long chunks of carrots, parsnips, potatoes, or sweet potatoes. Coat the vegetables with oil, and bake until tender at 400°F for potatoes and sweet potatoes or at 375°F for beets, carrots, and parsnips. Freeze. Microwave when ready to use.

- Roast sweet and hot peppers before freezing them. Broil each side until the skin chars. Remove from heat and let cool. Peel off the skin, and freeze the flesh.

- Cook and puree any kind of vegetable or fruit to use as a sauce or broth enricher for soups, stews, or casseroles. Then freeze.

You can skip blanching altogether for a number of different fruits and vegetables. You can freeze unblanched whole or quartered tomatoes, leeks, onions, and sliced peppers. Simply spread them out on a baking sheet and freeze. When they are solidly frozen, pack into freezer containers for continued storage. Do the same with banana chunks, blackberries, raspberries, sliced plums or persimmons, strawberries, and whole grapes. Let these fruits thaw slightly and enjoy as fruit ices. ❖ ❖ ❖

Preparing Fruit Syrups and Antidarkening Treatments

Fruits held at freezing temperatures will keep without the aid of a sweetener, but they may lose some of their flavor, texture, and color when packed dry. That's why most information on freezing fruits recommends freezing them with dry sugar or mixing them in a syrup of water, sugar, and sometimes an antidarkening agent. But you can also preserve them in honey or fruit juice syrups.

In general, you can substitute honey for sugar in recipes for freezing fruit. Honey will preserve the quality of the fruit best if you use the same amount of honey as you would have used of sugar. Stick with mild-flavored, light-colored honey instead of dark, strong-flavored honey. To coat the fruit thoroughly, use the fruit at room temperature and honey that's slightly warm.

For a thin honey syrup, blend ¼ cup honey with 2 cups very hot water. For a medium syrup, blend ½ cup honey with 2 cups very hot water. Let the syrup cool to room temperature before adding it, and use enough syrup to completely cover the fruit.

For a light sugar syrup for a 9-pint load, mix 1½ cups sugar with 5¾ cups water. For a medium sugar syrup, mix 2¼ cups sugar with 5¼ cups water.

How to Prevent Darkening

For apples, apricots, figs, nectarines, peaches, pears, and sweet and sour cherries, which darken easily during freezing and thawing, add ¼ teaspoon ascorbic acid powder (available in season at grocery stores or through your local drugstore) to each quart of chilled syrup to help prevent discoloration. You can also use bottled lemon juice, but it's not considered as effective as ascorbic acid. Start by adding lemon juice at twice the rate of ascorbic acid, and increase it according to taste. Cut the fruit directly into the syrup and place crumpled wax paper on the top to keep the fruit under the syrup. You also can blend 1 to 2 tablespoons of lemon juice in pure honey if you drizzle it over the fruit.

Or freeze fruits susceptible to darkening in orange juice. Slice fruit directly into thawed orange juice concentrate, coating the slices thoroughly to keep them light-colored.

If you don't want to use a sweetener, you can dip fruit in an antidarkening agent before freezing. Add ¼ teaspoon of ascorbic acid to a quart of water. Dip each piece of fruit into the solution before packing. Ascorbic acid is bitter, so use sparingly.

Thawing Fruits and Vegetables

When frozen foods thaw, microorganisms held dormant on them begin to multiply, and the produce starts spoiling. The higher the thawing temperature, the faster the growth of the microorganisms.

Don't let your frozen food spoil when it thaws! You can avoid the problem entirely by cooking your frozen food without thawing it first. You can cook most freezer foods in the microwave, oven, or boiling water. But when you have casseroles or ingredients that you need to mix thawed into other dishes, thaw them in their original containers in the refrigerator. Or, if you can't wait for hours for something to thaw, put it in the microwave and use the defrosting cycle. Once frozen foods are thawed, use them promptly because they'll decompose faster than fresh foods.

Don't Overcook Frozen Foods!

Because blanching followed by freezing softens tissues and changes the texture of vegetables, you only need to cook frozen vegetables one-third to one-half as long as fresh vegetables.

You can freeze fresh herbs in freezer bags. It's easiest to use frozen herbs if you bag enough for one meal (say, for putting in a soup, sauce, or salad dressing). Don't forget to label your bags with the type of herb and the date you froze it.

Freezing Herbs

You can freeze many herbs whole, as individual leaves or even sprigs. Wash off excess soil, lay the herbs on a baking sheet to freeze, then pack the frozen herbs in freezer bags. When you are ready to use an herb, pull out the crisp-frozen leaves and crumble them into the dish you're cooking. If you let the herbs thaw, they're likely to be soft-textured, and some may discolor, so they won't be good as garnishes. But the flavor is rich and full and can contribute to many dishes. Some herbs, like basil, will keep their color and flavor better if you blanch them before freezing. Place them in a strainer and pour boiling water over them for just a second.

Herb ice cubes are a convenient way to freeze and use herbs. Freeze chopped herbs and water or pureed herbs in an ice cube tray, then pop the frozen cubes into freezer bags. Use as needed.

Herb Ice Cubes
You can also freeze herbs in ice cubes. Herb ice cubes are particularly good if you make a lot of soups and stews—just pop one or two cubes in as your dish is cooking. To make the cubes, prepare your herbs by removing the stems and chopping the leaves, then pack 1 to 2 teaspoons into ice cube trays, cover with water, and pop into the freezer.

Herb Pastes and Butters
Instead of covering your herbs with water for ice cubes, you may want to cover them with oil to make a paste, or chop and mix them with butter. To make herb paste, take 2 cups of fresh, washed herbs such as parsley, basil, dill, or chives, and puree them in the food processor while drizzling in ½ to ¾ cup of olive oil. When the blend becomes a thick paste, pour or spoon it into ice cube trays and freeze. You can

spoon herb butter into ice cube trays, too, or you can roll the prepared butter into a log and wrap the log first in wax paper and then in freezer wrap. See page 274 for some recipes.

Herb pastes are good for making pasta sauces or herb breads like garlic breads, and for use in casseroles. Butters can be used the same way; they also make wonderful spreads for seasoning fish, grains, and vegetables.

❧ Freezer Failure

If, for any unfortunate reason (like a power failure or a freezer breakdown), your freezer stops functioning, don't run to it and open the door to check the contents. This is probably the worst thing you can do. First, try to determine approximately how long the freezer will be out of service. This may mean calling the electric company or the repairman. Do this as soon as possible after you discover the problem.

If your freezer will be off for 48 hours or less and it is packed full, you have nothing to worry about. The food will stay frozen as long as you don't open the door and let warm air enter. A freezer packed less than half full should cause more concern; it may not keep food frozen for more than 24 hours.

If you expect the food to start thawing before the freezer resumes operation, place dry ice (use gloves—dry ice "burns") inside the freezer, out of direct contact with food. To find dry ice, look in the Yellow Pages under "Ice" or "Dry Ice." Or call a neighborhood ice company and inquire if they stock dry ice—not every ice company does.

Place pieces of cardboard or wood on top of the food packages and put the dry ice on top of these. Close the freezer door and open it only to add more ice. If the dry ice is placed in the freezer soon after it has stopped running, 25 pounds should keep the food frozen for two to three days in a half-full, 10-cubic-foot freezer and three to four days in a fully loaded, 10-cubic-foot freezer.

If you have to remove some food to make room for the ice, store it in the refrigerator, and cook the food as it thaws. You can refreeze some foods that you moved to the refrigerator if your freezer starts operating sooner than you expected. But they must show no signs of spoilage, or they won't be suitable for refreezing. Mark refrozen foods appropriately, and use them before other frozen foods. You also can refreeze thawed food that you cook as long as you freeze it soon after cooking.

If no dry ice is available, you can always move your frozen food to a commercial locker plant or to a friend's freezer. Pack the food in ice chests or wrap it in thick layers of newspaper to prevent thawing during transportation.

Freezing Step-by-Step

Here are all the details you need to prepare and process your favorite vegetables. These are general directions; you'll find specific guidelines for freezing vegetables and fruits in "A Crop-by-Crop Guide to Freezing Vegetables and Fruits" on the opposite page.

1. Pick young, tender vegetables for freezer storage; avoid bruised, damaged, or overripe vegetables. Freezing doesn't improve poor-quality produce. As a rule, it is better to choose slightly immature produce over any that is fully ripe. Harvest in the early morning. Try to include some of the tastiest early-season crops; don't just wait for later ones.

2. Line up everything you'll need for blanching and freezing first. Nothing counts more than speed for holding on to freshness, taste, and nutritive value. If you have a lot to freeze at once, plan a family "Operation Deep Freeze." Have all hands on deck for fast help, and arrange equipment and containers in advance for a smooth production.

3. Blanch with care and without delay. Thoroughly clean and cut up vegetables, if desired. Then blanch to stop or slow down enzyme action. For water blanching, use at least 1 gallon of water to each pound of vegetable, preheated to the boiling point in a covered pot. If you're steaming, use a wire-mesh holder over 1 inch of boiling water in an 8-quart pot. The same wire-mesh holder is handy for plunging vegetables into boiling water, 1 pound at a time. Start timing when the water resumes boiling, following the recommended time listed for each vegetable or fruit. If you live in a high-altitude area, add $\frac{1}{2}$ minute to blanching time for each 2,000 feet above sea level.

4. Cool quickly to stop cooking when the time is up and to chill vegetables for the freezer. The extra time it takes your freezer to freeze warm vegetables results in bigger ice crystals and limper food. If you don't chill vegetables quickly to stop the cooking, they'll get overblanched and show a loss of color, texture, flavor, and nutritive value. Plunge blanched vegetables into cold water, ice water, or cold running water.

You also can use blocks of ice instead of cubes. They won't melt so fast or get mixed up with the vegetables. Early in the season, freeze blocks of ice in any extra containers you have around so that you have plenty when you need them. Or, to prevent blanched vegetables from losing some of their food value when soaking in water, put them into a pan sitting in a larger container filled with ice water. Then cover the vegetables with a bag of ice until they're cool to the touch.

5. Pack cooled blanched produce at once in suitable containers. Glass jars require a 1- to 1½-inch headspace; paper and plastic containers need a ½-inch headspace, except for vegetables like asparagus and broccoli that pack loosely and need no extra room. Work out air pockets by gently pressing on the food and its packaging, if it's flexible. Then seal tightly.

6. Label all frozen food packages; indicate vegetable, date of freezing, and cultivar. Then store with other foods of its type in the freezer for easier retrieval later on.

A Crop-by-Crop Guide to Freezing Vegetables and Fruits

Before starting any freezing operation, check these lists to see if your vegetable or fruit is recommended for freezing. If it is, follow these tips when it's time to freeze.

Preparing Vegetables for Freezing

You'll be surprised at how many vegetables you can freeze. And they'll all taste great if you follow these simple guidelines.

Artichokes

Select small artichokes or artichoke hearts. Cut off the top of the bud, and trim the thorny end down to a cone. Wash, then blanch in boiling water for 7 minutes or in steam for 8 to 10 minutes.

Asparagus

Use young, green stalks. Rinse and sort for size, then cut into convenient equal lengths to fit your containers. Blanch thick spears in boiling water for 4 minutes or thin spears for 2 minutes, or in steam for 3 minutes. Also see "Microwave Blanching Timetable" on page 43.

Avocados

Choose avocados that are ripe and perfect. Peel, halve, and remove pits. Scoop out the pulp and mash it, adding 1 tablespoon lemon juice per two avocados to prevent browning.

Beans, Dried

Freeze dried beans in plastic freezer bags.

Beans, Green and Yellow

Pick when pods are of desired length but before seeds take a shape that you can see through the pod. Wash in cold water and drain. Snip ends and cut, if desired. Blanch in boiling water for 3 minutes or in steam for 4 1/2 minutes. Also see "Microwave Blanching Timetable" on page 43.

Beans, Lima

Pick when pods are slightly rounded and bright green. Wash and blanch in boiling water for 2 minutes for small beans, 3 minutes for medium beans, and 4 minutes for large beans, or in steam for $3\frac{1}{2}$ to $5\frac{1}{2}$ minutes. Drain and shell. Rinse shelled beans in cold water.

Beets

Beets usually taste better canned, but you can freeze them if you cook them thoroughly first. Harvest while tender and mild-flavored. Wash and leave $\frac{1}{2}$ inch of the tops on. Cook whole until tender (about 25 to 30 minutes for small beets and 45 to 50 minutes for medium to large ones). Or cook a pound of beets in $\frac{1}{2}$ cup of water in the microwave for 15 to 20 minutes on high. Stir and rotate the dish three or four times. Let the beets cool for 3 to 5 minutes. When cool, remove the skin and cut or leave whole. No further blanching is necessary.

Broccoli

Select well-formed heads. Buds that show yellow flowers are too mature and should not be frozen (or canned). Rinse, peel, and trim. Split broccoli lengthwise into pieces not more than $1\frac{1}{2}$ inches across. If there's a chance that tiny green cabbageworms have invaded the buds, soak in cold salt water for 30 minutes. Then rinse well and pick over. Blanch in boiling water for 4 minutes or in steam for 6 minutes, depending on the size of the pieces. Also see "Microwave Blanching Timetable" on page 43.

Brussels Sprouts

Pick only green buds. Like broccoli, heads that are turning yellow are too mature to process. Rinse and trim, cutting off outer leaves. Blanch in boiling water for 3 minutes for small heads, 4 minutes for medium heads, 5 minutes for large heads, or in steam for 5 to 7 minutes. If there is a chance that insects have invaded the sprouts, soak in cold salt water for 30 minutes.

Cabbage

Trim off outer leaves. You can shred for tight packing, or cut into wedges. Blanch the shredded cabbage in boiling water for $1\frac{1}{2}$ minutes or in steam for 3 minutes. Blanch wedges in boiling water for 3 minutes or in steam for $4\frac{1}{2}$ minutes.

Cabbage, Chinese

Trim off coarse outer leaves. Cut heads into medium or coarse pieces, thin wedges, or separate leaves. Blanch in boiling water for $1\frac{1}{2}$ minutes, or in steam for 2 minutes.

Carrots

Harvest while still tender and mild-flavored. Trim, wash, and peel. Freeze small carrots whole. Cut others into ¼-inch cubes or slices. Blanch in boiling water for 2 minutes for small pieces, 3 minutes for larger pieces, and 5 minutes for whole carrots, or in steam for 4½ minutes for small pieces and 5½ minutes for larger ones.

Cauliflower and Broccoflower

Select well-formed heads free of blemishes. Wash and break into florets. Peel and split stems. If there is a chance that tiny green cabbageworms have invaded the head, soak in cold salt water for 10 to 15 minutes. Then rinse well and pick over. Blanch in boiling water for 4 minutes or in steam for 6 minutes. Also see "Microwave Blanching Timetable" on page 43.

Corn

Pick ears as soon as they ripen. The natural sugars in corn turn to starch quickly after ripening, so good timing is critical. Husk, de-silk, and wash the ears. If you are freezing whole cobs, choose cultivars that have small ears. Blanch three ears at a time in steam or boiling water for 7 to 11 minutes, depending on the ear size. Cool and pack separately or together, grouping enough for one meal. Wrap ears in freezer paper or in plastic freezer bags.

If you are freezing cut corn, it's still easier to blanch with kernels on the cob first. Blanch in boiling water for 4 minutes or in steam for 6½ minutes. Then cool and remove the kernels from the cob with a sharp knife or corn cutter. To cut corn kernels off the cob more easily, place the cob on a nail embedded in a block of wood, or push the cob into the hole of a tube pan. Either method will hold the cob firmly while you work. Also see "Microwave Blanching Timetable" on page 43.

Quality Conscious

CORN ON THE COB

Corn on the cob is the only vegetable that you should thaw before cooking to get the best flavor and texture. Once thawed, steam or roast it instead of boiling it. ❖ ❖ ❖

Cucumbers

Cucumbers don't freeze very well; they are much better stored as pickles. But you can freeze them as pickles. See "Freezer Pickles" on page 304 to find out how.

Eggplant

Eggplant is best frozen when it is partially prepared (sautéed, roasted, or breaded and baked) first. Select firm, heavy fruit of

Tired of trying to immobilize those slippery corn ears so you can cut the kernels off? Two easy ways to pin them down are to skewer the cob on a nail that's been hammered through a block of wood or to jam the end of the cob into the hole of a tube pan. Both techniques will hold the ear firmly in place while you work.

uniform dark purple color. Harvest before skin loses its gloss and the seeds become hard and dark. Wash and peel, since the skin toughens in storage. Cut into 1/3- to 1/2-inch slices or cubes. To prevent darkening, dip the slices or cubes in a solution of 1 tablespoon lemon juice to 1 quart water. Blanch in boiling water for 5 minutes or in steam for 6 1/2 minutes. Dip the eggplant slices or cubes again in lemon solution after cooled.

Garlic

For best results, store garlic in a cool, dry root cellar. But you also can freeze garlic chopped or in unpeeled cloves. Or puree garlic, shape it into a log, and wrap it in plastic wrap for freezing. Cut off as much as you need at a time while still frozen, and re-freeze the rest.

Greens

See "Spinach and Other Greens" on page 55.

Herbs

See "Freezing Herbs" on page 46.

Jerusalem Artichokes

Select firm, unblemished tubers, wash well, and peel. Blanch in boiling water for 3 minutes for small tubers or pieces, 4 minutes for medium tubers or pieces, or 5 minutes for large tubers or pieces.

Kale

See "Spinach and Other Greens" on page 55.

Leeks

Harvest while still tender. Wash and trim off outer leaves, tops, and base. You don't have to blanch leeks before freezing unless you plan to freeze them for more than nine months. Just slice and freeze. For longer keeping, blanch in steam for 2 minutes for sliced leeks and 3 minutes for whole leeks.

Mixed Vegetables

If you like to freeze mixed vegetables, cut and blanch each vegetable separately. Then mix and freeze them. Since blanching times vary according to the type of vegetable, blanching separately for the required time assures you that each vegetable is sufficiently—but not overly—precooked. See the recipes starting on page 244 for prepared foods and combination dishes for the freezer.

Okra

Select tender young pods. Wash and cut off stems so as not to rupture seed cells. Blanch in boiling water for 3 minutes for small pods or 4 minutes for large pods, or in steam for 5 minutes. Freeze whole or slice crosswise.

Onions

For best results, store onions in a cool, dry root cellar. But you also can freeze them. Like leeks, onions need no blanching before freezing, unless you plan to freeze them for more than nine months. Just peel, slice if they are regular-size onions, and freeze. For longer keeping, blanch in steam for 2 minutes for sliced onions and 3 minutes for small whole onions.

Parsnips

Root cellaring is the best storage method for parsnips, but you may also freeze them. Choose smooth roots; woody roots will be tough and tasteless. Remove the tops, wash, and peel. Cut into slices or chunks. Blanch in boiling water for 3 minutes or in steam for 5 minutes.

Peas, Garden and Black-Eyed

For garden and black-eyed peas, pick when seeds become plump and pods are rounded. Shell but don't wash. Freeze the same day they are harvested, as sugar is rapidly lost at room temperature. Discard

---

Quality Conscious

CHANGE IN ONION FLAVOR

The flavor of onions may change after freezing. Be sure to taste and adjust seasonings before serving previously frozen foods that have onions as an ingredient. ❖ ❖ ❖

immature and tough peas. Blanch green peas in boiling water for 2½ minutes or in steam for 3 minutes. Blanch black-eyed peas in boiling water for 2 minutes or in steam for 3 minutes. Also see "Microwave Blanching Timetable" on page 43.

Peas, Snap or Snow

You can harvest snap or snow peas any time before the pods fill out. Wash, trim off the flower end, and pull out the string. Blanch in boiling water for 2 minutes or in steam for 3 minutes. Also see "Microwave Blanching Timetable" on page 43.

Peppers, Sweet and Hot

Select when fully ripe. You can freeze green, red, or yellow peppers. The skin should be glossy and thick. Wash, halve, and remove the seeds and whitish membrane. Peppers do not require blanching, but you may blanch for 2 minutes in boiling water or steam for easier packing. Or roast peppers under the broiler until the skin chars and loosens. Peel the skin off and freeze.

Potatoes

Store potatoes in a root cellar; they don't freeze well, with just a couple of exceptions. Pan-fried cubed potatoes, often called home fries, freeze reasonably well. For home fries, choose a waxy or all-purpose potato; baking potatoes will disappoint you because they lose their shape when cooked this way. Scrub well, then bake, steam, or microwave potatoes until partially softened. Cool and chop into ¼-inch cubes. Put a few tablespoons of vegetable oil in a frying pan, heat over medium heat, and add the potatoes. Turn the heat to medium-low, and cover the pan. Turn potatoes when browned on one side. Brown on the other side, then cool, and pack for freezing. Cook the potatoes while still frozen; if you thaw them first, they will become watery and grainy.

Pumpkins and Winter Squash

Harvest when fully colored and hard-shelled. Wash, pare, and cut into small pieces. Bake at 375°F, microwave, or steam until soft and completely cooked.

Rhubarb

See "Rhubarb" on page 60.

Rutabagas

Harvest while tender and mild-flavored. Avoid any that are overmature. Wash and trim off the leaves. Peel and slice or dice into ½-inch or smaller pieces. Blanch in boiling water for 1 minute or in steam for 2 minutes.

Sorrel, French

Steam or sauté for 1 to 2 minutes until the leaf dissolves into puree. Freeze in ice cube trays. Then move to freezer bags for extended storage. Also see "Freezing Herbs" on page 46.

Soybeans, Green

Pick when pods are well rounded but still green. Yellow pods are too mature for processing. Even two or three days too long in the garden will result in overmaturity. Wash. Blanch in boiling water or steam for 5 minutes before shelling. Cool and shell; rinse in cold water.

Spinach and Other Greens

Harvest while still small and tender, leaf by leaf or plant by plant. Harvest entire spinach plant as long as it is not overly mature. Use only tender center leaves from old mustard and kale plants. Select beet, Swiss chard, and turnip leaves from young plants. Rinse well and trim off large midribs and leaf stems. Blanch in boiling water for 2 minutes or in steam for 3 minutes. Stir a few times to prevent leaves from matting. Cool and chop, if desired.

Sweet Potatoes

Use smooth, firm sweet potatoes. Wash and microwave, steam, or bake at 350°F until soft. Cool and remove skins, if you wish. Pack whole, sliced, or mashed. To retain bright color, mix 2 tablespoons lemon or orange juice into each quart of pulp, or dip potatoes in a solution of ½ cup lemon juice per quart of water for 5 minutes.

Swiss Chard

See "Spinach and Other Greens" above.

Tomatillos

Cook in chili, salsa, or meatless tomato dishes, and freeze.

Tomatoes

You can freeze tomatoes as sauce (see page 289) or whole and unblanched. Freeze whole tomatoes on baking sheets, and when frozen, store them in plastic bags. The skins will conveniently crack during freezing, making it easy to remove them once the tomatoes have thawed.

It's easy to freeze whole tomatoes. Put whole, unpeeled tomatoes on a baking sheet and freeze until they're hard, then pop them into a plastic freezer bag. When you're ready to use them, take out as many as you need, and run them under warm water for fast thawing and easy skin removal.

To save space and preparation time later, you may also stew tomatoes. Peel and then cut into quarters, and simmer slowly in a covered heavy pot until the tomatoes are soft and release their juices. Then remove the lid and cook as long as you like. You can cook the tomatoes down into a paste, but be sure to keep the heat low and stir frequently to prevent burning.

Or you can quick-blanch tomatoes, peel, and cut into quarters to freeze. To peel tomatoes, submerge them in boiling water for 30 seconds, then plunge into cold water and drain. The skins will slip right off. You can also run the dull side of a knife over the skin until it wrinkles, and then peel the skin away.

Zucchini and Summer Squash

You can shred zucchini before you freeze it. Quick-blanch it in boiling water. It's convenient to drop ½ cup of frozen shredded zucchini into any muffin mix you make, so that the muffins will be moist. Or you can add shredded zucchini to tomato sauce to thicken it. Slice or cube summer squash into ½-inch pieces, and blanch for 4 minutes, or until translucent.

Preparing Fruits for Freezing

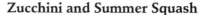

You'll find general instructions for freezing fruits in "Freezing Methods" on page 39. Review the information in "Preparing Fruit Syrups and Antidarkening Treatments" on page 44. Adapt for specific fruits as follows:

Apples

To freeze in slices, peel, core, and slice apples. Pack dry or in a 30 to 40 percent syrup, or mix with honey thinned with warm water or ½ cup sugar per 4 cups of fruit. Add lemon juice or ascorbic acid to any of these to prevent darkening. For applesauce, core (but leave skins on), either grind whole in a blender or cook until soft in an uncovered heavy pot, and put through a food mill. Add a sweetener to taste, if desired.

Apricots

Peel apricot skins before freezing because they tend to roughen during freezing. Dip a few fruits at a time into boiling water for 15 seconds, or until skins loosen. Chill quickly in ice water and peel. Cut in half and re-

Here's a great way to deal with gargantuan zucchini crops (or other megaharvests): Turn your vegetables into instant soup stock. Puree the zucchini with herbs and onions in a blender, then freeze until needed to make a thick, flavorful soup base.

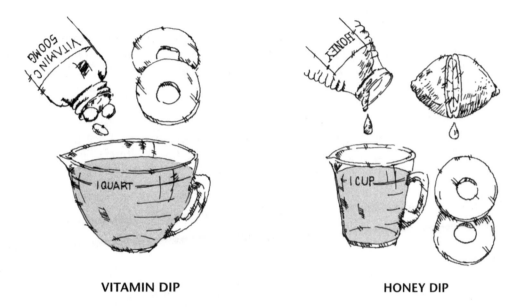

VITAMIN DIP **HONEY DIP**

Keep frozen apple slices from darkening by using one of these easy pretreatments.
Put cored, sliced apples in a vitamin C dip made from three 500-milligram vitamin
C tablets crushed and mixed into 1 quart of water. Or, dip your apple slices in a
honey dip made from 1 cup of honey, 1 cup of water, and the juice of one lemon.

move pits. Pack in a 40 percent syrup, or mix with honey thinned with warm water or ½ cup sugar per 4 cups of fruit. Add lemon juice or ascorbic acid to any of these to prevent darkening.

Bananas

Peel and freeze in chunks or as a puree. For chunks, freeze loose on baking sheets, and then bag when frozen. For puree, mash with a fork or potato masher or use a food processor, adding lemon juice or ascorbic acid to prevent browning.

Blackberries, Blueberries, Boysenberries, and Mulberries

(See individual entries for currants, gooseberries, raspberries, and strawberries.)

Pick out debris and wash. Pack dry or in a 30 percent syrup, or mix with honey thinned with warm water or ½ cup sugar per 4 cups of fruit.

Cherries, Sour

Wash and chill in ice water before pitting to minimize loss of juice. Pack dry or in a 30 to 40 percent syrup with lemon juice or ascorbic acid to prevent darkening.

Cherries, Sweet

Wash and chill in ice water before pitting to minimize loss of juice. Pack dry or in a 30 to 40 percent syrup with lemon juice or ascorbic acid added to hold color; light cultivars need more lemon juice or ascorbic acid.

Currants

Choose the larger cultivars for freezing. Stem and wash. Pack dry or in a syrup, or add a sweetener to taste.

Dates

Choose ripe, firm fruit. Wash and remove pits. Pack whole, or puree dates in a blender, food processor, or food mill.

Figs

Wash, sort, cut off stems, peel, and leave whole or slice. Cover with a 20 percent syrup, adding lemon juice or ascorbic acid to prevent brown-ing. For crushed figs, wash and coarsely grind in blender or food processor. Add a sweetener, if desired, and add lemon juice or ascorbic acid to prevent darkening.

Gooseberries

Freeze ripe berries for pies and underripe berries for preserves. Sort, wash, and trim. Pack dry for pies or preserves. For other uses, pack in a heavy syrup.

Grapes

Wash and stem. Leave seedless grapes whole. Cut in half and remove seeds from others. Pack dry or in a 20 percent syrup.

Frozen grapes make a great frozen snack. Just lay them out on a baking sheet in your freezer so that they freeze separately, and then bag them for snacking later. To peel frozen grapes, dip one at a time into cool water while still frozen hard. The skins will slip right off.

Guavas

Freeze as a puree or in slices. For puree, remove seedy portion and strain to remove seeds. Sweeten, if desired. For slices, pare, halve, and slice. Pack in a syrup.

Lemons and Limes

Peel and remove sections from the heavy membrane. Pack dry or add a sweetener to taste. If you have whole lemons that you won't use within a few weeks, you can freeze them. The skins will get soft when thawed, but the insides will be fine. Do this with limes, too.

Melons

Cut flesh in slices, cubes, or balls. Add a sweetener and lemon juice or ascorbic acid, if desired. The texture of the melon can best be preserved if you serve the fruit before it's entirely thawed. (See "Firm Frozen Fruit" on page 45.)

You can puree cantaloupes and honeydew melons with ¼ cup lemon juice for each quart, then freeze. Thaw, stir in 2 cups of chopped fruit, top with nonfat yogurt, and you'll have a lovely fruit dessert soup.

Nectarines

Freeze like peaches since they are really a fuzzless peach. Their disadvantage is that their skins aren't as easy to peel. Peel with a vegetable peeler or a small, sharp knife. See "Peaches" below for a tip on freezing whole nectarines.

Oranges and Grapefruit

Peel and remove sections from the heavy membrane. Pack dry or in a syrup, or add a sweetener to taste.

Peaches

Peaches taste better canned, but you can freeze them. Use ripe fruit. To avoid darkening, prepare only enough fruit for one container at a time. Wash, skin, pit, and freeze in halves or slices. Pack in a 30 to 40 percent syrup, or add a sweetener if desired and a small amount of lemon juice or ascorbic acid.

You can also freeze peaches and nectarines whole. This is good to know when time is short and you want to get the fruit into storage quickly, without peeling and slicing it first. Freezing them whole also preserves the color. To use, put frozen fruit in a strainer and pour boiling water over them until the skins crack. Then peel, pit, and slice as usual.

Pears

Pears retain better appearance and texture when you can them. If you wish to freeze them, choose ripe but firm (not hard) fruit.

Wash, peel, and remove cores. To avoid unnecessary darkening, prepare only enough fruit at one time to fill one container. Slice pears directly into a cold 30 to 40 percent syrup mixed with a small amount of lemon juice or ascorbic acid.

Persimmons

Sort and wash. Slice and freeze, press through a food mill, or blend in a food processor or blender for puree. Add a sweetener to taste and lemon juice or ascorbic acid to prevent darkening.

Plums

If freestone, wash, peel, and pit; halve or quarter. If cling-stone, pit and crush slightly, heat just to boiling, cool, and puree in a food mill. Or remove pits and skin, then puree in a blender or food processor. Pack in a 30 to 40 percent syrup, or add a sweetener to taste and lemon juice or ascorbic acid to prevent darkening.

Pomegranates

The tasty seeds of this fruit are what you really eat. Cut halfway into the fruit and then break it apart at this cut. Over a large bowl, tap on the back of the fruit with a wooden spoon to dislodge the seeds. Once frozen, sprinkle the seeds over fruit salad, cottage cheese, or whatever you like. They'll thaw quickly.

Quinces

Quinces are best used as jelly, jam, or sauce, but you can freeze them in chunks. Peel, quarter, and core. Cut into chunks and blanch in boiling water for two minutes or steam for four minutes. Cool by plunging into ice water, drain, and pack dry.

Raspberries

Clean and remove stems. Pack dry or in a 30 percent syrup, or add a sweetener to taste.

Rhubarb

Choose crisp, tender red stalks. Remove leaves and discard any woody ends. Wash and cut into 1-inch pieces. Blanch for $1^1/2$ minutes in steam or boiling water and pack dry, or pack fresh in a 40 percent syrup or a favorite sauce.

Strawberries

Wash and slice or cut in half. Pack in a 30 percent syrup, or add a sweetener to taste. First slice the berries into a bowl, then toss gently with the syrup.

You also can pack strawberries dry if you are freezing fully ripe berries. To pack dry, freeze whole on baking sheets and bag when frozen.

FREEZING SLICED STRAWBERRIES

Freeze sliced strawberries by first tossing them gently in a bowl with a syrup to coat them, then packing them in freezer boxes. Freeze whole strawberries on a baking sheet until they're hard, then store them in plastic freezer bags.

FREEZING WHOLE STRAWBERRIES

CHAPTER THREE

Canning

F OR MANY PEOPLE, canning *means* preserving. Most of us remember gleaming jars of beans, peaches, and tomatoes on
the shelves of Grandma's pantry. There's something heartwarming
about a farm stand with row after row of home-canned pickles,
piccalilli, beets, and chowchow. But often, when we try to capture
that special feeling in our own kitchens, what we end up with is a
hot, sticky mess. In this chapter, you'll find out how to can your
fruits and vegetables quickly, efficiently, and painlessly. Soon, you
can admire your own gleaming shelves of delicious produce!

Can-Do Canning

A lot of home gardeners have abandoned canning for freezing.
That's because, compared to the ease of freezing, canning seems
so old-fashioned, so cumbersome, and so much work. It keeps you
tied to the kitchen stove processing jars filled with food, often
during the hottest days of summer and early fall. And through the
entire lengthy process, you must be very precise to ensure that the
food will be safe. For these reasons, many people have traded in
their canning jars for freezer containers.

But there are ways to make canning easier. You may already
have many kitchen tools that take a lot of the work and time out
of canning. Your food processor, blender, and microwave can save
you time. You also can adapt other appliances. For instance, you
can preheat jars in a dishwasher. You can work with produce that
needs little preparation, such as fruits and vegetables that are seedless, easy to peel, and easy to boil down. Or choose recipes that
are uncomplicated. If you're a novice canner, stick with high-acid
foods like tomatoes that are less likely to spoil. You can process
them in a boiling-water–bath canner, which is less cumbersome
than the pressure canner needed for low-acid foods.

Quick Tip

PREPARATION SHORTCUTS

You can speed up food preparation with the following ideas.

- Use your microwave to heat up hot-packed foods or canning liquids and to cook fruits in their own juice.

- You also can save time by precooking hot-pack beets and sweet potatoes in the microwave.

- Use your blender or food processor to make vegetables, herbs, and fruits into purees or sauces.

- If you need to peel fruits, dip them in boiling water for a few seconds to loosen the skin.

- Use freestone plums, peaches, and nectarines or seedless grapes to minimize pitting. ❖ ❖ ❖

But canning still takes more time and effort than freezing or drying. It's time well spent if you have a large crop and limited freezer space. You may can until your basement bulges, whereas your freezer space is definitely limited. You need only invest in canning jars and, for processing, a large pot with a fitted rack for boiling-water–bath canning or a pressure canner for pressure canning, all of which can be used over and over again through many harvests.

Another plus for canning is that some foods taste better canned than frozen. Artichokes, carrots, and plums develop a rich flavor in the canning fluid. Canning tomato sauce, applesauce, and other fruit purees converts them to a convenient form that pours out without a fuss. Beets, peaches, pears, pickles, and sauerkraut maintain a better texture when canned instead of frozen. For all of the above, the quality and convenience may make your initial investment in time worthwhile.

When Canning Falls Short

There are a number of different fruits and vegetables that are suitable for canning. You'll find them listed in the timetables on page 88. But some kinds of produce lose quality during processing or submersion in liquids. For top quality, try alternative methods of preservation for the following items:

- Berries, including blackberries, boysenberries, dewberries, raspberries, and strawberries: freeze or preserve
- Broccoli: freeze or pickle
- Brussels sprouts: freeze or store in a root cellar (or cold place)

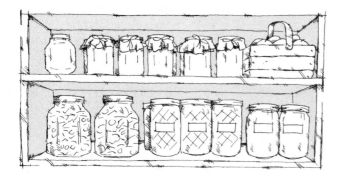

Colorful jars of home-canned produce bring back memories of summer in Grandma's garden—and in your garden, too.

* Cabbage: make into sauerkraut or store in a root cellar (or cold place)
* Cauliflower: freeze or pickle
* Celery: store in a root cellar (or cold place)
* Eggplant: pickle or freeze
* Peppers, hot: pickle or freeze
* Salsify: store in a root cellar (or cold place)
* Turnip, parsnip, rutabaga: store in a root cellar (or cold place)
* Zucchini or summer squash: pickle

How Canning Works

In simple terms, canning food means sterilizing it and keeping it sterile by sealing it in glass containers. The food is sterilized by heating the food and the jar until they're hot enough to kill all pathogenic and spoilage organisms that may be present in raw food. The amount of processing time and the temperature at which you hold the food and its container during processing depends on which food you're canning.

Safety First

High-acid foods, like pickled vegetables, acid-treated tomatoes, and fruits are vulnerable only to heat-sensitive organisms. This makes canning easier. You can kill off molds and yeasts with boiling temperatures achieved in boiling-water–bath processing. These temperatures are not high enough to destroy botulism-causing bacteria, but this lethal bacteria can't survive in high-acid foods with a pH of 4.6 or less anyway.

Other vegetables are low-acid foods, however. They are not only susceptible to heat-sensitive organisms but also to bacteria that can withstand temperatures above the boiling point of water. *Clostridium botulinum* forms a dangerous toxin that causes botulism and may be present in low-acid foods even after long boiling. This bacterium is so toxic that even the tiniest taste can kill. To assure that there are no possible traces of *C. botulinum,* you must process low-acid food at 240°F. Temperatures above the boiling point of water (212°F) can't be reached under ordinary conditions; you have to add pressure with a pressure canner. It's not safe to add extra acids to low-acid foods to avoid the extra time involved in pressure canning. Don't attempt it! There's no way to know if the food is acid enough to eliminate the risk of botulism.

Jars sealed by heat processing in a boiling-water bath or pressure canner makes it impossible for destructive organisms to invade the food and reinfect it. In addition, sealing creates a vacuum inside the container. This vacuum protects the color and flavor of the food, helps to retain the vitamin content, and prevents rancidity due to oxidation.

You can see why the success of preserving the taste, appearance, flavor, nutritional value, and safety of foods depends on the

Quick Tip

SHORTCUTS FOR MAKING TOMATO PASTE, KETCHUP, AND THICK SAUCE

Most recipes for pastes, ketchups, and thick sauces direct you to cook the puree slowly in a heavy pot over low heat, stirring frequently so that the bottom of the puree doesn't burn. This is a fine method as long as you have the time and patience to watch your pot carefully. But if patience isn't one of your virtues, try one of these alternative methods.

Method 1

Use a slow cooker (such as a Crock-Pot) during the final cooking-down stage when making tomato paste or ketchup. Cook down peeled and seeded tomatoes and spices in a heavy pot on the stove, and puree according to the recipe in a food mill, blender, or food processor. Cook the puree down some more if it needs to be a little thicker, then pour it into your slow cooker and set the cooker on high. Keep the lid off so that water can evaporate. Hours later, your puree will be nice and thick, with no stirring and no burned bottom of the pan.

Method 2

Use a colander or sieve. Wash, peel, seed, and quarter your tomatoes and other vegetables and, without chopping or squeezing, simmer slowly in a heavy pot with spices. Don't stir. You'll notice that the water separates out of the tomatoes and rises to the top. When this happens, gently pour the contents of the pot through a colander or sieve, saving the light liquid for soup stock. Run the pulp that's left through a food mill, blender, or food processor. If not quite thick enough, cook down over low heat, stirring frequently.

Method 3

Use your oven instead of the stove, following a standard recipe. Make a large batch and cook it all in a roasting pan, first with the lid on until the tomatoes break down. Process into a puree and bake again, this time with the lid off, so that the water can evaporate and the puree can thicken. Set the oven at 350°F for the first stage and to 300°F for the last cooking-down stage. ❖ ❖ ❖

THE TOMATO CONTROVERSY

There has been a good deal of controversy about whether or not all tomatoes are acidic enough to be canned by the traditional boiling-water–bath method. That is because tomatoes, while generally considered high-acid foods, have a pH range of 4.3 to 4.9, depending on the cultivar and on growing and harvesting conditions. Since any food that has a pH over 4.6 is considered low-acid for canning purposes, tomatoes are pretty close to the borderline. Overripe tomatoes or those that are damaged in some way could actually have an even higher pH.

So for safety's sake, be sure to use only prime, properly ripened fruit. Do *not* use overripe tomatoes. Give your canned tomatoes an extra acid boost by adding bottled lemon juice: 4 tablespoons for each quart and half that amount for each pint, or ½ teaspoon citric acid per quart and ¼ teaspoon citric acid per pint. We also suggest that you can all tomatoes, tomato sauce, and tomato juice with the hot-pack method, eliminating the raw-pack option altogether for these foods. And process tomatoes for a longer time, as the canning timetable on page 90 indicates. ❖ ❖ ❖

complete sterilization of foods and their containers and also on perfect seals. It's essential to follow the canning instructions that follow closely.

Canning Supplies

When produce begins ripening in the garden, gather all the supplies and equipment you'll need. Getting organized ahead of time will let you fly through the canning process while your vegetables have only been off the vine for minutes, or at most, a couple of hours. You can capture them at their freshest and best, and you'll be thankful for it with every jar you open.

Picking Produce—and Water

Even more than when you're eating them fresh, when you're canning, it's critical to use only the best, freshest fruits and vegetables. For maximum quality and safety, always follow these guidelines.

• Use only fresh food in tip-top condition.
• Sort foods for size and maturity so that they will heat up evenly and pack well.
• Don't bring hot food into contact with aluminum, copper, iron, or chipped enamel.
• If possible, use soft water (as opposed to hard water) for canning.

Keeping hot food away from metal and using soft water help prevent a chemical reaction between the minerals in hard water and the foods or metal utensils. This kind of chemical reaction can make some foods darker or gray-tinted—unpleasant but not unsafe.

Even when you follow these guidelines, water with an acidic or alkaline pH can affect the color or texture of certain vegetables. Dr. Kenneth Hall, professor of nutritional sciences and extension food scientist for the University of Connecticut, notes that alkaline water can turn canned onions yellow. Also red cabbage, red plums, and many other red vegetables and fruits will turn greenish blue. Acidic water, common near his home in Connecticut, makes red vegetables and fruits more pink. Canning in acidic water also tends to keep fruits more firm, Hall says. He explains that pectin is most stable at pH 4.0 to 4.5, which is quite acidic. In water with a more neutral to alkaline pH of around 7.0 to 7.5, fruits and vegetables get softer with less cooking. Check your water pH so you'll have some idea of how it may influence your canned goods. A simple litmus test will give you an indication of water pH.

You can buy litmus paper at a garden center, hardware store, or scientific supply store. Just pour your water into a sterile jar, put a strip of litmus paper into the jar, and leave it in for about a minute. Then remove the paper and match its color to a color on the chart that comes with the paper. The pH rating will be on the chart next to the color.

While you're at it, test your water to be sure it's safe to consume before you begin canning with it. If you have a well, get your water checked every year or two. You also should have your water tested for lead, a dangerous element that could be leaching out of your plumbing and could cause developmental problems in children. You can find do-it-yourself test kits that identify lead levels in hardware or water treatment stores.

If you have doubts about your well water or city water, substitute good-quality bottled or distilled water so you won't have to worry. (But don't forget to test its pH before you start!)

The Boiling-Water-Bath Canner

Only high-acid foods, which include all fruits (except figs), tomatoes supplemented with extra acid like lemon juice, and pickled vegetables, should be processed in a boiling-water bath. (This is not the same as a simmering-water bath; the water should be boiling rapidly the entire processing time.) With a few exceptions, these foods can be packed either raw (sometimes called cold) or hot in jars before processing. See "Raw and Hot Packing" on page 73.

Any large pot will do for a water-bath canner as long as it meets these requirements.

• It should be deep enough to have 1 to 2 inches of water over the top of the jars and 1 to 2 inches of extra space for boiling.

• It should be large enough so that you can fit in enough jars to make it worth your while.

• The jars should fit in so that none of them are touching any others; you need room for the water to circulate freely among them. If you wedge them in too tightly, there is a good chance they will crack as they push against one another and the sides of the canner when they expand with the heat.

• The canner should have a snug-fitting cover.

BOILING-WATER–BATH CANNER

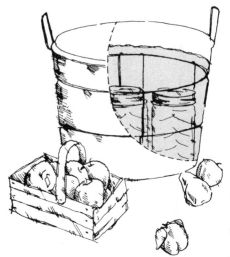

Use a boiling-water-bath canner to can high-acid foods like tomatoes, fruits, and pickled vegetables. You can use any large pot for water-bath canning, including a large stockpot or pressure canner. The pot should be able to hold at least five jars without touching, hold 1 to 2 inches of water over the tops of the jars, plus room for an additional 1 to 2 inches of air space (called headspace) for boiling. Make sure your water-bath canner has a snug lid and a rack to hold jars off the bottom.

PRESSURE CANNER

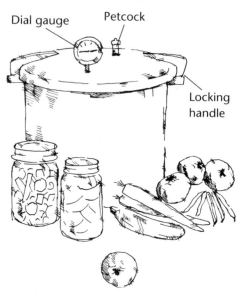

Use a pressure canner to can all vegetables except tomatoes. Pressure canners can have weighted gauges that show three pressure settings—5, 10, and 15 pounds—or can have dial gauges, which monitor rises in pressure from 5 to 15 pounds.

• There should be a metal rack to keep the jars from touching the bottom of the pot. Plan on a second rack between layers of jars if you want to do double-decker canning in your pot.

There's no need to go out and buy a special pot if one you already have can serve double duty. A large stockpot will do nicely; so will a pressure canner. A pressure cooker, though, probably won't be big enough. If you use your pressure canner for water-bath canning, just set its cover in place without fastening it. Be sure to have the petcock open wide (if yours has a dial gauge) or remove the weighted gauge so that the steam escapes freely and no pressure builds up.

The Pressure Canner

All vegetables, except pickles and acid-treated tomatoes, are low-acid foods and must be processed at 240°F. For this you need a pressure canner, not a pressure cooker. A pressure cooker isn't as reliable at maintaining proper pressure, and it's not big enough to hold most canning jars. You need a canner especially made for pressure processing. It must be in good working condition, and it must contain a rack to keep the jars up off the bottom of the pot. Check the safety valve and petcock opening on the canner regularly to make sure that they are not stopped up with food or dirt. You can clean them by drawing a string or piece of cloth through them.

Your canner will probably have a weighted gauge, although some canners have dial gauges. A weighted gauge has three markings: 5 pounds, 10 pounds, and 15 pounds pressure. It is usually more reliable for indicating the correct pressure than a dial gauge, which has markings to indicate pressure from 5 to 15 pounds.

The advantage of the dial gauge is most appreciated by those who live in high-altitude areas, where it's necessary to increase the pressure by 1/2 pound for each 1,000 feet above sea level. With a weighted gauge all that you can do is increase the pressure by the next mark, which means that if your food requires 5 pounds of pressure at sea level (which is how most charts are figured) and you live high in the mountains, process at 10 pounds instead; if it calls for 10 pounds, process at 15 pounds, and if it calls for 15

Quick Tip

SHOPPING FOR CANNERS

You can find different sizes of canners. Select one that won't take up too much cupboard space but will still process enough jars for your needs. Average canners will hold 7 quart jars or up to 9 pint jars. Small canners hold 4 quart jars. Large canners can handle up to 18 pint jars, but only half as many quart jars. ❖ ❖ ❖

OPEN-KETTLE CANNING: OLD-FASHIONED AND DANGEROUS

Open-kettle canning brings to mind those great iron pots simmering over the stove. Lots of people used to do it, and some people still do it, but that doesn't make it safe. Open-kettle canning has fallen out of favor for good reason. In theory, food is sterilized by bringing it to a boil and then kept sterile by placing it immediately in sterile jars covered with sterile caps. When the screw band is tightened over the lid, a vacuum is created, sealing the food and keeping it safe from spoilage.

That's the theory. In reality, there is a chance that bacteria or mold spores can get into the food after it's been heated through but before it's been covered with that sterile cap by means of a less-than-sterile piece of equipment, your hand, or even the air.

We don't take chances, and we don't think that you should either. Forget tradition in this case, and stick with the boiling-water or pressure-canning methods, depending upon your food. This even goes for most jams and jellies, the last holdout for the open-kettle method. As you'll see in Chapter 4, we no longer recommend that you seal jellies, jams, and preserves with paraffin because paraffin can be used only with open-kettle canning. ❖ ❖ ❖

pounds, then increase the pressure a bit so that the marker goes past the 15-pound point.

If your pressure canner has a dial gauge, check it each year for accuracy. Instructions for checking should come with the canner. If not, the home economist at your county extension office should be able to help you find a place to get your gauge checked. A weighted gauge needs only thorough cleaning. Also, make sure the canner is clean before using it.

Jars and Caps

Use only pint or quart jars made for canning. These are manufactured to be sturdy and safe and to fit efficiently into your canner without wasting space. Although you can find canning jars in half-pint, pint, pint-and-a-half, quart, and half-gallon sizes, most recipes call for pint or quart jars. Be sure your recipe calls for the size of jars you plan to use so you can be sure the processing time is right. Substituting another size isn't safe unless you process the food as long as required for a larger jar—and then the food can overcook.

You can reuse your old standard canning jars as long as they're in perfect condition. Discard any jars with cracks, nicks, or chips. Even slight imperfections may prevent proper sealing.

TWO-PIECE CAP

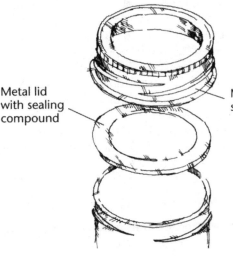

Metal lid
with sealing
compound

Metal
screw band

The easiest cap for can-
ning is the modern two-
piece type—a metal
screw band that holds
down a metal lid with a
rubber sealing compound
on the underside.

When buying new jars, you can choose between styles with wide- or narrow-mouth openings. Use whichever you prefer. The wide-mouth jars can be easier to pack with whole produce and to empty. Narrow-mouth jars have a sleeker look.

You'll seal either kind of jar with a two-piece cap. This has a flat metal disk lined with a ring of rubber (the flange) that fits snugly against the rim of the jar when processed properly. Use the metal lid only once; throw it out when you've eaten the food in that jar so you won't use the lid again by mistake.

A metal screw band holds the lid down during processing and cooling. It's only there to support the lid; it doesn't seal the jar.

Safety Stop

CAP PREPARATION

Before you're ready to can, you need to prepare your caps. Wash them in hot soapy water or in the dishwasher, and rinse them well. Then simmer the metal lids to soften the rubberized flange, re-move from heat, and leave in hot water until ready to use. ❖ ❖ ❖

NARROW-MOUTH JAR

WIDE-MOUTH JAR

Choose narrow- or wide-mouth jars to suit your
canning needs, but remember that it's easier to
remove food from and clean a wide-mouth jar.

You can use metal screw bands over and over again as long as they are in perfect condition with no dents or rust on them. You'll screw the band over the lid fingertip tight before processing. But don't tighten it after taking the jar from the canner; the lid should be tightly sealed without it. Remove the band after the contents of the jar are cold, usually after 24 hours. (But don't force the band off; you might break the seal if you do.) If it won't come off easily, store the jar with the band on. You also can leave the band on if you have to move sealed jars and want extra protection for the seals. Unfortunately, this could make the band rust and become unusable. You'll also have to check the food carefully before you use it. (See "Signs of Spoilage—Throw It Out!" on page 77.)

Canning Basics

Recipes usually don't explain why you follow different procedures and how you choose which one is right for you. So all that vital information is here for you. Read on for a behind-the-scenes tour of canning.

Headspace

Headspace is the space between the contents and the top of the jar. You want to leave enough headspace so that the food can swell and move about as it's heated without running up and over the sides of the jar. But you don't want so much headspace that there's an unnecessarily large quantity of air to force out to create a good vacuum during processing. The problem with food being forced out of the jar because of insufficient headspace is more than just the mess it makes in the canner. Food that winds up outside on the rim of the jar can interfere with a good, tight seal. And food that winds up around the lid and is not entirely washed off can harbor mold, which in turn can grow its way right into the jar and break the seal.

Most vegetables and fruits—either in pint or in quart jars—need a ½- to 1-inch headspace, but don't assume that this is standard for them all. Headspace requirements change with the density, shape, and cooking characteristics of individual foods. Always follow headspace requirements in a recipe, and for individual foods, check the processing timetables on page 88.

SWEETENER CONVERSIONS

You can mix and match sweeteners, using the following conversions.

- 1 cup sugar = 1 cup mild-flavored honey

- 1 cup sugar = 2 cups corn syrup (substitute no more than 50 percent of the total sweetener to add gloss) ❖ ❖ ❖

HOT-PACKED PEACHES

RAW-PACKED PEACHES

Jars hold more produce when the food is precooked (or hot-packed). A full jar of uncooked (or raw-packed) produce fills only two-thirds of a jar after processing, so you'll get more in every jar if you hot-pack.

Sterilizing Jars

The latest research has shown that presterilizing jars is essential if you are processing jellies, juices, pickles, or relishes in a boiling-water bath for less than ten minutes. But it's a good idea to sterilize jars no matter how long you're processing.

Use warm, soapy water or the dishwasher to wash jars and any utensils that you'll be inserting into the jars as you fill them. Then cover the jars and utensils with warm water, bring to a boil, and boil for ten minutes. Add an extra minute to the boiling time for every 1,000-foot increase in elevation. Keep the sterile equipment in the hot water until you are ready to use it.

Raw and Hot Packing

Our canning timetables on page 88 call for raw packing (inserting produce into jars when it's fresh and cold) and hot packing (inserting precooked produce) where it's appropriate to use both methods. When you have a choice, use hot packing. According to Dr. Kenneth Hall, extension food scientist at the University of Connecticut, hot packs produce better quality canned goods by driving air out of the foods (which can hold up to 30 percent air), inactivating enzymes, and setting colors. Hot packing also reduces the chance of ending up with excess headspace.

When packing foods hot, you can insert them into jars more easily because they're not so rigid. They've already shrunk slightly during the initial heating. And, because foods are already hot, they need less processing time in the boiling-water bath. But if you need to pressure-can the food, you won't save any time using hot packing. It takes about the same length of time for both hot- and raw-packed foods to reach the proper pressure. A disadvantage of hot packing is that foods may initially lose some of their food value when they're precooked. But over the next few months of storage, they'll lose fewer nutrients to oxidation than raw-packed foods will.

Raw packing can be better for foods with delicate textures that may suffer less damage when packed raw. And raw packing leaves you with one less pot to clean, a big advantage when your kitchen counter is covered with jars, caps, and produce. Be careful, however, to put raw-packed jars into a canner that's filled with hot—not boiling—water. If you put them into boiling water, the cool jars may crack. One big disadvantage of raw packing is that air can be trapped in the jar.

In as little as two months, trapped air can make the produce lose quality and discolor.

Fruit Syrups

When canning fruits, you can pack them in sweet syrup, fruit juice, or water. Many people prefer to pack fruit with sweeteners, which help fruits hold their shape, color, and flavor. Some sweetener recommendations are listed under individual fruits in the timetable on page 88. But don't use artificial sweeteners before processing fruits. Under the high temperatures of canning, they can develop an off-taste or lose their sweetness.

You also can mix and match sweeteners to suit your own taste. Make a honey syrup using 1 cup mild-flavored honey with 2 cups very hot water. If you prefer to use sugar, for a 9-pint load, make a sugar syrup. For a very light syrup (10 percent), combine 6$\frac{1}{2}$ cups water and $\frac{3}{4}$ cup sugar. For a light syrup (20 percent), combine 5$\frac{3}{4}$ cups water and 1$\frac{1}{2}$ cups sugar. For a medium syrup (30 percent), combine 5$\frac{1}{4}$ cups water and 2$\frac{1}{4}$ cups sugar, and for a heavy syrup (40 percent), combine 2 cups water and 3$\frac{1}{4}$ cups sugar. Use a heavy syrup to sweeten tart fruits and a lighter syrup for sweeter fruits.

For fruits such as apples, apricots, figs, nectarines, peaches, and pears that darken after cutting, you can blend antidarkening agents such as ascorbic acid powder (available in season at grocery stores or through your local drugstore) or bottled lemon juice into the syrup. Other recipes for a lightly sweet, antidarkening syrup is 1 cup apple or pineapple juice, 1 tablespoon bottled lemon juice, and 2 cups water. For a heavy syrup, use 1 cup frozen apple or pineapple juice concentrate, 1 tablespoon bottled lemon juice, and 1 cup water.

If you don't want to can fruit in a sweet syrup, you can pretreat it in a solution of $\frac{1}{2}$ teaspoon ascorbic acid powder or 1 teaspoon lemon juice (add more lemon juice as needed to taste) to 2 quarts of water. Place fruit in the solution as soon as you've washed and sliced it. Can promptly in fresh water or natural juices. Or place the fruit in a solution of 1 tablespoon vinegar to 2 quarts of water, and let it soak for up to 20 minutes. Rinse in cold water, and can in fresh water or natural juices.

Creative Cooking

FRUIT SAUCES AND FRUIT SYRUP TREATS

• Cook down clean apple, peach, and pear peelings that you have left over from canning. Puree them in the food processor for apple, peach, or pear sauce.

• Turn leftover syrup from jars of fruit into frozen fruit bars for the kids or fancy ice cubes for herb tea, punch, or iced tea by freezing it in ice cube trays. ❖ ❖ ❖

Label every canning jar with the date, type of food, and cultivar name. Then you can use the jars with the oldest dates first, making sure your canned produce is up-to-date. And you can compare the flavor and texture of different cultivars, so you'll know which ones to plant next year.

Checking Seals

After processing and cooling canned foods, make sure they are tightly sealed. Press down on the center of the lid. If it doesn't bounce when you press on it, the seal is airtight and proper.

Labeling Containers

After you cool your processed jars and remove the screw bands from the two-piece caps, mark the type of food and the canning date on top of the containers. You can write directly on canning lids with a permanent pen; you don't need to use stick-on labels. Then you can use up the older jars first. If you've canned different varieties of the same food, include the fruit or vegetable's cultivar name. Next year, you'll be able to compare which cultivars you liked best.

Quality Conscious

DON'T DISCARD THE LIQUID

The liquid in canned fruits and vegetables is an important source of nutrients. If you discard it, you're throwing out a good part of the vitamins and minerals in the jar. Normally, fruit and vegetable solids make up about two-thirds of the total contents of the container; the rest is water. Soon after canning, the water-soluble vitamins and minerals distribute themselves evenly throughout the solids and liquid. So about one-third of the water-soluble nutrients is in the liquid portion. Use vegetable liquids in soups, stews, and sauces; add fruit liquids to orange juice for a fruit punch, or add a splash to iced tea to make iced-tea punch. ❖ ❖ ❖

INGENIOUS STORAGE SPACES

If you're short on space but long on garden goods, look for unused nooks and crannies that could hold some of the produce you can. Here are some ideas.

- Pack jars into boxes, and store them under the basement stairs.

- Place jars in vertical racks or stacking baskets in the back of the coat closet.

- Slip a few jars behind your desks, dressers, chests of drawers, or file cabinets.

- Line up jars on the attic steps.

- Put jars in peach crates, and slide them under your bed.

- Install shelves inside the doors on your broom closet and put jars there. ❖ ❖ ❖

Storing Canned Foods

Store canned produce in a cool, dry, dark place for best keeping. The higher the temperature of the storage area, the more chance of vitamin loss in the canned product. But you don't want to store the food in a place so cold that it freezes. Food expands when it freezes, which could break the seals. Dryness is important because humidity can corrode canning lids. And darkness prevents the food from losing its color due to fading in sunlight or artificial light.

Spoiled Food

When canned produce goes bad, it usually provides a few warning signals. Look for a bulging lid, liquid oozing out from under the lid, mold at the top of the canning liquid, air bubbles in the liquid, and browning produce. Don't take a chance on bad produce (and food poisoning)—when in doubt, throw it out.

If you see a jar that shows signs of spoilage (see "Signs of Spoilage—Throw It Out!" on the opposite page), don't even open it. Put the jar in a pan and cover it with water. Boil for 30 minutes. Then wrap the jar in several layers of plastic bags, sealing it well, and bury it so it can't be unearthed by animals or kids. If the contents of the jar have escaped, take care to sanitize your hands, counters, and utensils with hot, soapy water. This may seem like a lot of trouble, but the botulism bacteria are so toxic that a taste may be fatal. Don't release it into the environment where you don't know who'll come into contact with it.

Signs of Spoilage—Throw It Out!
Evaluate every jar before you use it, checking for the following signs of serious contamination.

• A jar that is soiled or moldy on the outside indicates that food has seeped out during storage, which means that air and bacteria, yeasts, and molds could have gotten in. (Jars right out of the canner might be a bit soiled from some of the liquid that was drawn out with the air. This is okay as long as half the contents of the jars aren't floating outside in the canning water! If you've wiped the jars as you should have done, the jars would have gone clean into storage and any food on the outside of the jars now is not okay.)

• A significant change in color, most notably a much darker color, can mean spoilage. Some brown, black, or gray discoloring may be due to minerals in the water or in the cooking utensils; while it may detract from the looks of the food, there is no harm done otherwise.

• A change in texture, especially if the food feels slimy, is a sure sign that the food isn't fit to eat.

• Mold in the food or inside the lid—sometimes nothing more than little flecks—is not a good sign.

• Small bubbles in the liquid or a release of gas, however slight, when you open the can means foul play. Sometimes you get a strong message: Liquid actually spurts out when you release the seal. Other times the gas is more subtle.

Safe but Unsightly

Some fruits and vegetables take on an unusual, but nontoxic, appearance when canned. Here are some common changes that may look strange but are not harmful.

Cauliflower color changes. Cauli-flower that develops a pinkish hue in the jar during storage might look a bit odd, but it's safe to eat. The color change means that it was overly mature when it was canned. Pickled cauliflower may change color because some cultivars react with the vinegar.

Garlic color changes. Garlic added to vegetables before canning has a tendency to turn blue and may share its new color with the rest of the can. No harm done.

Pear color changes. The pinkish color of some canned pears is caused by heating the natural tannins in the fruit. It's harmless.

Separated tomatoes. It's not unusual for the pulp in canned tomatoes or tomato juice to separate from the liquid during storage. The culprit is an enzyme in the

---

Safety Stop

BOIL BEFORE EATING

You can boil any home-canned vegetables for 10 minutes—or up to 20 minutes for corn, spinach, and vegetables of a thicker consistency like sweet potatoes—before serving them. This helps eliminate any unseen spoilage. ❖ ❖ ❖

COMBINATION FOODS

Some older canning books recommend combining different vegetables and processing as if for the ingredient that needs the longest time. But that is not safe in every case and is no longer recommended. Dr. Kenneth Hall, extension food scientist from the University of Connecticut, notes that when you mix two vegetables, you change the solids content of the canned good and may need more heating time. If you want to can vegetable combinations, find reliable, modern recipes such as those included in this book, and follow those processing instructions. ❖ ❖ ❖

vegetable that breaks down the peeled tomatoes if the tomatoes sit too long before being processed—unsightly, but safe.

Buckled lid. If you have a newly canned jar that has a lid with a "buckle" in it, refrigerate it and eat it within a few days. Or reprocess the jar using a new lid, even if the buckled lid is sealed tightly on the jar. The buckling means that there is still some air inside the jar because you screwed the band on too tight; all air must vent from the jar during processing to create a vacuum seal.

Mineral deposits. Dark smudges on the underside of the lid are black, powdery deposits that form when some vegetables react with the metal on the lid. They are harmless as long as you processed the food according to directions. Such deposits are more likely to occur with raw-packed foods than with hot-packed ones.

Floating fruit. Canned fruit that floats is safe to eat. It floats because it's lighter than its syrup. You can prevent the problem next time by trying a few different things. Heat the fruit first to drive out some of its air or switch to a lighter syrup. Or try rolling the jar on its side after it's been canned and the jar is cool. This may cause the fruit to reabsorb some of the liquid it lost during the vacuum process of canning, making the fruit heavier.

Headspace Headaches

Sometimes the liquid level in canned food drops during processing, leaving the jar with a big headspace. To avoid this problem next time, try one of the following:

• Be sure to remove all air bubbles by carefully running a non-metallic spatula around the inside of your jar and adding more liquid as necessary to reach desired headspace level.

• Don't pack the food too tightly or fill the jar too full; if this happens, the food can boil over and take some of the liquid with it.

• Be sure that the lids are centered on the jar and the bands are screwed down fingertip tight. Partial seals allow liquid to escape. If liquid loss occurs during pressure canning, be sure that

SALSA

RELISH

Make your own garden-fresh salsa, relish, and succotash. It's easy to can these flavorful condiments and side dishes. Just make sure you have all the ingredients on hand before you start.

SUCCOTASH

the pressure is held constant and that the jars are allowed to cool slowly. Be particularly careful about sterilizing jars, screw bands, and any other equipment that might have come in contact with the food. Wash your hands with soap and hot water and rinse well.

Canning Step-by-Step

Once you've familiarized yourself with the canning process, equipment, and basics, it's time to graduate to the actual techniques of boiling-water–bath and pressure canning. Here's how they're done.

Boiling-Water–Bath Canning: For High-Acid Foods

This is the easiest kind of canning, with the least chance for error. It's a good way to get started in canning—as long as you follow these directions carefully.

1. Fill the boiling-water canner with enough water to cover the jars completely. There should be 1 to 2 inches of water over the tops of the jars and at least 1 to 2 inches of headspace in the canner above the water.

2. Turn on the heat so the water can heat up. If you're raw packing, be careful not to let the water go over about 140°F or boil to prevent the jars from cracking because of the sharp temperature difference. For hot packing, bring the water temperature up to about 180°F.

3. Wash and rinse the jars and screw bands, and put them into hot water until needed. Sterilize jars and packing utensils by boiling them for 10 minutes if you'll be processing the food for less than 10 minutes. Place lids in water and bring to a simmer. Remove from heat and leave in hot water until ready to use. If you are using closures that have rubber rings, wash the rings in hot water and rinse well. Keep rings in hot water until you are ready to use them.

4. Prepare syrup, if it is to be used.

5. Prepare fruit, pickled vegetables, or tomatoes for canning.

6. Pack the produce, either raw or hot, into jars. If you haven't read it already, go back and read "Raw and Hot Packing" on page 73. You'll see that with some foods you can pack either way, but with others you have no choice and must follow specific recipe directions or directions in the timetable on page 88.

7. Add hot syrup, juice, or water to fill jars, leaving recommended headspace as noted in the timetable or in the specific recipe.

8. Remove the air from the jars by running a nonmetallic spatula along the inside, pressing the food as you do so. Add more liquid, if necessary; the correct amount of liquid helps to create a good vacuum. Wipe the jars, paying particular attention to any food or liquid that might have spilled onto the rim; any food left there could ruin your chances of a good seal. Then close the jars (see "Jars and Caps" on page 70).

9. Place the closed jars upright on a rack in the canner so that none of them are touching any others, allowing the water to circulate freely. If there is room for two layers of jars, place a rack between the two levels and stagger the containers so that none are directly over any of those below. Water should be 1 to 2 inches over the tops of the jars. Add water, if needed (boiling water if hot packing, and hot water if raw packing). Be careful not to pour water directly on the jars. Allow 1 to 2 inches headspace in the canner for water to boil without running over.

10. Put the cover on the canner and bring the water to boiling.

11. Begin to count time as soon as the water starts to boil and process for the time recommended for each specific food and size of jar in the timetable on page 88. The processing times given in the timetable are for altitudes less than 1,000 feet above sea level. For high-altitude areas, increase the processing time two minutes for each 1,000 feet above sea level. For example, if you live 3,000 feet above sea level, process six minutes longer than the recommended time. Leave the lid on the canner, but remove it periodically to make sure the water is boiling gently and steadily. Add more boiling water as needed to keep jars covered.

12. As soon as the processing time is up, remove the jars from the canner. Place them upright, out of drafts, on a wood rack or board, or on several thicknesses of a dry towel so that they are not in direct contact with cold or wet surfaces, either of which might cause very hot jars to crack. Be sure that the jars are an inch apart so that air can circulate under, over, and around each one. Let them cool by themselves; don't tamper with them until they are cool.

13. In the jars, the last bit of air is drawn out as the food cools, creating the vacuum you want. The common two-piece cap is self-sealing; you'll hear a reassuring high-pitched sound of the metal lid snapping down on the glass rim when the vacuum is complete and the jar seals itself. You can tell if the two-piece cap is sealed by pressing down on the center of the lid. If it is down already or stays down when pressed, the seal is good. If it fails to stay down, reprocess the jar with a new lid, or, place in the refrigerator and use within the next few days, or freeze the jar.

Safety Stop

STIRRING SMARTS

Use a nonmetallic spatula, not a knife or other sharp utensil, for removing air bubbles. If you slide a knife around inside a canning jar, you could make tiny scratches or nicks in the glass. The dramatic temperature swings of canning stress the glass, and it could break along those weak spots. ❖ ❖ ❖

Step-by-Step

BOILING-WATER—BATH CANNING

1. Wash and rinse your canning jars and caps,
and keep them in hot water until you need them.

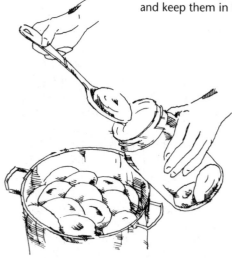

2. Pack fruit, tomatoes, or
pickled vegetables into the jars.

3. Add hot syrup or juice, leaving
the recommended headspace.

5. Wipe the jar rims to remove any spilled food or liquid, then close the jars.

4. Remove air from the jars by running a rubber or other nonmetallic spatula along the inside of the glass. Add more liquid, if necessary, making sure all jars have the correct headspace.

6. Place the jars on a rack in the canner, making sure none are touching. There should be 1 to 2 inches of water above the jars.

7. When the processing time is up, remove the jars and place them on a folded towel or wood rack to cool. Make sure the jars aren't touching—they'll cool faster if air can circulate around them.

Pressure Canning: For Low-Acid Foods

If you like canning and don't mind investing in a pressure canner, you can expand your options using the following method.

1. Put 2 inches of hot water in the bottom of the canner.

2. Wash and rinse jars and screw bands and put them into hot water until needed. Place lids in water and bring to a sim-mer. Remove from heat and leave in hot water until ready to use.

3. Prepare vegetables for canning as suggested in the timetable on page 91. It is not necessary to precook or blanch vegetables intended for canning as you do for freezing and drying since the enzymes that would otherwise break down the food are killed by the heat in the canning process.

4. Pack vegetables, either raw or hot, into jars, leaving recommended headspace, as noted in the timetable. Pour in enough boiling water to cover the vegetables. Run a nonmetallic spatula around the inside of the jar to remove any air bubbles from the jar. Add more liquid if necessary to bring the water level up to the recommended headspace level. Wipe tops and rims of jars, paying particular attention to any food or liquid that might have spilled onto the rims; any food left there could ruin your chances of a good seal. Then close the jars (see "Jars and Caps" on page 70).

5. Set the closed jars on a rack in the canner so that steam can circulate around them freely. If there is room for two layers of jars, place a rack between the two levels and stagger the containers so that none are directly over any of those below.

6. Fasten the cover of the canner securely so that no steam escapes except at the open petcock (if your canner has a dial gauge) or the weighted gauge opening.

7. Allow steam to escape from the opening for ten minutes so all the air is driven out of the canner. Then close the petcock (if your canner has a dial gauge) or put on the weighted gauge and let the pressure rise. When the pressure climbs close to the pressure you need (see the timetable), turn the heat down a bit and let it rise a bit more slowly to where you want it. (If you live in a high-altitude area, you need to increase the pressure by $1/2$ pound for each 1,000 feet above sea level. See "The Pressure Canner" on page 69 for a discussion of adjustments for high altitudes.)

8. Start counting time as soon as 10 pounds pressure is reached, and process for the required time listed in the timetable on page 91. When the proper pressure is reached, turn the heat down a bit, since all you need to do now is maintain that temperature (which affects the pressure), not raise it. Watch the gauge carefully to be sure it stays at the right pressure. Avoid changing the heat suddenly because it will affect the pressure. Don't leave the kitchen even though you might be using a timer; you'll want to be close by to check the gauge frequently. If you *do* leave the kitchen and return to find that the pressure has dropped, start timing again from the beginning.

NOTE: Fluctuating pressure can cause liquid to be pulled from the jars, which might affect the seals. If this happens, check the seals after the jars have cooled. If the liquid level is low, but the canning seals are good, no need to worry.

9. At the end of the processing time, gently remove the canner from the heat.

10. Let the canner stand until the pressure returns to zero. Do not try to bring the pressure down quickly by running cold water over the canner in the sink. The shock could be enough to crack the jars. Wait a minute or two, but no more, then slowly open the petcock (if your canner has a dial gauge) or remove the weighted gauge.

11. Wait 2 minutes, then unfasten the cover and open it away from you so the steam doesn't hit you in the face. Remove the jars and set them upright, out of drafts, on a wood rack or board or on several thicknesses of a dry towel so that they are not in direct contact with cold or wet surfaces, either of which might cause very hot jars to crack. Be sure that the jars are an inch apart so that the air can circulate under, over, and around each one. Let them cool by themselves; don't tamper with the caps until they're cool.

12. Check the seal. You can tell if the two-piece lid is sealed by pressing down on the center of the lid. If it is down already or stays down when pressed, the seal is good. If it fails to stay down, reprocess the jar with a new lid, or, place in the refrigerator and use within the next few days, or freeze the jar.

Step-by-Step

PRESSURE CANNING

1. Wash and rinse your canning jars and caps, and keep them in hot water until you need them.

2. Pack vegetables into the jars, leaving the recommended headspace.

3. Pour in enough boiling water to cover the vegetables.

4. Remove air from the jars by running a rubber or other nonmetallic spatula along the inside of the glass.

5. Wipe the jar rims to remove any spilled food or liquid, then close the jars.

6. Put the jars on a rack in the canner. You can stagger the jars in two rows with a rack between them.

7. Fasten the cover on the canner and allow steam to escape for ten minutes.

9. Remove the cover by opening it away from you so steam doesn't billow up into your face.

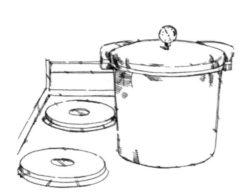

8. Start counting the processing time once the dial or weighted gauge reads 10 pounds. When the time is up, remove the canner from the heat and let it stand until the pressure returns to zero.

10. Take the jars out and place them on a folded towel or wood rack to cool. Make sure the jars aren't touching—they'll cool faster if air can circulate around them.

Timetable for Processing High-Acid Foods

If raw pack and hot pack work well for a specific food, we give directions for both. Otherwise, we describe the preferred method only. See the step-by-step directions on page 80 for instructions on canning in a boiling-water bath.

Product	Directions	Processing Time Glass Jars	
		Pints (min.)	Quarts (min.)
Apples	HOT PACK. Peel, core, and cut into pieces. To keep from darkening, place in water containing lemon juice, ascorbic acid, or vinegar (page 74). Drain, then boil for 5 minutes in syrup, juice, or water. Pack into jars. Cover with boiling syrup, juice, or water, leaving ½-inch headspace.	20	20
Applesauce	HOT PACK. Make applesauce according to your own recipe or one that appears on page 274; pack hot into jars to ½ inch of top.	15	20
Berries, except Strawberries	Because of their delicate texture and flavor, berries are better frozen than canned.		
	RAW PACK. This is preferred for blackberries, boysenberries, dewberries, loganberries, and raspberries. Wash berries and drain well. Fill jars, shaking berries gently. Cover with syrup, juice, or water, leaving ½-inch headspace.	15	20
	HOT PACK. This is preferred for firmer berries: blueberries, cranberries, currants, elderberries, gooseberries, and huckleberries. Wash berries and drain well. Add ¼ cup honey to each quart fruit. Cover pan and bring to boil. Pack into jars. If the berries haven't made enough of their own juice, cover them with boiling syrup, juice, or water, leaving ½-inch headspace.	15	15
Cherries	RAW PACK. Wash; remove pits in sour or pie cherries. Sweet cherries need not be pitted, but do prick their skins with a pin or tip of a knife so that they don't burst during processing. Fill jars, shaking cherries down gently. Cover with boiling syrup, juice, or water, leaving ½-inch headspace.	25	25
	HOT PACK. Wash; remove pits if desired (see raw pack). Add ¼ cup honey to each quart of fruit. Add a little water to unpitted cherries. Cover pan and bring to a boil. Pack hot into jars, and add boiling syrup, juice, or water, leaving ½-inch headspace.	15	20
Figs	HOT PACK. Use ripe figs only. Wash, but do not remove skins or stems. Cover with boiling water and simmer for	45	50

Product	Directions	Processing Time Glass Jars	
		Pints (min.)	Quarts (min.)
Figs— *Continued*	5 minutes. Pack hot into jars, and add 1 tablespoon lemon juice to each pint. Add boiling syrup, juice, or water, leaving 1/2-inch headspace. If lemon juice is not used, jars must be pressure-canned at 5 pounds pressure for 10 minutes for pints.		
Fruit juices	See Chapter 7.		
Fruit puree	**HOT PACK.** Use sound, ripe fruit. Wash; remove pits, if desired. Cut large fruit in pieces. Simmer until soft; add a little water, if needed. Put through a strainer or food mill. Add honey to taste. Heat to simmering and pack into jars to 1/4 inch of top.	15	15
Grapefruits, Oranges, and Tangerines	**RAW PACK.** Remove fruit segments, peeling away the white membrane that could develop a bitter taste in the canning process. Seed carefully. Pack into jars and cover with boiling syrup, juice, or water, leaving 1/2-inch headspace.	10	10
Grapes	**RAW PACK.** Wash and stem seedless grapes. Pack tightly into jars, but be careful not to crush. Add boiling syrup, juice, or water, leaving 1-inch headspace.	15	20
	HOT PACK. Prepare as for raw pack. Bring to a boil in syrup, juice, or water. Pack into jars without crushing, and add boiling syrup, juice, or water to 1/2 inch of top.	10	10
Mixed fruits	**HOT PACK.** Prepare peaches, pears, and pineapples by peeling and cutting into uniform 1/2-inch pieces. Add slightly under-ripe seedless grapes, if you wish. Cook in syrup, juice, or water for 3 to 5 minutes, or until slightly limp. Pack hot into jars, and cover with boiling syrup, juice, or water, leaving 1/2-inch headspace.	20	—
Peaches, Apricots, and Nectarines	**RAW PACK.** Wash fruit and remove skins. About 20 seconds in boiling water makes skins easier to remove. Remove pits. To keep from darkening, place in water containing lemon juice, ascorbic acid, or vinegar (page 74). Drain. Pack into jars. Cover with boiling syrup, juice, or water, leaving 1/2-inch headspace.	25	30
	HOT PACK. Prepare fruit as for raw pack. Heat fruit through in hot syrup, juice, or water. If fruit is very juicy, you may heat it with 1/2 cup honey to 1 quart raw fruit, adding no liquid. Pack into jars to 1/2 inch of top.	20	25

(continued)

Timetable for Processing High-Acid Foods — *Continued*

Product	Directions	Processing Time Glass Jars	
		Pints (min.)	Quarts (min.)
Pears	**HOT PACK.** Peel, halve, and core fruit. To keep from darkening, place in water containing lemon juice, ascorbic acid, or vinegar (page 74). Heat fruit through in hot syrup, juice, or water. If fruit is very juicy, you may heat it with 1/2 cup honey to 1 quart raw fruit, adding no liquid. Pack into jars to 1/2 inch of top.	20	25
Pickled vegetables	See Chapter 5. For specific recipes and processing times, see page 300.		
Plums and Italian prunes	**RAW PACK.** Wash. To can whole, prick skins. Freestone prune varieties may be halved and pitted. Pack into jars. Cover with boiling syrup, juice, or water, leaving 1/2-inch headspace.	20	25
	HOT PACK. Prepare as for raw pack. Heat slowly to boiling to bring out juices. If fruit is very juicy, you may heat it with 1/2 cup honey to 1 quart raw fruit, adding no liquid. Pack into jars. Cover with boiling syrup, juice, or water, leaving 1/2-inch headspace.	20	25
Rhubarb	**HOT PACK.** Wash, trim, and peel only if stalks are not young and tender. Discard all leaves—they are poisonous. Cut into 1/2-inch pieces. Add 1/4 cup honey to each quart rhubarb, and let stand for 3 to 4 hours to draw out juice. Bring to boiling. Pack into jars to 1/2 inch of top.	15	15
Strawberries	Strawberries don't can as well as they freeze. Freeze them or make jams and preserves instead, when possible. **HOT PACK.** Wash and hull berries. Using 1/4 to 1/2 cup honey for each quart of berries, spread berries one layer deep in pans and drizzle honey over them. Cover and let stand at room temperature for 2 to 4 hours to draw out the juice. Then place berries and the juice in a saucepan, and simmer for 5 minutes, stirring to prevent sticking. Pack into jars without crushing, and cover with extra boiling syrup if berries didn't produce enough juice of their own, leaving 1/2-inch headspace.	10	15
Tomatoes	Because tomatoes are borderline low-acid foods, hot pack them only. Add 4 tablespoons bottled lemon juice per quart, or 1/2 teaspoon citric acid. **HOT PACK.** Wash tomatoes. Place a few at a time in boiling water just long enough to loosen skins. Then dip in cold water. Leave tomatoes whole or cut into quarters. Bring tomatoes to boiling and pack into jars to 1/2 inch of top, adding extra boiling water or juice if tomatoes have not made enough juice of their own to cover.	40	45

Timetable for Processing Low-Acid Vegetables

If raw pack and hot pack work well for a specific food, we give directions for both. Otherwise, we describe the preferred method. The step-by-step directions on page 84 give you the basics for pressure canning; read them before following these directions.

Raw-pack or hot-pack foods following directions. Place jars on a rack in the pressure canner containing 2 inches of boiling water. Fasten canner cover securely. Let steam escape for ten minutes before closing the petcock on dial gauge canners or putting on the weighted gauge. Note for high-altitude canners: For each 1,000 feet above sea level, increase the pressure by ½ pound. For more specific directions, see "The Pressure Canner" on page 69.

Product	Directions	Processing Time at 10 lbs. Pressure (unless otherwise noted) Glass Jars	
		Pints (min.)	Quarts (min.)
Artichokes	HOT PACK. Trim and wash artichokes. Be sure that you trim enough so that the chokes fit into a wide-mouth jar. Cook for 5 minutes in a solution of ¾ cup vinegar to 1 gallon water. Then discard the solution and pack into jars. Cover with a brine made from ¾ cup lemon juice and 3 tablespoons salt to 1 gallon water, leaving ½-inch headspace. (To make pulling the chokes out of the jar easier and prevent them from falling apart when you do, tie a string firmly around the bud.)	25	30
Asparagus	RAW PACK. Wash asparagus; trim off scales and tough ends and wash again. Cut into 1-inch pieces. Pack into jars to ½ inch of top as tightly as possible without crushing.	30	40
	HOT PACK. Prepare as for raw pack; then cover with boiling water and boil for 2 to 3 minutes. Pack loosely into jars, and cover with boiling water, leaving ½-inch headspace.	30	40
Beans, dried, with molasses sauce	HOT PACK. Sort and wash dried beans. Cover with boiling water; boil for 2 minutes, remove from heat, and let soak for 1 hour. The beans should expand to twice or a bit more in volume after soaking. Heat to boiling and drain, reserving liquid for molasses sauce, if desired. Fill jars full with hot beans. To make molasses sauce, mix 1 quart liquid from beans, 3 tablespoons dark molasses, 1 tablespoon vinegar, and ¾ teaspoon dry mustard. Heat to boiling. Fill jars to 1 inch of top with molasses sauce.	65	75
Beans, green and yellow	RAW PACK. Wash beans. Trim ends and cut into 1-inch pieces. Pack tightly into jars. Cover with boiling water, leaving 1-inch headspace.	20	25

(continued)

Timetable for Processing Low-Acid Vegetables — *Continued*

| Product | Directions | Processing Time at 10 lbs. Pressure (unless otherwise noted) Glass Jars | |
		Pints (min.)	Quarts (min.)
Beans, green and yellow— *Continued*	**HOT PACK.** Prepare as for raw pack. Then cover with boiling water and boil for 5 minutes. Pack loosely into jars. Cover with boiling liquid and water, leaving ½-inch headspace.	20	25
Beans, lima	**RAW PACK.** Shell and wash beans. Pack the beans loosely into jars. Cover with boiling water, leaving 1-inch headspace.	40	50
	HOT PACK. Shell the beans. Cover with boiling water and bring to a boil. Pack loosely into jars. Cover with boiling water, leaving 1-inch headspace.	40	50
Beets	**HOT PACK.** Sort beets for size. Cut off tops, leaving a 1-inch stem and root to prevent color bleeding. Then wash. Boil or microwave until skins slip off easily. Skin, trim, cut, and pack into jars. Cover with boiling water, leaving 1-inch headspace.	30	35
Cabbage	See "Sauerkraut Grandma's Way" on page 123.		
Carrots	**RAW PACK.** Wash and scrape carrots. Slice, dice, or leave whole. Pack tightly into jars. Cover with boiling water, leaving 1-inch headspace.	25	30
	HOT PACK. Prepare as for raw pack, then cover with boiling water and bring to boil. Pack into jars. Cover with boiling liquid, leaving ½-inch headspace.	25	30
Corn, cream style	**HOT PACK.** Husk corn and remove silk. Wash. Cut corn from cob at about center of kernel and scrape cobs. Add 1 pint boiling water to each quart of corn. Heat to boiling. Pack into jars, and add liquid, leaving 1-inch headspace.	85	—
Corn, whole kernel	**HOT PACK.** Husk corn and remove silk. Wash. Cut corn from cob at about two-thirds the depth of kernel. Add 1 cup hot water, heat to boiling, and simmer for 5 minutes. Pack loosely into jars to 1 inch of top with mixture of corn and liquid.	55	85

Product	Directions	Processing Time at 10 lbs. Pressure (unless otherwise noted)	
		Glass Jars	
		Pints (min.)	Quarts (min.)
Okra	**HOT PACK.** Choose young, tender pods only. Wash and trim stems. Leave whole or cut into 1-inch slices. Cover with boiling water and boil for 1 minute. Drain, reserving liquid. Pack into jars, and cover with hot liquid, leaving 1-inch headspace	25	40
Onions, small white	**HOT PACK.** Choose onions of uniform size, about 1 inch in diameter. Peel, trim off roots and stalks, and wash, if necessary. Cover with boiling water, and cook gently for 5 minutes. Pack loosely into jars, and cover with boiling liquid, leaving $\frac{1}{2}$-inch headspace.	25	30
Peas, edible pods	**RAW PACK.** Trim and wash pea pods. Pack loosely into jars, and cover with boiling water, leaving 1-inch headspace.	20	25
Peas, garden	**RAW PACK.** Shell and wash peas. Pack loosely into jars. Cover with boiling water, leaving 1-inch headspace.	40	40
	HOT PACK. Prepare as for raw pack. Cover with boiling water and bring to a boil. Pack loosely into jars. Cover with boiling water, leaving 1-inch headspace.	40	40
Peppers, sweet	**HOT PACK.** Remove stem, core, seeds, and inner white membrane. Remove skins by plunging into boiling water for a few minutes, running under cold water, and taking off the now-split skins with a sharp knife or potato peeler. Slice peppers or flatten whole halves and pack carefully in layers into jars. Cover with boiling water, leaving $\frac{1}{2}$-inch headspace. You can add $\frac{1}{2}$ tablespoon of lemon juice or 1 tablespoon of vinegar per pint, if you wish.	35	—
Potatoes	**HOT PACK (cubed).** Wash, peel, and cut into $\frac{1}{2}$-inch cubes. Dip cubes in 1 teaspoon salt to 1 quart water or $\frac{1}{2}$ teaspoon ascorbic acid to 1 quart water to prevent darkening. Drain. Cook for 2 minutes in boiling water. Pack into jars, and cover with boiling water, leaving 1-inch headspace.	35	40
	HOT PACK (whole). Use potatoes 1 to $2\frac{1}{2}$ inches in diameter. Wash, peel, and cook in boiling water for 10 minutes. Pack into jars, and cover with hot liquid or boiling water, leaving 1-inch headspace.	35	40

(continued)

Timetable for Processing Low-Acid Vegetables — *Continued*

Product	Directions	Processing Time at 10 lbs. Pressure (unless otherwise noted)	
		Glass Jars	
		Pints (min.)	Quarts (min.)
Pumpkins and Winter squash	Because pureed squash is so dense, it's difficult to get good heat penetration. Can only cubes and freeze puree. **HOT PACK.** Wash pumpkin or winter squash, remove seeds, and peel. Cut into 1-inch cubes. Boil for 2 minutes. Pack into jars, and cover with hot liquid or boiling water, leaving 1-inch headspace.	55	90
Soybeans, green	**HOT PACK.** Shell beans, then cover with boiling water and bring to a boil. Drain, reserving liquid. Pack loosely into jars, and cover with hot liquid, leaving 1-inch headspace.	40	50
Spinach and other greens	**HOT PACK.** Pick over and wash thoroughly. Cut out tough stems and midribs. Place about 2½ pounds of spinach in a cheesecloth bag and steam for about 10 minutes, or until well wilted. Pack loosely into jars. Cover with boiling water, leaving 1-inch headspace.	70	90
Sweet potatoes	**HOT PACK.** Wash and sort for size. Boil or steam for 20 to 30 minutes or microwave to facilitate slipping of skins. Cut into uniform-size pieces. Pack loosely into jars, pressing gently to fill air spaces. Cover with boiling water, leaving 1-inch headspace.	65	90
Vegetable soups (vegetable, dried bean)	Prepare according to your favorite recipe but cook only half or less the time suggested; let the soup do most of its cooking during processing. Pack into jars, leaving 1-inch headspace.	60	75
Zucchini and Summer squash	None of these are particularly good canned or frozen, but you can do both. You can also pickle zucchini, and you'll find a good recipe for such pickles on page 315. **RAW PACK.** Wash and slice; do not peel unless squash is large and skin is tough. Cut into ½-inch slices and halve or quarter slices that are extra large in diameter. Pack tightly into jars, and cover with boiling water, leaving 1-inch headspace.	25	30
	HOT PACK. Prepare as for raw pack. Cover with boiling water and bring to a boil. Drain, reserving liquid. Pack loosely into jars, and cover with hot liquid, leaving ½-inch headspace.	30	40

CHAPTER FOUR

Preserving

Jellies, Jams, Preserves, Fruit Butters, and Marmalades

*L*ET SPARKLING JARS of homemade jellies and jams spice up your breakfasts. They're a perfect gift for family and friends, too—everybody loves that rich fruit flavor! Homemade preserves, a natural with a peanut butter sandwich, are a great way to store extra berries and fruits. Once you get started, you may enjoy making preserves so much that you'll grow fruits and berries just for jelly making.

If you have shied away from making your own preserves because you don't have a lot of extra time, you'll be glad to know that there are several easy ways to make preserves fast. You can use commercial pectin and ripe fruit to make jellies and jams in minutes. Or make low-sugar freezer spreads that you don't even have to cook. Then, if you have a quiet spell on a rainy day, you can relax and cook the old-fashioned way, using the delicious, natural elements in fruits to make rich, flavorful spreads.

Start the habit of making preserves whenever you have extra fruit left over from canning or freezing. Preserve any fruit that's too small or too large, too ripe or not ripe enough. Use delicious ripe fruit with recipes that call for adding commercial pectins. Slightly underripe fruit contains more natural pectin and acid—the key ingredients for jelling—than you'll find in ripe or overripe fruit. That's why you'll include some underripe fruit in a recipe for cooked-down jellies and jams.

You'll learn several different methods for preserving in this chapter, along with specifics on how to use both honey and sugar as sweeteners. Sugar is easy to use and bonds readily with pectins to make jellies and jams jell. Mild-flavored honey, used sparingly, can make a unique, natural product. Where possible, we call for using honey in smaller amounts than the sugar equivalent. When you use less, you leave more opportunity for the good fruit flavor to come through. If you haven't had strawberry jam or raspberry preserves that really zing with a taste that's more fruity than sweet, you're in for a very pleasant surprise.

How Preserving Works

Jellies, jams, and other preserves are a safe and effective way to preserve fruit color and flavor. The naturally high acid and sugar levels in most fruit, combined with natural or added pectin, make delicious spreads for toast or sandwiches or fillings for desserts or breads. Better yet, preserves are easy to freeze, refrigerate, or can in a boiling-water bath.

You may need to add extra pectin, either commercial pectin or fruits naturally high in pectin, to fruits like strawberries and apricots that don't have much natural pectin in them. You also can add pectin to cut down on cooking time when using honey instead of sugar. Jellies made with added pectin also require less fruit than the cooked-down type to make the same amount of finished produce.

The traditional cooked-down method of jelly and jam making simply uses fruit, a liquid such as water or fruit juice, and a

HOW TO TEST PECTIN AND ACID LEVELS

Making cooked-down preserves jell can be a little tricky because you never know just how much acid and pectin are in any batch of fruit. If you want to have a better idea of what you're starting with and what you can do to make them better for jelling, try the following tests.

The acid test. Taste the prepared fruit mixture to see if it is as sour as 1 teaspoon lemon juice diluted in 3 tablespoons water and ½ teaspoon sugar. If it is not, add up to 1 tablespoon lemon juice per cup of fruit mixture until the acidity matches.

The pectin test. This test uses rubbing alcohol, which is poisonous, to determine the pectin level needed to jell fruit preserves. Cook the fruit mixture for five minutes and let it cool. Then combine 1 teaspoon rubbing alcohol and 1 teaspoon of the fruit mixture. Shake them together and let the blend rest for one minute. Pour into a saucer. If the blend becomes solid or full of flakes, the pectin levels are adequate. If it's runny, you may want to add extra pectin. Don't taste the mixture—it's poisonous once you add the alcohol. ❖ ❖ ❖

sweetener. It only works with fruits that have plenty of natural pectin (see the list on page 98), and even then, you need to use a blend of three-quarters fully ripe fruit and one-quarter slightly underripe fruit. You may have to do a little guessing when making jellies and jams this way because of natural variations in pectin, acid, and sugar levels. (To learn how to test pectin and acid levels in fruit, see "How to Test Pectin and Acid Levels" on the opposite page.) If the fruit you're working with is low in acid, recipes will call for adding lemon juice or citric acid.

Jelly or Jam?

Using either added pectin or the cooked-down method, you can make jellies, jams, preserves, conserves, and marmalades. But all five are distinct because they use different raw materials. Here's how they differ.

- Jellies are made from fruit juice into a clear or translucent gel.
- Jams are purees made with fruit. They're thick but not as firm as jellies.
- Preserves, conserves, and marmalades are made with bits of fruit, cooked with sweeteners and pectin until translucent. Preserves are generally made with a single kind of fruit. Conserves are made with fresh and dried fruits or nuts. Marmalades are made from one or many kinds of citrus fruits.

Fruit Butter Facts

Fruit butters are not jelled at all but instead are thick purees. What's really great about fruit butters is that you don't need a special knack to make them. They aren't as delicate as jams and jellies. You don't have to get them off the stove at exactly the right moment for fear they won't jell properly. You won't have to worry about testing your fruit for acid or pectin or to find out if the mixture is thick enough or not. This is because fruit butters don't jell at all. Instead they thicken naturally as they cook down. You can leave them unamended or add sweeteners and spices.

Refrigerator Jams

Uncooked jellies and jams are often called refrigerator jellies and jams because they are not sterilized by boiling and will spoil unless you refrigerate or freeze them. These spreads don't use pectin for thickening—instead they substitute agar, a natural thickening agent made from seaweed, or gelatin.

Preserving Methods at a Glance

Product	Difficulty	Flavor
Cooked-down jam and jellies	Challenging	Full fruity flavor
Added-pectin jam and jellies	Moderate	Sweet
Refrigerator jam and jellies	Easy	Firm, mild
Fruit butters	Easy	Rich and fruity

Preserving Supplies

Here are the supplies and equipment you'll need for making preserves. Gather them together first so that when you actually start to cook you can proceed without delay.

Fruit First

The essential ingredient in all preserving is fruit. For the best preserves, use fresh, healthy fruit in an appropriate blend of ripe and underripe for the recipe you've chosen. Picking the right fruit is especially important if you plan to make cooked-down preserves. For these, start with fruits that are naturally high in acid and pectin.

Pectin levels go up when growing conditions are dry, so midsummer droughts are a good time to experiment with this method. Pectin levels also peak in most slightly underripe fruits but are especially high in the following: tart apples, underripe blackberries, crabapples, cranberries, red currants, gooseberries, 'Concord' grapes, underripe guavas, sour plums, and underripe quinces.

Still other fruits, especially ripe ones, are naturally low in pectin. Use the following fruits for recipes where you'll be adding pectin: apricots, blueberries, ripe figs, ripe mangoes, mulberries, nectarines, peaches, pears, raspberries, and strawberries.

Frozen Fruit

Feel free to use frozen fruit instead of fresh fruit for jams and preserves. At the Rodale Food Center, we were delighted to find that jams and preserves made from frozen fruit tasted and looked just as good as the ones made from fresh fruit.

Knowing that you don't have to drop all those other projects to make jams right when the fruit is ready could really be a godsend. You'll still have the work of cleaning and slicing the fruit for

To make jelly, you'll need fruit, a sweetener such as honey or sugar, usually pectin to help the fruit jell, and jelly jars. Gather your supplies before you start for fast, flawless jelly making.

the freezer, but you can postpone the cooking and mashing for another time so that you don't have to do it when you're also attempting to freeze your bumper crop of tomatoes and plant your fall peas. And with frozen fruit, you've got the advantage of being able to be creative by making up combinations of fruits that don't come into season at the same time.

Using Frozen Fruit in Jams and Preserves

Fruit that you intend for jam or preserves later on should be dry-packed, which means it should be frozen without sweetening or syrup of any sort. This is because fruit thaws faster without a syrup, and the measurement of sweetener will be more precise if it's added when you're making your jam or preserves. Remove stems, blemishes, pits, and skins where appropriate. Make sure you premeasure the fruit and mark the amount on the container. Don't bother to thaw the fruit before preserving (although you can thaw it if you wish). Thawing fruit may turn brown, but you can prevent some of this if you thaw it quickly over heat in a saucepan.

Jams are made from fruit purees. You can puree the frozen fruit in a food processor. If you don't have a processor, then you're going to have to partially thaw it first and chop it in a blender or mash it with a fork, potato masher, or pastry blender. Measurements in our recipes are for whole, prepared fruits, that is, cups of whole berries, sliced peaches, and so forth. After the fruit has been pureed, it will measure somewhat less. For instance, 1 cup of strawberries will yield ³/₄ cup of puree.

Preserves are made with chunks of whole fruit. To make them from frozen fruit, place the whole fruit, still frozen, in a saucepan. Add a little fruit juice—about ¹/₄ cup to each quart of fruit. Cover the pan and warm it over very low heat until the fruit is softened and its juices have been released. You may then want to crush some of the fruit, particularly if the pieces are very large. Proceed from here with any recipe as if the fruit was fresh.

More juice may drain from the frozen fruit than from fresh fruit, which is ideal for making preserves because it combines with the sweetener to make the clear, syrupy part of the preserves.

Sweeteners

Most recipes for preserves call for sugar, which helps to form the jell and preserve the product. But for no-cook freezer preserves and fruit butters, you also can use honey or maple syrup—natural sweeteners with unique flavors of their own. We also have recipes that use honey in jams and jellies, but they're a bit trickier to make than conventional sugar-based jellies and jams. To jell, you have to cook honey-based preserves longer than if they were made with sugar—about 8 to 10 minutes for pectin-added jellies and jams and even longer for the cooked-down ones that have no extra pectin added. But don't go over 20 minutes or the pectin will break down and your preserves will be runny. And don't be surprised if honey-based preserves are a little less firm than sugar-made jells because of the extra liquid in honey.

Because the kind of sweetener is intimately involved with how the product jells, don't swap sweeteners in any recipe, except gelatin-based spreads or fruit butters, which don't rely on pectin to thicken them.

Pectins

You can use several different kinds of pectins for your jellies, jams, and preserves. Decide if you want to work quickly and easily—if so, use added liquid or powdered pectin. Or, if you want rich fruit flavors to shine, use natural pectins in the fruit or add homemade pectin. You also can eliminate pectin entirely in fruit butters (see "Flavorful Fruit Butters" on page 112) and low-calorie gelatin- or agar-based spreads.

Here are the differences in the kinds of pectins.

Powdered pectin. This commercial product is easy to find in grocery stores. It makes a large batch of jelly or jam in only a few minutes of cooking time. But it requires lots of sugar—up to 60 percent of the preserve's contents.

Liquid pectin. This is another commercial product, which works even faster than powdered pectin (in about one minute of cooking) but also requires a lot of sugar.

Natural pectin in fruit. Check the list of fruits that are naturally high in pectin and acid on page 98 to get an idea of which fruits have the most. You'll have to cook them longer, up to 20 minutes, and can get a lower yield than with commercial pectins.

HOW TO MAKE HOMEMADE PECTIN

If you happen to have a bumper crop of apples, you'll like the idea of using some of the surplus to make your own pectin. It's one more good use for that large supply.

You can make pectin—often called apple jelly stock—ahead of time and preserve it for later use if you enjoy making combination jellies or blending it with other fruits in season when fresh apples are not available. Or, if you are lucky enough to have fresh apples at the same time as the other fruits, you can use the pectin immediately.

Apple thinnings—those small, immature green apples sold in the early summertime—are rich in both acid and pectin. They will make good jelly stock and will give a snappy tartness to your jelly. However, if you prize the clarity of the jelly, be warned that such apples will not produce as clear and transparent a jelly as pectin made from fully mature apples.

Whatever type of apples you're using, here's what to do. Wash the apples carefully, but don't peel or core them, as pectin is concentrated just under the skins and in and around the seeds. Trim off bad parts, and cut the pieces into thin slices. Measure 1 pint of water for every pound of apples. Place the slices in a kettle, and boil for 15 minutes.

Strain off the free-running juice through one thickness of cheesecloth, without attempting to squeeze the pulp. Return the pulp to the kettle, and add the same measure of water again. This time, cook the mixture at a lower temperature for 15 minutes. Allow it to stand for 10 minutes, then strain the second batch of juice through one thickness of cheesecloth. Again, do not attempt to squeeze the pulp.

Allow the pulp to cool enough so that you can handle it. Squeeze out the remaining juice, and combine all the batches of strained juice. There should be about 1 quart of juice for every pound of apples you used.

You can use this stock immediately for blending with other fruit juices to make jelly or jam, or you can preserve it for future use. If you wish to can the stock, heat it to the boiling point, and pour it immediately into hot, scalded canning jars, leaving $1/2$ inch headspace. Cap, process in boiling water bath for 15 minutes. Use within a few months. Or, invert the jars to cool in the refrigerator. Use within four days.

If you prefer to freeze the stock, allow it to cool in the refrigerator, and then pour into freezer containers, leaving 1 inch of headspace. Use within 6 months.

Four cups of homemade pectin will replace approximately one-half of a bottle or 3 ounces of commercial liquid pectin in most recipes. ❖ ❖ ❖

Homemade pectin. Making your own pectin takes some time and trouble but will result in more flavorful jellies. Try it sometime and see. You'll need a lot of homemade pectin—it takes about 4 cups to equal 3 ounces of liquid pectin—but you can make a big batch ahead of time and freeze it for later. (See "How to Make Homemade Pectin" above.)

Gelatin and agar. These are not really pectins and don't need to be cooked, only dissolved.

Whichever pectin you use, be sure to have fresh pectin on hand before you begin making preserves. When pectin gets over about a year old—including the time it sits on the grocery store shelf—it becomes less reliable.

Jars, Caps, and Processing Equipment

Use wide-mouthed, 8- or 12-ounce glass canning jars to safely process and store your preserves. Top the jars with standard two-piece caps, not wax.

Food preservation researchers once thought that any jelly or jam that was firm enough could be sealed safely with paraffin. That is no longer the case, no matter how much or what kind of sweetener you use. It's been discovered that wax seals fail more often than the common two-piece caps, inviting molds and other contaminants inside. People used to scrape off the top layer of jelly or jam when they noticed mold, but this isn't advised any more because we know that some molds produce toxins that can seep below the surface and go deep into the food.

Sterilize the jars before filling them if your recipe calls for processing for less than ten minutes. Then process in a boiling-water–bath canner. For details on sterilizing and processing, see page 110.

You also can freeze most preserves and spreads in standard freezer bags or containers. Let them thaw before using. For more information on freezing, see Chapter 2.

Labels

Be sure to mark the kind of jelly or jam and the date you made it on the jar or freezer container. If you make more than one batch per day, indicate the batch number so you can tell them apart. Write in permanent ink on the top of the lid or invest in some decorative labels that will beautify and personalize your preserves.

Preserves in the Microwave

Use the microwave oven to warm fruit before extracting juice for jellies—it can save you time. Or, use your microwave to make preserves, from start to finish, following a recipe adapted for microwave use. You need a special recipe because microwave techniques are a little different than conventional ones. Here are some reasons why and some tips to help you succeed.

• With a microwave, less moisture evaporates out of the mixture. So begin with fruit that has been washed and dried for the fastest results.

• Because of the way microwaves cook, cut fruit up into uniform pieces, or if you microwave fruit whole, prick the skin so it won't explode.

• Use smaller quantities for quicker results.

• Cooking times can vary according to the power of the oven, the recipe you use, and the condition of the fruit. So check the preserves often to see how they're coming along.

Creative Cooking

UNCOOKED PRESERVES

Enjoy delicious fruit spreads without dealing with the jelling process by making uncooked refrigerator or freezer jams. These use gelatin or agar and as little or as much sweetener as you'd like. They can't be cooked, and certainly not boiled, because high temperatures affect the gelatin or agar that's used to create the gel. You won't find agar (which is a natural thickening agent made from seaweed) in many supermarkets, but you shouldn't have much trouble finding it in a natural food store, an Asian market, or a mail-order food catalog.

You can't can most uncooked jams and jellies. Instead, pour them into sterilized jars with tight-fitting lids and refrigerate for up to three weeks, or store in the freezer for up to six months. If you're going to freeze them, remember to leave $\frac{1}{2}$ inch of headspace for expansion, and let them cool in the refrigerator for at least ten hours so they can set up before going into the freezer.

Uncooked Jam with Agar

This recipe was developed for agar flakes. Agar comes in other forms, but the flakes are the most convenient to use.

1 tablespoon lemon juice

3 cups prepared mashed fruit, at room temperature

$\frac{1}{2}$ cup cold water

3 tablespoons plus $1\frac{1}{2}$ teaspoons agar flakes

$\frac{1}{2}$ cup mild-flavored honey, such as clover (the amount of honey can be adjusted 3 tablespoons either way, according to taste)

Stir the lemon juice into the fruit, and set aside. Place the water in a small saucepan, and stir in the agar flakes. Without further stirring, wait 1 minute, then bring the agar to a simmer over medium-low heat. Once it's simmering, stir for at least 2 minutes, or until the agar is completely dissolved. Then stir in the honey. Use a heatproof rubber spatula to scrape the sides and bottom of the pot.

Pouring with one hand and stirring with the other, add the agar mixture to the fruit (do not add the fruit to the agar). Continue stirring until it's completely mixed. Taste at this time and add more honey, if desired. Pour into hot, scalded half-pint jars, leaving $\frac{3}{4}$ inch of headspace, and seal.

You can keep jam that will be used within 3 weeks in the refrigerator, but freeze the rest. To freeze, leave $\frac{1}{2}$ inch of headspace, and allow the jam to cool in the refrigerator for 10 hours before freezing. Thaw jam in the refrigerator.

Yield: 4 half-pints

• Preserves can boil over and make a big mess. Eliminate that problem by using a glass or microwave-safe ceramic container that's large enough to accommodate the rapid boiling of your preserves.

• Top the container with a fitted microwave-safe lid, or for quicker cooking, use microwave-safe plastic wrap left open in one corner as a vent.

• Stir often to keep the sweet spreads from sticking or burning on the sides of the container and to encourage even cooking.

Now you're ready to try a quick recipe for jam prepared in the microwave, such as "Unconventional Refrigerator Jam" below.

Creative Cooking

UNCONVENTIONAL REFRIGERATOR JAM

We call this unconventional because it breaks all the rules we gave you about what an uncooked jam or jelly should and should not do. Contrary to convention, this does not use gelatin or agar, and so, contrary to convention, it can be canned.

Refrigerator Apricot Jam

The Rodale Food Center found this jam to be tasty and tart. It also is suitable as a filling for baked goods.

2 cups dried apricots

2 cups water

4 tablespoons lime juice

2 tablespoons maple syrup

$\frac{1}{2}$ teaspoon almond extract

In a 1-quart microwave-safe dish, combine the apricots and water. Cover with a lid or plastic wrap. Microwave on high for 6 to 7 minutes, or until apricots are soft, stirring after half the cooking time. Drain the apricots, reserving 3 tablespoons of the liquid. Puree the apricots in a blender or food processor. Return to the baking dish, and add the lime juice, maple syrup, and almond extract. Cover and microwave on high for 1 minute, or until heated through. Refrigerate.

To can: Pour into hot, scalded half-pint jars, leaving ¼-inch headspace, and seal. Process for 10 minutes in a boiling-water bath.

To freeze: Prepare the recipe as directed. Pour into freezer containers, leaving ½-inch headspace. Cool in the refrigerator for 10 hours before freezing.

Yield: 3 half-pints

Jelly Step-by-Step

If you're a novice jelly and jam maker, follow these procedures carefully. You'll need to do every step "just so" for best results. But once you begin to get some experience, you'll be able to progress without pausing to glance at this book every few minutes. Preserving can become as natural and easy for you as making muffins.

Here are some procedures that will make following jelly recipes easier.

Extracting Juice for Jelly

Before you make jelly, you must first extract juice from your fruit. You can use your own canned or frozen fruit juice (see how to make your own on page 106). Or you can use any unsweetened, commercial fruit juices as long as you have a recipe that calls for added pectin.

You also can extract juice with a cloth jelly bag, available at most hardware stores during the canning season. Or you can use several thicknesses of cheesecloth. Dampen the jelly bag or cheesecloth before you use it. For the clearest jelly, let juice drip through the bag without squeezing it. You can get more juice by twisting the jelly bag slightly and squeezing the juice out, but strain the pressed juice again through a new jelly bag without squeezing. If the juice yield is slightly short and you need a bit more for your recipe, add a little water to the pulp in the jelly bag and let it drain through. When you're finished with the jelly bag, wash it out well so your next batch of jelly won't pick up a sour or musty taste from old fruit or fermenting juice.

You'll get the clearest jelly if you let the juice drip out of the fruit overnight instead of squeezing it out. Use a jelly bag or cheesecloth. If you're using cheesecloth, dampen several sheets of cheesecloth, place your fruit pulp in the center of the sheets, and gather the cloth into a bag with a piece of string. Loop the string over a kitchen cabinet knob and suspend the bag over a bowl. By the next morning, all the juice will have dripped into the bowl.

A Fruit-by-Fruit Guide to Juicing for Jelly

Different fruits require slightly different juice-extracting procedures. Try the following methods.

For 5 pounds of apples: Remove blossoms and stem ends. Chop coarsely. Add 5 cups water; cover and simmer for 10 minutes, stirring occasionally. Then crush and simmer for 5 more minutes. Pour into a jelly bag, and let juice drip through. This yields about 10 cups.

For 3 pounds of grapes and fruits with pits, such as cherries, plums, and peaches: Remove pits (this isn't necessary for grapes) and chop finely. Add 1/2 cup water, cover, and simmer for 5 to 10 minutes, stirring occasionally. Pour into a jelly bag, and let juice drip through. This yields about 5 1/2 cups.

For 2 1/2 quarts of berries: Puree or mash. Pour into a jelly bag, and drain. This yields about 5 1/2 cups.

Cooking the Fruit Mixture

Heat the juice you've extracted for jelly. Time when you add the pectin to the juice according to the kind of pectin you use. When using powdered pectin, mix it with the unheated fruit juice before cooking. If you're using liquid pectin, add it to the juice and sweetener mixture once it's boiling. After adding liquid or powdered pectin, bring the mixture to a full boil that can't be stirred down. Slow boils make disappointing jams and jellies. Cook for the recommended length of time but not longer. Pectin is activated by heat but deactivated by long cooking.

When Is It Done?

Jellies that use added pectin are done when they have been boiling rapidly for the time required by your recipe. But jellies without added pectin are less reliable. You can use a candy/jelly thermometer to check for doneness: When it reads 220°F (subtract 2° for each 1,000 feet above sea level), it's done.

If you don't have a jelly thermometer, you can test for doneness by doing a jelly test. There are a couple of different tests you can use. While you're preparing to test, remove the jelly from the heat so that it doesn't continue to cook.

The Spoon or Sheet Test

The spoon or sheet test is the most traditional but perhaps not the easiest test. To make a spoon or sheet test, dip a cold metal spoon in the boiling jelly mixture. Raise it at least a foot above the kettle, out of the steam, and wait 20 seconds. Then turn the spoon so

This jelly thermometer is easy to read when inserted in a boiling batch of fruit juice or crushed fruit.

Step-by-Step

MAKING JELLY, JAM, OR PRESERVES

1. If you're using powdered pectin, mix it with the unheated fruit juice (for jelly) or crushed fruit (for jams and preserves) before cooking *(left)*. But if you're using liquid pectin, add it to the boiling juice or cooked fruit off the heat *(right)*.

2. Bring the juice-pectin or fruit-pectin mixture to a full boil, and cook for the recommended time.

3. If you're making jelly, remove it from the heat when it reaches 220°F on a jelly thermometer, and do a jelly test.

5. Ladle the mixture into jars set on a towel. Make sure there's enough space between the jars for air to circulate and speed cooling.

4. Skim off the foam.

that the syrup runs off to one side. If the syrup forms two drops that flow together and fall off the spoon as one sheet without breaking or dripping, the jelly should be done.

The Freezer Test

You can also try a refrigerator test. Pour a small amount of boiling jelly on a cold plate, and put it in the freezer compartment of a refrigerator for a few minutes. If the mixture has a good jellylike jiggle to it when you shake it, it has passed the test.

The Metal Bowl Test

Then there's the method that the Rodale Food Center particularly likes. We call it the metal bowl test. Float a light metal mixing bowl in a larger bowl, pot, or basin filled with cold water or ice water. Drop a teaspoon of jelly mixture in the bottom of the metal bowl. Because metal conducts heat quickly, the jelly mixture will cool quickly. Once cool, run your finger through the jelly. It's ready if it doesn't run back together.

If the jelly test you conduct fails, cook the jelly mixture a little longer and try again. Keep cooking and testing for a bit until your jelly passes. Don't overcook, though. If you do, your jelly may get gummy.

Canning Jelly in a Boiling-Water Bath

Once you've cooked the jelly and tested for doneness, follow these steps to can it.

1. Fill a boiling-water canner with enough water to cover the jars completely. There should be about 1 to 2 inches of water over the tops of the jars and at least 1 to 2 inches of headspace in the canner above the water. Turn on the heat so the water can heat up.

2. Wash and rinse the jars and screw bands, and sterilize them in boiling water. Leave them in hot water until needed. Place new lids in water and bring to a simmer. Remove from heat and leave in hot water until ready to use.

3. Prepare the jelly for canning.

4. Spoon the jelly into jars, leaving recommended headspace. Wipe the jars, paying particular attention to any food or liquid that might have spilled onto the rim; any food left there could ruin your chances of a good seal. Then close the jars (see "Jars, Caps, and Processing Equipment" on page 102).

FAST FRUIT CHOPPING

Try out some of the different food processor blades to chop fruit fast for jelling. Make fruit chunks by pulsing with the S-shaped blade. Grind with the S-shaped blade by holding pulse bursts for two seconds. Use specialized shredding and slicing blades for shredding and slicing citrus rinds or nuts, according to the manufacturer's instructions. ❖ ❖ ❖

5. Place the closed jars upright on a rack in the canner so that none of them is touching any others, allowing the water to circulate freely. If there is room for two layers of jars, place a rack between the two levels and stagger the jars so that none are directly over any of those below. Water should be 2 inches over the tops of the jars. Add water, if needed. Be careful not to pour water directly on the jars. Allow 1 to 2 inches headspace in the canner for water to boil without running over.

6. Put the lid on the canner and bring the water to boiling.

7. Begin to count time as soon as the water starts to boil and process for the time recommended in the individual jelly recipes. For high-altitude areas, increase the processing time 2 minutes for each 1,000 feet above sea level. For example, if you live 3,000 feet above sea level, process 6 minutes longer than the recommended time. Leave the lid on the canner, but remove it periodically to make sure the water is boiling gently and steadily. Add more boiling water as needed to keep containers covered.

8. As soon as the processing time is up, remove the jars from the canner. Place them upright, out of drafts, on a wood rack or board or on several thicknesses of a dry towel so that they are not in direct contact with cold or wet surfaces, either of which might cause very hot jars to crack. Be sure that the jars are an inch apart so that air can circulate under, over, and around each one. Let them cool by themselves; don't tamper with them until they are cool.

9. In the jars, the last bit of air is drawn out as the food cools, creating the vacuum you want. The common two-piece cap is self-sealing; you'll hear a reassuring high-pitched sound of the metal lid snapping down on the glass rim when the vacuum is complete and the jar seals itself. You can tell if the two-piece cap is sealed by pressing down on the center of the lid. If it is down already or stays down when pressed, the seal is good. If it fails to stay down, reprocess the jar with a new lid, or place in the refrigerator and use within the next few days, or freeze the jar.

If Your Jelly Fails

There are many factors involved in making jellies and jams, so it's often hard to pinpoint one single factor that's responsible for a poor jelly. Such is the challenge of making jellies and jams. A good grape jam or apple jelly of just the right firmness, with beautiful color and good fruit flavor, needs one special ingredient that you'll also find in a finely textured, light yeast bread, a fluffy soufflé, and a crisp homemade pickle—experience. And the best way to get experience is to learn from your mistakes and try again.

Here are some common problems, how to avoid them, and what to do about them.

It's runny. Jellies and jams made with honey tend to be softer than those made with sugar because honey contains so much more moisture. If your jelly was too runny and you used added liquid pectin, use the powdered kind next time. It generally jells better with honey than liquid pectin does. Maybe you didn't use enough pectin. Or you could have boiled the jelly too long or too slowly—you need a steady, rapid boil that can't be stirred down.

It's too stiff. If, on the other hand, your jelly is too stiff, you may have used too much pectin. If you were making a jelly with fruit that required no extra pectin, perhaps you cooked it too long. (Perhaps some underripe fruit in the batch contributed extra pectin to the product.) If the jelly is gummy, you may have overcooked it.

It's spoiled. If jelly is improperly sealed, fermentation may occur or mold may develop. Throw out any jelly that has mold growing on it.

Its color changes. Jellied fruit products made with honey are generally a bit darker than those made with sugar. However, if

---

Creative Cooking

PRESERVES THAT DON'T JELL

The biggest problem that comes with making jams and jellies is when the finished product doesn't jell. If this happens to you, think of it as a blessing in disguise. Freeze or can the "syrup" with new lids for the same amount of time as you did the jam or jelly, and use it on pancakes, waffles, ice cream, or sponge cake. Pour it over fruit, mix it with yogurt, or use it as a sauce for meat or fish.

Or, if you're determined to make this particular preserves work, you can try to make the jelly jell again. Take 4 cups of the jelly juice, add $1/2$ cup water, $1/4$ cup sugar, 2 tablespoons lemon juice, and 4 teaspoons dry pectin. Boil for 30 seconds, skim off the foam, then process according to the recipe directions, using sterilized jars and screw bands and new lids. ❖ ❖ ❖

your jellies or jams darken at the top of the jar, it might be because you stored them in too warm a place or because a faulty seal allowed air to enter the jar. The color of jellies and jams can also fade if you store them in too warm a place or if you keep them in storage for too long. Red fruits, such as strawberries or red raspberries, are especially likely to fade.

It has floating fruit. If you've stirred your jams and preserves properly before canning them, you should have no trouble with fruit floating to the surface. If you find fruit floating in your preserves, stir the preserve mixture gently for five minutes after removing it from the heat the next time you make some. Also, make sure that you've used fruit of the proper ripeness, that it was cooked long enough, and that it was properly crushed or ground.

It's separated. Sometimes part of the liquid will separate from the jellied mass during storage. This could be the result of having too much acid in the fruit or keeping the preserves in too warm a place. Separation is more common in preserves made with honey or those that contain less sweetener than in preserves made using traditional recipes. This is because sugar has a tendency to hold the liquids and solids in the preserves together. But if there is no evidence of mold or spoilage, the preserves are still safe to eat.

Just for Jam

Making jam is pretty much like making jelly. You simply add pectin to fruit, cook the mixture, pour the jam into sterilized jars, and can it. But there are some special steps you'll need to make it jam. Here's what to do.

Preparing the Fruit

You can use fresh or frozen fruit to make jam. (See page 98 for more information on preparing frozen fruit.) Crush fresh fruit with a potato masher, which leaves some small pieces of fruit in the blend, or puree it in a food processor for a smoother mixture.

Cooking the Fruit Mixture

Add powdered pectin to the unheated crushed fruit before cooking. Add liquid pectin to the cooked fruit and sweetener mixture off the heat. Cook according to the recipe directions. Use a full, rolling boil, in which bubbles form over the entire surface of the jam mixture. The jam is done when a spoonful holds shape in a cold bowl or spoon. Can as detailed on page 108.

 ## Preserves, Conserves, and Marmalades

Because preserves, conserves, and marmalades aren't as common as jams and jellies, they make wonderful gifts. Again, jelly making forms the basis for making preserves, conserves, and marmalades. But there are a few key differences.

Preparing the Fruit

Chop, grind, slice, dice, or cut fruit into chunks according to recipe directions. Gather together citrus rinds, raisins, nuts, and other ingredients as needed.

Cooking the Fruit Mixture

Add pectin as you would to jams (see page 111). Once you've finished cooking, stir the mixture gently for about five minutes before ladling into jars. This lets the mixture cool so the fruit is less likely to float to the top of the liquid. Can as detailed on page 108.

Flavorful Fruit Butters

Fruit butters are a great option for folks who like intense fruit flavor but don't want the uncertainty that sometimes comes with making jams and jellies jell. Fruit butters take a little patience because they have to be cooked for a long time. But they don't have to be tiresome if you use a slow cooker like a Crock-Pot.

You can use any kind of sweetener you'd like for fruit butters. But you may not need any at all if you use ripe or slightly overripe fruits, which are rich in natural sugars. Wait until the butter is done, then taste it and decide what kind and how much sweetener to use.

Quick Tip

SPICED-UP FRUIT BUTTERS

Spice up your fruit butter with allspice, cinnamon, cloves, and other flavorings when it has almost finished cooking. Add stick cinnamon about 40 minutes before you think the butter will be finished, and add powdered spices about 15 minutes before the butter's done. ❖ ❖ ❖

Equipment for Fruit Buttering

You can cook your fruit butter in the oven or in a slow cooker; neither demands close watching. Any slow cooker is good. If you want a big batch, too much for your slow cooker to handle, cook the fruit mixture down to a loose puree on top of the stove in an uncovered pot. Then finish it in the slow cooker.

When you make fruit butter in the oven, as in the recipe for apple butter on page 291, use a large roasting pan. This exposes the maximum amount of surface area to heat and encourages good evaporation. Use stainless steel, glass, or enamel pans, but stay away from aluminum.

Stove-Top Cooking

If you're making fruit butter on top of the stove, watch it closely and stir frequently so it won't burn or scorch. Scorched fruit butter is awful.

A large kettle or pot with a heavy bottom is best for making fruit butters on the stove. Because they take so long to cook down and the quantity is considerably reduced after all that cooking, you'll probably want to start with a good amount of fruit to make it worth your while, so a big pot is essential. It needs a heavy bottom because the thicker the butter gets, the more chance it has of scorching. Heavy bottoms don't mean you don't have to stir frequently, though, especially toward the end.

How to Make Fruit Butters

Prepare fruit according to recipe directions and boil it down. You'll know it's done when it's as thick as you'd like it. Or put a dab of the fruit butter on a plate and let it sit for a few minutes. If the dab doesn't separate—if you don't notice liquid at the edges of the butter—then you're ready to can the butter in a boiling-water bath or to freeze it.

It's incredibly easy to make apple butter in a slow cooker. Rather than standing over the stove while the butter thickens, pour the cooked apple-and-cider mixture into a slow cooker. Cook on high for ten hours, leaving the lid off. Stir occasionally, pushing the outer edges into the middle of the butter.

CHAPTER FIVE

Pickling

Freezer pickles are super-easy since you don't have to can them or soak them in brine. Instead, just layer cucumber slices in a plastic freezer box, then pour a mix of oil, vinegar, honey, water, and garlic over the cukes, and freeze. They'll keep for three months in the freezer.

PICKLING IS an old Chinese invention that allows you to take ordinary vegetables and fruits and turn them into something extraordinary—flavorful condiments and culinary extras. Pickling also preserves the texture of vegetables such as cucumbers, zucchini, and cauliflower, which wilt under ordinary canning.

But while pickles taste good and add zing to meals they accompany, they aren't particularly nutritious. With traditional pickles, the long brining or fermenting process may indeed preserve cucumbers and other foods, but it does nothing to preserve their food value. Water-soluble nutrients leach out into the brine, never to be heard from again. Vitamin B losses can be as high as 75 to 85 percent, and forget the vitamin C—almost 100 percent of it is lost during brining.

Honestly, though, no one eats pickles to get the daily minimum requirement of any vitamin or mineral. Pickles are hardly mainstays, only condiments, so food loss isn't a big concern. Of bigger concern than food value, however, is the amount of salt in pickles. A raw cucumber contains about 6 milligrams of sodium; a large dill pickle boasts close to 2,000 milligrams. Eat one big pickle, and you're eating all the salt you should eat in an entire day.

If you're salt-conscious because of the link between salt and high blood pressure, check our no- or low-salt pickling recipes. You're sure to like our low-salt sweet pickles, and you might enjoy the dills, too, especially if you're used to a low-salt diet already. But for die-hard pickle fans, we also have a few classic salty recipes made by brining. And in between these extremes are our easy-to-make quick pickles with moderate amounts of salt. Find all of these recipes, starting on page 300.

 ## How Pickling Works

Any food that's preserved with vinegar or some other acidic solution is a pickle or pickled product, but there are actually six distinct kinds of pickles.

Brined pickles. Brined pickles are the old-fashioned kinds that are cured or aged in salt. The salt encourages fermentation, the growth of friendly lactic-acid–producing bacteria naturally found on the food. This lactic acid raises the acidity high enough to prevent the growth of any not-so-friendly bacteria that would otherwise cause the food to spoil while it's curing, before it's canned. Brining takes time and attention because you must skim off the scum that sits on top of the brine each day. But it's the only way to make sauerkraut and kim chee, a Korean version of sauerkraut, both of which are actually brined pickles.

Quick pickles. Fresh-pack or quick-process pickles are the easiest to prepare. Sometimes you'll soak them in a low-salt brine for several hours or overnight. Then drain and process them with boiling-hot vinegar, spices, herbs, or other seasonings. Or you might skip the brining and process your produce directly in spiced vinegar. Unlike brined pickles, vinegar, not lactic acid, provides the acidity in these pickles.

CHOICE PICKLING CUCUMBER CULTIVARS

The cucumber cultivar you use for pickling can affect the crunch of your pickles. Seedless or burpless cucumbers that are longer and lighter than the others stay crunchy because they don't lose texture around the seed section. And small, whole cucumbers stay crunchier than larger ones that are cut into spears or slices. Here are a few favorite pickling cucumber cultivars.

- 'Edmonson', an 80-year-old heirloom cultivar from Kansas, is especially durable and produces crunchy, 4-inch-long cucumbers.

- 'Lemon' cucumbers are round heirlooms that make extra-crisp pickles. Though they're lemon-shaped, they only turn yellow when overripe.

- 'Little Leaf' is able to produce cucumbers without insect pollination, so you can grow plants under floating row covers and escape cucumber pests. The fruit has no bitter compounds and tolerates extremes in temperatures.

- 'Saladin', an All-America award winner, is extra-reliable because it resists diseases and is highly productive. ❖ ❖ ❖

SLICING
CUCUMBER

PICKLING
CUCUMBER

GHERKIN

When deciding which cucumber cultivars to grow, think about how you plan to use them. Slicing cukes are the best for salads, while pickling cukes are the cultivars of choice for pickling—unless you want whole baby cukes for sweet pickles. Then choose a gherkin. Seed catalogs will tell whether each cuke is a slicer, pickler, or gherkin.

Fruit pickles. Fruit pickles are usually prepared from whole fruits—pears, peaches, and crabapples are good choices. Watermelon rind is also a popular choice for fruit pickles. To make them, you simmer the fruit in spicy, sweet-sour vinegar syrup, then pack and process.

Relishes. Relishes are mixed fruits and vegetables that you chop, season, and then cook, pack, and process. Relishes may be hot and spicy or sweet and spicy. Familiar ones include piccalilli, chutneys, corn relish, and Pennsylvania Dutch chow-chow.

Salt-free pickles. Salt-free pickles don't need brining. Instead, like quick pickles, you'll can them immediately in a strong vinegar solution. It's this vinegar that does the preserving. Saltless pickles can be just as crunchy as salt pickles if you take care to pick your vegetables when they make the best pickles, which is not necessarily when they are best for fresh eating. For more information on selecting vegetables, see "Fruits and Vegetables" below.

Herb vinegars. Herb vinegars are a simple blend of herbs soaked in vinegar. The herbs infuse the vinegar with fragrance, flavor, and sometimes color.

Pickling Supplies

When you're ready to start pickling, take the sensible approach. Gather together all your supplies and equipment first. Then run out and harvest your vegetables or fruits so you can preserve them fast, fresh, and firm.

Fruits and Vegetables

Pick young, firm, choice fruits and vegetables in prime condition. Their quality will shine through when the pickling is done.

Be sure to check your recipe to see what size of produce it requires. Some recipes need cucumbers as small as $1\frac{1}{2}$ inches long;

others call for larger cucumbers. Always pick cucumbers before they get overripe. Look for solid fruits with green skins that don't show any sign of yellowing. Once yellowing starts, the skin gets tough, the seeds grow, and hollow areas may develop inside. Also, don't use any fruits or vegetables that are moldy or diseased. You need to use top-quality produce to get high-quality pickles.

Freshness is especially important for cucumbers; they deteriorate rapidly after picking. If you must delay pickling for an hour, store the cucumbers in a cool basement instead of the refrigerator, which is so cold that it can damage the cukes.

It's also a good idea to hold off harvesting for at least 12 hours if you get a heavy rain. When you harvest promptly after a downpour, the produce tends to be waterlogged and less crisp.

When the time is right for picking, cut cucumbers off the vine, leaving a short stem on the fruit. If you pull the cucumbers off, you may break the stem loose from the skin and encourage rotting at the stem end.

If you want to make an especially good batch of pickles, sort the produce for uniform size so every piece cooks and cures evenly. This is one of the secrets of meticulous canners—the people who win prizes at county fairs.

Vinegar

There's one hard-and-fast rule when it comes to choosing a vinegar for pickles. Use a good grade of 40- to 60-grain-strength vinegar (4 to 6 percent acetic acid). Most commercial vinegars meet this criterion, but homemade vinegars may not.

Most pickling recipes call for clear, distilled vinegar, which is inexpensive and won't discolor pickles. But on occasion, you may substitute red or white wine vinegars, which have a fruity, mellow flavor and are especially good for herb vinegars. Or try rice wine vinegar, which is sweet and mild. Occasionally recipes call for apple cider vinegar, which has a good flavor and aroma but can discolor white pickles made with onions, Jerusalem artichokes, or cauliflower.

Sweeteners

In most recipes that call for sweeteners, you'll use white sugar. But we also include recipes that use light honey, such as clover, orange blossom, and alfalfa. These are very

---

Quick Tip

CHOOSE HONEY OR SUGAR

Because sweeteners are not used as preservatives in pickles, you can substitute sugar for honey, or vice versa, depending on how you want the finished pickle to taste. The Rodale Food Center says you can substitute equal amounts of honey and sugar. ❖ ❖ ❖

mild in flavor and for that reason are good to use for canning or pickling. If you use dark, stronger-flavored honey (like wildflower and buckwheat) in pickling, you might find that the flavor will overpower the flavors of the other ingredients. If you like maple syrup, you can also use it for sweetening pickles. But it has a strong flavor and may make the brine dark and cloudy.

No matter what kind of sweetener you use, we suggest that you taste your syrup as you add the sweetener to it. If you think that the syrup is sweet enough, stop adding sweetener even though you may not have reached the amount suggested in the recipe. Those amounts are intended to be guidelines only, not hard-and-fast rules. Your best guide is your tastebuds.

Unlike jams and jellies, you can alter a recipe to replace the sweetener because, in pickles, honey or sugar is added just for taste, not for texture or keeping quality. Use 1 cup honey or

Rodale Whole Pickling Spice

We've found that this blend gives pickles a wonderfully spicy flavor with a touch of heat.

2 tablespoons bay leaves

1 tablespoon cardamom seeds

1 tablespoon dried ginger

1 stick cinnamon

1½ whole dried chili peppers (more if you like it hot)

2 tablespoons mustard seeds

1 tablespoon whole allspice

1 tablespoon coriander

1 tablespoon peppercorns

Crush bay leaves. If you have cardamom in the pod, pound it with a mortar and pestle to extract the seeds. Also pound the dried ginger, and break the cinnamon stick into small pieces to distribute the flavors. Dried chilies can be broken or crushed into small pieces.

Combine bay leaves, cardamom seeds, ginger, cinnamon, chili peppers, mustard seeds, allspice, coriander, and peppercorns. Blend, and store in an airtight glass container in a cool, dark place. Use as directed in recipes.

Yield: 4 ounces

maple syrup for each cup of sugar called for. If using sugar, you'll need to boil the syrup—vinegar, spices, and sugar—to allow the sugar to dissolve completely. Boiling also allows the spices to flavor the syrup.

If you're altering a recipe to use honey rather than sugar, remember that heating honey tends to break down its sugars and change its flavor. You can heat honey to high temperatures for short periods without causing too much damage, but it will not stand sustained boiling. So boil the vinegar and spices together for the stated time, then add the honey, tasting the syrup as you add it to determine sweetness. Bring the syrup to a boil, and pour it over the pickles. Process as directed.

Seasonings

Always use whole, fresh herbs and spices—the fresher the better. Avoid ground herbs and spices, which tend to darken pickles. For some recipes, you'll tie the herbs and spices in a cheesecloth or muslin bag or put them in a stainless steel spice or tea ball so you can remove them before packing the pickles. Recipes call for this if the whole spices may cause an off-flavor in the pickles. In other recipes, you'll leave dill sprigs, mustard seeds, peppercorns, and other herbs and spices in with the finished pickles.

Make a habit of tasting the pickling liquid before you can it. You'll find that spices vary considerably in strength, and you may need to correct the blend before using it. Keep unused spices in airtight jars in a cool, dry place because heat and humidity tend to sap their quality.

Water

For the best-looking pickles, we recommend that you use soft water. Iron or sulfur in hard water will darken pickles; calcium and other salts can interfere with the fermentation process. If you have especially hard water running from your tap, you might find that one of the bottled waters you can buy in the supermarket is softer water. But be careful. Many bottled waters have a very high mineral content—look for distilled water.

Don't use chlorinated water when making fermented pickles because the chlorine will discourage friendly microbial growth. You can dechlorinate tap water either by leaving it in an uncovered bowl or pot overnight or whizzing it in an uncovered blender for ten minutes so that the chlorine can oxidize. Or replace tap water with unchlorinated bottled water.

Salt

Use plain pickling or canning salt that doesn't contain iodine or noncaking agents found in regular, iodized table salt. Iodine can cause darkening, and the noncaking agent sometimes causes a cloudy brine. Kosher salt is fine because it's pure and contains no iodine. You can measure it most accurately by weight because it's a coarse salt that doesn't pack down in a measuring cup. But if you need to use volume measurements, substitute $1\frac{1}{2}$ cups kosher salt for 1 cup pickling salt.

We don't recommend that you use sea salt because it's high in minerals and can darken and discolor foods. And don't use rock salt or any other salt meant to melt ice on sidewalks and driveways—this is not sold for human consumption and shouldn't be used for anything but its intended purpose.

Pickling Equipment

Use the same equipment for pickling that you use for other canning projects. Use unchipped enamel or stainless steel for heating pickling liquids on the stove or microwave-safe ceramics for heating them in the microwave. Don't use copper, brass, galvanized iron, or aluminum utensils. These metals react with acids and salts in the liquids and may cause undesirable color changes in your finished pickles. For storing pickles, use canning jars with two-piece caps for canned pickles or freezer containers for frozen pickles.

Quick Tip

HOW MUCH DOES IT WEIGH?

To figure how much produce you'd need to reach a weight required in a recipe, here are some general weight-to-volume conversions. You can see at a glance how much 1 cup of a particular fruit or vegetable weighs when cut up. To be more specific, you'll need a kitchen scale.

Vegetables		Fruits	
Beans, green	$1/2$ pound/cup	Apples	$3/4$ pound/cup
Beets	$3/4$ pound/cup	Cherries, unpitted	$2/3$ pound/cup
Carrots	$3/4$ pound/cup	Peaches	$2/3$ pound/cup
Cucumbers	$1/2$ pound/cup	Pears	$2/3$ pound/cup
Okra	$1/2$ pound/cup	Plums	$1/2$ pound/cup
Tomatoes	$3/4$ pound/cup		

For fermenting or brining, use a crock, stone jar, plastic container, unchipped enamel pan, or large glass jar, bowl, or baking dish. Find a heavy plate or large glass lid that fits snugly inside the circumference of the container. Then gather some weights, such as a glass jar filled with water, to hold the lid down and keep the vegetables in the brine. Instead of a lid and a weight, you may be able to cover the vegetables with a large plastic bag filled with brine ($1\frac{1}{2}$ tablespoons pickling salt for every quart of water). Just be sure the bag or lid completely covers the food and is tight against all the edges of the brining container.

Although most instructions here call for measuring ingredients by volume, occasionally you'll have to know the weight of ingredients. For this, you'll need a small household scale. A scale is especially important if you're making large quantities of sauerkraut—with a scale, you'll be sure you're using the proper proportion of salt and cabbage.

Pickling Techniques

To make delicious pickles, you'll need to use special techniques like curing and brining. It helps to know why recipes call for certain procedures and how to do them right. Here's a look at what these pickling methods are and how they work.

Preparing Produce

You'll need to wash and, in some cases, chop up your cucumbers and other fruits or vegetables for pickles, chutneys, and other relishes. Wash the produce thoroughly under running water. Scrub the food with a soft brush or your hands. Rinse well so that all soil drains off. Drain your produce on a dish towel or dish drainer. Wipe them dry, if you wish, but be careful not to bruise them.

Handle the food gently so it doesn't become bruised; this is especially important for cucumbers or soft fruits like peaches or pears—unless you pick them slightly underripe for pickling. Be sure to remove the blossom ends from cucumbers, since they may be a source of enzymes that cause spoilage. If the cucumber still has a long length of stem attached, cut it back to about $\frac{1}{8}$ inch.

To make large batches of pickles faster, use your food processor to cut cucumbers and other fruits or vegetables into slices or chunks or to shred cabbage. But you'll have to make long slices, quarters, or diced pieces yourself unless you buy a specialized food chopper that can handle that task. Always use a stainless steel knife for all the hand trimming you do.

Curing Pickles

Curing, or soaking produce in salted brine, adds another step to the pickling process that you may or may not find to be worth the effort involved. It's a matter of personal opinion. If you make quick pickles or relishes, you may skip the curing process entirely. Or, with some quick pickles, you might cure the produce briefly—not over 24 hours. Not curing at all saves you time, but a short curing treatment can result in crisper pickles because the brine pulls some moisture out of the produce.

Old-fashioned pickles and sauerkraut go through a longer brine-curing process. They soak in salty brine until they ferment, producing acid that causes pickling. This method is more difficult and time-consuming than quick pickling and usually produces pickles that are higher in salt than quick pickles.

If you are an experienced pickle maker, if you're ready for a new challenge, or if you love the taste of brine-cured pickles, you'll find details of the brining process in "Brine Pickles" below and a recipe on page 308. But if you're new to pickling or don't have a lot of time, try quick pickles—see the recipes on pages 304 and 305.

Brine Pickles

You can cure just about any vegetable in brine, including green and yellow beans, broccoli, cabbage, carrots, cauliflower, cucumbers, Jerusalem artichokes, onions, and green tomatoes. By covering foods with brine and keeping them in a moderately warm room, you can create ideal conditions for the lactic-acid–forming bacteria that actually pickle the produce. These bacteria exist on the vegetable's surface and feed on the sugar naturally present in the food. You should cover fermenting pickles with a clean towel to help keep insects and molds out, however.

The lactic acid will continue to grow as the batch ferments until enough has formed to kill any bacteria present that would otherwise cause the food to spoil. Lactic acid, which aids digestion and helps to kill harmful bacteria in the digestive tract, gives the brined food a slightly acid, tangy flavor. You'll find a recipe for brine-cured pickles on page 308.

Sauerkraut

Sauerkraut used to be one of the only winter sources of vitamin C, and it was used as a cure for scurvy on sea voyages. In addition, like other cured vegetables, sauerkraut contains beneficial lactic acid.

Sauerkraut Grandma's Way

Try this old-fashioned fermenting method to produce excellent kraut. Follow the directions carefully for the best results.

15 pounds cabbage

9 tablespoons pickling salt

Harvest the cabbage and let it sit at room temperature for one day. Remove the outer leaves and any undesirable portions from firm, mature heads of cabbage; wash and drain. Cut into halves or quarters; remove the cores. Use a shredder or sharp knife to cut the cabbage into thin shreds about the thickness of a quarter.

In a large container, thoroughly mix 3 tablespoons of salt with 5 pounds of shredded cabbage. Let the salted cabbage stand for several minutes to wilt slightly. This allows packing without excessive breaking or bruising of the shreds.

Pack the salted cabbage firmly and evenly into a large, clean crock. Using a wooden spoon, tamper, or your hands, press down firmly until the juice comes to the surface. Repeat the shredding, salting, and packing of cabbage until the crock is filled to within 4 or 5 inches of the top.

Cover the cabbage with a piece of plastic wrap, and tuck the edges down against the inside of the container. Cover with a plate that just fits inside the container so that the cabbage is not exposed to the air. Put a weight on top of the cover so the brine comes to the plate but not over it. Two glass jars or two heavy-duty plastic bags filled with brine (½ tablespoons salt per 1 quart water) make good weights. The amount of brine in the plastic bags or jars can be adjusted to give just enough pressure to keep the fermenting cabbage covered with brine.

Formation of gas bubbles indicates fermentation is taking place. A room temperature of 70° to 75°F is best for fermenting cabbage. Fermentation is usually completed in three to four weeks.

To can: Turn to Chapter 3 for details on canning. Then heat well-fermented sauerkraut to simmering (185° to 210°F). Pack hot into jars. Cover with boiling juice, leaving ½-inch headspace. Seal and process pints for 10 minutes and quarts for 15 minutes in a boiling-water bath.

Sauerkraut making has come a long way since the days of the "cabbage board"—a wooden board with a cutting blade in the middle. Now you can cut a head in wedges and toss them into the food processor. Instant shredding!

Sauerkraut is packed in a dry salt, not covered in a salt-water solution. This is because cabbage contains a great deal of water and forms its own brine when the salt draws out water from its shredded leaves. After fermentation, you may can sauerkraut in a boiling-water bath or store it in the container in which it was made. If you're just storing it in the container, be sure to keep it in a cold place. Temperatures just above freezing are best. Low temperatures will discourage the growth of surface scum. Even so, check the kraut periodically and remove any scum.

Making Mustards and Herb Vinegars

Because mustards and herb vinegars both contain vinegar, they're included here in the pickling chapter. Both products are easy to make and can add terrific flavors to ordinary foods.

Mustards

Mustards combine dry mustard, which is pulverized mustard seed, with different kinds of vinegars and delicious extras like honey, herbs, and spices. Some recipes require cooking; others don't. When blended, you can process your mustards in canning jars, or make a small batch and store it in the refrigerator for a month or more.

Herb Vinegars

Herb vinegars capture the full flavor of fresh herbs and preserve that flavor in a vinegar solution. To make herb vinegars, you can use any of the vinegars mentioned for pickling—white distilled vinegar, red and white wine vinegars, rice wine vinegar, and apple cider vinegar—and you can also use homemade vinegar. But learn how different vinegars taste so you can find herbs that will compliment them. Two excellent vinegars to start with are white wine and rice wine vinegars, which are mild and light-colored. They let the herbal flavor shine through and take on a pretty color if you're using purple basil sprigs or nasturtium or chives flowers. (If you like the distinct flavor of apple cider vinegar but find its strong flavor masks the more subtle flavor of herbs, you can dilute it. Mix it with milder-tasting white distilled vinegar before adding herbs.)

To make herb vinegars from a single herb, add a handful of fresh sprigs of herbs like tarragon, rosemary, basil, or dill. Or make a blend of several of your favorites herbs. When combined, the herbs mellow and blend together in the bottle, so you can use

Chutneys and mustards are delicious condiments that are easy to make at home with vinegar and spices.

just about any combination and not go wrong. Try these herb vinegar suggestions.

- Basil and garlic
- 'Dark Opal' basil (for a purple-tinted vinegar)
- Dill (both seeds and leaves) and rosemary
- Orange mint (for fruit salads)
- Tarragon and basil

You can let the herbs remain floating in the bottled vinegars if you think they're pretty, or strain them out after they've soaked for a couple of weeks. Wait until you can smell the herb aroma, then pour the vinegar into another clean jar—a decorative one if you like.

If you only have dried herbs around, you can still make a good herb vinegar. Crumble about 3 tablespoons of dried leaves in a jar. If you're adding herb seeds such as dill or anise, crush them well first. Then warm your vinegar in a stainless steel, enamel, or microwave-safe ceramic container. Avoid metals other than stainless steel, which could react with the vinegar and give it a bad appearance and taste.

Pour the warmed vinegar over the herbs. The warm vinegar will break down the leaves and extract oil from the herbs more quickly than cool vinegar. Let the vinegar and herbs sit for two to four weeks in a covered bottle. Sample the vinegar and see if it's

---

Creative Cooking

INNOVATIVE USES FOR PICKLES, RELISHES, CHUTNEYS, MUSTARDS, AND VINEGARS

In addition to slicing pickles on your hamburger or setting them beside your Reuben sandwich, you can incorporate them into other foods to add a burst of flavor. Here are some ideas.

- Use pickled garlic to replace fresh garlic in recipes.

- Add relishes to tuna, egg, or chicken salad.

- Spread chutney instead of mustard on a roast beef or turkey sandwich. Or use it as a sauce for grilled chicken.

- Use pickled fruits with roasted meat or to replace fresh or canned fruits in baked goods.

- Chop up pickled beets or eggplant and blend with steamed chopped potatoes or rice for a flavorful dish.

- Use homemade mustards in salad dressings and meat glazes.

- Use herb vinegars in meat marinades or salad dressings, to replace lemon juice in any recipe, or to add extra flavor to soups. ❖ ❖ ❖

Herb vinegar makes a beautiful gift when you package it in a lovely bottle with a few decorative herb sprigs inside. For a lovely pink or reddish vinegar, use one of the purple-leaved basil cultivars to make the vinegar.

flavorful enough yet. If so, strain it into sterilized jars, cap airtight, and store until you're ready to use it. If not, add some more herbs and let them soak for a week more. For other herb vinegar ideas, see page 317.

Canning Pickles

Pickles are high-acid foods that you can in a boiling-water bath. Fill the jars as recommended in the recipes, leaving the necessary headspace. Pack jars firmly and uniformly, but avoid packing so tightly that there's no room for the brine or syrup to fit around and over the food—the brine or syrup is necessary for flavor and good keeping. Wipe the rims of the jar with a clean, damp cloth, and cap. Screw on the bands fingertip tight. Be careful not to over-process the pickles; they'll get soft if you do.

In Chapter 3, you'll find detailed information on canning jars and boiling-water–bath canners. Refer to specific recipes, starting on page 300, for canning times and headspace requirements.

Creative Cooking

DILL AND NASTURTIUM BUD VINEGAR

For an unusual vinegar with a clear, sharp flavor, blend 1 tablespoon nasturtium buds, several sprigs of fresh dill, and a pint of hot white wine vinegar. Combine them in a ceramic, enamel, or stainless steel container, cover, and let steep for one week. Filter into one hot, scalded quart bottle or two pint bottles. Cap or cork tightly. ❖ ❖ ❖

Storing Pickles

Store pickles, mustards, vinegars, and so forth in cool, dark, dry places. Extreme fluctuations of temperature may cause a breakdown of texture, resulting in an inferior product. It might also cause the pickles to expand and break the jar or the seal. Light makes pickles fade and become less appetizing in appearance, but it doesn't spoil them.

You can keep canned pickles in the basement if it's cool, dark, and dry. Don't store canned products like pickles in a root cellar or in a place where you're storing whole vegetables or fruits that need to be kept moist. Dampness may rust caps and cause spoilage.

We found that our canned pickles kept fine for a year, but after that their flavor

COMPARING PICKLE STORAGE TECHNIQUES

Just as there are many different ways to pickle your garden harvest, there also are many ways to store your pickles. You can process and can them, store them in the refrigerator without processing, or freeze them.

Canned pickles. The conventional method of storing pickles—quick and brine pickles as well as relishes—is to keep processing the jars brief (usually for 10 minutes) in a boiling-water bath. This takes a little more time than freezing or refrigerating but results in top-quality, easy-to-use pickles. And it allows you to make a big batch of pickles and store the extra jars in an out-of-the-way place.

Refrigerator pickles. But if you just want a few jars of pickles and don't want to spend time processing, you can put most pickles in sterilized jars, and store them in the refrigerator for a month or more. Just let the jar sit unopened for several weeks to let the flavors blend and mellow.

Freezer pickles. Freezer pickles are just as fast as refrigerator pickles, but the cucumbers tend to get softer after freezing. If this bothers you, experiment with recipes. You may come across a recipe that works better for you. Or try pickles made of fruits or vegetables besides cucumbers and zucchini that will come through freezing without a problem. ❖ ❖ ❖

started to suffer. Most spices tended to lose their punch after a year, but a few, notably ginger, got stronger.

 What Went Wrong?

If for some reason your pickles don't turn out the way you'd like them to, try again with another recipe as long as you still have fresh produce. Hopefully, you can learn from your mistakes. Here are some common causes of pickle and sauerkraut failure and how you can correct them.

Pickle Problems

Check this list of potential problems if your pickles aren't as good as you'd hoped or if something has definitely gone wrong. Next time, you'll know what to do.

Shriveled pickles. If your pickles are shriveled, you may have used too strong a vinegar or salt solution at the start of the pickling process. Shriveling may also be caused by overcooking or overprocessing. Your pickles may not look too good, but they're okay to eat.

Hollow pickles. Hollowness in cucumber pickles usually results from one or several of the following: poorly developed cucumbers, cucumbers that were too ripe, holding the cucumbers too long before pickling, too rapid fermentation, or too strong or too weak a brine during fermentation. Again, these pickles are safe to eat.

Dark pickles. Dark pickles are not spoiled pickles; however, if you pride yourself on the looks of your home-canned products, darkening can be annoying. Darkening may result from over-cooking or from the use of too much spice, iodized salt, hard water containing lots of minerals (especially iron), iron utensils, maple syrup, or cider vinegar instead of white (distilled) vinegar. Go ahead and eat the pickles, but make adjustments next time.

Pickled cauliflower may turn pink; this is a result of a red pigment in the vegetable released by the acid in the vinegar. This is more likely to occur if you used overly mature cauliflower. Commercially, the bleaching agent sulfur dioxide is used to prevent the problem. It's not harmful to eat such cauliflower, and not all cultivars will turn pink in vinegar.

Slippery pickles. Soft or slippery pickles are spoiled pickles. Don't eat them. This condition is generally a result of microbial action that caused the spoilage; it's irreversible. Proper processing should halt microbial activity. But if it happens, here's a checklist of things you might have done wrong.

- Used too little salt or acid
- Failed to cover your cucumbers completely with brine during fermentation
- Let scum scatter through the brine during fermentation
- Processed the pickles for too short or too long a time
- Didn't seal the jar airtight
- Used moldy garlic or spices

Also, if you failed to remove the blossoms from the cucumbers before fermentation, they may have contained mold or yeasts responsible for the softening action.

There are also improper canning or storage procedures that can result in spoiled canned foods of any kind. See "Signs of Spoilage—Throw It Out!" on the opposite page for details.

Spoiled Sauerkraut

Your sauerkraut has gone bad if it develops a soft texture, an undesirable color, or off-odors. If your kraut has spoiled, here's what you might have done wrong.

Soft kraut. Soft sauerkraut may be due to insufficient salt. Try using more salt next time. Another cause of softness is high temperatures during fermentation. Uneven distribution of salt may also be a cause of softness—be sure that your salt is well mixed with the kraut next time. Air pockets caused by improper packing may make your kraut soft. Your crock or jar may have had air spaces that caused poor fermentation; this can be remedied by packing the jar or crock tightly and being sure to weight it properly.

Pink kraut. Pink kraut is caused by the growth of certain types of yeast on the surface of the kraut. These yeasts may grow if there's too much salt, if there's an uneven distribution of salt, or if the kraut is improperly covered or weighted during fermentation.

Dark kraut. Darkness in kraut may be caused by improperly trimmed cabbage, insufficient brine in the fermenting process, or high temperatures during fermentation, processing, or storage. Be sure that the brine completely covers the fermenting cabbage. Exposure to air or a long storage period in the crock after fermentation is complete may also result in darkened kraut.

Rotted kraut. Rotted kraut is usually found at the surface where the cabbage has not been covered sufficiently to exclude air during fermentation. This scum doesn't cause trouble as long as you skim it off before it stops fermentation. Remove it every day or two.

SIGNS OF SPOILAGE—THROW IT OUT!

Like any canned good, pickles can go bad. If you notice any of the following conditions in your pickles or relishes, don't eat the food: Destroy it. Boil the closed jar for 30 minutes, wrap it in several sealed plastic bags, and bury it where no child or animal will come into contact with it. If the contents of the jar have escaped, wash the counter, your hands, and anything else it touched with warm, soapy water. Here are the signs to look for.

Dirty or moldy jars. A jar that is soiled or moldy on the outside indicates that food seeped out during storage, which means that air along with bacteria, yeasts, and molds could have seeped in. (Jars that have come right out of the canner might be a bit soiled from some of the liquid that was expelled with the air; this is okay as long as half the contents of the jars aren't floating outside in the canning water! If you wiped the jars, they would have gone clean into storage and any food on the outside of the jars now is not okay.)

Color change. A significant change in color, most notably a much darker color, can mean spoilage.

Texture change. A change in texture, especially if the food feels slimy, is a sure sign that the pickle isn't fit to eat.

Mold. Mold in the food or inside the lid—sometimes nothing more than little flecks—is not safe to eat.

Bubbles. Small bubbles in the liquid or a release of gas, however slight, when you open the can means foul play. Sometimes you get a strong message: Liquid actually spurts out when you release the seal. Other times, the gas is more subtle. But either way, your food is spoiled and you should dispose of it. ❖ ❖ ❖

CHAPTER SIX

Drying

CAMPERS DO IT . . . backpackers do it . . . and more families than ever before are doing it. They're drying their own produce. Drying is an easy and space-saving way to make delicious snacks, desserts, teas, convenience foods, and seasonings. Trail mixes have shown us all how delicious dried fruits are, and now dried veggie chips are starting to edge into the old potato-chip niche as flavorful, crunchy treats without the chemicals and fat.

When you dry foods, you take out their water content. And by removing the water, you reduce 10 pounds of fresh food into about 2 pounds of highly concentrated food. This dried "superfood" has more flavor and nutrients, pound for pound, than fresh food.

That means that besides tasting good, dried foods are good for you. The nutritional value of dried foods is similar to that of frozen food. Dried produce loses some vitamin A and C while drying, but the major losses occur during blanching, just like with frozen foods. As far as nutrients are concerned, drying can be better than canning, which loses up to 65 percent of the original vitamin C, thiamine, and riboflavin in the high processing temperatures, but its success varies with each crop.

Herbs are the easiest foods to dry. The flavor of homegrown herbs, whether you dry or freeze them, is more fresh and pungent

It's easy to make your own dried soup mixes. Just mix your favorite dried beans with dried vegetables and herbs to taste, and store. When you want soup, the soup will be ready to cook.

Quality Conscious

NUTRITION WATCH

If you're nutrition-conscious, you can get more vitamins and minerals from the same amount of some dried foods than you'll get from canned or frozen foods—sometimes a *lot* more. Yellow and orange fruits and vegetables are particularly nutritious dried because they concentrate large amounts of vitamin A as well as other nutrients.

For example, you can dry 12 pounds of peaches, reducing it to about 1 1/4 pounds when dried. If you analyzed the nutritional value of 100 grams of those dried peaches, you'd find they had 63 milligrams (mg) of vitamin C, 22,680 mg of vitamin A, 0.43 mg of riboflavin, 15.9 mg of iron, and 81 mg of calcium. Frozen and canned peaches fall far behind in all nutrients. One hundred grams of canned peaches have 13 mg of vitamin C, 1,950 mg of vitamin A, 0.11 mg of riboflavin, 1.4 mg of iron, and 18 mg of calcium. Compare 100 grams of frozen peaches and you'll find 50 mg of vitamin C, 2,950 mg of vitamin A, 0.18 mg of riboflavin, 2.3 mg of iron, and 18 mg of calcium.

For a green vegetable, though, you're better off nutritionally with canned or frozen produce. For example, 8 pounds of fresh peas will produce about 3/4 pound of dried peas. If you analyzed 100 grams of those dried peas, you'd find 20 mg of vitamin C compared to 40 mg in canned peas and 60 mg in frozen peas. Dried peas would have 4,020 mg of vitamin A compared with 2,040 mg of vitamin A in canned peas and 3,020 mg in frozen peas. But when you reconstitute the peas to use in soups or stews, you'll dilute the nutrient levels so they fall below canned and frozen peas. ❖ ❖ ❖

NOTE: Nutritional and weight data is taken from *All About Drying Foods,* Ohio State University Cooperative Extension Service.

than most commercially processed herbs. What makes them even better is that you can grow the most flavorful cultivars, preserve them with your favorite technique, and store them in ways that maximize their essential oil content. (And the essential oils are what give herbs their flavor and fragrance.) Just take them out of the jar and sprinkle them on food while cooking or just before serving. You can even blend dried herbs into other foods, making instant seasonings or gourmet prepared foods. You'll save money and get better results.

How Drying Works

When you're drying food, you're removing a good part of its moisture through evaporation. Air movement is the key. But the drier and, up to a point, the warmer the air is, the faster and more complete the evaporation of the water.

At its simplest, drying is incredibly basic. You can place small pieces of food out in the warm sun on a dry day. Warm, dry air passing over, under, and around the food pulls the moisture from it.

Safety Stop

DON'T DRY FOOD IN A MICROWAVE

Microwaves are good for many things, like blanching vegetables before you freeze or dry them. Use microwave drying for small quantities of herbs only. Microwaves are not suitable for drying other foods. ❖ ❖ ❖

And that's it. If the air is dry enough, if the sun is hot but not scorching, if the food is cut properly, and if there are no insects, dust, or other pollutants, you'll get a pretty good dried food with hardly any effort at all.

In cool, humid, or wet weather, relying on warm dry air won't work. Your food may mildew or mold before it dries. To be sure your efforts yield good results, use an electric dehydrator, designed to provide just the right amount of heat and maximum air movement all the time. Or you can use your oven to do the work. Achieving very low, steady temperatures and good air circulation might take a little practice to master, but at least you don't have to worry about having enough sun.

When foods are properly dried, they can't support the growth of spoilage organisms. Bacteria, yeasts, and molds can't live in fruits that have 80 percent of the water removed and in vegetables with almost 90 percent of the water removed. So drying eliminates spoilers, but you also have to deactivate the enzymes that speed up the natural deterioration of vegetables. The simple way to do this is by blanching your produce. Enzymes can change produce color, texture, and flavor unless you blanch most vegetables before drying them. Blanching also helps set color and flavor, plus it softens tissues so that water is released more readily during drying. Blanching is easy—see page 142 to find out how to do it.

Drying Supplies and Options

What kind of equipment you should have for drying depends on what kind of produce and the weather you have. Review this section to find out exactly what you'll need. Plan ahead so you can have everything ready to make drying work the first time and every time.

Choosing Vegetables, Fruits, and Herbs

Start with perfect produce; blemished or bruised vegetables and fruits won't keep as well and may turn the whole tray of drying produce bad. Make sure fruit is fully ripe with the sugar content at its peak. If you have overripe fruit, use it for fruit leathers. (See page 151 to find out how to make them.)

Next, determine which drying method is appropriate for the produce you have. Thin or dry-fleshed vegetables and herbs can

When you dry fruits like bananas and cherries, you not only remove a lot of water, but you also concentrate nutrients, flavor, and sweetness in a compact package.

air-dry fairly easily. But those thick, plump, juicy vegetables and fruits may need extra heat and ventilation to get thoroughly dry.

Among the crops that are easy to dry naturally are herbs with thin, narrow, or needlelike foliage. These include rosemary, sage, summer and winter savory, tarragon, and thyme. Among the vegetables, it's easy to air-dry mature beans, black-eyed peas, cayenne peppers, fava beans, field corn, and lima beans—as long as the weather cooperates. A few fruits are naturally suited for air-drying, including apricots, dates, and prunes.

A second group of crops are fleshier and may need to be dried in a dehydrator or oven. These include herbs such as basil, lovage, and parsley. Most of the succulent fruits and vegetables, except the ones listed above, also are in this group.

And then there are the herbs and vegetables that simply don't dry well. They may lose flavor or accumulate unpleasant tastes, aromas, or textures that make them worthless. These include herbs such as chervil, chives, cilantro, lemon balm, and salad

Quality Conscious

FREEZE DRYING: GOOD, BUT NOT AT HOME

Freeze drying substantially reduces the weight and volume of foods and preserves them for two years without much loss of nutrients, color, or flavor. Unfortunately, freeze drying is a sophisticated process that requires special equipment—large, bulky equipment that's too expensive for home gardeners. To compare freeze drying with conventional drying, here's how it works.

In commercial freeze drying, water is removed from frozen foods that have been sliced, diced, powdered, granulated, or liquefied. The frozen food is spread out on trays and placed in a vacuum cabinet. The door is closed and the pressure is lowered, creating a vacuum. Heat is applied, and the ice within the food disappears in the air and is taken out of the cabinet with a pump.

Freeze drying takes about ten hours (during drying, the food is kept frozen) and almost all of the water is removed from the food. The moisture content is usually 2 percent or lower. The food is taken from the drying chamber and tightly packaged so it will stay dry until used. ❖ ❖ ❖

burnet, and vegetables such as brussels sprouts, cucumbers, lettuce, radishes, and squash. Consider freezing, canning, or pickling these crops instead of trying to dry them.

Providing Heat and Ventilation

You need to maintain a proper and steady temperature to prepare good dried produce. If the temperature's too high, your food can quite literally cook. What usually happens is that the food cooks on the outside, forming a dry skin that traps moisture inside. You can prevent this problem by making sure temperatures don't get too hot, especially in the first few hours of drying.

High temperatures, up near 145°F, also will destroy significant amounts of vitamins. Lower temperatures save more vitamins, but if drying gets too low, down near 90°F (and especially if conditions are humid), there's a greater chance of bacteria and mold growth on fruits and vegetables. (But 95°F

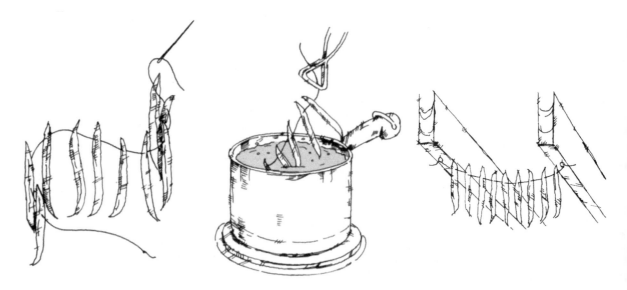

Here's an old-fashioned but effective way to store dried string beans. String green beans on a heavy thread (left). Blanch the strung beans as you would any vegetable, then towel-dry, moving the beans so they're not touching on the string (center). Then hang the strings in a warm, dark, well-ventilated place like an attic (right). Once the beans are dry, you'll see why they're called leather britches.

is ideal for most herbs, which lose flavorful oils at higher temperatures.)

For your convenience, most commercial dryers are designed to keep food at a low-medium temperature of 95° to 145°F, and this is a good target for homemade dryers and oven drying as well: 140°F is ideal. But ovens may not be easy to set at temperatures this low. (See oven-drying details on page 138.)

Another element you need for fast, efficient drying is good ventilation. The aim is not to heat the food but to remove moisture from it by circulating warm, dry air over the maximum amount of surface area. This is why the best drying trays let air through, top and bottom, and why dryers should be well ventilated.

Drying Outdoors

The cheapest and sometimes the easiest way to dry is to let the sun do all the work. But drying outdoors works well only if you live in an area that has long, hot, sunny days and low humidity, not to mention clean, unpolluted air. If you can't depend on about three good drying days in a row, or if you live in an industrial area or near a heavily traveled highway (both of which usually mean poor air quality), turn to the section on indoor drying on page 137.

To dry outdoors, you'll need drying trays. Set the crop out early in the morning after the dew has dried so that it will have a full day to dry and won't be too wet the first night. Place the trays in a comparatively pest-free location, on racks raised above the ground so that air can circulate freely under as well as over the food.

Cover the trays at night to prevent dew from settling on the food. Move them to a sheltered place, or cover them with clean, chemical-free cardboard (cartons are fine), heavy towels, an old shower curtain, or anything that will keep moisture out. Obviously, if you expect rain, make sure the cover is really waterproof. Secure it tightly because many insects are nocturnal and will try to get into the food after the sun goes down.

Be sure to exclude insects and animals from the drying area during the day, too. Turn the food often, and dry only on sunny days. When the food is dry enough to bring in, try to do it in the middle of a hot day to make sure that surface moisture has evaporated.

Making and Using Drying Trays

Drying trays, which hold drying foods and let air circulate around them, can be made of just about anything that has a good-sized flat surface. But the best trays are those that have ventilated bottoms made from cheesecloth, nylon screening, or fine wooden slats.

You can buy trays made especially for drying food or make them yourself. Construct wooden frames and stretch nylon mesh, cotton sheeting, or cheesecloth over them. If you're using cheesecloth, make the frames at least 1 to 2 inches under 36 inches because most cheesecloth comes in 3-foot widths. Reinforce mesh or cheesecloth underneath with string tacked diagonally between the corners of each frame.

Although they're convenient, don't use wire mesh or window screening alone. The metal can interact with the food (especially high-acid foods like fruits and tomatoes) and either destroy some of the vitamins or introduce a questionable metal onto the food itself. If you're using wire mesh or window screening, cover it with tightly woven cotton fabric, brown paper, or freezer paper. Each time you dry new produce, replace the paper and wash the cheesecloth and mesh or screening. Scrub the wood.

Drying trays are a must if you're drying produce outdoors. But you may want to make your trays so that they'll fit into your oven or a food dryer, too. That way you're covered if you hit a rainy spell and decide to dry indoors instead or become impatient with the sun and want to speed things up with extra controlled heat.

Put food on the tray one piece deep. If one side of your piece of food is covered with skin, put that side down on the tray. (Peeled foods dry faster.) By the time it's ready to be turned, the side without the skin will be dry enough to have lost its stickiness. Then place a piece of cheesecloth or other fine-meshed material like wire mesh or window screening over (but not touching) the food, keeping it slightly above the food with blocks of wood or clean stones.

You can stack drying trays for convenience if you separate them so air can circulate around each tray. Here, 3-inch-thick wooden blocks are used as spacers for the trays. Cover the trays with cheesecloth or another fine-mesh cloth to keep out bugs.

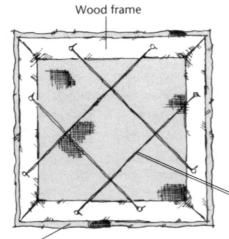

Wood frame

Cheesecloth
tacked and stretched
over frame

String to add support
to cheesecloth

Here's a homemade drying tray that's easy to make. Since cheesecloth comes in 1-yard widths, make the wooden frames 1 to 2 inches under 36 inches so you can tack or staple the cheesecloth to the underside of the frame. Tack crisscrossed strings on the underside of the frame to reinforce the cheesecloth tray.

Out in the open, carefully lay strips of wood or stones on the edges of the cheesecloth or other screening material to prevent the material from blowing off. When you've finished drying a batch, remove the covering, wash it well, and let it dry before you set out more produce. Scrub any sticky wooden surfaces as well.

Solar drying (collecting the sun's rays in a solar box using a reflectant such as aluminum foil or glass to elevate the temperature 20° to 30°F) is not recommended for food safety and quality reasons.

Drying Indoors

Many parts of the country are not blessed with many warm and dry days on a consistent basis. If such is the case where you live, you'll probably have more luck if you do your drying indoors.

Drying with controlled heat in a kitchen oven or in a dryer has several advantages. The drying goes on day and night, in sunny or cloudy weather. Controlled-heat dryers shorten the drying time and extend the drying season to include late-maturing varieties. Better yet, vegetables dried with controlled heat cook up into more appetizing dishes than do sun-dried vegetables. They also have higher vitamin A content and better color and flavor. And you have no insects to worry about.

Oven Drying

Drying produce in your oven takes hours, during which you can't use the oven for cooking and you heat up the house. But using the oven is better than letting food spoil in wet weather. And it's great for finishing up nearly dry produce.

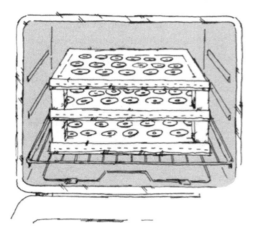

You'll get better-quality dried fruits and vegetables if you use drying trays in the oven instead of baking sheets. That's because the trays will allow warm air to circulate evenly around the produce as it dries, for faster, more uniform drying. Separate the trays by placing small blocks of wood at each corner when stacking them.

Each square foot of shelf space in an ordinary oven will hold about 1 to 2 pounds of produce. This comes out to be, for instance, a little more than a quart of peas or four medium apples. Of course, the poundage depends on how thick the slices of fruit or vegetables are, and a lighter load will dry faster than a heavier one.

Place food directly on oven racks one piece deep, or if the slats are too far apart, cover them first with fine wire cooling racks, cotton sheeting, or cheesecloth, and then place the food on top. You also can use regular baking sheets, but because they're solid, they won't expose the food to drying heat on all sides. Alternatively, you can buy or make special drying trays described on page 136.

It's very difficult to give more than general guidelines for time and temperature. Set your oven to bake no higher than 160°F. This will be tricky with many ovens, since the lowest setting is often 200°F. If this is the case with yours, set it to "warm" and use an oven thermometer to check the real temperature inside. If you can't get the temperature to stay between 140° and 160°F, you ought to consider other ways to dry food. Don't broil your produce! If your oven uses the broiling element when baking, put a baking sheet on the top shelf to protect the food below.

Don't place any food closer than about 6 inches from either the top or bottom of your oven. Check food drying in the oven often, especially during the end of the drying time. Rotate the trays periodically for more even drying. If your oven isn't vented (and many electric ones aren't), leave the oven door slightly ajar to get good air circulation: 4 to 6 inches for an electric oven and 1 to 2 inches for a gas oven. Check the temperature to make sure the oven is 140°F, the ideal temperature for drying. Try propping the door open with a folded towel or hot mat.

Don't overload your oven in an attempt to save energy. Extra food just means extra drying time, and it might mean a lot longer drying time because of poor air circulation from crowded food. Sliced fruits and vegetables and small whole berries can take from 4 to 12 hours to dry in a warm oven.

As when drying outside, put produce skin-side down. By the time you're ready to turn the fruit, the more moist exposed side should have dried out a bit and lost some of its tackiness so there's less chance that it will stick to the tray.

Dehydrators

Dehydrators are easy and effective to use for all kinds of produce. You'll probably spend about $100 for a good-quality dehydrator, although prices range higher and lower depending on the size and features of the dehydrator. The initial expense is worthwhile if you intend to dry produce regularly. Dehydrators work faster than the oven and are more dependable. And they don't heat up your house or monopolize cooking space.

Evaluate the models you find by size, construction, and quality control features so that you're sure you get one that you can use for years. Here's what to look for.

Size. If you have a big garden and plan to do a lot of drying, get a big dehydrator that can handle all your harvest. If you're just planning to dry a few fruits and herbs, you'll probably get by with a smaller dehydrator.

Calculate the space you'll need as follows. Each square foot of shelf space will hold 1 to 2 pounds of sliced produce or herb sprigs. To determine the drying space of a dryer, multiply the inches of shelf length by shelf width and then by the number of shelves. Then divide that number by 144. For example, a three-shelf, 12 × 12-inch dehydrator would have 3 square feet of drying space and could handle 3 to 6 pounds of produce at a time.

Finish and noise level. If you have plenty of counter space and intend to keep your dehydrator on the kitchen counter, buy one that looks good, matches your decor, and is quiet. If you're going to

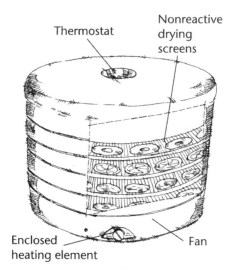

Thermostat

Nonreactive drying screens

Enclosed heating element

Fan

If you're serious about drying food, it pays to buy the best dehydrator you can afford. A top-quality dehydrator will have all the features shown above, increasing both safety and efficiency.

MAKE YOUR OWN DRYER

If you only want to dry small batches of food at a time or wish to experiment with preparing and using dried foods, make this simple, inexpensive dryer designed by Rodale Technical Services. It's easy to make and will save you money since you won't have to buy an expensive dryer or dehydrator.

You'll need a cardboard carton or wooden box, without a lid and at least 8 inches deep, one or more 60-watt bulbs, a socket base and cord, a stainless steel baking sheet or piece of stainless steel sheet cut to fit the box, some aluminum foil, and a few brushfuls of black paint.

Start by painting the back side of the baking sheet or metal sheet black for maximum heat absorption. While it's drying, line your box with aluminum foil, shiny side out. Then place your bulb setup in the center of the box, angling the bulb at 45 degrees. (To help diffuse heat evenly, you might also put a little aluminum-foil "shade" on the top of the bulb.)

After notching the top corner of the box so the cord can exit, place the tray over the box (black side down) so it's suspended a few inches over the light bulb. Then coat the tray with a little vegetable oil to prevent the food from sticking to it (or put a layer of nylon or fiberglass netting or cheesecloth over the tray), fill the tray with a layer of sliced fruit or vegetables, and plug it in. In about 12 hours (more time on a humid day, much less time for herbs and foods cut into fairly small pieces, or perhaps longer for high-moisture foods like most fruits), you'll have a trayful of dried goodies for storage or snacking.

Our prototype dryer features a cardboard fruit box that's 12 × 18 inches and 8¼ inches deep. It uses a 1-inch-deep baking sheet, which fits the top exactly. The baking sheet was purchased at a hardware store and will hold about 1½ pounds of raw prepared food.

For Larger Quantities

To dry larger amounts at one time, simply increase the size of your box and tray. For every 2 to 3 square feet of tray you add, use one additional 60-watt-bulb setup, taking care to space the bulbs carefully for even heating. This should keep your surface tray temperature at about 125° to 130°F—cool enough so you can just bear to touch it, but hot enough to dry your harvest slowly and surely without scorching or experiencing the kind of nutrient loss that begins at around 140°F.

This indoor dryer is simplicity itself. While not very large or sophisticated, it costs practically nothing to build and will quickly give you a sense of the food-drying technique in action. You also can use it for other things. Here are a few suggestions.

- You can put pans of bread dough on top of it to provide low heat for rising.

- Put your milk and yogurt starter mixture inside and use the gentle heat to make yogurt.

- Use it to liquefy crystallized honey, to make limp crackers crisp again, and to soften butter. ❖ ❖ ❖

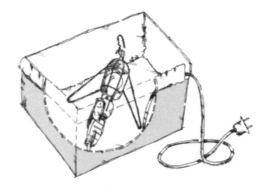

Make this simple, inexpensive, but functional dryer in minutes from household odds and ends. Just line a cardboard box with aluminum foil, insert a cord and lightbulb with an aluminum-foil shade, and set a baking sheet on top of the box.

put the dehydrator in some out-of-the-way place, these options don't matter as much.

Thermostat. Be sure the dehydrator you buy has an enclosed thermostat that can measure temperatures from 85° to 160°F. This keeps the dehydrator at a steady, preset temperature so the food dries at the right rate without burning.

Fan. For fast, efficient drying, a dehydrator must have a fan or blower to improve ventilation and carry away the water vapor given off by the dehydrating produce. Dryers without fans may have hot spots, which lead to cooked or burned food.

Shelf construction. Be sure the shelves are made of an inert material that won't discolor the food or give it an off-flavor, are easy to handle, and have holes small enough to hold your produce. Thin nylon-mesh screens over plastic or aluminum frames are lightweight and easy to clean. Solid wood or metal shelves will block airflow and hinder dehydrating.

Storage Containers

Once you get produce dry, you need to keep it dry. Seal it in airtight packages that allow no moisture to leak through. If you are occasionally visited by mice or cupboard-browsing insects, you'll need containers that are rigid enough to keep pests out. Glass canning or recycled food jars are ideal on both counts, but they let sunlight through, which can fade the dried goods inside.

You also can store dried produce in freezer bags and containers. But be extra careful to seal them tightly—one tiny leak can let in enough humidity to spoil most dried foods. To keep out pests, store the plastic bags in old coffee cans, jars, or other rigid containers.

You can use new, brown paper bags free of adhesives, inks, or other chemicals to store dried herbs that are not yet stripped. These herbs may not be dry enough for sealing airtight, but they will keep adequately with the ventilation provided in paper bags. Finish drying them in the oven before sealing them airtight. You also can store dried legumes and corn in paper bags; see "Super-Easy Dried Beans, Peas, and Corn" on page 162.

 Drying Techniques

Here's the background you need to know to dry your fruits and vegetables. For specifics on drying herbs, see "Drying Herbs" on page 154.

Cutting Up Fruits and Vegetables

The entire batch of produce will dry fast and at almost the same time if you cut it up into small, uniform pieces. If you're preparing big batches, you can use your food processor to slice vegetables and fruits. Find the appropriate blades and insert the food at the right angles to get the most uniform pieces. Check your operating manual for more information. If you're doing small batches, you may be more precise if you slice and dice by hand.

You also may have to trim some vegetables, like asparagus and broccoli, so you dry only the choice parts. This can be a fairly fast job with a hand-held knife. For more details on each food, see page 160.

Blanching

As when you're freezing produce, you should blanch or precook most vegetables. You'll blanch foods for drying for a shorter time than for frozen foods because you cut the pieces up small and thin. And you can skip chilling the food after blanching because the heat left over from blanching will start the drying process more quickly. Blanch them in steam or boiling water after you slice them. We recommend steaming because it dissolves fewer nutrients into the cooking water and adds less extra moisture to the food. Meanwhile it sets food colors, hastens drying by softening the tissues, stops the ripening process, and prevents undesirable changes in flavor during drying and storage.

You can steam-blanch vegetables in a pressure cooker or a large, heavy pot. Place a shallow layer of vegetables, not over 2 inches deep, in a vegetable steamer, in a wire basket with legs, or in a basket that rests on the inner rim of the pot so that it doesn't let the vegetables sit in the water. Or put them in a stainless steel or enamel colander. Fill the pot with 2 or more inches of boiling water, and set the steamer, basket, or colander in the pot. Cover tightly, and keep the water boiling rapidly. Steam for the required time.

If there's no convenient way of steaming, boiling is second best. Use a large amount of boiling water and a small amount of food so that the temperature of the water will not be lowered much when you add the food. Use about 3 gallons of water to every quart of vegetables. Place the vegetables in a wire basket and immerse them in the boiling water for the required time.

You also can blanch vegetables in a microwave oven. Follow the directions in "Microwave Blanching" on page 42 and in the timetable on page 43.

No matter which method you use, when blanching time is up, gently roll the vegetables in a towel to soak up moisture. For specific blanching times, see "A Crop-by-Crop

---

Quick Tip

NO BLANCHING NEEDED

Don't bother to blanch some vegetables before drying; they keep their quality nicely without precooking. These include garlic, leeks, onions, peppers, and tomatoes. ❖ ❖ ❖

Guide to Drying Vegetables, Herbs, and Fruits" on page 160.

Fruit Pretreatment

Dried fruit is delicious eaten right out of your hand or plumped up with extra water and added to baked goods. But most fruit also needs some form of pretreatment to maintain top quality once dried. Commercially, some fruit is pretreated with sulfur to preserve its color, but sulfur can add a sour or acid taste, and some people are allergic to sulfur.

A healthy and easy alternative that will keep apples and bananas from browning and peaches from discoloring is to dip them in an antidarkening agent such as ascorbic acid powder (available in season at grocery stores or through your local drugstore), lemon or pineapple juice, or honey solutions. Although we mention some fruits specifically, you can use these dips with any fruit. Here's how.

• Dip fruits like apples, apricots, and peaches for 3 to 5 minutes in an ascorbic acid solution (mix 1 teaspoon powdered ascorbic acid—3000 mg of vitamin C tablets crushed—in 2 cups of water).

• Make a honey-lemon dip with 1 cup honey, 1 cup water, and the juice of one lemon. Then dip fruits in that.

• Dip any kind of fruit into a honey syrup made of 1/2 cup sugar and 1 1/2 cups boiling water cooled, then 1/2 cup honey added.

Another pretreatment you might consider for faster fruit drying is blanching to crack fruit skins so the moisture inside can readily escape. Blanch whole or halved fruits such as berries, cherries, or grapes in steam for one to two minutes or in boiling water for 15 seconds to one minute. The length of time depends on the thickness of the skin and the size of the fruit. Then quickly plunge the fruit into cold water. The skins should crack with the shock of the temperature change.

When Is It Dry?

To keep dried food from spoiling, you need to be able to tell when the fruit is about 80 percent dry and vegetables are about 90 percent dry, enough to drop below the moisture levels that support decomposers. One of the best ways is by feel. With the exception of papayas and bananas, fruit should feel dry and leathery on the outside but slightly moist inside. It should be pliable and delicious to eat as is.

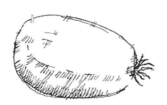

FRESH TOMATO

HALF-DRIED TOMATO

DRIED TOMATO

Make sure your produce is fully dried before you store it.

Herbs should be crackling crisp, like a newly opened box of cornflakes. If any less dry, they'll quickly mildew in storage. Beans, peas, and corn should be very hard; leafy and thin vegetables should be leathery or crisp. For more specifics on each food, see page 160.

Check your drying trays regularly and remove any food that is dry. Don't wait until everything is dry to clear out the whole tray. If you're not sure if the produce is dry enough, leave the food on the drying trays a little longer, but lower the temperature in an oven or dehydrator so the food won't scorch. Then remove a few pieces from the heat—they will feel less moist when cool.

Conditioning Dried Fruits and Vegetables

When you think the fruits and vegetables are dry, store each type in a separate, closed, airtight container at room temperature. Glass jars, freezer containers, or all-purpose storage containers are some good options. But don't use aluminum containers if you're drying fruits; aluminum can react with the acid in the fruits. Wood is not a good idea either because it's porous and can retain moisture.

Stir the contents thoroughly each day for seven to ten successive days. This brings the drier particles in contact with some that are more moist and distributes the moisture content more evenly. If, at the end of this conditioning period, the food seems too moist, return it to the dryer or leave it in the sun for further drying, stirring and checking daily.

Pasteurizing Produce

After the effort you've put into drying your produce, make sure it doesn't become home to a brood of insects. When you dry produce outdoors or uncovered indoors, insects may lay their eggs on the food. Destroy them by heat or cold pasteurization before you store the food away. Pasteurizing food before drying can prevent contamination. But pasteurization isn't as important for foods you wash well, seal in a dehydrator indoors, or peel, which removes most hidden insect eggs.

You can pasteurize your food by either heating it or freezing it. But freezing is better because it destroys fewer vitamins than heating. To freeze-pasteurize dried food, place it in plastic bags or food containers and hold it at or below 0°F, if possible, for a minimum of 48 hours. To pasteurize with heat, spread dried food 1 inch thick on baking sheets or trays, and heat for 30 minutes in a 160°F oven. Then cool thoroughly.

Quality Conscious

LONGER STORAGE

Dried foods will keep for the longest possible time if you put them in the freezer. But if you're ultimately going to put the foods in the freezer, you may wonder why you shouldn't just freeze them fresh and not bother drying them first. The reason is that dried foods take up practically no space compared with fresh-frozen foods—something to keep in mind if your freezer space is at a premium. ❖ ❖ ❖

Storing Dried Foods

When thoroughly and uniformly dry and pasteurized, pack the food for storage. Promptness is important here because dried food will immediately start to pick up moisture from the air. There's also plenty of humidity in the refrigerator, so don't put dried goods in there unless they're sealed airtight.

Store in airtight, sterilized glass jars, in heavy-duty plastic bags, or in metal cans (with tight-fitting lids) that are lined with new brown paper bags to keep food out of contact with the metal. Or put brown paper bag liners in clear plastic bags and glass jars to keep the light out. If you don't use a light-blocking liner, then make sure the storage area is dark. And if storing dried foods in paper bag–lined plastic bags, make sure the area is rodent-proof!

Squeeze excess air out of plastic bags or pick jars that are just big enough to hold your food. Half-filled jars are also half filled with air, and it's air and the natural moisture in it that you want to avoid. Store only one type of food in each container, even if each is wrapped in separate plastic bags within that container, so that flavors and smells don't mix.

It's generally best to package small quantities—enough, say, for one meal. Then if one package spoils, only a small amount of food will be wasted. Several brown paper bags of dried foods can be stored inside one larger heavy-duty plastic bag. After the foods are packaged, place a label on each container indicating the kind of food and the date it was packaged so that you can use your foods in the order in which you dried them. The rule for dried as well as for all preserved foods is: first in, first out.

After labeling, store dried foods in a dark place in a cool (below 60°F), dry basement or pantry. During warm, humid weather, dried foods retain their quality best if refrigerated.

It's a good idea to examine dried foods occasionally for mold. If you find any, the food's a loss; throw it out. It probably wasn't dried sufficiently in the first place. Live and learn. If, on the other hand, upon examination you find that it's more limber and moist than you remember, but there's no mold at all, you can stick it in the oven or food dryer to dry it out. Use it sooner rather than later.

(continued on page 148)

Storage Times for Dried Foods

Dried foods keep well for anywhere from a month to two years, depending on the food and how well it was stored. Check this table to find out how long you can keep specific foods at room temperature (70°F) and at a cooler temperature, close to the temperature of unheated basements (52°F). You can see that dried foods store considerably longer at the lower temperature.

Food	Months Stored at 70°F	Months Stored at 52°F
VEGETABLES		
Asparagus	2	4–6
Beans, green and yellow	4	8–12
Beans, lima	4	8–12
Beets	4	8–12
Broccoli	1	2–3
Cabbage	1	2–3
Carrots	6	12–18
Cauliflower	1	2–3
Celery	2	2–3
Corn	4	8–12
Eggplant	2	4–6
Garlic	4	8–12
Horseradish	4	8–12
Okra	4	8–12
Onions, Leeks	4	8–12
Parsnips	4	8–12
Peas	4	8–12
Peppers, chili	8	16–24
Peppers, sweet	8	16–24
Potatoes, white	4	8–12
Pumpkins	1	2–3
Spinach, Kale, Swiss chard	2	4–6

Food	Months Stored at 70°F	Months Stored at 52°F
VEGETABLES		
Sweet potatoes	1	2–3
Tomatoes	3	6–9
Turnips	2	4–6
Zucchini, Summer squash	1	2–3
FRUITS		
Apples	6	18–24
Apricots	8	24–32
Bananas	4	12–16
Blueberries	6	18–24
Cherries	12	36–48
Citrus peels	6	18–24
Coconut	1	3–4
Dates	12	36–48
Figs	6	18–24
Grapes	6	18–24
Papayas	6	18–24
Peaches, Nectarines	6	18–24
Pears	6	18–24
Pineapple	8	24–32
Plums	8	24–32
Rhubarb	4	12–16
Strawberries	6	18–24

Using Dried Fruits and Vegetables

The flip side of drying and storing fruits and vegetables is eating them. Many fruits and some vegetables are good right from the bag. But all dried food is good cooked, and some of it is *only* good cooked. With dried food, though, it's not just a question of throwing the food in the pan. Fruits in particular need presoaking to rehydrate them before cooking. That way, they'll cook at the same time as your other ingredients. Here are the techniques you need to get the most out of your dried foods.

Rehydrating Fruits

Many dried fruits are delicious eaten dried. Eat them as they are, or chop them up to mix in trail mixes or sprinkle on cereals and desserts. However, you may want to return dried fruits to their original moist form, putting the water back in them for use in

---

Creative Cooking

FRUIT PUREES

Make fancy, richly fruity sauces and sweeteners for baked goods, frozen yogurt toppings, or flavoring for yogurt using reconstituted dried fruits. Just pull out as much fruit as you need, soak it as specified on page 150, and puree in the food processor. For the best flavor, consider whether you are starting with sweet or tart fruit, as indicated in the table below.

When preparing fruit puree from a tart fruit, as shown in the table, add some sweet fruit rather than honey to sweeten it. Apple is ideal for this, as it blends well with other fruits.

Begin by coarsely chopping each desired fruit alone in a blender. In a saucepan, combine the fruit with water to cover. Cook, uncovered, over low heat for about 30 minutes, or until the fruit is tender. Stir frequently. For faster cooking, you can microwave four medium apples on high for about eight minutes, or according to your microwave manufacturer's directions.

Return the fruit to the blender and puree to the desired consistency. Puree berries well or they'll be gritty. You can leave some chunks in softer fruits such as apples, peaches, or pears.

Sweet Fruits		Tart Fruits
Apples	Figs	Apricots
Bananas	Grapes	Cherries
Blackberries	Pears	Nectarines
Blueberries	Pineapple	Peaches
Cherries	Plums	Plums
Coconut	Raspberries	
Dates	Strawberries	

SUBSTITUTING DRIED FOOD FOR FRESH

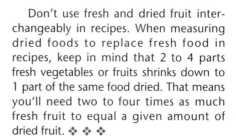

Don't use fresh and dried fruit inter-changeably in recipes. When measuring dried foods to replace fresh food in recipes, keep in mind that 2 to 4 parts fresh vegetables or fruits shrinks down to 1 part of the same food dried. That means you'll need two to four times as much fresh fruit to equal a given amount of dried fruit. ❖ ❖ ❖

baked goods, fruit stews and soups, and compotes. Once dried, fruits such as citrus peels and grapes (raisins) are best left in their dried form.

To rehydrate fruits, place them in a pot or microwave-safe container, and pour boiling water over them. Don't add the food to the water; it's not the same. Cover the container, and keep it hot but not boiling—not even simmering. Let them soak until they've absorbed the water.

The water should just cover the food. Too much water will take a lot of the flavor out of the food. You can always add more boiling water if it needs more, so it's better to add too little at the start than too much. Check "Soaking Times for Dried Fruits" on page 150 for the suggested amount of water you should pour over each food; they all don't need the same amount. Don't add sugar to fruits at this stage because it will cause them to absorb less water than they normally would.

"Soaking Times for Dried Fruits" also gives suggested soaking times. But the times are only suggestions. If this is your first time rehydrating a certain food, you might want to lift the lid now and then to check how things are coming. Taste it after a while to see how you like it and how it looks. Remember that the rehydrated fruit should look pretty much like fresh fruit does after it's been cooked. When done correctly, all the water will be soaked up.

For faster results, you can plump up fruit in the microwave. Put them in a microwave-safe container, cover with boiling water, and put in the microwave. Use high for 4 to 5 minutes and then medium-low for 4 to 10 minutes, depending on the kind of fruit and the power of the microwave.

Soaking Times for Dried Fruits

The recommendations below are based on our experiences in the Rodale Food Center. Unless otherwise noted, pour boiling water over the fruit to rehydrate it. As we've said before, there are no hard-and-fast rules for using dried foods. Use our recommendations as a starting point, and experiment from there.

Apples. Use equal amounts of apples and water; soak for 10 minutes. Reconstituted apples are very similar to baked apples. The flavor is good, and the flesh is soft but holds its shape. Although more flavor will be lost this way, you can also reconstitute apples by soaking in cool water. Keep the apple surfaces in contact with the water. It will take 10 to 30 minutes to rehydrate, depending on the size of the slices.

Apricots, dates, and figs. Use equal amounts of fruit and water; soak for 15 minutes. The flavor is good. Apricot flesh is soft but has body; color darkens a bit. Apricots do not reconstitute well in cool water.

Bananas. Use equal amounts of bananas and water; soak for ten minutes. Reconstituted bananas are very soft, limp, and sweet; they have the dark color of very ripe bananas. They do not reconstitute well in cool water.

Blueberries. Use equal amounts of berries and water; soak for 10 to 15 minutes. Do not reconstitute in cool water.

Cherries. Use equal amounts of cherries and water; soak for ten minutes. They'll be dark in color and soft with almost a mushy texture, but they'll hold their shape. Rehydrated cherries taste sweet like cooked cherries. They do not reconstitute well in cool water; much flavor is lost, and it takes over an hour for them to become tender.

Peaches, nectarines, and papayas. Use equal amounts of fruit and water; soak for about five minutes. Flavor is good; flesh becomes soft but holds its shape.

Pears. Use equal amounts of pears and water; soak for ten minutes. Flavor is good; the flesh is soft, but it darkens in color a bit. Pears also reconstitute well in cool water; soak for ten minutes.

Pineapple. Use equal amounts of pineapple and water; soak for ten minutes. Good in all respects; it is a bit mushy, but it holds its shape. Pineapple does not reconstitute well in cool water.

Plums. Dried plums are prunes. To reconstitute, use equal amounts of plums and water, and soak for 20 minutes. Plums reconstitute well in cool water. Flavor and color are good, but

Use dried apples as is in trail mix. Or soak them in hot water, apple juice, or cider to reconstitute them, then use them in baked treats like fruit breads, muffins, and pies.

they're a bit slimier than when soaked in boiling water. Different kinds of plums give very different results.

Strawberries. Use equal amounts of strawberries and water; soak for ten minutes. Strawberries do not reconstitute well in cool water; make sure you use boiling water.

Fruit Leathers

Like trail mixes, fruit leathers have revolutionized how we snack. Instead of eating fast foods high in salt and fat, many people are just as happy to nibble on sweet, flavorful fruit leathers that have the texture of chewy candy. They're called leathers because they feel (but don't taste!) something like leather—soft and pliable. You

---

Creative Cooking

Apple Leather

Making delicious apple leather is no harder than making apple butter. Here's what you'll need.

1 gallon apples, peeled and cored

1 cup apple cider (or more)

$^1/_2$ to 1 cup mild-flavored honey

2 tablespoons lemon juice or $^1/_2$ teaspoon ascorbic acid

Ground cinnamon, cloves, and/or nutmeg, added to taste (optional)

Place the apples and their juice in a large, heavy pot, and add the apple cider. (Apples are drier than other fruits and will scorch as they are heated if you don't add liquid to the pot.) Place the pot over low heat, and bring the apples to a boil. (The USDA recommends heating fruit to 160°F to kill bacteria.) Add more cider if needed to prevent the apples from sticking to the bottom of the pot. If the apples are tart, add honey and lemon juice when the mixture looks somewhat clear and is boiling well. Then add the spices, if you wish.

When the mixture reaches the consistency of a very thick sauce, remove it from the heat and run it through a food mill, blender, or food processor. Return to the heat and cook to the consistency of thick applesauce. Spread the pulp about ¼ inch thick on oiled baking sheets or baking sheets lined with freezer paper or plastic wrap. Dry, cool, and store as indicated on page 152.

Yield: 4 sheets, each about 10 × 5 inches

Step-by-Step

MAKING FRUIT LEATHER

Fruit leather is surprisingly easy to make. And it's delicious on the trail or as a snack. Here's how to do it.

1. Puree cooked fruit in a blender, then pour the pureed fruit onto an oiled baking sheet. (The USDA recommends adding ½ teaspoon ascorbic acid or 2 tablespoons lemon juice to every 2 cups of fruit.)

2. Spread the puree with a spatula until it covers the tray in a ¼-inch-thick layer, then dry it in a food dryer or on low in the oven.

3. After the puree has dried into fruit leather, pull it from the baking sheet in a single layer.

4. Place the leather on a cooling rack until both sides are thoroughly dry.

5. Dust the dried leather with cornstarch or arrowroot powder to prevent sticking. Then roll the leather between two sheets of wax paper to store.

make them by drying cooked pureed fruit on a baking sheet until a good part of the moisture and stickiness is gone and you're left with a thin sheet of fruit. (The USDA recommends that fruit used for leathers be brought to 160°F before drying to kill spoilers.) Any single fruit is good, and combinations can be quite delicious. Spices and sweeteners are optional.

Fruit leathers are usually dried in a very low-heat oven (see the recipes on pages 151 and 333), but you can also dry them in a food dryer. Some models even come with special fruit-leather drying trays. To prevent sticking, pour the puree on oiled trays or trays lined with freezer paper or plastic wrap. Don't use wax paper or aluminum foil; the leather will stick to it. Spread the puree so it's 1/8 to 1/4 inch thick. It will dry in six to eight hours in an electric food dehydrator. If it's any thicker, it will take a very long time to dry. You'll know the leather is done when the center is no longer sticky. If it's brittle, it has overdried.

Once the fruit leather is dry, remove it from the tray, place it on a cake rack, and leave it there for a few hours so that you're sure both sides are dry. Then dust with cornstarch or arrowroot powder before you roll it up or stack it in layers with wax paper, freezer paper, or plastic wrap between each sheet. Store fruit leathers in a cool, dry place for 1 to 2 months or in the refrigerator or freezer for 1 year.

Fruit Flour

Make some fancy baked goods with your own homemade fruit flour. Use extra-dry fruits, and grind them in a coffee mill or food processor to a flourlike consistency. For every cup of flour called for in your recipe, add up to 1/2 cup fruit flour. Blend it with the other dry ingredients. You may need to add 1 to 2 tablespoons extra liquid to the recipe.

You can also use fruit flour to make custards and puddings. For custard, use about 1 cup fruit flour to 4 cups milk and three eggs. In pudding, use about 1 cup fruit flour to 4 cups milk and 6 tablespoons cornstarch.

Cooking Dried Vegetables

Some vegetables, like dried beet, carrot, parsnip, sweet potato, tomato, and zucchini chips, make flavorful snacks fresh from the bag. But most dried vegetables need to be cooked. It's best to use vegetables while dried or to put them directly into soups, stews, and sauces—letting them plump back up as you cook them.

In taste tests we conducted at the Rodale Food Center, we found

Make sure you label your dried soup mixes so you'll know what's in them at a glance. List the ingredients, date dried, and how to use the mix.

To make "instant" home-made soup, add dried vegetable flakes, small pasta, diced dried root crops, dried herbs to taste, and boiling water to a thermos.

that the best way to use dried vegetables is to cook them in soups and stews. The color and aromas are appetizing, the textures are soft, and the flavor is good. What's more, dried vegetables—except beans and peas—don't need to be rehydrated before cooking them this way. (You'll learn how to handle dried peas and beans on page 162.)

For stew, use 1 cup of water for every cup of dried vegetables. For soup, use at least 2 cups of water for every cup of vegetables. Combine ingredients, bring to a boil, cover, and reduce the heat to low. Simmer for about 20 minutes. The dried vegetables that we like best for soups and stews are green beans, lima beans, beets, broccoli, cabbage, carrots, cauliflower, celery, corn, eggplant, garlic, onions, peas, chili peppers, sweet peppers, potatoes, spinach, and summer squash.

Instant Dried Vegetable Soup

A simple way to use dried vegetables is to make them into instant soup. Make yourself a steaming thermos of soup by adding 5 tablespoons mixed dried vegetables, 1 tablespoon macaroni or other small pasta, some spices or herbs, and a few drops of soy sauce to 2 cups boiling hot stock (vegetable, chicken, beef, or whatever you'd like). Cap the thermos and let it sit to "cook" for a few hours.

Don't add grains, peas, or beans to your soup unless you cook them first. We tried other ingredients like dried lentils, brown rice, and split peas but were disappointed with the results because they were undercooked.

Drying Herbs

You haven't heard a lot about drying herbs up to this point because you need to handle them slightly differently than vegetables and fruits. But you may end up using your drying skills more often to preserve herbs than for any other use. Dry choice cultivars of herbs from your garden and store them in jars, ready to sprinkle into any food you're cooking. Or blend them into easy-to-use mixes for different kinds of dishes, like Mexican, Italian, Indian, and, of course, classic French.

Drying Herb Leaves

If you live in an arid climate, you can dry small bunches of herbs by hanging them in a well-ventilated area free from strong light, such as an attic or garage. This will work even if your climate is slightly humid as long as you use herbs that dry well naturally. See "Choosing Vegetables, Fruits, and Herbs" on page 132.

Keep air-dried herbs away from the kitchen, where humidity rises every time you boil water and oil can splatter on decoratively hung herbs. If you hang them in out-of-the-way places, like attics or spare bedrooms, be sure the herbs won't get dust or insulation fibers on them. One way to keep them clean is to hang them in paper bags with holes punched in the sides.

But there are other ways to air-dry herbs—any way that keeps air circulating freely around the herbs and keeps them out of sunlight, dust, grime, and moisture will do. If you don't want to hang them up, remove their stems and dry them on baking sheets, on window screens covered with clear sheeting or cheesecloth, or even on a towel.

You can also dry herbs in a food dryer. But be certain that the screen or netting on the tray is very fine so that no leaves can fall through its openings. You may have to line your racks with sheeting or cheesecloth. For best flavor, the temperature inside the dryer should stay between 95° and 115°F. When thoroughly dry, remove the leaves from the stems, but don't crush them unless you plan to use them right away. There's no sense in releasing precious oils—the part that adds flavor and fragrance—and having them degenerate in storage.

For best flavor, harvest herb leaves before the plants flower.

Drying Herb Seeds

Spread seed pods from herbs such as anise, caraway, coriander, cumin, dill, and fennel one layer thick on drying trays just as you do the leaves. When they seem thoroughly dry, rub the pods between the palms of your hands, and the seeds should fall out easily. You can also dry the seeds by hanging the whole plant upside down inside a paper bag to dry. As the seeds dry and fall from the pods, the paper bag will catch them.

You can give the dried seeds, especially dill seed, a light threshing to separate the pods from the seeds. Rub the seeds between your palms. Then pick a day when there is a light breeze, go outside, and pour the seeds slowly from a 2-foot height into a large bowl, bucket, or any container big enough for the job. Put a clean sheet under the

Quick Tip

FRESH AND DRIED HERB MEASUREMENTS

When substituting dried herbs for fresh ones in recipes, use this equivalence guide: 1 tablespoon of fresh herbs equals 1 teaspoon of dried, crumbled herbs or ½ teaspoon of dried, powdered herbs. ❖ ❖ ❖

To air-dry herbs, hang them in bunches from a drying rack or wooden laundry rack. Put the rack in a dark, dry, well-ventilated place. For fast, even drying, use a dehydrator at a lower temperature than you would for vegetables and fruits.

To dry herb seeds, hang a bunch of herbs upside down in a dark, dry, well-ventilated place. Put a sheet down to catch the dried seeds as they fall. Remove dropped seeds regularly, storing them in glass bottles.

bucket in case the breeze is too strong and carries a lot of the seeds with it. Because pods are lighter than seeds, the breeze should blow them away while the seeds fall into the container below. You will probably need to repeat this a few times until the seeds are free of pods.

Drying Herb Roots

You can use the dried roots of plants such as angelica, burdock, ginger, and ginseng for candy, teas, and cold beverages. These roots are much thicker than the delicate seeds, flowers, and leaves of other plants, so they take longer to dry. Place small or thinly sliced pieces of root one layer deep in a food dryer or low-temperature oven to dry.

Resist the urge to dig and dry the roots of the sassafras tree for sassafras tea. It's not safe to eat or drink foods containing sassafras because it contains safrole, a substance found to cause cancer in laboratory rats.

Storing Dried Herbs

You can crush herb leaves before storing them, but they'll retain their oils better if you keep them whole and crush them as you use them. But be sure the leaves are crackling

DRYING HERB FLOWERS

You can dry herb flowers to add color and flavor to dishes. Harvest lavender buds for French Herbes de Provence, marigolds for their pungent aroma and golden color, chamomile heads, bee balm, and rose petals for tea, dill flowers for salads and dips, and thyme spikes for herb wreaths.

Cut flowers you plan to use in cooking on the first day they open. If you use the petals alone, remove them from the base and spread them on a tray. For rose petals, remove the claws (the narrow white portions at the base of each leaf). Dry chamomile heads whole. ❖ ❖ ❖

dry before storing them, so they won't mildew. Likewise, keep seeds whole during storage—they deteriorate quickly when the seed shell is broken.

Store herb leaves, seeds, flowers, and roots in tightly sealed jars in a warm place for about a week. At the end of that time, examine the jars. If there's moisture on the inside of the glass or under the lid, remove the contents and spread the herbs out for further drying so they won't mold. Checking the jars is especially important when you're storing dried roots because it's difficult to know when they're completely dry.

Keep the sealed jars in a cool place, out of strong light, either in dark glass jars, in tins, or behind cabinet doors. Herbs deteriorate after a while in storage. It's best to throw them out after a year and restock with fresh ones.

Herb Blends

Instead of storing all of your dried herbs separately, you might like to make some herb blends. During storage, the distinct aromas and flavors of the different herbs can blend together and form delightful herb mixtures. Sprinkle them on foods, or tie them in cheesecloth bags and plunge them in soups and stews while they're simmering. Here are some flavorful blends for you to try.

Fines herbes. Traditionally, fines herbes is a mixture of finely chopped fresh herbs that you sprinkle on food during the last few minutes of cooking or just before serving. But you can do something similar with your dried herbs. Blend equal amounts of any of the following herbs: basil, chervil, chives, marjoram, mint, parsley, rosemary, sage, sweet savory, tarragon, and thyme. Chop them up finely in your food processor or blender, and store them in an airtight glass jar until ready to use.

Bouquet garni. This is a mixture of fresh or dried herbs (and sometimes spices) that you tie in a cheesecloth bag or put in a spice ball and suspend in soups or stews while cooking. Remove the herbs when you take the dish off the heat. You can use any blend of herbs you want, but traditionally, you should include one fresh herb, such as parsley.

Creative Cooking

Italian Seasoning

*Here's a simple
but delicious Italian herb mix.*

Yield: 6 or 7 tablespoons

2   tablespoons basil

2   tablespoons oregano

1   tablespoon sweet
    marjoram

1   tablespoon thyme

1   teaspoon sage

When they are dried crackling crisp, pulverize the herbs into
tiny flakes, and mix them together. Store in an airtight glass jar
in a cool, dry place.

SALAD DRESSING MIX

INDIAN MIX

MEXICAN MIX

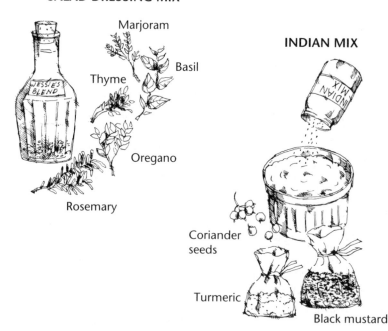

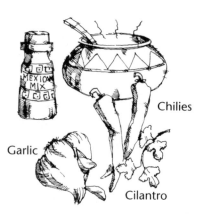

*Make your own delicious herb mixes at home with dried herbs from your garden.
It's easy to mix up your own salad dressing, Indian, and Mexican blends like those
shown here. Experiment until you find the perfect mix for your taste.*

Dried chamomile flowers make a soothing herb tea. Drinking a cup before bedtime is a good way to calm down.

Try these combinations, then start experimenting with your own. For meat and vegetable soups and stews, mix together 1 part sage, 1 part thyme, 2 parts marjoram, 2 parts rosemary, and 2 parts savory. For fish stews and soups, mix together ¼ part oregano, ½ part dill, ½ part thyme, 1 part basil, 1 part lemon balm, and 1 part savory.

Herb teas. Herb teas have come into their own as light, refreshing drinks served hot or iced. But there's no reason to spend money on fancy packaged blends when you can make them easily from the herbs in your garden. You can use a single dried herb, such as chamomile, lemon verbena, peppermint, or spearmint. Or try your hand at custom herb blends. When you've mixed up one you really love, give it a special name and package it prettily for hostess gifts, party favors, and Christmas baskets. You'll find plenty of combinations to start you off in "Herb Teas for All Occasions" below and on page 346.

Creative Cooking

HERB TEAS FOR ALL OCCASIONS

Herb teas can be soothing, stimulating, mild, or spicy. Some are cool and refreshing while others are warming—perfect for a snowy day. Make several blends to match your mood and taste. (Remember, you can mix spices, citrus peel, and even dried fruit with your herbs.) Here are some of our favorites.

- Blueberries, spearmint leaves, and chamomile flowers
- Chamomile flowers and rosemary and borage leaves
- Fennel and dandelion root
- Hibiscus flowers, lemon grass, and alfalfa
- Lemon balm, lavender, and rosemary leaves
- Lemon grass and cloves
- Orange peel and chicory root
- Orange peel, cinnamon, and cloves
- Peppermint and spearmint leaves and lemon peel
- Peppermint leaves and chamomile flowers
- Pineapple sage leaves and ginger
- Rose hips, ginger, and orange peel
- Rosemary leaves, lemon peel, and cinnamon
- Sage leaves, cinnamon, and nutmeg
- Spearmint leaves and orange or lemon peel
- Thyme and bergamot leaves and ginger

A Crop-by-Crop Guide to Drying Vegetables, Herbs, and Fruits

As with any technique, you can't just give blanket recommendations for drying produce. It's true that there are just a few basic techniques, but you'll get the best results if you treat each crop individually. Look up the crop you want to dry on the pages that follow to find out the best ways to prepare and dry it, plus how to tell when it's dry.

Drying Vegetables and Herbs

Here are the specifics you'll need to know to dry garden vegetables and herbs for soups, stews, and seasonings.

Asparagus

Use only the top 3 inches of the spear. Boil or steam for about 5 minutes, or until tender and firm. When dry, asparagus will be very tough to brittle.

Beans, Dried

See "Super-Easy Dried Beans, Peas, and Corn" on page 162 for information on how to dry beans.

Soaking and then cooking dried beans takes several hours, but you can plan ahead and have presoaked beans ready for dinnertime cooking. Soak a couple of pounds of dried beans at a time. Rinse and drain them very well and freeze in bags. When ready to cook, bang the bag against a hard surface to separate the beans, and pour the amount you want into boiling water. The beans will cook a little more quickly than if they had not been frozen.

Leftover cooked beans can also be frozen, but they tend to fall apart when they're cooked again. This hardly matters, though, if you're making a soup with them.

You also can soak beans relatively quickly in a microwave. Put 2 cups of beans in a large baking dish, and cover with water. Cover and cook on high for 10 minutes, or until the water boils. Let the beans stand for one hour, pour out the water, and cook.

Beans, Green and Yellow

Use tender beans only. Cut them into short pieces and boil for 4 minutes, or steam for $5\frac{1}{2}$ minutes. When dry, they will be brittle and crisp. See also page 162 for more information on drying beans, peas, and corn.

Beans, Lima

Shell and blanch for 5 minutes. When dry, limas will be hard and brittle. See also page 162 for more information on drying beans, peas, and corn.

Beets

Remove tops (leaving ½ inch) and roots, and cook until tender. Boil for 30 to 45 minutes, or microwave for about 20 minutes until cooked through. The time depends on the size of the beets. Cool, peel, trim, and cut into ¼-inch cubes or slice very thin. When dry, beets will be tough to brittle.

Broccoli

Trim and slice into small ½-inch strips. Boil for 4 minutes, or steam for 5½ minutes. When dry, broccoli will be crisp and brittle.

Cabbage

Cut into long, thin slices. Boil for 4 minutes, or steam for 5½ minutes. When dry, cabbage will be brittle.

Carrots

Wash and slice thinly. Steam or boil for 4 minutes. When dry, carrots will be tough to brittle.

Cauliflower

Use only the florets. Remove them from the core and split the stems. Boil for 4 to 5 minutes, or steam for 5½ to 6½ minutes. When dry, cauliflower will be crisp and slightly browned.

Celery

Cut stalks into ¼-inch pieces. Boil or steam for 4 minutes. When dry, celery stalks will be very brittle. You also can dry the leaves to use like an herb. Wash well and dip in boiling water before drying. They'll be crisp when dry.

Corn

Husk and remove the silk. Boil the whole cob for 4 minutes, or steam for 5 minutes to set the milk. Cut the cob deeply enough to obtain large kernels, but be careful not to cut so deeply as to include any cob. When dry, corn will be dry and brittle. Also see directions for drying corn on the cob without blanching on page 162.

Eggplant

Peel and cut into ½-inch slices. Boil for about 4 minutes, or steam for 5½ minutes. When dry, eggplant will be leathery to brittle.

SUPER-EASY DRIED BEANS, PEAS, AND CORN

Let nature do the work of drying, indoors or out, with the following vegetables.

The easiest way to air-dry beans is to just leave them in the garden until the pods become papery and the beans are dry. But don't try this unless you usually have a spate of dry, sunny days around harvest time.

Field Drying Beans and Peas

Let fava beans, lima beans, peas, soybeans, and other dried beans dry right in the garden on the vine or stalk. For this to work, you need a long growing season so the crop can stay on the vine until the pods are thoroughly dry but untouched by frost. You also need dry weather; wet weather might cause the seeds to rot or sprout. And plan to get out to collect your dried beans or peas before the pods split open and scatter the bean seeds all over the ground. Watch limas and soybeans carefully as they near the dried stage as their pods split easily when dried.

Air Drying Beans and Peas

A good alternative to field drying is air drying. Pick legume pods when mature and spread them out in shallow layers in the attic, covered porch, or spare bedroom to dry. Blanch as detailed on page 142.

Or cut entire bush bean or pea plants when most of the pods are mature and hang them upside down in a dry, well-ventilated place.

Shelling Dried Beans and Peas

To shell dried beans and peas, place them in cloth bags and beat them with a mallet or stomp on them. This cracks the pods so you can sort the beans or peas from the shells. Or put them in a clean pillowcase, tie it closed, and put it in a clothes dryer on low

Garlic

Peel and cut into thin pieces. No blanching is necessary. When dry, garlic will be crisp.

Herbs

Wash leafy herbs briefly but thoroughly in cold water if they are dirty or have been thickly mulched (otherwise, don't wash). Shake off any excess water and hang the herbs, tied in small bunches, in the sun until the water evaporates from them. Or wrap them up in a thick towel to absorb the extra water.

To dry beans outdoors, lay them on a raised screen and cover the beans and screen with a floating row cover to keep insects out. Use rocks to weight down the sides of the row cover.

for a half hour. The heat and tumbling encourages the pods to break open. Soybeans and chickpeas have tougher pods, though. You'll probably have to shell them by hand.

Storage Pretreatment

Before storing beans or peas, heat them in the oven to kill any insect eggs they may contain. Lay them on shallow trays and heat in a 160°F oven for 30 minutes, or freeze at 0°F for 48 hours.

How to Store

Put completely dry beans and peas in paper bags and enclose them in airtight plastic bags. Or, to keep rodents and insects out, put the paper bags in metal coffee cans or similar cans with tight-fitting lids. Or simply store them in sterilized glass jars with tight-fitting lids. For extra protection from weevils and other insects, put a dried chili pepper in with your legumes.

Drying Corn

Pick the corn, remove the leafy husk, and sun- or oven-dry the corn cob until the kernels are too hard to squeeze. To shell the dried corn, hold the cob between both hands and twist in opposite directions, letting the kernels fall into a container below. You can also store corn on the cob, but it will take up less space and be more convenient to use later if you shell, pasteurize (treat with heat or cold), and store it like beans and peas. ❖ ❖ ❖

Gather seedpods of herbs such as anise, caraway, coriander, cumin, dill, and fennel when the seedpods or heads have changed color but before they begin to shatter.

Dig roots of herbs such as angelica, ginger, and ginseng while the plants are dormant, usually in the fall or winter months. Cut off tender roots—never more than a few from each plant. Scrub them with a vegetable brush to remove all dirt. If roots are thin, you can leave them whole, but slice thick roots lengthwise.

Dry all of these as recommended in "Drying Herbs" on page 154.

Label your dried herbs with the date dried, cultivar name, and type of herb. Store tightly sealed jars of herbs in a dark cabinet or use dark glass bottles.

Horseradish

Trim tops off and grate or slice root. No blanching is necessary. When dry, horseradish will be brittle.

Kale

See "Spinach, Kale, and Swiss Chard" on page 167.

Leeks

See "Onions and Leeks" below.

Okra

Cut off tips and slice. Blanch for 4 minutes. When dry, okra will be tough to brittle.

Onions and Leeks

Peel and dice. Blanch for 4 minutes. When dry, onions and leeks will be brittle.

Parsnips

Trim off tops, peel, and slice. Blanch for 5 minutes. When dry, parsnips will be tough to brittle.

Peas

Shell peas. Boil for 4 minutes, or steam for 5½ minutes. When dry, peas will be wrinkled and brittle. See also directions for drying peas in the pod on page 162.

Creative Cooking

USING DRIED HORSERADISH

To use dried horseradish in dips and spreads, soak in an equal amount of warm water for 30 minutes. ❖ ❖ ❖

Peppers, Chili

If possible, do not pick chili peppers until they are mature and fully red. However, if frost threatens, harvest your crop even if some are still green; many should ripen while drying. If using a food dryer, you can dice them up for faster drying, but wear rubber gloves. There's no need to blanch chili peppers.

You may also string peppers by running a needle and thread through the thickest part of the stem. Hang them outdoors or in a sunny window to dry. They will shrink and darken considerably and will be leathery when dry. Although you can hang dried chilies in a dry place for months, they may deteriorate with accumulated dust or humidity. For best flavor, store the chilies in airtight jars. Grind a few peppers into flakes every now and then to sprinkle on food.

Peppers, Sweet

Clean and slice into thin strips. Blanch for 4 minutes. When dry, peppers are leathery to brittle.

Potatoes

Wash and slice into 1-inch rounds. Peeling is optional. Boil for 7 minutes, or steam for $8\frac{1}{2}$ minutes, and then soak in $\frac{1}{2}$ cup lemon juice and 2 quarts cold water for about 45 minutes to prevent potatoes from oxidizing during drying. When dry, potatoes are brittle.

Pumpkins

Clean and cut into 1-inch strips, and then peel. Blanch for 4 minutes, or until slightly soft. When dry, pumpkin will be very tough to brittle.

Soybeans

See "Super-Easy Dried Beans, Peas, and Corn" on page 162 for information on how to dry beans.

Soybeans aren't like other dried legumes—they need special attention. Soak them overnight in the refrigerator, throw out their soaking water, then cook for one to two hours in fresh liquid before using in recipes. Soybeans contain an antinutritional enzyme and should be eaten only after they are completely cooked.

MAKE A CHILI PEPPER WREATH

Store and display dried chili peppers in this colorful wreath. To make a chili pepper wreath, you'll need the materials shown here. The wreath base and floral wire should be available at florist and craft shops. Here's how to make the wreath.

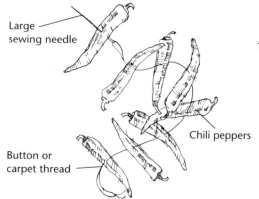

Large sewing needle

Chili peppers

Button or carpet thread

1. Harvest chilies on a dry day, after the dew has evaporated. Make sure a bit of stem is attached to each pod. Thread the needle, doubling the thread and knotting the end. Run the needle and thread through the center of each chili to make a long string, leaving about 1 inch of space between each pepper.

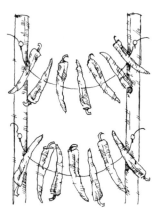

2. Make enough chili strings so you'll have about 100 peppers for your wreath. Then hang the strings in a warm, dark, well-ventilated place until the chilies are dry.

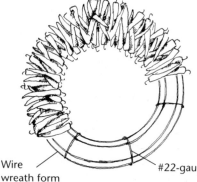

3. Push the dried peppers close together on the strings, then tie the strings together, cutting off excess string. Using floral wire, tie the string of chilies to the wire wreath base until it's entirely covered.

Wire wreath form

#22-gauge floral wire

Spinach, Kale, and Swiss Chard

Cut very coarsely into strips. Boil spinach and Swiss chard for 4 minutes, or steam for $4^1/2$ minutes. Spread strips not more than $^1/2$ inch thick on trays. When dry, they will be crisp and crumble easily.

Sweet Potatoes

Wash, and then grate, slice, or dice. Peeling is optional. Boil for 3 minutes, or steam for 6 to 10 minutes. When dry, potatoes are tough to brittle.

Tomatoes

Slice and blanch briefly to loosen skins for easy peeling, if you wish. When dry, tomatoes will be leathery. See also "Sun-Dried Tomatoes" below.

Turnips

Trim off tops and roots, and slice. Blanch for 5 minutes. When dry, turnips will be very tough to brittle.

Creative Cooking

SUN-DRIED TOMATOES

They cost a fortune in the store, and they're almost worth it because they're so good. But you can make sun-dried tomatoes at home for next to nothing. When air drying, use paste tomatoes because they're meatier and will dry faster than salad tomatoes. But if you have a dehydrator, any kind of tomato will do.

Slice the tomatoes in half lengthwise, or in thirds if they're huge. Dip the slices in a solution of 1 teaspoon citric acid and 1 quart water for 10 minutes. Place cut side up on screens outdoors or in an electric food dryer set at 120°F for 24 hours. Outside, count on a few days of drying; bring the tomatoes in at night. Well-dried tomatoes should be leathery but pliable, not stiff. Store in glass jars with tight lids.

Use dried tomatoes like herbs. Crumble them over pasta, in sauces, or in dressings for a sweet, rich flavor. Or pour a mixture of equal parts vinegar and boiling water over them and let them sit for a few minutes until they soften to a chewy consistency. Drain and cover with olive oil seasoned with a sliver of garlic. Let them marinate in the refrigerator for at least 24 hours before sampling. They'll keep fine refrigerated in this oil for about a month (do not store them at room temperature). Their concentrated flavor is delicious with pasta, in an antipasto, or mixed with tomato sauce. ❖ ❖ ❖

Zucchini and Summer Squash
Don't peel but slice into thin strips. Steam-blanch for 4 minutes. If you're making zucchini chips to eat right away, don't bother to blanch them. When dry, squash is leathery to brittle.

Drying Fruits

Here are the crop-by-crop specifics you need to know to dry fruits for snacks, baking, and desserts.

Apples
Use firm fruit. Don't peel unless the apples have been heavily sprayed. If they've been sprayed or you're not sure, peel them. Then core and cut into thin slices or rings. Pretreat as described in "Fruit Pretreatment" on page 143. When dry, apples will be soft and pliable and slightly tough. Apples are excellent eating dried.

Apricots
Cut in half, remove pits, and slice. Pretreat as described in "Fruit Pretreatment" on page 143. When dry, apricots will be soft and pliable. Apricots are excellent eating dried.

Bananas
Peel and slice thinly. Pretreat as described in "Fruit Pretreatment" on page 143. When dry, bananas will be pliable to crisp. Bananas are excellent eating dried.

Blueberries
Remove stems and blanch quickly to break skins. When dry, blueberries will be leathery and pliable, something like raisins. Blueberries are good eating dried.

Cherries
Cut in half, pit, and remove stems. (If you don't pit them, the dried cherries will taste like the seeds.) Blanch to crack the skin. When dry, cherries will be pliable and leathery, something like raisins. Cherries are good eating dried.

Citrus Peels
Wash well with hot, soapy water, and scrape out the white bitter pith inside. When dry, the peel will be crisp.

To make zest, lightly grate the colored part of a lemon or orange peel, being careful not to grate the bitter white pith. Using a home food dryer, lay grated zest on racks. You may need to cover the racks with cheesecloth to prevent the zest from falling through the slats in the racks. Dry zest according to your food dryer manufacturer's directions, or follow oven-drying directions below. Zest should be crisp in 1 to 2 hours.

Or try oven drying. Dry zest with the oven door slightly open and oven temperature at 145°F. Use an oven thermometer to regulate the heat and keep it at 145°F. You will need to turn the trays if one area of the tray is drying more than another. Zest will be crisp in 1 to 1¼ hours.

One orange yields 2 teaspoons dried zest, and one lemon yields 1 teaspoon dried zest.

Dates
When dry, dates will be leathery and a deep russet color. Dates are excellent eating dried.

Figs
Cut in half. Pretreat as described in "Fruit Pretreatment" on page 143. When dry, figs will be leathery. Figs are excellent eating dried.

Lemon zest is often called for in recipes. But what is lemon zest? It's actually finely grated lemon peel—but only the colored part of the peel, not the bitter white part underneath.

Grapes

Use seedless grapes only. Remove stems and crack skins by blanching quickly or nicking with a knife. If halved, pretreat as described in "Fruit Pretreatment" on page 143. When dry, grapes are raisins. Grapes are excellent eating dried.

Nectarines

See "Peaches and Nectarines" below.

Papayas

Remove seeds, peel, and slice. When dry, papayas will be leathery to crisp. Papayas are good eating dried.

Peaches and Nectarines

Quickly blanch to crack skins, then remove them. Pit, slice, and pretreat as described in "Fruit Pretreatment" on page 143. When dry, peaches and nectarines will be soft, pliable, and leathery. Peaches and nectarines are excellent eating dried.

Pears

Peel and cut into slices or rings. Pretreat as described in "Fruit Pretreatment" on page 143. When dry, pears will be soft, pliable, and leathery. Pears are good eating dried.

Grapes and other tough-skinned fruits will dry faster if you nick the skin with a knife. Use a sharp knife and cut a slit through the skin. Make sure you don't cut into the pulp.

Pineapple
Peel and core. Cut into rings. When dry, pineapple will be leathery and no longer sticky. Pineapple is excellent eating dried.

Plums
Pit and cut into thin slices. Pretreat as described in "Fruit Pretreatment" on page 143 unless drying whole. When dry, plums will be pliable and leathery. Plums are excellent eating dried.

Raspberries
Wash and dehydrate whole. Pretreat as described in "Fruit Pretreatment" on page 143. When dry, the berries will be light and crunchy.

Rhubarb
Cut into thin strips about 1 inch wide, and blanch for three minutes. When dry, rhubarb will be tough to crisp.

Rosehips
Let the hips partially dry on the stem. Remove both ends and slice thinly. When dry, rosehips will be crisp. Use for tea.

Strawberries
Remove stems and cut in halves or thirds. Pretreat as described in "Fruit Pretreatment" on page 143. When dry, strawberries will be pliable and leathery. Strawberries are good eating dried.

Juicing

YOU MAY HAVE DRUNK your orange juice faithfully every morning as a child. It was every mother's prescription for good health and a full day's vitamin C. As you grew up, you probably added apple, cranberry, grape, and tomato juice to the list. And now, the grocery stores are overflowing with exciting (and pricey) juice blends. We don't need to be convinced that juices are delicious and nutritious. The great news is that they're easy to make at home.

Making juice of freshly harvested fruits and vegetables is so popular that it's touted as a way to cure assorted ailments. And while we can't prove that this is true, we do know that drinking fresh juices will help you meet dietary requirements for fruits and vegetables. And you can be sure that your homemade juice is free of any undesirable additives, preservatives, and artificial flavoring or coloring.

According to the USDA, you should be eating at least five servings of fruits and vegetables daily, which can be difficult for busy folks who sometimes rely on fast food to keep going. The beauty of juices, especially for folks like this, is that they provide the nutrition and flavor of fresh fruits and vegetables without the bulk. You can drink a healthy portion of required vitamins and minerals in a modest-size glass. But juices lack fiber, which is also important to your diet. So juices can supplement but never replace whole fruits and vegetables.

You'll also find that homemade juices can add exciting new flavors to everyday cooking. Use juices to replace water when you cook rice, prepare cream soups, or make broth for meat or seafood. Cook down thick juices made from tomatoes or other vegetables to use as sauces for pasta or sautéed vegetables. Use fruit juices in yogurt-based desserts, as a liquid in baked goods, for sorbets, and as fruity ice cubes for iced tea or children's drinks.

What's even better is that juicing provides you with an alternative way of putting your garden extras to good use. If you've done all your canning and freezing for the year but still have some fruits and vegetables ripening outdoors, you can convert fairly large quantities into manageable amounts of juice. For the best nutrition, drink them right away. Or save extra juice by freezing or canning it to use in future recipes.

Juicing Economics

By juicing your own homegrown fruits and vegetables, you get good nutrition and pure, chemical-free juice. But if you're buying the produce to make it, you'll probably spend more than you would for commercial juices. You'd come out ahead, though, if you bought produce to make unusual juice not readily available in most stores.

 # How Juicing Works

When you extract the juice from your fruits and vegetables, you draw out flavorings and sugars. You also extract nutrients such as B-carotene, folic acid, vitamin C, and minerals such as calcium, magnesium, and potassium. The nutrient levels vary according to the kind of produce you use, but all fresh vegetables and fruit are rich in beneficial ingredients. Unfortunately, once extracted from the body of the vegetable or fruit, nutrients and minerals begin to deteriorate. Drink them immediately, if possible. Or preserve them—with some nutrient loss—by refrigerating, freezing, or canning.

Quality Conscious

FLAVOR CHANGES IN COMMERCIALLY PROCESSED JUICES

Have you noticed how much more complex and delightful freshly squeezed orange juice tastes by comparison with frozen concentrate? The reason is that frozen concentrates are made by heating to evaporate and remove the excess moisture. Unfortunately, heat destroys some of the finer flavor elements. Frozen concentrate will lose even more flavor if it's allowed to thaw and refreeze during shipping or when it's displayed in the store. ❖ ❖ ❖

When you extract the juice, you leave the bulk of the produce behind. A pound of carrots becomes an 8-ounce glass of juice. Seven medium tomatoes make a drink for two. The juice from a pound of spinach will fill a small juice glass half full.

The bulk that's lost contains fiber, which is a very valuable thing to eat in abundance every day. Fiber helps keep you regular and helps you maintain a healthy weight. It also lowers your chance of developing cancer and other serious health conditions, according to experts. So drink juice as a healthful alternative to soda and coffee, but make sure you also eat lots of fruits and vegetables whole.

Juicing Supplies

If you're making juice to drink fresh, juicing is a snap. All you need is fresh fruits or vegetables and something to juice them with. If you plan to can or freeze your juice, you'll need an extra step and a few more pieces of equipment. Get organized before you harvest your fruits and vegetables so you can make and enjoy juice without delay.

Choosing Fruits and Vegetables

Theoretically, you can juice just about any crop. But fruits are easier, and some fruits are easier than others. Grapes and citrus fruits, for instance, are naturals for juicing. Bananas and avocados are another story; they turn into a mash rather than a juice and are best used to fortify other fruit juices. Tomatoes are the easiest of the vegetables to juice. Carrots, cabbage, and celery also make classic vegetable juices, at their best when they're mixed with one another or with other juices.

But you also can use less common but delicious juicing fruits such as apricots, blackberries, melons, plums, and strawberries. Or experiment with healthy blends of vegetables such as asparagus, beets, carrots, celery, fennel, garlic, ginger, onions, parsley, peppers, and radishes. Try asparagus, beet, or onion juice to add a unique zest to cooked dishes.

Use ripe, unblemished produce of any shape or size. Start with top quality to give you the best flavor. But if you're going to use a juicer or extractor, be sure it can accommodate the kind of produce you have in mind. Some juicers only work on citrus fruits; you need an extractor for more difficult vegetable and fruits. And even then, some models won't handle tough items like currants, rhubarb, or woody roots. Read the manufacturer's information for details.

Quick Tip

YIELDS VARY

The amount of juice that any fruit or vegetable will yield depends on how much fluid is in that kind of produce and on the method of extraction. For example, apples and berries, which contain higher amounts of solids and pectin, will give a lower juice yield than grapes. And more powerful juice extractors tend to do a better job of pulling every last bit of juice out of produce than smaller and weaker extractors. ❖ ❖ ❖

Juicing Equipment

The equipment you need to extract juice depends on the kind of produce and the budget you have. With grapefruit, lemon, lime, and orange juice, you can twist fruit halves on the familiar cone-shaped citrus juicer quite effectively. Or, cut citrus fruit into quarters and squeeze them by hand.

For soft, juicy fruits and vegetables like tomatoes, you can extract the juice manually without much trouble. Get a large pot for heating the produce and a strainer or cheesecloth for separating pulp from juice. For firmer fruits and vegetables, you may want to buy a heavy-duty juice extractor.

To save extra juice by freezing or canning, you'll need standard airtight freezer containers or canning jars with two-piece caps.

Juicers

If you're going to make juice regularly, it could be worth investing in an electric juice extractor. Juice extractors work quickly and efficiently without cooking the produce, which saves nutrients. Find an extractor that's big enough to accommodate the quantity of produce you expect to juice. And be sure you get a model that's easy to use and clean. For your convenience, look for a machine that has an automatic pulp injector, few parts to clean, and wide feeder tubes for easy produce insertion, plus allows easy dismantling and produces enough power to handle tough jobs. You can choose from decent extractors for as low as $60 to deluxe machines that run up to $300. Here's what to look for.

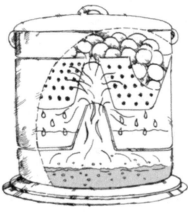

Use a steam juicer for easy one-pot juicing, without the mashing and stirring needed for hand juicing. Put the fruit into the top section of the juicer, which is perforated like a colander, and put water in the bottom section. When the water boils, steam rises through the center section of the juicer into the top. Fruit juice drains through the perforations into the bottom of the middle section, where it drains out through a tube into a bottle or bowl.

Quick Tip

JUICE FROM FROZEN FRUIT

If you have an abundance of fruit in the freezer, you can thaw a portion and turn it into juice. This is handy to know when you run out of fresh juice and don't have time to run to the store. ❖ ❖ ❖

Centrifuge juicer. Most juicers on the market that are designed to extract juice from carrots, celery, and other vegetables as well as from fruits are centrifuge juicers. They whorl around, grinding the food with a blade at high speeds and releasing the juice. The centrifugal action throws the juice off while the pulp is trapped on the strainer. The better models have an automatic pulp ejector that forces the pulp from the strainer into a separate compartment so that the strainer is free to accept more pulp. This is a nice feature because it means you don't have to continually stop the machine to clean off the strainer as you're juicing. We tested a half-dozen such juicers and found that they all have their strengths and weaknesses. So get a personal recommendation or check a buyer's guide before you buy.

Liquefier or pulverizer. We don't know what else to call this machine because it's not technically a juicer, although it does make thick juice. You may know it as a Vita-Mix, which is a brand name and the most popular of this type of machine. It mashes fruits or vegetables—skin, seeds, and all—into a thick homogeneous liquid, which then gets strained through a strainer bag. This juicer isn't cheap; it costs more than most other types, but it does more than make juice. The Vita-Mix can perform many tasks in addition to juicing, including making ice cream, grinding grain, and kneading dough.

Steam juicer. Steam juicers are hard to find these days, having been replaced by many models of centrifuge or liquefier juicers. But they remain the favorite of Anita Hirsch, Rodale Food Center nutritionist. The earliest steam juicers were all made of aluminum, a metal we don't think much of for preparing foods, especially acid foods that are heated for some time as juice is. Acids react with aluminum to form an aluminum salt that can then be transferred to food by the liquid. Look for enamel and stainless steel steam juicers instead of aluminum.

A steam juicer makes the juicing process a whole lot easier because everything happens in one pot, and you don't need to mash and stir the fruit along the way. It looks something like a double boiler. The bottom holds boiling water. The top section is really two parts: there is a colander-like basket that holds the fruit and a pan below it to catch the juice. As the water in the bottom boils, it creates steam that rises into the basket above. When exposed to the hot steam, the fruit easily yields its clear juice, which is caught in a pan below the colander that has an outlet for draining off juice into bottles.

To use a steam juicer, just wash the fruits or vegetables thoroughly and cut up the larger or firmer foods for quicker extraction of the juice. This is a marvelous timesaver when juicing elderberries or other small fruits that go into the juicer stems, seeds, pits, skins, and all.

🌿 Juicing Techniques

It's easy to turn fresh fruits and vegetables into nutritious, flavorful juices. If you make more than your family can drink in a day or two, juice keeps beautifully when it's frozen or canned. Here's what to do.

Preparing Fruits and Vegetables

Wash all produce well. Use hot, soapy water if you bought your fruits or vegetables at the grocery store. Peel off the skin or peel on bananas, beets, citrus fruits, imported tropical fruits, kiwifruits, and melons. You also should peel any fruit or vegetable that's been coated with wax and may contain pesticide residues on the skin. (See page 169 for more about this.)

Remove the pits or seeds from apples, apricots, cherries, nectarines, peaches, and plums. Cut off inedible greens from carrots, peppers, radishes, rhubarb, and tomatoes. You can leave the foliage on beets, broccoli, garlic, and onions. If you're using a juicer, cut the produce up into sizes that will easily fit into the machine.

Extracting Juice

You can extract juice with power juicers, described on the opposite page, or you can juice some fruits and vegetables manually. Here's how. Simply squeeze grapefruit, lemon, lime, and orange juice out by hand. Cut the fruit into quarters, and squeeze it until no more juice is released. Other fruits and tomatoes are easy to juice once they've been heated. Heat breaks down the tissues and allows the juice to flow freely.

You'll find specific directions in some of the juice recipes, starting on page 344, but the procedure is just about the same for all of them. Basically all you do is simmer tomatoes or fruit in water or in its own juice in a stainless steel, glass, or enamel pot. (Don't use aluminum because the metal can react with the food acid.) Cook the fruit until it's tender,

---

Creative Cooking

NEW LIFE FOR PULP

Leftover pulp is great to toss on the compost pile. But you also may be able to find other uses for it. For example, use carrot pulp for carrot bread or cake. And try peach, nectarine, or apple pulp for fruit butters, or use them in fruit breads or muffins. ❖ ❖ ❖

Quick Tip

CITRUS JUICERS

If you get tired of juicing by twisting citrus fruits on cone-shaped citrus juicers, you can buy small electric citrus juicers for as little as $20. They work much like your hand juicer but are powered by an engine instead of your arm muscles. ❖ ❖ ❖

then press it through two layers of cheesecloth or through a food mill or colander. Straining through cheesecloth will give you the clearest juice.

The juice may not need sweetening if you started with ripe fruit. If you do want to sweeten it, though, add honey or sugar to taste. Usually $\frac{1}{2}$ cup is sufficient for each gallon of juice. You also can add lemon juice to peach and apricot nectar or to sweet cherry and apple juice to add a little zing and help preserve the color. But wait to add spices and sweeteners until after you make your juice. Then you can adjust the flavorings according to the richness and sweetness of the juice.

Storing, Freezing, or Canning Juice

Fresh juices are at their best if you drink them immediately after extracting the juice. Nutrient levels drop from the moment the juice is released and exposed to air. But if you've made more than you can use right away, you can store juices in the refrigerator for a day or two. Or you can freeze or can most juices.

Because most vegetables aren't as juicy as fruits, it takes a lot of produce to make a little vegetable juice. For example, you need a pound of fresh carrots to make an 8-ounce glass of carrot juice.

Fast Freezing

Freezing juice is easiest, but big containers of juice will take up a lot of space in your freezer. If you've already heated the juice, don't bother to blanch it before freezing. Just pour it into clean glass jars or freezer containers, leaving $^1/_2$ inch of headspace (in quarts) for expansion. Seal and freeze right away. You can also pour the juice into ice cube trays, freeze, and then transfer the juice cubes to plastic freezer bags.

If you didn't heat the juice when you made it, you can flash-pasteurize it, just like commercial juices. Quickly heat it to 185°F, cool it right away, and freeze. The secret is to work in small quantities so that the heating and cooling go fast. Heat about a quart at a time to 185°F, which is to simmering, not boiling. Use a jelly thermometer to get an accurate reading of the temperature. Then pour the hot juice into freezer containers, leaving $^1/_2$ inch of headspace, and freeze. Don't let the juice cool down on the counter. You want to cool it quickly, and putting it in the freezer is the easiest and quickest way to do this.

Creative Cooking

Homemade Lemonade Syrup

It's easy to make your own frozen lemonade concentrate. Here's how.

Yield: 1$^1/_2$ cups

$^1/_3$ cup honey

Juice of 8 lemons (about 1$^1/_2$ cups lemon juice)

Slice of lemon (garnish)

Fresh mint (garnish)

Warm the honey in a small saucepan over medium heat. Add the lemon juice, and cook, stirring, for another 30 seconds. Remove from the heat, and let the mixture cool. Freeze it in ice cube trays (an ice cube is about 2 tablespoons), and when frozen, transfer the cubes to plastic freezer bags. To use, combine 4 tablespoons syrup or 2 frozen cubes with 1 cup water. Add more sweetening, if desired. Garnish with a lemon slice or fresh mint.

If you have a simple food mill, you don't even need a juicer to make tomato juice. Just simmer the tomatoes in water until they're tender, then put them through the mill.

Canning

Canning procedures for fruit juices vary from food to food, so check specific directions in the recipes, starting on page 344. However, the delicate flavor of most fruit juices can be spoiled by the high temperatures of a long boiling-water bath.

Tomato juice flavor isn't damaged by boiling-water–bath canning, though. Other vegetable juices may need processing in a pressure canner. For more information on canning, see Chapter 3.

CHAPTER EIGHT

Root Cellaring

STORING PRODUCE in a root cellar can be a bargain if you have the right kind of vegetables and fruits and a humid, cold location. Root cellaring, also called cold storage, cool storage, and underground storage, takes advantage of the natural coldness of late fall and winter and the insulating coolness below the ground to keep your harvest fresh for a couple of weeks or an entire winter.

Root cellaring is incredibly easy, but it isn't foolproof. That's because the low temperatures aren't powered by electricity, so they'll vary and so will the length of time your produce will last. As a result, you'll have to check the food regularly, adjusting temperature and humidity if you can and removing any fruits and vegetables that are starting to spoil. Be especially vigilant if you're new to root cellaring and still learning how to make the system work well.

Store only top-quality, sound produce without blemishes, bad spots, or wounds. Any weakness can invite decay or disease, which can spread to other fruits and vegetables. And only store produce suited for long cold storage. Good choices for root cellaring are apples, cabbages, pears, firm cool-season root crops, and hard-shelled squash—the crops that seem to last forever if forgotten in the back of the refrigerator.

Handle produce destined for storage with great care during and after harvesting so you won't cut or bruise it. Don't wash the fruits or vegetables, even if they're dirty. Instead, just rub soil off with a soft cloth or glove, or rinse it off gently under running water. Then let the water evaporate before storing. And if you harvest on a warm autumn day, let the food chill in the refrigerator before you put it into storage. Otherwise it will take a long time to cool down and could spoil in the process.

How Root Cellaring Works

We've come to rely on our refrigerators for storing just about anything. There's hardly a single home without a refrigerator, and some homes have several refrigerators. It's hard to believe that just a few generations ago, your ancestors used their root cellar for a similar purpose. But why should you bother to use a root cellar in our technological age?

For one thing, your refrigerator probably is crowded with other things, and you simply won't have enough space to store the fall harvest from a medium- or large-size garden. Secondly, the conditions in a root cellar can be even better than refrigeration for crops such as garlic, onions, and potatoes.

But a big part of what you can do when root cellaring depends on your storage conditions. You can keep produce in a barrel buried in the garden, in a styrofoam ice chest in an unheated garage, or in boxes or bags in your basement. If you don't have space or time to make an extra-cold and extra-humid area, you can still keep many vegetables in your basement or in an unheated room. If the temperature stays about 50°F, it's great for pumpkins, sweet potatoes, and winter squash and tolerable for eggplant, garlic, onions, potatoes, tomatillos, and green tomatoes. You can make a storage area in any convenient place where temperature is low, ideally 32° to 40°F, and the humidity is high, 80 percent or more. Let's look at these conditions more closely.

Safety Stop

REGULAR INSPECTION

No matter where you store your food, you've got to check it regularly to make sure it doesn't decay, start growing, or shrivel. If it does, take this action to stop any further deterioration.

• Remove any decaying food as soon as you notice it.

• Eat any vegetable that starts to sprout—as long as it's still good. Try to lower the temperature to prevent more food from sprouting.

• Wrap up shriveled food, place it in closed containers, or sprinkle it with water to keep it from drying out any more. ❖ ❖ ❖

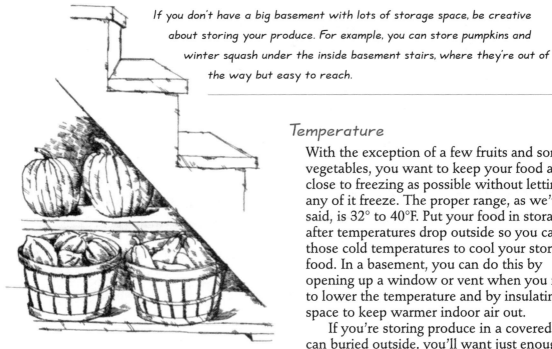

If you don't have a big basement with lots of storage space, be creative about storing your produce. For example, you can store pumpkins and winter squash under the inside basement stairs, where they're out of the way but easy to reach.

Temperature

With the exception of a few fruits and some vegetables, you want to keep your food as close to freezing as possible without letting any of it freeze. The proper range, as we've said, is 32° to 40°F. Put your food in storage after temperatures drop outside so you can use those cold temperatures to cool your stored food. In a basement, you can do this by opening up a window or vent when you need to lower the temperature and by insulating the space to keep warmer indoor air out.

If you're storing produce in a covered trash can buried outside, you'll want just enough soil over and around the container to keep it cold but not freezing. Styrofoam chests are their own insulators. For more on these storage techniques, see pages 187 and 188.

Humidity

Most vegetables, except onions and winter squash, shrivel rapidly unless stored in a moist atmosphere where the humidity is between 80 and 95 percent. In a storage room you can keep the humidity up either by keeping the air quite moist or keeping the food moist in rustproof cans, pails, or barrels.

To keep the air in the storage room moist, spray water regularly right on the cement or dirt floor. Or you can sprinkle the floor with water from a watering can. (If you've got a dirt floor, think about building a wooden slat floor over it so that you won't be walking around in wet dirt. Or, lay down a layer of coarse, well-washed gravel 3 inches thick, and keep that moist.) Be careful not to water so much that puddles collect; these could easily encourage the growth of molds and bacteria. You'll have to sprinkle each time the relative humidity of the air falls below 80 percent (a hygrometer will tell), which could be quite often.

A corner of an unheated porch makes another great winter storage site when you're short on space. You can store carrots in a bucket of slightly moist sand. Apples will keep best if wrapped individually in paper before storing.

You can also get large shallow pans, place them around the room, and keep them filled with clean water.

If you can't or don't want to go through the trouble of keeping the entire storage room humid, store vegetables that are particularly likely to shrivel, like root crops, in closed rust-proof containers layered in damp sand, burlap, or sphagnum moss. Large crocks, metal cans, tight wooden boxes, and barrels are all suitable.

Ventilation

Good ventilation is important to keep airborne bacteria and molds that like humid conditions from thriving. It's not so important when you're just storing a small amount of food in a buried barrel as it is when you're storing a large amount in a storage room. To ventilate, let in fresh, cold outside air, which also helps bring your storage room temperature down to 32° to 40°F.

Light

Keep your fruits and vegetables in the dark. Light will hasten the food's deterioration.

 ## Root-Cellaring Supplies

Get together everything you'll need for root cellaring so you can bring your produce right from the garden into storage without shifting it from container to container. You'll save time and minimize handling, which keeps the produce in better condition. Luckily, you don't need a lot of fancy equipment for root cellaring. All you need are the fruits and vegetables you want to store, containers to store them in, and packing materials like hay or leaves to cushion and separate the produce in storage.

INDOOR HERBS

Instead of drying or freezing all of your herbs, you can dig a few up and grow them indoors in your sunny windows. Uproot whole basil, parsley, and summer savory plants, or take divisions of chives, mint, oregano, tarragon, and thyme.

Plant the herbs in pots that are large enough to accommodate the roots comfortably. Move the herbs into a cool area with lots of sun, water when the soil begins to dry out, and harvest new growth regularly. ❖ ❖ ❖

Crates, Bins, Trash Cans, and Other Containers

Containers need to be clean as well as easy to clean and air out again after the storage season is over, but they don't have to be new. Here's a great opportunity to put your recycling creativity to work with the following containers.

• Wooden boxes, originally designed to store and ship apples and other fruits, make ideal storage units for root cellars or larger storage areas. You can stuff them with leaves (dry and crisp), hay, straw, sphagnum moss, or crumpled burlap. When stacking wooden boxes for storage, be sure to place furring strips between the boxes and the floor and between individual boxes to permit good air circulation.

• Homemade storage bins are another good option. You can build bins right into storage areas so that there is no chance of water seeping in from the floor. Make the lowest bins 4 inches off the floor for good air circulation. And make the storage containers removable so you can take them outdoors at the end of the storage season to wash them thoroughly and air them out.

• Plastic and metal trash cans, large pails, and barrels are fine as long as they're rustproof. Leave them open or cover the food with leaves, sphagnum moss, or straw. If these containers are waterproof, you can use them in pit storage areas. Layer packing material and produce alternately, finishing with 2 inches or more of packing at the top.

• Styrofoam ice chests, with their lids removed, make fine containers. A crack or two will do no harm.

• Orange crates and mesh bags are excellent for storing onions and other produce that need good air circulation.

Sites for Root Cellaring

You could opt for partitioning off your basement to build a cold storage room there, or take a look at some other, simpler ideas. A basement root cellar is lovely to have because it is so convenient to use, but it can be expensive to build and may just cancel out any savings you'd gain from storing your harvest instead of buying fresh from the grocery store during the winter. Instead, you can fashion cold-storage areas from anything that will meet

---

---

the temperature, humidity, ventilation, and no-light requirements. If, after reading about these ingenious ideas for smaller storage spaces, you still want a basement storage area, you'll find information about constructing one on page 188.

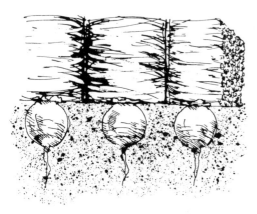

The easiest way to store root crops through the winter is to leave them in the ground. Cover the area with mulch so the soil doesn't freeze, then put a plastic sheet over the mulch to keep it dry for fast, as-needed harvesting.

The Garden

The easiest way to keep vegetables in cold storage is to leave them where they are growing during the late fall and early winter. This only works with extra-hardy crops such as winter-keeper cultivars of beets, carrots, parsnips, rutabagas, and turnips as well as durable greens such as brussels sprouts, evergreen scallions, and parsley. And it requires a well-drained soil that won't encourage the roots to rot. If you have a cold frame, you can also grow arugula, corn salad, Swiss chard, winter lettuce, and other cool-season greens. For more details on in-garden storage, see the individual crop storage descriptions on page 190.

The Cellar Steps

You can make a small but simple and inexpensive storage area by taking advantage of the steps that lead from your basement to the outside basement door. Install an inside door to keep out basement heat at the bottom of the steps. If you want to create an even larger storage area, build inward into the basement, but take care to insulate this extra interior wall space from the rest of the basement. Temperatures in the stairwell will go down as you go up the steps, and a little experimenting will help you determine the best levels for the different crops you are storing. If the air is too dry, set pans of water at the warmest level for extra humidity.

Styrofoam Ice Chests

Styrofoam ice chests may be all you need to store a few root crops for a short period of time as long as you have an unheated space that does not freeze, such as a garage or porch. Prepare vegetables as described on page 190, and put a different one in each chest (don't mix different types of produce). Put the lid in place and keep it out of the sun, which might heat up the chest. Vegetables kept this way will probably be good for several weeks.

Simple In-Ground Storage

When we speak about in-ground storage, we mean burying or partially burying containers filled with food, preferably a different food in each container. The earth provides insulation and humidity control, and it keeps out light. But it doesn't keep out rodents and other animals; only a secure container can do that. And it's a good idea to provide some kind of drainage so that water doesn't seep into the container and create problems.

Areas of the country that have moderate winters without extreme temperature swings are the best for this kind of cold storage. The earth acts as a pretty good insulator, but there's no guarantee that it's going to keep out subzero temperatures that will freeze your food or springlike temperatures that could cause food to spoil. Two simple ways to store produce below ground are in a wooden box or a sunken trash can.

A Buried Box

Use 2 × 4s to make a wooden box that's 3 feet wide, 6 feet long, and 2 feet deep. Line the inside with 1-inch hardware cloth, carefully kept tight against the sides to keep out rodents. Make a neat wooden lid for the top.

At harvest time in late autumn, select beets, carrots, parsnips, potatoes, turnips, and the like for storage. Rinse them free of soil, but be careful not to bruise the skin. (Let excess water evaporate before storing.) Make a pit to put the box in, preferably on sloping ground so excess water will drain away. Put the box inside and lay a layer of clean, sharp builder's sand (washed sand) on the box bottom. Then place a layer of root vegetables on top of this, resisting the temptation to just dump vegetables into the pit. Cover this first layer of root crops with a layer of sand, then continue layering like this until you fill the box, finishing with a layer of sand.

Try to keep different vegetables separate from one another. (You may want to sketch out a map to keep track of where to find different ones.) For insulation, close the lid and cover it with bales of straw, and then cover this with a plastic sheet to keep out rain and snow. In the summer, when all the food has been taken from the box, clean everything out and let in sunshine and fresh air.

A Built-In Basement Storage Room

Centrally heated homes with concrete-floor basements are generally too warm to be used just as they are for food storage, since most vegetables and many fruits require temperatures between 32° and 40°F. But with a little ingenuity and a little investment, part of almost any basement can be converted to a root cellar.

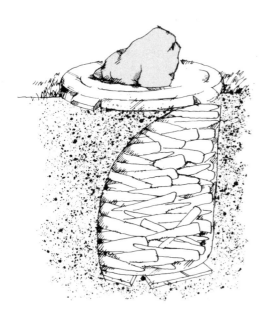

Prepare a room that's separated from the rest of the basement, is reasonably well insulated, and has a window or other means of allowing cold outside air in on occasion to cool the space. You could try a storage room, 8 × 10 feet, which should be large enough for most families who plan to store both vegetables and fruits. A room this size will hold 60 bushels of produce. Where practical, locate the storage room either in the northeast or northwest corner of the basement and away from the chimney and heating pipes. The northeast corner takes advantage of the two coldest walls of a house; the northwest corner is second best. You have the added advantage when building into a corner of only having to construct two interior walls to enclose your storage space.

Even this setup won't give you total control over temperature; that depends largely on the outside weather conditions. In early fall and late spring, daytime temperatures may be higher than you want in the storage area. So close the windows to keep the warmth

Another easy in-ground storage technique is trash-can storage. Dig a pit the size of the can and sink the can into the ground, leaving the rim aboveground. Fill the trash can with layers of a single type of crop, like carrots or turnips. Then put on the lid, weighting it with stones to keep out animals (and the elements). In cold-winter areas, you can add a bale or two of hay or other mulch over the top for insulation.

out. Open the windows whenever the storage room temperature is over 40°F and the outside temperature is lower. Close them when the room temperature drops to 32°F.

To block light from the stored foods, cover the windows with opaque material. Wide wooden shutters fitted to the outside of the window frame will help if you need to open the windows during the daytime. Cover shutters (or cover open windows, if you don't use shutters) with screening to keep out insects and animals.

Keep the storage room clean to prevent problems with bacteria and molds. Use easy-to-clean materials for the walls, floor, and ceiling, and make the bins removable. Sweep underneath shelves and planking to remove dead leaves, stalks, and other debris. During dry summer days, clean the room from top to bottom, and leave the windows open so it can air out.

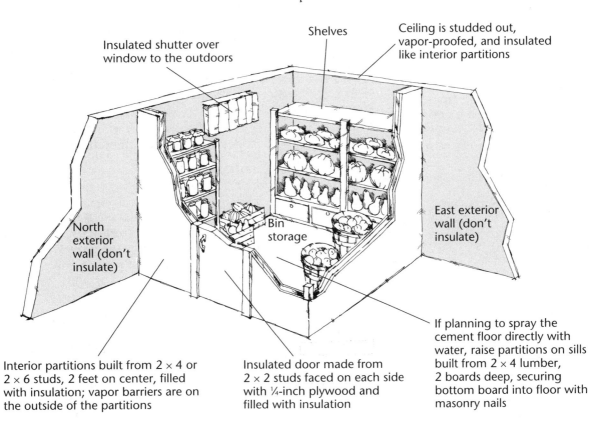

Insulated shutter over window to the outdoors

Shelves

Ceiling is studded out, vapor-proofed, and insulated like interior partitions

North exterior wall (don't insulate)

Bin storage

East exterior wall (don't insulate)

Interior partitions built from 2 × 4 or 2 × 6 studs, 2 feet on center, filled with insulation; vapor barriers are on the outside of the partitions

Insulated door made from 2 × 2 studs faced on each side with ¼-inch plywood and filled with insulation

If planning to spray the cement floor directly with water, raise partitions on sills built from 2 × 4 lumber, 2 boards deep, securing bottom board into floor with masonry nails

If you're handy with tools, you can convert a corner of an unfinished basement into an ideal root cellar. (Modern basements are often too warm and dry for good vegetable and fruit storage.) Build it on the north and east walls—the coldest—and insulate the interior walls. Make sure you build in plenty of storage space!

A Crop-by-Crop Guide to Storing Vegetables and Fruits

Think about which method or methods of root cellaring will work well for you: Which methods suit your available space and are also suitable for the crops you're growing? To find out if your favorite crops will store well with the technique you have in mind, check the crop-by-crop guide on the following pages.

By root-cellaring some of your produce, you'll free up freezer space for other kinds of produce and save the time and trouble of canning. Since root-cellar conditions vary and it's hard to predict how long food will stay good, start out small the first year. Learn from your mistakes, and you'll begin to get a feel for how to make root cellaring a success.

Vegetables for Root Cellaring

These crops will keep well in a root cellar. Times noted here assume you can maintain constant recommended temperature and humidity, which can best be achieved in a root cellar, either underground or built into a basement. Storage times in other storage areas—like cellar steps, buried boxes, and barrels—will vary. Vegetables not listed here do not keep well in underground storage. And some cultivars of those that are listed will store better than others. Refer to the chapters on freezing, canning, preserving, pickling, drying, and juicing for other methods of preservation.

Beans, Dried

Dried beans keep indefinitely. You can keep dried beans in your pantry or in a dry part of your underground storage room. Keep the beans in airtight jars or containers so they won't pick up moisture from the air. For more on drying beans, see page 162.

Beets

Beets stored at 32°F will keep for four to six months. Harvest beets in late November, after 30°F nights. Remove most of the greens, which might otherwise rot, but leave a 2-inch stub. Never cut off the greens right at the root; you might very well cut the vegetable, inviting quick decay. Do not wash. Pack the beets in containers surrounded by straw or in moist sand for keeping in any outdoor storage pit or a root cellar. Place them in an area just above freezing, with 95 percent humidity.

You can also leave beets in the garden where they grew. If you choose in-garden storage, make winter digging easier by covering the rows with leaves or straw, then a layer of plastic, and then another layer of leaves or straw. The plastic keeps the bottom layer of mulch dry so that you won't have to hack away frozen leaves or straw when you want to dig up some beets. Make the top cover of mulch a foot deep, and weigh it down with chicken wire and rocks.

Brussels Sprouts

You can keep brussels sprouts in the garden a remarkably long time, sometimes right up to New Year's Day in areas that enjoy moderate winters. If you are not blessed with such weather, create a basement "garden" of brussels sprouts so that you can pick them as you need them. To do so, don't pick the sprouts off the stem, but dig up the whole plants carefully, keeping the roots and the soil clinging to them. Plant them upright by burying the roots in a box of soil. Water lightly and pick sprouts as needed.

Cabbage and Chinese Cabbage

Late cabbage stored at 32°F will keep for five to six months, while early cabbage stored at 32°F will keep only a few weeks. So choose a late cabbage cultivar. Prepare these for storage by removing loose outer leaves. You can store individual heads, separately wrapped, or entire plants. If you store only the heads, wrap them with newspaper, burlap, or other material, and store in boxes or bins at a temperature just above freezing in a damp area.

If you want cabbage heads to stay crisper longer, leave the roots on and store outdoors in a container of damp sand or soil. Cabbage emits a strong odor during storage that you probably won't like in the house, so most people prefer to store it in an outdoor storage arrangement.

Carrots

Carrots stored at 32°F will keep for seven to nine months. Store like beets (on the opposite page).

Celery

Celery stored at 32°F will keep for two to three months. To maintain celery best, pull the crop, leaving the roots intact. Don't cut it off at ground level. Leave the tops dry; do not wash. Place the roots in slightly moist sand or soil, and keep the plant at 32° to 34°F. To avoid odor contamination, don't store with cabbage or turnips. In areas without very severe winters, you can leave celery in the garden, covered with a thick layer of leaves or straw.

Endive or Escarole

Stored at 32°F, endive or escarole will keep for two to three months. Store this leafy vegetable, which goes under both names, like celery, with its roots in slightly moist sand or soil.

You can also use your basement to store the roots of witloof chicory until they sprout delicate, mild heads of Belgian endive. Here's how. Grow the chicory all summer in your garden and harvest it in late fall. Put the roots in a box of moist sand and set them in total

---

Step-by-Step

HOW TO MAKE A GARLIC BRAID

Garlic braids are a beautiful and practical way to store your harvest. But garlic will keep best in a cool, dry place, so resist the urge to hang your garlic braids in the kitchen.

1. Wrap 3 garlic bulbs together with twine.

2. Begin to braid the stems.

3. Work in another bulb about every inch along the braid.

4. If desired, you can remove the twine after the braid is complete.

5. Hang your finished braid in a pantry or on a wall where it's handy but protected from light.

darkness in your 50° to 60°F basement. After several weeks, small endive heads will sprout. Harvest them before they reach 6 inches tall.

Garlic

Stored in a dry place at 40°F, garlic will keep for six to seven months. Just like onions, you must cure garlic before storing it. Dry garlic thoroughly, making sure the bulbs aren't in direct sunlight. If you've grown large quantities of garlic, lay the plants in the garden with their tops covering the bulbs. If you have small quantities, bunch, tie, or braid them and hang them in a well-ventilated cool room to store and dry. Or remove the tops and roots with a knife or shears, leaving 1 inch of roots on the bulb, and store like onions in a cool, slightly humid (60 to 75 percent) area.

Horseradish

Whole roots can keep for one to two months at 32°F. Dig out whole horseradish roots and store in a root cellar in damp sand in a bucket or plastic bag. Or leave the roots in the ground throughout the winter. To make digging easier, cover the rows with about 1 foot of leaves or straw before the ground has frozen. Horseradish roots are thin-skinned and the quality deteriorates once dug up, so you might dig up no more than a two weeks' supply at a time.

Jerusalem Artichokes

Store like horseradish (above).

Kohlrabi

Stored at 32°F, kohlrabi will keep for two to three months. Remove leaves and roots, and store in an area with about 95 percent humidity.

Onions

Winter-storage onions will keep throughout the winter if stored in a cool, dry place. Pull the vegetable when its top falls over, shrivels at the neck of the bulb, and turns brown. Keep the bulbs off the ground in the shade, or bring them inside out of direct sun for about two weeks before storing. Then remove the tops and place in bins or string bags, or braid their tops together. Store onions at temperatures ranging from 33° to 45°F in an area with about 60 to 75 percent humidity. Your attic might be a good storage area as long as it's cool.

Parsley
Keep this leafy herb right in the garden, protected from frosts by a layer of mulch 1 to 2 feet deep. You can also cover it with an inverted basket or pail, stuffed with chopped cornstalks, leaves, or hay.

Parsnips
Stored at 32°F, parsnips will keep for six months. Store like beets (see page 190).

Peas, Dried
Store liked dried beans (see page 162).

Peppers, Chili
Once dry, chili peppers will keep throughout the winter and maybe longer. If mature, pick chili peppers just before frost. Dry them and store in an airtight jar in a cool, dry place. Do not store them in cellars, which are too damp. For drying information, see page 165.

Potatoes
Stored at 40°F at 95 percent humidity, potatoes will last throughout the winter. Leave tubers in the ground for about two weeks after the vines have died—as long as the weather is dry—to make sure that the potato skins have toughened up for storage. Then dig the potatoes, and store in a dark, humid place at about 40°F. Lower temperatures tend to turn starch to sugar and change the flavor. Never store with apples, which give off ethylene gas and encourage potatoes to sprout.

Pumpkins and Winter Squash
Stored at 50° to 60°F in a dry place, pumpkins and winter squash will keep for two to six months, depending on the cultivar. Be sure that the pumpkins and squash have matured completely on the vine before you harvest them. The skin should be hard and not easily punctured with your nail. Cut the fruit off with a portion of the stem attached. Then leave them in the field for two weeks after picking if the days are not cold. If weather is near freezing,

cure squash instead in a room with a temperature of about 80°F for several days. After curing, place them gently on shelves, separated from each other, in a 50° to 60°F dry place. Examine them every few weeks for mold. If you find some, wipe the squash carefully with a cloth made slightly oily with vegetable oil.

Radishes, Winter
Stored at 32°F, winter radishes will keep for up to four months. Store like beets (see page 190).

Rutabagas
Stored at 32°F, rutabagas will keep for up to four months. Store rutabagas like beets (see page 190). You can also wrap them well in plastic wrap that clings tightly to protect their skins and keeps their strong odor contained.

Salsify
Stored at 32°F, salsify will keep for four to five months. Store like beets (see page 190).

Sweet Potatoes
Stored in a warm (55° to 60°F) room that is well ventilated and the humidity is 85 to 90 percent, sweet potatoes will keep throughout the winter. Only store sweet potatoes that are free from injury. But before you do, cure them for one to two weeks in a place that's warm (85° to 90°F) and humid (80 to 90 percent) until the skins toughen and the wounds at either end grow a protective, corky coating.

Tomatoes and Tomatillos
Green but full-size tomatoes will ripen in one to three weeks if held at 55° to 70°F in moderate humidity. Ripe tomatoes don't store well, but you can hold green ones in storage and encourage them to ripen there. Harvest all tomatoes that are of good size, both ripe and still green, just before the first killing frost. Remove from the plants, wash, and allow to dry before storing. If you remove the stems, there's less chance that the tomatoes will puncture one another. Separate green tomatoes from those that show red, and pack green tomatoes no more than two deep in shallow boxes or trays for ripening.

Tomatillos are slow-ripening and keep well in a root cellar. You can peel back the husks and braid them like garlic. (See "How to Make a Garlic Braid" on page 192.)

Turnips

Stored at 32°F, turnips will keep for four to five months. Store like beets (see page 190). As with rutabagas, you can wrap turnips in plastic wrap that clings tightly to protect their skins and keeps their odor contained.

Fruits for Root Cellaring

Many major fruits don't store well for extended periods of time. Of the ones that do—most notably apples and pears—the keeping quality of the cultivars varies. So grow long-keeping cultivars if you know that you will be storing many of them.

If you've got a root cellar, partition off a section for fruits, or at least make sure that they are in separate bins, away from vegetables. Never store fruits with potatoes, turnips, or cabbage. The ethylene gas released from apples and pears during respiration can cause potatoes to sprout. Cabbage and turnips can transmit their odors to apples and pears.

If the fruit you wish to store is not listed here, it doesn't lend itself to long-term storage. Refer to the chapters on freezing, canning, preserving, pickling, drying, and juicing for alternative preservation methods.

Apples

Depending on the cultivar, apples will keep for two to six months stored at 32°F. Apples are among the better-keeping fruits, especially cultivars like 'Granny Smith' that can last up to six months in cold storage. Next in keeping quality are 'Stayman Winesap' and 'Rome Beauty'. Normal storage ranges from four to six months with these cultivars. You can keep 'Jonathan', 'McIntosh', and 'Delicious' (red or yellow) for shorter periods. There are other factors that influence keeping qualities of different apple cultivars, such as locality ('McIntosh' apples grown in New England store better than those grown in the mid-Atlantic states), seasonal conditions, maturity when picked, and length of time between picking and storing.

And you'll increase good keeping qualities with careful handling to prevent bruising. Store most cultivars at 32°F and 85 to 95 percent humidity. Wrap each fruit in oiled or shredded paper to help prevent storage scald (a general texture breakdown and browning of the fruit), acknowledged to be apples' most serious storage disorder.

Grapes

Grapes will keep for one to two months at 32°F. Cool grapes to 50°F as soon as possible after picking and spread them out in single layers. Allow the fruit to remain in this condition until the stems shrivel slightly. Then place the grapes in trays no more than 4 inches deep in a cellar that is slightly humid and has a temperature of about 32°F. Try to keep grapes separate from other foods since they can absorb odors, especially from vegetables. If you have some left over after a month or two, you can turn them into jams and jellies.

Oranges

You can keep Florida oranges for three to eight weeks at 38° to 48°F with 85 to 90 percent humidity. California oranges will keep for six to eight weeks at 35° to 37°F; they are subject to rind disorders at lower temperatures.

Peaches

Peaches are fairly perishable and can usually be stored only several days to two weeks in a cool cellar.

Pears

Pears store from one to three months, depending on the cultivar. 'Anjou', 'Easter Beurre', and 'Winter Nelis' keep better than 'Bosc', 'Bartlett', 'Comice', 'Hardy', and 'Kieffer'. Harvest pears in a condition that would seem to be immature. If allowed to begin to yellow on the tree, pears develop hard, gritty cells in the flesh. You want to pick them when the dark green of the skin just begins to fade to a yellowish green and the fruit begins to separate more or less readily from the tree. Pears often keep somewhat better in home storage if you wrap them in newspaper or other paper. Keep them at a temperature as close to 32°F as possible and in high relative humidity, ranging from 85 to 90 percent.

Pears ordinarily do not ripen as satisfactorily at storage temperatures as apples. For the highest eating quality, remove them from storage while they are still comparatively hard and green. Then let them ripen at room temperature with a high relative humidity.

Quinces

This fruit will keep for two to three months if you pick it before it is thoroughly ripe and hold it in a cool, moist storage area.

RECIPES FROM THE GARDEN

How to Use
These Recipes

*N*OW THAT YOU KNOW how to harvest and preserve garden-fresh fruits and vegetables, here's a banquet of recipes to try. Most are easy to make and don't require a lot of special ingredients. You can make some recipes ahead and store them in the freezer or pantry for a day when you don't have time to cook. Some recipes make the most of produce you've previously canned or frozen. Others call for just-picked fruits and vegetables that you can prepare in exciting new ways to enjoy their garden freshness.

You'll find all the recipes you're looking for listed by the kind of dish—Salads and Vegetables; Soups and Stews; Casseroles; Meals in Minutes; Sauces; Jams, Jellies, and Fruit Butters; Pickles, Condiments, and Relishes; Seasonings; Desserts; and Beverages. Within each group, recipes are grouped by their main ingredient (for example, apples or tomatoes). This makes it easy for you to find a recipe when you have a bumper crop of that particular fruit or vegetable.

To have these recipes turn out best, you'll need some background on when to harvest and how to handle the produce; refer to Chapter 1 on page 2. To prepare and store frozen foods properly, see Chapter 2 on page 31. It's especially important to use correct methods when canning, making jellies and jams, or pickling. So refer back to Chapters 3, 4, and 5 on pages 62, 95, and 114 for those specifics. You will also want to review Chapter 6 on drying on page 130, Chapter 7 on juicing on page 172, and Chapter 8 on root cellaring on page 181. With all this information at your fingertips, prepare to enjoy your garden harvest.

Salads and Vegetables

Baked Beans

Use this easy slow-cooker method to turn your dried beans into delicious baked beans. Freeze what's left over for a summer picnic.

2 quarts dried beans (marrow, navy, Great Northern, or field peas), soaked overnight

15 cups water

3 medium onions

2½ cups dark molasses

3 teaspoons dry mustard

Drain the beans and discard the soaking water. Put the beans in a 6- to 8-quart slow cooker. Add 15 cups of water and the whole onions. Cover the pot and cook on low for 9 to 10 hours or until the beans are tender. When the beans are tender, drain the liquid and reserve 3 cups. Add the molasses and dry mustard to the beans; stir. Add reserved bean liquid; stir. Cover and simmer the beans on low for 2 to 3 more hours.

To freeze: Prepare the recipe as directed. Cool quickly, then pack in freezer containers, leaving 1-inch headspace, and freeze. To serve, thaw the frozen beans in the refrigerator. Transfer the beans to a saucepan, cover, and warm over low heat until heated through. Or, microwave on medium until warm, stirring at least once, and then on high until hot.

NOTES: *During the last hour of cooking, you may want to add 1½ teaspoons ground cinnamon and ¾ cup catsup.*

You can divide the recipe in half if you have a smaller 4-quart slow cooker.

Yield: 5½ quarts

Savory Lima Beans

Fresh lima beans are sweet and absolutely exciting with this combination.

Yield: 6 servings

3 cups lima beans

1 cup minced red onions

1 cup halved cherry tomatoes

¼ cup apple cider vinegar

2 tablespoons olive oil

1 clove garlic, minced

1 teaspoon Dijon mustard

½ teaspoon dried savory

¼ teaspoon black pepper

Blanch the beans in boiling water for 5 minutes. Drain and transfer to a large bowl. Add the onions and tomatoes. Toss to combine.

In a small bowl, whisk together the vinegar, oil, garlic, mustard, savory, and pepper. Pour over the vegetables and toss to combine. Allow to marinate for 30 minutes before serving.

Sizzling Beans with Peanuts

These oriental flavorings add zest to fresh green beans.

Yield: 8 servings

6 cups green beans

1 tablespoon minced fresh ginger

1 tablespoon low-sodium soy sauce

1 teaspoon peanut oil

1 clove garlic, minced

3 tablespoons chopped roasted peanuts

Steam the beans for 4 minutes, or until just tender.

In a cup, combine the ginger, soy sauce, oil, and garlic. While the beans are cooking, heat a large cast-iron frying pan over medium heat until hot, about 4 minutes. Add half of the beans and half of the ginger mixture. Sauté for 5 minutes. Transfer to a platter and keep warm. Repeat with the remaining beans and ginger mixture. Sprinkle with the peanuts.

To freeze: Prepare the recipe as directed but don't add the peanuts. Cool quickly, then pack in freezer containers, and freeze. To serve, place frozen beans in a frying pan, cover, and cook over moderate heat until warm, stirring occasionally. Sprinkle with peanuts. Or, microwave frozen beans on high for 4 to 5 minutes, or until heated through. Sprinkle with peanuts.

Green Beans and Potatoes

This colorful salad is bursting with flavor. Use it to impress your guests!

6 to 8 small red potatoes

1½ cups green beans

2 sweet red peppers

8 cooked artichoke hearts, halved

⅓ cup tarragon vinegar

3 tablespoons olive oil

1 teaspoon Dijon mustard

1 clove garlic, minced

½ teaspoon dried marjoram

¼ teaspoon freshly ground black pepper

¼ teaspoon Worcestershire sauce

Steam the potatoes for 15 minutes, or until tender. Cool to warm and slice thinly. Place the sliced potatoes in a large bowl.

Blanch the beans in boiling water for 5 minutes. Drain and add to the bowl. Broil the peppers until charred on all sides. Let cool slightly, then peel, seed, and dice them. (See Roasted Sweet Peppers on page 213 for more details on roasting peppers.) Add the peppers and artichokes to the bowl and toss to combine.

In a small bowl, whisk together the vinegar, oil, mustard, garlic, marjoram, black pepper, and Worcestershire sauce. Pour over the vegetables and toss to combine. Chill or serve warm.

Yield: 4 servings

Spicy Beet Salad

Sweet, tender beets make a delicious marinated salad that will keep for days in the refrigerator.

8 medium beets

2 tablespoons tarragon vinegar

2 tablespoons olive oil

2 teaspoons low-sodium soy sauce

¼ teaspoon dry mustard

¼ teaspoon ground ginger

1 cup shredded carrots

2 tablespoons sliced scallions

2 tablespoons minced fresh parsley

In boiling water, in a 3-quart saucepan, cook the beets for 45 minutes, or until tender. Drain and rinse under cold water. Slice off the tops and squeeze the beets to remove the skins. Cut the beets into ½-inch slices and place them in a large bowl.

In a small bowl, whisk together the vinegar, oil, soy sauce, mustard, and ginger. Pour over the beets and toss to combine. Arrange the beets on a platter. Sprinkle with the carrots, scallions, and parsley. Chill or serve warm.

Yield: 4 servings

Broccoli Parmesan

Use your microwave to turn broccoli into a delicious dish in minutes.

Yield: 4 servings

1 small head broccoli

2 tablespoons water

¼ teaspoon dried thyme

2 tablespoons grated Parmesan cheese

Trim and peel tough stalks. Cut the broccoli into thin spears. Arrange on a large plate in a circular pattern, with the florets in the center and the stems at the rim. Sprinkle with the water and thyme. Cover with vented plastic wrap. Microwave on high for 4 minutes. Rotate the dish a half turn. Microwave on high for 3 minutes, or until the stems are easily pierced with a sharp knife. Do not overcook. Allow to stand for 5 minutes. Drain, then sprinkle with the cheese.

To freeze: Prepare the recipe as directed, but undercook the broccoli slightly and don't sprinkle it with cheese. Cool quickly, then pack in freezer containers, and freeze. To serve, place the frozen broccoli in a frying pan with a little water, cover, and cook over low heat until the broccoli is tender. Or, microwave on high for 2 to 4 minutes. When hot, sprinkle the broccoli with cheese.

Broccoli with Parsley Sauce

This vitamin-rich combination of parsley and broccoli tastes great and is good for you.

Yield: 4 servings

1 cup fresh parsley

1 small onion, minced

2 tablespoons part-skim ricotta cheese

½ cup buttermilk

6 cups broccoli florets

In a food processor, finely chop the parsley with the onions and ricotta. With the motor running, pour in the buttermilk and continue to process just until combined. Steam the broccoli for 8 minutes, or until tender. Drizzle the sauce over the broccoli.

Carrots and Parsnips

Brimming with nutrients, this vegetable puree is naturally sweet.

Yield: 8 servings

4 or 5 medium carrots, diced

4 medium parsnips, diced

1 ripe pear, chopped

2 tablespoons minced fresh chervil or parsley

In a 3-quart saucepan, steam the carrots and parsnips for 10 minutes, or until tender. Reserve the steaming liquid. Transfer the carrots and parsnips to a food processor. Add the pear. Puree until smooth, adding just enough cooking liquid to facilitate blending. Reheat gently before serving. Stir in the chervil or parsley.

To freeze: Prepare the recipe as directed but omit the chervil or parsley. Cool quickly, then pack in freezer containers, and freeze. To serve, place frozen vegetables in a saucepan, cover, and warm over low heat until heated through. Or, microwave on high until hot. Then sprinkle the vegetables with chervil or parsley.

Citrus-Marinated Carrots

These sweet and tangy carrot sticks make great appetizers. And you can store them in the refrigerator for days.

Yield: 6 to 8 servings

4 or 5 medium carrots

1 onion, thinly sliced and separated into rings

3 cups vinegar

Juice of 1 orange

Juice of 1 lemon

Juice of 1 lime

1 tablespoon low-sodium soy sauce

2 teaspoons sesame oil

½ teaspoon black peppercorns

Cut the carrots into 3-inch sticks. Blanch in boiling water for 5 minutes, until crisp-tender. Drain and transfer to a large glass jar. Add the onions.

In a large bowl, combine the vinegar, orange juice, lemon juice, lime juice, soy sauce, oil, and peppercorns. Pour into the jar to cover the carrots. Cover and refrigerate for at least 4 hours. To serve, drain off the liquid.

Honey-Glazed Carrots

Cooked carrots never tasted so good. These are perfect for a last-minute side dish.

Yield: 4 servings

4 or 5 medium carrots, thickly sliced diagonally

1 cup defatted chicken stock

2 tablespoons honey

1 tablespoon Dijon mustard

In a large frying pan, combine the carrots, stock, honey, and mustard. Cover and cook over medium-high heat, stirring often, for 5 minutes, or until the stock has been reduced to a glaze.

To freeze: Prepare the recipe as directed. Cool quickly, then pack in freezer containers, and freeze. To serve, place the frozen carrots in a saucepan, cover, and warm over low heat until heated through, stirring occasionally. Or, microwave on high until hot.

Quick Tip

MARINATED SALADS

Creating colorful marinated vegetable salads is a snap using the microwave. You can cook your vegetables in one bowl, add dressing, and refrigerate the salad until dinner time.

Remember that foods keep cooking after they are removed from the microwave. So after you've cooked vegetables to just the right point, you may want to rinse them under cold water to stop the cooking process. Pat the veggies dry so dressing will adhere well, and sprinkle on your choice of dressing. Toss well to coat. Chill until serving time. The vegetables will taste "just-picked" fresh, and the colors will remain vibrant.

If you choose vegetables with similar textures, you can cook them together. For a salad that contains many different vegetables, cook the most dense varieties—such as carrots, winter squash, parsnips, or turnips—first. Cut them into uniform pieces and microwave for two or three minutes. Then add less-dense, quicker-cooking

vegetables like cauliflower, celery, broccoli, or fresh asparagus. Cook them another two minutes.

Save the quickest cookers—mushrooms, zucchini, tomatoes, or scallions—for the end and zap them briefly, about one minute.

Exact times will depend upon the sizes, shapes, and quantities of your vegetables. Just be careful not to overcook your selections. It's better for your salad to be crisp-tender than mushy. To make a colorful presentation, choose contrasting garnishes. Try finely chopped red, yellow, or orange peppers on green or white vegetables. Or, try minced parsley and chives with yellow, orange, or white vegetables.

For an unusual marinated salad, shred red beets, rutabagas, or turnips, and combine with a small amount of lemon juice. Microwave briefly, turning and tossing after every minute, until just tender. Rinse, as above, toss with vinaigrette, and refrigerate until ready to serve. ❖ ❖ ❖

Herb-Flavored Corn on the Cob

If you've only boiled or steamed corn until now, you'll be pleasantly surprised by this dill-flavored grilled corn.

Yield: 8 servings

8 ears corn with husks

¼ teaspoon olive oil

1 teaspoon dill weed

Butter-flavored sprinkles

Pull down the husks of each ear of corn, but don't remove them. Remove and discard the silk. Very lightly rub each ear with the oil, then lightly dust with the dill and sprinkles. Replace the husks, making sure that all the corn kernels are covered. If necessary, secure the husks with damp kitchen string.

Prepare an outdoor grill. When the coals are hot, place the ears around the edge of the grill, about 5 inches from the hottest coals. Grill for about 20 minutes, flipping the ears occasionally, until cooked through.

VARIATION: *You may also microwave the corn. Prepare the ears as above, then arrange 4 of them in a square pattern on a large, flat plate. Microwave on high for 2 minutes. Turn the plate and rotate the ears. Repeat 3 times for a total of 8 minutes. Microwave the remaining ears the same way.*

Succotash

You can freeze or can succotash, an old-fashioned country favorite.

Yield: 7 or 8 pints

12 ears corn

6 cups lima beans or green snap beans

Butter (optional)

Paprika (optional)

Chopped parsley (optional)

Boil the corn for 5 minutes. Cut the kernels cleanly from the cobs; do not scrape. Steam the beans until tender. Mix the hot corn with an approximately equal amount of beans. Season the mixture with butter, paprika, or parsley, if desired.

To can: Fill hot, scalded pint jars with the corn-bean mixture, leaving 1-inch headspace. Seal and process in a pressure canner at 10 pounds pressure for 60 minutes.

To freeze: Prepare the recipe as directed. Cool quickly, then pack in freezer containers, leaving ½-inch headspace, and freeze. To serve, thaw the frozen vegetables in the refrigerator. Place in a saucepan, cover, and warm over low heat until heated through, stirring occasionally. Or, microwave on high until hot, stirring at least once.

Cucumber Salad

This creamy cucumber salad has a rich flavor, but it's fat-free.

Yield: 4 servings

3   medium cucumbers

2   scallions, sliced

1/2 cup nonfat yogurt

1   tablespoon minced sweet red peppers or shredded carrots

1   tablespoon minced parsley

2   teaspoons minced fresh dill

1/2 teaspoon dry mustard

Peel, cut lengthwise, seed, and slice the cucumbers. Place the cucumbers in a medium serving bowl. Add the scallions, yogurt, peppers or carrots, parsley, dill, and mustard, and toss to combine. Refrigerate until serving time.

Garlic Grilled Baby Eggplant

Baby eggplant soak up the flavors of sesame oil, soy sauce, and garlic to make a delicious grilled vegetable that's low in salt.

Yield: 8 servings

8   baby eggplant

1   tablespoon sesame oil

4   teaspoons low-sodium soy sauce

4   garlic cloves, minced

2   teaspoons white wine vinegar

2   teaspoons no-salt lemon-herb blend

1/2 teaspoon freshly ground black pepper

Place the eggplant on a flat cutting surface. With a sharp knife, make parallel lengthwise cuts 1/4 inch apart that run from the tops to within 1 inch of the stem ends. Place in a single layer in a large baking dish or roasting pan; fan out the slices slightly, making sure to keep them attached to the stem.

In a small bowl, combine the oil, soy sauce, garlic, vinegar, herb blend, and pepper. Brush over the eggplant. Let stand for 15 minutes. Flip the pieces and brush with the remaining marinade. Let stand for 15 to 30 minutes.

Prepare an outdoor grill. When the coals are hot, place a mesh grill rack over the top. Add the eggplant. Grill for 5 minutes. Flip the pieces; grill for 5 to 10 more minutes, or until tender.

Grilled Summer Salad

Enjoy the bold flavors of endive and radicchio brought to life on a grill and drizzled with sweet, aromatic balsamic vinegar.

4 heads Belgian endive, halved lengthwise

2 heads radicchio or romaine lettuce, quartered lengthwise

2 medium zucchini, thickly sliced on the diagonal

2 teaspoons olive oil

2 teaspoons minced fresh basil

2 large, firm tomatoes

¼ cup balsamic vinegar

Place the endive, lettuce, and zucchini in a large baking dish. Drizzle with the oil. Sprinkle with the basil. Toss lightly to combine and to coat the vegetables with oil. Cut the tomatoes in half through their cores. Trim the cores. Cut each half lengthwise into 1-inch-wide wedges.

Prepare an outdoor grill. When the coals are hot, arrange the zucchini slices over the hottest coals. Surround them with the endive and lettuce. Add the tomatoes, positioning them near the outer edges of the rack. Grill for 3 minutes. Carefully flip the pieces and grill for 3 to 5 more minutes, or until browned and soft.

Remove the pieces with a metal spatula and divide among 8 plates. Sprinkle with the vinegar, and serve.

Yield: 8 servings

Red and Green Salad

Use this colorful mix of vegetables, fruit, and low-fat dressing for brunch.

1 large head romaine lettuce, torn into bite-size pieces

3 cups diced tart red apples

2 cups diced celery

¼ cup chopped walnuts

1 ounce blue cheese, crumbled

1 cup nonfat mayonnaise

1 cup nonfat yogurt

½ teaspoon freshly ground black pepper

In a large bowl, combine the lettuce, apples, celery, walnuts, and blue cheese. In a small bowl, whisk together the mayonnaise, yogurt, and pepper. Pour over the salad and toss well. Serve or chill until serving time.

Yield: 12 servings

Dilled Vegetables

A dill dressing brings out the flavor of tender-crisp garden vegetables.

Yield: 4 to 6 servings

2 large carrots, julienned

2 small yellow summer squash, julienned

12 ears canned baby corn, halved lengthwise

5 scallions, julienned

2 tablespoons vinegar

2 teaspoons Dijon mustard

1 teaspoon dill weed

1 clove garlic, minced

2 heads Belgian endive

Blanch the carrots in boiling water for 40 seconds. Drain, pat dry, and transfer to a large bowl. Blanch the squash for 20 seconds. Drain, pat dry, and add to the bowl. Add the corn and scallions.

In a small bowl, whisk together the vinegar, mustard, dill, and garlic. Pour over the vegetables and toss to coat well. Chill. Separate the Belgian endive into leaves and line a large platter with them. Add the vegetables.

Quick Tip

MIXED VEGETABLE COMBINATIONS

Here are some suggestions for vegetables that go well together. Blanch each vegetable in the following combinations separately, pack them together in freezer containers and then label appropriately. (Don't bother to blanch fruits, herbs, and spices.)

- Baby peas and mint

- Brussels sprouts, carrots, and cloves

- Carrots, peas, and pearl onions

- Carrots, turnips, and peas

- Julienne of carrots and zucchini with onion wedges

- Cauliflower, broccoli, and carrots

- Celery, carrots, and broccoli

- Corn, sweet red peppers, green peppers, and onions

- Corn, lima beans, and scallions

- Eggplant, tomatoes, onions, and garlic

- Green beans and cherry tomatoes

- Sliced parsnips, carrots, and green beans

- Red beets and their tops with oranges and a stick of cinnamon

- Yellow squash and raisins

- Yellow squash, prunes, and carrots

- Zucchini, tomatoes, onions, and garlic ❖ ❖ ❖

Cidered Parsnips

Try this sweet treat as an alternative to sweet potatoes.

Yield: 4 servings

6 medium parsnips, thinly sliced

1 cup apple cider

Steam the parsnips for 10 minutes, or until tender. In a large frying pan, over medium-high heat, boil the cider until it is reduced to ⅓ cup. Add the parsnips and toss to coat. Serve warm.

To freeze: Prepare the recipe as directed. Cool quickly, then pack in freezer containers, and freeze. To serve, place frozen parsnips in a frying pan. Cover and warm over medium heat until warmed through, stirring occasionally. Or, microwave on high for 3 to 5 minutes, or until hot.

Sesame Snow Peas

Sesame gives a twist of oriental flavor.

Yield: 4 servings

2 cups snow peas

1 carrot, julienned

1 tablespoon toasted sesame seeds

1 teaspoon sesame oil

½ teaspoon grated orange rind

Steam the snow peas and carrots for 4 minutes, or until tender. Transfer to a medium bowl. Add the sesame seeds, oil, and orange rind. Toss to combine, and serve warm.

Savory Stuffed Snow Peas

Make a fancy filling for sweet snow peas.

Yield: 9 to 12 servings

4 cloves garlic

2 cups nonfat yogurt

1 teaspoon dill weed

1 teaspoon dried savory

36 snow peas

Boil the garlic for 2 minutes, then mash to a paste. In a medium bowl, mix the garlic, yogurt, dill, and savory. Pour into a strainer lined with cheesecloth. Cover with a piece of plastic wrap, set over a bowl, and allow the yogurt to drain overnight.

Boil the snow peas for 2 minutes. Drain and cool. Open one long side of each pod. Using a small spoon or a pastry bag fitted with a decorative tip, fill each pod with the yogurt mixture.

Good-Luck Peas

Even if this dish doesn't bring good luck, it will bring good health because it's vitamin-packed and low in fat.

Yield: 4 servings

2 cups cooked black-eyed peas

2 cups shredded carrots

1 cup shredded kale

1 cup minced leeks

2 tablespoons lemon juice

2 tablespoons red wine vinegar

2 tablespoons olive oil

1 teaspoon dried basil

½ teaspoon dried sage

¼ teaspoon dry mustard

In a large bowl, combine the peas, carrots, kale, and leeks. In a small bowl, whisk together the lemon juice, vinegar, oil, basil, sage, and mustard. Pour over the vegetables and toss to combine. Serve or chill for later.

Compote of Raspberries and Roasted Red Peppers

Rich, roasted peppers, sweet berries, and bold radicchio make a flavorful salad.

Yield: 8 servings

2 sweet red peppers

2 cups raspberries

1 tablespoon balsamic vinegar

1 teaspoon olive oil

1 small head radicchio lettuce

1 loaf whole wheat French bread, thinly sliced

Broil the red peppers until blackened on all sides. (See Roasted Sweet Peppers on the opposite page for more details on roasting peppers.) Allow to cool, then remove and discard the peel and seeds. Chop the peppers and place in a medium bowl. Add the raspberries, vinegar, and oil. Toss to combine.

Separate the lettuce into individual cup-shaped leaves. Divide the compote among them. Serve with the bread.

Roasted Sweet Peppers

Roasting brings out full flavor in sweet peppers and makes it easy to remove the skins.

Yield: 8 peppers

8 large sweet peppers

Set the peppers 4 at a time on a broiler pan, so they are about 5 inches below the broiler element. Broil, turning often, until the peppers are well blistered and charred on all sides.

Place the peppers in a paper bag; close the bag tightly. Let them rest 18 to 20 minutes to loosen the skins. Remove the peppers from the bag and strip off the skins. Cut the peppers lengthwise into quarters. Remove and discard the stems and seeds. Cut the peppers into 1-inch strips.

To freeze: Prepare the peppers as directed. Pack them in freezer containers and freeze.

USES FOR ROASTED PEPPERS

Roasted peppers are delicious in salads, pasta dishes, marinades, and many other dishes. Try these for starters.

- Use in green salads, or rice or pasta salads.
- Cook in a little olive oil. Toss with hot pasta and grated cheese.
- Add to an antipasto or appetizer tray; decorate with hard-cooked egg wedges.
- Try roasted peppers on homemade pizza.

- Puree peppers with tuna. Add olive oil. Use to garnish hot pasta, tomatoes, and cold meats.

- Marinate roasted peppers in any vinaigrette. The ones on page 203 are very good. Marinated, roasted peppers will keep about three days in the refrigerator and much longer in the freezer. Thaw desired quantity of frozen marinated peppers in the refrigerator overnight and then allow them to stand at room temperature until the oil melts. ❖ ❖ ❖

Garden-Puff Potatoes

These low-calorie stuffed potatoes resemble twice-baked potatoes but have a fraction of the fat.

4 large baking potatoes
1½ cups bite-size broccoli florets
½ cup diced green peppers
¼ cup diced onions
1 cup shredded carrots
⅓ cup buttermilk
2 teaspoons dill weed
1 tablespoon snipped chives

Bake the potatoes at 375°F for 1 hour, or until easily pierced with a fork. Steam the broccoli for 3 minutes. Add the peppers and onions. Steam for 2 minutes. Cut a thin slice off the top of each potato. Scoop out the pulp, leaving a ¼-inch-thick shell. Reserve the shells and transfer the pulp to a blender or food processor. Add the carrots, buttermilk, and dill. Whip on high speed for 5 minutes, or until light and fluffy. Add more buttermilk, if needed.

Transfer to a medium bowl. Fold in the steamed vegetables. Spoon the potato mixture into the reserved shells. Broil about 4 inches below the broiler element for 5 minutes, or until lightly browned. Sprinkle with the chives.

To freeze: Prepare the recipe as directed. Freeze the stuffed potatoes on a baking sheet until firm. Wrap them in freezer wrap or foil, or place in freezer bags. To serve, unwrap the potatoes and place them on a baking sheet. Bake in a 350°F oven for 30 to 40 minutes, or until heated through and lightly browned. Sprinkle with chives. Or, microwave one potato on high for 5 to 7 minutes, or until hot.

Yield: 4 servings

Curried Potato Salad

Potato salad takes on a new flavor.

3 medium potatoes
¼ cup raisins
2 scallions, minced
3 tablespoons sliced almonds
½ cup nonfat yogurt
2 tablespoons chutney
1 teaspoon curry powder

Cut the potatoes into 1-inch chunks. Steam for 12 minutes, or until tender. Transfer to a large bowl. Stir in the raisins, scallions, and almonds.

In a small bowl, whisk together the yogurt, chutney, and curry powder. Pour over the potatoes and combine well. Serve warm.

Yield: 4 servings

Potato and Raspberry Salad

Let fruit replace sour cream or mayonnaise for excellent potatoes that are low in fat. too.

Yield: 4 servings

3 medium potatoes

1½ cups raspberries

½ cup snipped chives

2 tablespoons canola oil

1 tablespoon raspberry vinegar

1 tablespoon orange juice

¼ teaspoon Dijon mustard

⅛ teaspoon grated nutmeg

Steam the potatoes for 15 minutes, or until easily pierced with a fork. Set aside to cool, then cut into bite-size pieces.

In a large bowl, combine the potatoes, raspberries, and chives. In a small bowl, whisk together the oil, vinegar, orange juice, mustard, and nutmeg. Pour over the potatoes and toss gently.

Squash Salad with Buttermilk Dressing

This bright. colorful salad will make you glad your summer squash is prolific.

Yield: 4 servings

2 medium yellow summer squash, julienned

2 tomatoes, cut into wedges

⅓ cup broccoli stems, julienned

¼ cup buttermilk

1 teaspoon Dijon mustard

½ teaspoon dried basil

⅛ teaspoon curry powder

2 cups shredded red cabbage

Steam the squash for 2 minutes, or until tender. Transfer to a large bowl. Add the tomatoes and broccoli.

In a small bowl, whisk together the buttermilk, mustard, basil, and curry powder. Pour over the squash mixture and toss well to combine.

Place the cabbage on a serving platter. Spoon on the squash mixture. Serve warm.

Spaghetti Squash in a Flash

Spaghetti squash is a vegetable wonder that is low-fat and low-calorie with the sensory pleasure of pasta.

1 medium spaghetti squash

Cut the squash in half and remove the seeds. Place each half, cut side down, on a separate plate. The squash is moist enough to cook without any added liquid. Microwave each half separately on full power for 6 to 8 minutes, or until the flesh is tender and can be easily pulled from the shell in strands.

Remove the squash strands from the shell gently, using a fork. Top with any sauce suitable for pasta, including pesto. Do not stir with a spoon; instead, lift the strands with a fork and toss with the topping until the sauce is well distributed.

Yield: 4 servings

Spiced Squash Puree

This tasty alternative to applesauce enhances roast pork and lamb.

12 cups peeled, seeded, shredded squash (acorn, crooked neck, yellow, or whatever you have on hand)

12 ounces unsweetened frozen apple juice concentrate

1 teaspoon ground cinnamon

1/4 teaspoon ground allspice

1/4 teaspoon ground ginger

Combine the squash, juice concentrate, cinnamon, allspice, and ginger in a large, heavy-bottom saucepan and simmer until the liquid evaporates and the squash is translucent. Allow to cool, then puree in a blender or food processor.

To freeze: Prepare the recipe as directed. Cool quickly, then ladle into freezer containers, leaving 1-inch headspace, and freeze. To serve, transfer frozen squash to a saucepan, cover, and warm over low heat until heated through, stirring frequently. Add 2 to 3 tablespoons of water if the consistency is too thick. Or, microwave on medium until warm, stirring at least once.

VARIATION: *Substitute 1 1/2 teaspoons Chinese Five Spice Powder (available in Asian food markets) for cinnamon, allspice, and ginger.*

Yield: 12 servings

Maple Sweet Potatoes

You can serve these sweet potatoes as a vegetable, but they're also delicious for dessert.

Yield: 4 servings

4 large sweet potatoes

¼ cup nonfat yogurt

3 tablespoons maple syrup

3 tablespoons orange juice

Bake the potatoes at 375°F for 1¼ hours, or until easily pierced with a fork. Slice in half lengthwise. Scoop out the pulp, leaving a ¼-inch-thick shell. Reserve the shells and transfer the pulp to a large bowl.

Mash the pulp and stir in the yogurt, maple syrup, and orange juice. Spoon the filling into the reserved shells.

Return to the oven and bake for 5 minutes to heat through.

To freeze: Prepare the recipe as directed. Place the filled potatoes on a baking sheet and freeze until firm. Wrap them in freezer wrap or foil or place them in freezer bags. To serve, unwrap the frozen potatoes and place them on a baking sheet. Heat in the oven for 15 minutes at 400°F, or until heated through. Or, microwave 1 potato on high for 5 to 7 minutes, or until hot.

French-Style Chard

Swiss chard becomes an exciting side dish with this French technique.

Yield: 4 servings

4 cups coarsely shredded Swiss chard

2 cloves garlic, minced

1 tablespoon olive oil

2 tablespoons grated sapsago or Parmesan cheese

In a large no-stick frying pan, sauté the chard and garlic in the oil for 5 minutes, or until the chard is wilted. Sprinkle with the cheese.

Stuffed Cherry Tomatoes

Your guests—and even your kids—will love these. Don't be too surprised if they want to run out to the garden to get more tomatoes so you can make another batch.

Yield: 8 servings

24 red or yellow cherry tomatoes

½ cup dry-curd cottage cheese

¼ cup minced spinach

1 tablespoon minced fresh basil

2 teaspoons snipped chives

Slice off the very tops of the tomatoes. Use a small spoon to remove the insides; discard. Turn the tomatoes upside down to drain while you prepare the filling.

In a small bowl, mix the cottage cheese, spinach, basil, and chives. Spoon into the tomatoes (or place in a pastry bag fitted with a large decorative tip; pipe the filling into the tomatoes).

VARIATIONS: For variety, replace the cottage cheese filling with pureed chicken, tuna, or salmon salad. For brunch, use scrambled eggs and garnish with tiny herb sprigs. For a Mexican flavor, try guacamole.

You may also turn these cold hors d'oeuvres into warm ones. For best results, use firm-walled tomatoes that won't collapse when heated. Prepare the filling as directed, but replace the cottage cheese with 3 tablespoons dry bread crumbs plus 2 ounces softened Neufchâtel cheese. Blend well, then pipe the filling into the tomatoes. Arrange the tomatoes in a baking dish and bake at 350°F for 15 minutes, or until the tomatoes just begin to soften. Do not overbake, or the tomatoes will split. Let stand for about 10 minutes, or until just barely warm, before serving.

Dill-Zucchini Spears

This marinated zucchini salad will keep for days.

Yield: 6 to 8 servings

2 tablespoons white wine vinegar

2 cloves garlic, minced

½ teaspoon Dijon mustard

3 tablespoons canola oil

1 teaspoon dill weed

3 small zucchini, cut lengthwise into spears

In a small bowl, combine the vinegar, garlic, and mustard. Slowly whisk in the oil until thoroughly combined. Whisk in the dill. Arrange the zucchini in a shallow dish. Pour the dressing over the zucchini. Cover and chill for at least 3 hours.

Zucchini Fries

Zucchini fries have a great flavor that french fries can't rival, and they use much less fat.

Yield: 4 servings

2 small zucchini, 1-inch diameter

2 small yellow squash, 1-inch diameter

1/2 teaspoon oil

1 teaspoon minced fresh basil

Cut the zucchini and squash into fries about 2 inches long and 1/2 inch thick. In a large no-stick frying pan, over medium-high heat, sauté the vegetables in the oil for 5 minutes, or until lightly browned. Sprinkle with the basil.

Zucchini with Caraway

Caraway, parsley, onions, and garlic give zucchini a fabulous flavor.

Yield: 4 servings

1 tablespoon olive oil

3 medium zucchini, thinly sliced

1/4 cup chopped onions

1/4 cup sliced mushrooms

2 cloves garlic, minced

1/4 teaspoon caraway seeds, crushed

1 tablespoon minced fresh parsley

In a large no-stick frying pan, over medium-high heat, heat the oil. Add the zucchini, onions, mushrooms, garlic, and caraway seeds. Sauté for 8 minutes, or until the zucchini is tender and a bit brown. Sprinkle with the parsley.

Soups and Stews

Asparagus Soup

⚘

This soup stretches the great flavor of asparagus, making even small harvests seem big.

7 cups defatted chicken stock

½ cup white wine vinegar

2 teaspoons honey

6 or 7 asparagus spears, cut into 1-inch pieces

7 ounces canned baby corn, drained

¼ cup snipped chives

In a 3-quart saucepan, combine the stock, vinegar, and honey. Bring to a boil. Reduce the heat to a gentle simmer. Add the asparagus and corn. Simmer until the asparagus is tender but still vibrant green, about 3 minutes for thin stalks. Serve sprinkled with the chives.

To freeze: Prepare the recipe as directed but don't sprinkle with chives. Cool quickly, then ladle into freezer containers, leaving 1-inch headspace, and freeze. To serve, transfer the frozen soup to a saucepan. Cover and warm over low heat until heated through, stirring frequently. Or, microwave on medium until the soup is warm, stirring at least once, and then on high until hot.

Yield: 8 servings

Black Bean Soup

Use this soup for a light lunch with crusty French bread or as the first course of a full dinner.

1 cup dried black beans, soaked overnight

4 cups water

4 bay leaves

2 cloves garlic, whole

1/4 teaspoon dry mustard

1 1/2 teaspoons chili powder

4 whole cloves

2 medium onions, chopped

Low-sodium soy sauce

Lemon slices (garnish)

Hard-cooked eggs, sliced (garnish)

Drain the beans and discard the soaking water. Bring the water to a boil. Add the beans, bay leaves, garlic, mustard, chili powder, cloves, and onions. Simmer for 1 to 1 1/2 hours, or until the beans are tender. Puree in a blender or food processor and serve. Add soy sauce to taste and garnish with lemon slices and sliced eggs.

To freeze: Prepare the recipe as directed, omitting the soy sauce, lemon slices, and sliced eggs. Cool quickly, then ladle into freezer containers, leaving 1-inch headspace, and freeze. To serve, transfer the frozen soup to a saucepan, adding a little water to the pan. Cover and warm over low heat until heated through, stirring frequently. When hot, add soy sauce, lemon slices, and sliced eggs.

Yield: 4 servings

Cuban Bean Stew

Wake up your taste buds with this spicy stew.

1/2 cup dried black beans, soaked overnight

4 cups defatted chicken stock

1 large onion, chopped

1 stalk celery, thinly sliced

2 hot chili peppers, seeded and minced

1/4 cup minced fresh parsley

1 tablespoon peeled, minced ginger

1 tablespoon low-sodium soy sauce

4 cloves garlic, minced

1 teaspoon dried thyme

1 bay leaf

Drain the beans and discard the soaking water. Place them in a 3-quart baking dish. Add the stock, onions, celery, peppers, parsley, ginger, soy sauce, garlic, thyme, and bay leaf. Bring to a simmer on top of the stove. Transfer to the oven and bake at 375°F for 2 hours, or until the beans are tender. Discard the bay leaf and serve.

Yield: 4 servings

Broccoli-Buttermilk Soup

꩜

Collect the broccoli florets from sideshoots to make this nutritious soup.

Yield: 4 servings

6 cups broccoli florets

1 cup sliced onions

4 cloves garlic, whole

2 cups buttermilk

Steam the broccoli, onions, and garlic for 12 minutes, or until the broccoli is tender. Transfer the vegetables to a blender or food processor and puree. Stir in the buttermilk.

To freeze: Steam and puree vegetables as directed. Cool quickly, then put in freezer containers, leaving 1-inch headspace, and freeze. To serve, thaw the vegetable mixture in the refrigerator. Place in a saucepan, add buttermilk, and warm over low heat until heated through, stirring frequently. Or, microwave the thawed vegetable mixture and buttermilk on medium just until warm, stirring at least once.

Iced Cantaloupe Soup

꩜

If you grow more cantaloupe than you can eat for breakfast, make one into soup for lunch.

Yield: 4 servings

1 large cantaloupe

1½ cups low-fat milk

2 tablespoons maple syrup

¾ teaspoon ground cinnamon

¾ teaspoon ground coriander

½ cup nonfat yogurt

Remove the seeds and rind from the cantaloupe. Cut the flesh into cubes. In a blender, combine the cantaloupe, milk, maple syrup, cinnamon, and coriander. Blend well. Transfer to a large bowl. Cover and chill for 1 hour.

While the soup is chilling, spoon the yogurt into a cheesecloth-lined sieve. Let it drain over a bowl to thicken.

Whisk the yogurt into the soup.

Cream of Carrot Soup

1 large onion, sliced

1 teaspoon canola oil

2 cups defatted stock

1 cup carrots, sliced

1 large potato, cubed

1/2 teaspoon dried thyme

3/4 cup skim milk

You've never tasted cream of carrot soup until you've made it with sweet, home-grown carrots!

In a 2-quart saucepan, sauté the onions in the oil for about 5 minutes, or until softened. Add the stock, carrots, potatoes, and thyme. Simmer for 25 minutes, or until tender. Puree in a blender or food processor. Stir in the milk.

To freeze: Prepare the recipe as directed but don't add the milk. Cool quickly, then ladle the pureed mixture into freezer containers, leaving 1-inch headspace, and freeze. To serve, thaw the pureed mixture in the refrigerator. Place the thawed puree and milk in a medium saucepan, and warm over low heat until heated through, stirring frequently. Or, microwave the thawed puree and milk on medium for 7 to 9 minutes until heated through, stirring at least once.

Yield: 4 servings

Quick Tip

MICROWAVE SOUP

Microwaving enhances the flavor of vegetables, yielding soups that taste fresher than conventionally cooked soups. Use these guidelines to convert your favorite recipes to the microwave.

- Cut meat and vegetables into small, uniform pieces so they'll cook evenly and quickly.
- Microwave clear soups or brothy chicken-and-vegetable soups on high power to keep them clear. A lower setting may cloud the soup.
- Use medium power and longer cooking times for soups based on less-tender cuts of meats, such as beef cubes. Start by covering the beef in liquid and cooking until tender. Then add vegetables and seasonings.
- Making very thick pureed soups is easy in the microwave. Conventional thick soups made on the stove must be cooked over low heat and stirred often to prevent sticking. Since sticking is not a problem with the microwave, such soups can be cooked on high and stirred only two or three times throughout cooking.
- Reduce the amount of liquid in your conventional recipe by one-fourth, since very little liquid evaporates during the short time it takes to microwave soup. Exceptions are soups made with dried peas or beans. These need the full amount of liquid to rehydrate the legumes. (Also, some of the water will evaporate during the longer microwaving time needed for these types of soup.)
- When precooking vegetables for pureed soups, use high power and little or no liquid. ❖ ❖ ❖

Cream of Celery Soup Mix

Use homemade dried soup mix instead of high-salt commercial mixes.

Yield: About 7 packets, each making 1 serving

2 2/3 cups instant powdered milk

1/2 cup celery powder (from dried stalks and leaves, not seeds)

3 tablespoons arrowroot powder or cornstarch

3 tablespoons onion flakes

1 tablespoon dried, crushed parsley flakes

1/2 teaspoon paprika

1/4 teaspoon white pepper

Stir together all ingredients. Divide the mixture into individual packets, each containing 7 tablespoons. Small pieces of plastic wrap or aluminum foil, small plastic bags, or even paper envelopes will work well as containers. Close securely and mark. Store in airtight jars.

Quick Cream of Carrot Soup

Here's how to turn celery soup mix into cream of carrot soup.

Yield: 1 serving

1 cup water

1 packet Cream of Celery Soup Mix (above)

2 tablespoons dried carrots or 1/4 cup raw, sliced carrots

In a small saucepan, mix the water, soup mix, and carrots. Stirring frequently, simmer, uncovered, at medium-high heat for 20 minutes, or until thick and creamy.

Quick Cream of Celery Soup

You can make this soup fast!

Yield: 1 serving

1 cup water

1 packet Cream of Celery Soup Mix (on the opposite page)

In a small saucepan, whisk together the water and soup mix. Stirring frequently, simmer, uncovered, over medium-high heat for 15 minutes, or until thick and creamy.

Quick Cream of Potato Soup

For a change of pace, try almost-instant potato soup.

Yield: 1 serving

1 cup water

1 packet Cream of Celery Soup Mix (on the opposite page)

¼ cup shredded raw potatoes

In a small saucepan, mix the water, soup mix, and potatoes. Stirring constantly, simmer, uncovered, over medium-high heat for 15 minutes, or until thick and creamy.

Bouillabaisse

This classic fish stew calls for plenty of garden-fresh vegetables.

1 cup sliced carrots

1 cup sliced celery

1 cup sliced red onions

1 cup sliced fresh fennel

1 tablespoon olive oil

2 cups peeled, seeded, and chopped tomatoes

1 clove garlic, minced

¼ teaspoon saffron

2 quarts defatted stock

2 bay leaves

½ teaspoon fennel seed

½ teaspoon dried oregano

1 pound red snapper, cut into 1-inch chunks

1 pound scallops

24 shrimp, peeled and deveined

In a 4-quart pot, over medium-high heat, sauté the carrots, celery, onions, and fennel in the oil for 5 minutes. Add the tomatoes, garlic, and saffron. Sauté for 5 minutes.

Add the stock, bay leaves, fennel seed, and oregano. Bring to a boil. Reduce the heat, cover, and simmer for 30 minutes. Add the snapper, scallops, and shrimp. Cover and simmer for 5 to 7 minutes, or until the seafood is tender. Discard the bay leaves.

To freeze: Prepare the recipe as directed. Cool quickly, then ladle into freezer containers, leaving 1-inch headspace, and freeze. To serve, transfer frozen soup to a saucepan. Cover and warm over low heat until hot, stirring frequently. Or, microwave on high for 9 to 10 minutes until hot, stirring at least once.

Yield: 6 servings

Quality Conscious

TIPS FOR SAVORY STOCK

A good stock is the foundation upon which full-bodied soups, stews, and sauces are built. In addition, it gives extra flavor to marinades and perks up vegetables lightly cooked in it, so you're not tempted to spruce them up with butter or a high-calorie sauce.

• Save vegetable trimmings when you are preparing other dishes, and store them in the freezer until you have enough to make a hearty stock.

• Cut vegetables like onions, carrots, potatoes, and celery into large pieces so they won't fall apart during cooking and cloud the stock.

• Get rich, deep color by adding onion skins to the pot. ❖ ❖ ❖

Savory Chicken Vegetable Soup

Put some chicken soup away for winter weather and the cold and flu season.

8 cups defatted chicken stock

1 clove garlic, minced

½ teaspoon dried basil

½ teaspoon celery seeds

¼ teaspoon ground ginger

1 teaspoon ground savory

½ teaspoon finely ground black pepper

1 cup cubed carrots

1 cup cubed potatoes

1 medium onion, cut in half and sliced

2 cups cubed cooked chicken

1 large tomato, seeded and chopped

1 cup corn

1 cup peas

1 cup green beans, cut in half lengthwise

Bring the stock to a boil. Reduce the heat and simmer with the garlic, basil, celery seeds, ginger, savory, and pepper for 20 minutes. Add the carrots and potatoes and cook for 10 minutes. Then add the onions and cook for 5 minutes, or until just tender. Add the chicken, tomatoes, corn, peas, and beans. Cook, covered, for 15 minutes, or until the vegetables are tender.

To freeze: Prepare the recipe as directed but don't add the potatoes and peas (cook them separately before serving). Also, cut the final cooking time from 15 minutes to 5 minutes to avoid overcooking the vegetables. Cool quickly, then ladle into freezer containers, leaving 1-inch headspace, and freeze. To serve, transfer the frozen soup to a saucepan. Cover and warm over medium heat until the vegetables are tender, adding the cooked potatoes and peas when the soup is almost heated through. Or, microwave on medium until warm, stirring at least once, and then on high until hot. Taste the soup and adjust the seasonings, if necessary.

Yield: 10 servings

Tuscan Minestrone

Every region of Italy has its version of this hearty soup.

½ cup dried white beans (marrow, navy, or Great Northern), soaked overnight

½ cup chopped onions

½ cup chopped leeks

1 cup coarsely chopped carrots

½ cup coarsely chopped celery

2 cups coarsely chopped zucchini

1½ cups chopped escarole or Swiss chard

1½ cups green beans, cut into 1-inch pieces

1 cup shredded cabbage

2 cloves garlic, minced

1 tablespoon fresh or 1 teaspoon dried thyme

1 tablespoon fresh or 1 teaspoon dried rosemary

1 tablespoon fresh or 1 teaspoon dried basil

½ teaspoon freshly ground pepper

1½ cups canned Italian tomatoes, undrained and chopped

2 sprigs parsley

1 bay leaf

3 cups water

1 cup whole wheat elbows, shells, or ditalini

1 tablespoon fresh basil (garnish)

1 tablespoon fresh parsley (garnish)

½ teaspoon minced garlic (garnish)

Drain the beans and discard the soaking water.

Place the beans, onions, leeks, carrots, celery, zucchini, escarole, green beans, cabbage, garlic, dried herbs (if using dried instead of fresh), pepper, tomatoes, parsley, bay leaf, and water in a 4-quart slow cooker. Cover and simmer on low heat for 8 to 10 hours, or until the vegetables are tender. If using fresh herbs, add them during the last 2 hours of the cooking time. Remove and discard the parsley sprigs and bay leaf.

To freeze: Prepare the recipe as directed but omit the pasta. Cool quickly, then ladle into freezer containers, leaving 1-inch head-space, and freeze. To serve, transfer frozen soup to a 4-quart saucepan, adding a little water to the bottom of the pan to prevent sticking. Cover and warm over low heat until heated through, stirring frequently. Or, microwave on medium until thawed and then on high until warmed through. Cook the pasta separately and add to the warm soup; reheat, if necessary. Adjust the seasonings, if necessary. Garnish with fresh basil, parsley, and garlic.

Yield: 10 servings

Vegetable Soup Mix

꙰

Use dried ingredients for this mix.

Yield: About 8 packets, each making 1 serving

¼ cup dried carrots

¼ cup dried celery

1 tablespoon crushed parsley flakes

2 teaspoons onion flakes

1 teaspoon crushed thyme

1 teaspoon crushed basil

½ teaspoon white pepper

Stir together all ingredients. Divide the mixture into individual packets, each containing 4 teaspoons. Small pieces of plastic wrap or aluminum foil, small plastic bags, or even paper envelopes will work well as containers. Close securely and mark. Store in airtight containers.

Hearty Vegetable Soup

꙰

Here's a fast and easy soup that's really good for you.

Yield: 1 serving

1 cup water

1 packet Vegetable Soup Mix (above)

½ cup tomato juice or vegetable cocktail juice

¼ cup diced cooked chicken or beef

1 teaspoon butter

In a small saucepan, stir together all ingredients. Bring to a boil and reduce heat to simmer. Cook, covered, for 20 minutes.

Vegetable Macaroni Soup

Add macaroni for a soup that your kids will love.

Yield: 1 serving

1 cup water

1 packet Vegetable Soup Mix (page 229)

2 tablespoons whole wheat elbow macaroni

1 teaspoon butter

In a small saucepan, stir together all ingredients. Bring to a boil and reduce heat to simmer. Cook, uncovered, until macaroni is tender. Stir occasionally.

Tomato Vegetable Soup

Have this soup with a sandwich for lunch or make it for a late afternoon snack.

Yield: 1 serving

1 cup water

1 packet Vegetable Soup Mix (page 229)

½ cup tomato juice or vegetable cocktail juice

1 teaspoon butter

In a small saucepan, stir together all ingredients. Bring to a boil and reduce heat to simmer. Cook, covered, for 20 minutes.

Cool Peach Soup

~❧~

This cool, fruity soup is good for lunch on hot days.

1 cup white grape juice

1 cup water

⅓ cup apple juice concentrate

1 teaspoon vanilla extract

¼ teaspoon ground cinnamon

2 teaspoons lemon juice

4 large peaches

1 pint raspberries

In a 1-quart saucepan, bring the grape juice, water, apple juice concentrate, vanilla, and cinnamon to a boil. Simmer for 2 minutes. Remove the pan from the heat and stir in the lemon juice.

Peel the peaches by immersing them in boiling water for about 1 minute, then running them under cold water. The skins will slip off easily. Chop 2 of the peaches and place them in a blender or food processor. Add the liquid and puree until smooth. Transfer to a larger bowl.

Cut the remaining peaches into ½-inch wedges. Add to the bowl, making sure the slices are covered with puree so they won't discolor. Refrigerate the soup for at least 1 hour, or until well chilled. Serve in shallow bowls and top with raspberries.

Yield: 4 servings

Irish Vichyssoise

~❧~

Make this nutritious potato soup ahead and freeze it.

3 large potatoes, diced

1 large bunch broccoli, chopped

1 large onion, sliced

½ teaspoon dried thyme

¼ teaspoon ground rosemary

¼ teaspoon ground cumin

2 cups evaporated skim milk

1 cup defatted stock

Steam the potatoes and broccoli for 10 minutes, or until tender. In a 3-quart saucepan, sauté the onions in the oil for 5 minutes. Add the thyme, rosemary, and cumin. Cook for 1 minute.

In a blender or food processor, working in batches, puree the potatoes, broccoli, and onions with the milk and stock. Return the soup to the saucepan and heat through.

To freeze: Prepare the recipe as directed. Cool quickly, then ladle the soup into a freezer container, leaving 1-inch headspace, and freeze. To serve, transfer frozen soup to the top of a double boiler over simmering water. Cover and warm over medium heat until heated through. Stir or beat if the mixture separates. Or, microwave on medium until the soup is warm, stirring at least once.

Yield: 4 to 6 servings

Clam Chowder Base

Use your garden-fresh vegetables and herbs to make this ahead.

2 dozen chowder clams
3 tablespoons vegetable oil or butter
1 cup finely chopped onions
½ cup chopped celery
1 bay leaf
2 sprigs parsley
2½ cups diced potatoes
½ cup chopped carrots
Dash of ground thyme
2 tablespoons lemon juice

Steam the clams open (discard any clams that don't open). Reserve the clam broth. Chop the clams.

In a kettle or large saucepan, heat the oil or butter. Add the onions and celery and sauté for 3 to 4 minutes. Add enough water to the clam broth to measure 6 cups and add it to the onion mixture along with the bay leaf and parsley. Bring to a boil. Reduce heat. Add the clams and simmer for 15 minutes. Then add the potatoes and carrots and boil gently for 5 minutes. Remove the bay leaf and parsley. Add the thyme and lemon juice.

To freeze: Prepare the recipe as directed. Cool quickly, then ladle the base into freezer containers, leaving 1-inch headspace, and freeze.

Yield: 6 pints

New England Clam Chowder

This is the classic creamy chowder version.

3 pints Clam Chowder Base (above)
3 cups milk
1 cup light cream
1 tablespoon butter
⅛ teaspoon ground thyme
Paprika

If frozen, thaw the chowder base in refrigerator. Then place it in a saucepan, cover, and heat slowly over low heat to a simmer. Add the milk, cream, butter, and thyme. Heat through but do not let boil. Serve with a sprinkling of paprika.

VARIATION: *For a thicker chowder, melt 1 tablespoon butter in a small saucepan. Stir in 1 tablespoon whole wheat flour. Remove from heat. Whisk in 1 cup milk and ½ cup light cream. Cook over low heat, stirring constantly, until thickened. Add to the chowder base with 2 cups milk, ½ cup cream, and ⅛ teaspoon thyme. Heat through.*

Yield: 10 to 12 servings

Manhattan Clam Chowder

On a hectic day, just pull out your premade base for wonderful clam chowder.

Yield: 10 to 12 servings

3 pints Clam Chowder Base (on the opposite page)

3 cups chopped canned or cooked tomatoes

$1/8$ teaspoon ground thyme

3 tablespoons chopped parsley

If frozen, thaw the chowder base in the refrigerator. Then place it in a saucepan, cover, and heat slowly over low heat to a simmer. Add the tomatoes and thyme and simmer for 5 to 7 minutes. Serve with a sprinkling of parsley.

VARIATION: *Add other vegetables, such as cooked corn or peas.*

Pumpkin Soup

This flavorful soup is fun to serve at a Halloween party or fall luncheon.

Yield: 4 servings

1 large onion, minced

2 cups defatted chicken stock

$1 1/2$ cups pureed cooked pumpkin

$1/2$ teaspoon dried oregano

$1/4$ teaspoon hot pepper sauce

$1/4$ cup toasted pumpkin seeds

In a 2-quart saucepan, cook the onions in 2 tablespoons of the stock until limp. Add the remaining stock, pumpkin, oregano, and hot pepper sauce. Simmer over low heat for 15 minutes. Serve sprinkled with pumpkin seeds.

To freeze: Prepare the recipe as directed but omit the hot pepper sauce and toasted pumpkin seeds. Cool quickly, then ladle into freezer containers, leaving 1-inch headspace, and freeze. To serve, thaw the soup in the refrigerator. Place it in a saucepan, cover, and warm over low heat until heated through, stirring frequently. Or, microwave on high for 8 to 10 minutes, stirring at least once. When warm, add hot pepper sauce and toasted pumpkin seeds.

Velvety Sweet Potato Soup

🌿

If you can't store fresh sweet potatoes long, freeze them in this rich, thick soup. It is especially welcome in the middle of winter.

2 medium yams or sweet potatoes

2 medium leeks

2 tablespoons defatted chicken stock

½ teaspoon dried dill

1½ cups evaporated skim milk

Peel the yams or sweet potatoes and slice into ¾-inch chunks. Place in a 1½-quart casserole dish. Trim the leeks, slit them lengthwise, and wash them well to remove all grit. Coarsely chop them and add to the dish. Stir in the stock and dill.

Microwave on high for 5 minutes, or until the yams or sweet potatoes are just tender. Let stand for 4 minutes.

Transfer the mixture to a blender or food processor. Pour the milk into a 2-cup glass measure and microwave on high for 2 minutes, or until warm. Add to the blender or food processor and puree.

To freeze: Prepare the recipe as directed. Cool quickly, then ladle into freezer containers, leaving 1-inch headspace, and freeze. To serve, transfer the frozen soup to a double boiler over simmering water. Cover and warm over medium heat until heated through, stirring frequently. Add water if too thick. Or, microwave on medium until warm, about 8 to 9 minutes, stirring twice.

Yield: 4 servings

Creamy Tomatillo Soup

🌿

The combination of tomatillos, garlic, and cilantro gives this soup a unique Mexican flavor.

1 tablespoon margarine

1 cup chopped scallions

3 tomatillos, quartered

2 garlic cloves, minced

1½ cups low-sodium vegetable stock

¼ cup frozen lima beans, thawed

¼ cup chopped fresh cilantro

3 cups frozen corn, thawed

½ cup spicy vegetable cocktail juice

2 teaspoons brown sugar or 1 teaspoon honey

1 teaspoon lemon juice

Pinch of ground red pepper

In a 3-quart saucepan, over medium heat, melt the margarine. Add the scallions, tomatillos, and garlic; cook, stirring frequently, for 4 minutes. Stir in the stock, beans, cilantro, and 2 cups of the corn. Cook for 1 minute.

Working in batches, puree the mixture in a blender or food processor until smooth. Return the mixture to the pan. Stir in the vegetable juice, sugar or honey, lemon juice, pepper, and the remaining 1 cup corn. Simmer for 10 to 15 minutes to blend the flavors.

To freeze: Prepare the soup as directed. Cool quickly, then ladle into freezer containers, leaving 1-inch headspace, and freeze. To serve, transfer frozen soup to a saucepan, cover, and warm over low heat until heated through, stirring frequently. Or microwave on medium until warm, about 10 minutes, stirring at least once, and then on high until hot.

Yield: 4 servings

Chunky Tomato Soup

This tomato soup is full of herbs and low in salt.

2 leeks

2 large onions, diced

3 cloves garlic, minced

1 tablespoon olive oil

3 cups defatted chicken stock

2 cups diced tomatoes

1/2 cups minced fresh parsley

1/2 teaspoon dried thyme

1 bay leaf

2 teaspoons low-sodium soy sauce

2 teaspoons honey

Remove and discard the tough green leaves and root end of the leeks. Cut the leeks in half lengthwise. Wash well to remove any dirt from between the layers, then chop coarsely.

In a 3-quart saucepan, over medium heat, sauté the leeks, onions, and garlic in the oil for about 7 minutes, or until translucent. Add the stock, tomatoes, parsley, thyme, and bay leaf. Cover and simmer for 20 to 30 minutes. Discard the bay leaf. Stir in the soy sauce and honey.

To freeze: Prepare the recipe as directed. Cool quickly, then ladle into freezer containers, leaving 1-inch headspace, and freeze. To serve, transfer frozen soup to a saucepan. Cover and warm over low heat until heated through, stirring frequently. Or, microwave on medium until warm, about 10 minutes, stirring at least once, and then on high until hot.

Yield: 4 servings

Casseroles

Black Beans and Rice

This flavorful dish hints of Mexican fare.

1 tablespoon olive oil

2 sweet red peppers, finely chopped

1 large onion, finely chopped

1 stalk celery, finely chopped

2 cloves garlic, minced

¼ teaspoon dried thyme

2 cups cooked black beans

2 tablespoons apple cider vinegar

2 cups hot cooked rice

1 cup nonfat yogurt

Heat the oil in a large, no-stick frying pan. Add the peppers, onions, celery, garlic, and thyme. Sauté over medium heat for 10 minutes, or until the vegetables are fragrant and tender. Add the beans and vinegar. Cook for 3 minutes, or until the beans are hot. Divide the rice among shallow bowls. Top with the beans and yogurt.

To freeze: Cook and freeze the rice separately from the beans. Pack in freezer containers, leaving 1-inch headspace, and freeze. To serve, place frozen beans and rice in separate saucepans. Cover, and heat on low, adding a little water to the bottom of the pan to prevent sticking, until warm. Stir frequently. Or, sprinkle the rice with 4 tablespoons of water and microwave it on high for 4 to 7 minutes, stirring once. Stir again, cover, and let stand 1 minute. Microwave the bean mixture on medium until warm, stirring at least once, and then on high until hot.

Yield: 4 servings

Mexican Bean Pie

These flavorful individual pies make fast and fun dinners.

4 corn tortillas

½ cup sliced scallions

2 green peppers, diced

2 cloves garlic, minced

1 tablespoon olive oil

2 cups cooked pinto beans, mashed

2 tomatoes, chopped

2 teaspoons chili powder

1 teaspoon ground coriander

¾ cup egg substitute

¼ cup shredded low-fat Monterey Jack cheese

Heat the tortillas at 350°F for 5 to 8 minutes, or until crispy. Break into pieces, then pulverize in a blender. Coat four 5-inch-wide shallow baking dishes with no-stick spray. Cover with the tortilla crumbs and reserve any extra.

In a large no-stick frying pan, sauté the scallions, peppers, and garlic in the oil for 5 minutes, or until tender. Add the beans, tomatoes, chili powder, and coriander. Sauté for 5 minutes. Remove from the heat and stir in the egg substitute. Divide among the prepared pans. Sprinkle with the reserved crumbs. Bake at 375°F for 20 minutes. Top with the cheese.

To freeze: Prepare the recipe as directed but don't top with the cheese. Wrap with freezer wrap or foil or place in freezer bags and freeze. To serve, preheat oven to 375°F. Bake frozen pies for 30 to 40 minutes, or until heated through. Sprinkle with cheese.

Yield: 4 servings

Baked Broccoli

This cheesy broccoli will melt in your mouth.

3 to 4 cups broccoli

1 cup pearl onions

2 eggs, beaten

1 cup part-skim ricotta cheese

1 tablespoon minced scallions

Freshly ground black pepper, to taste

½ cup grated cheddar cheese

¼ cup bread crumbs

Trim the broccoli and peel the tough stalks. Parboil the broccoli and onions for 7 minutes, drain, and arrange in a 1½-quart, buttered baking dish. Mix the eggs, ricotta cheese, scallions, pepper, and ¼ cup of the grated cheese. Pour over the broccoli and onions. Sprinkle bread crumbs and the rest of the grated cheese over the casserole. Bake at 350°F for 45 minutes.

Yield: 6 to 8 servings

Classic Ratatouille

This is the perfect midsummer dish to try when eggplant, tomatoes, peppers, and basil are so plentiful. Make a double batch and freeze the extra.

¼ cup olive oil

2 medium onions, chopped

2 cloves garlic, minced

2 small eggplant, cut into 1-inch cubes

3 small zucchini, sliced

1 sweet red pepper, cored, seeded, and cut into ½-inch cubes

1 green pepper, cored, seeded, and cut into ½-inch cubes

2 stalks celery, thinly sliced

4 plum tomatoes, seeded and quartered

1 tablespoon fresh or ½ teaspoon dried basil

2 tablespoons packed, minced fresh parsley

1 teaspoon dried oregano

¼ teaspoon dried thyme

In a heavy frying pan, over medium heat, heat 2 tablespoons of the oil. Add the onions and garlic. Cook until soft, but not browned. Add the eggplant, zucchini, red peppers, green peppers, celery, and remaining oil. Cover and cook gently over low heat for 30 minutes.

Add the tomatoes, basil, parsley, oregano, and thyme. Cover and cook for 10 minutes, or until most of the liquid has evaporated and the mixture is thick.

To freeze: Prepare the recipe as directed. Cool quickly, then pack in freezer containers, leaving 1-inch headspace, and freeze. To serve, thaw the frozen ratatouille in the refrigerator. Place in a saucepan, cover, and warm over low heat until heated through, stirring frequently. Or, microwave on high until hot.

Variations: Ratatouille serves up beautifully in many ways. Reheat over low heat and try the following suggestions:
- *Use as a topping for whole wheat pizza; top with grated mozzarella cheese.*
- *Use in an omelet: Make a 4-egg omelet (4 eggs, 1½ tablespoons cold water, 2 tablespoons butter), and spoon ¾ cup heated ratatouille on top. Cook until the omelet is almost set. Fold or serve flat.*
- *Spoon heated ratatouille onto whole wheat toast and top with a poached egg. Garnish with chopped fresh tomatoes.*
- *Serve as a sauce over pasta.*
- *Serve warm or at room temperature in hollowed-out eggplant or zucchini shells, or on crackers or pita bread.*

Yield: 8 to 10 servings

Potato-Cheese Casserole

If you can't store all your potatoes in the cellar, this is one good way to freeze the extras.

12 medium potatoes

1/4 pound butter

1/4 cup low-fat milk

1/2 pound low-fat cream cheese, at room temperature

1/2 cup shredded cheddar cheese

1/2 cup grated Romano or Parmesan cheese

1 green pepper, chopped

1/2 cup snipped chives

1/4 cup pimiento

Freshly ground black pepper, to taste

Steam the potatoes until tender. Peel. Pulse in a food processor until almost pureed. Melt the butter; add the butter, milk, cream cheese, cheddar cheese, Romano or Parmesan cheese, green pepper, chives, pimiento, and pepper, and pulse until well combined. Pour into three 1-quart baking dishes and bake one or more, uncovered, in an oven preheated to 350°F for 1½ hours, or freeze unbaked.

To freeze: Prepare the recipe as directed. Wrap the casseroles in freezer wrap or foil, or place in freezer bags, and freeze. To serve, thaw one or more of the casseroles in the refrigerator and bake, uncovered, in an oven preheated to 350°F for 1½ hours, or until the top is browned and the mixture is bubbly.

Yield: 6 servings per casserole

Raspberries with Wild Rice

The sweet, tart flavor of raspberries blends well with wild rice.

1½ cups defatted chicken stock

3/4 cup wild rice

2 teaspoons canola oil

1/8 teaspoon dried marjoram

1 cup raspberries

2 tablespoons minced parsley

In a 1-quart saucepan, bring the stock to a boil. Transfer to the top of a double boiler. Add the wild rice, oil, and marjoram. Cover and cook over boiling water for 1 to 1½ hours, or until the liquid has been absorbed and the rice is tender. Transfer to a serving bowl. Fold in the raspberries and parsley.

Yield: 4 servings

Spinach Croquettes

Turn extra spinach into sandwich fillings or side dishes for now or later.

Yield: 5 croquettes

12 quarts young spinach leaves (lightly packed)

½ cup whole wheat bread crumbs

1 egg, beaten

1 small onion, chopped

½ teaspoon dried thyme

Dash of nutmeg

Vegetable oil

Wash the spinach until free of sand. Place the wet leaves in a saucepan, cover, and cook over medium heat for 4 to 6 minutes, or until tender. Chop coarsely.

In a large bowl, combine the spinach, crumbs, egg, onions, thyme, and nutmeg. Mix together and shape into 3-inch-round patties. In a frying pan, sauté the patties briefly on each side in the vegetable oil until light brown.

To freeze: Prepare the recipe as directed. Freeze the croquettes on a baking sheet until firm. Wrap the croquettes in freezer wrap or foil or place in a freezer bag with double sheets of freezer wrap between the patties. To serve, heat the frozen croquettes on a baking sheet for 25 minutes, or until heated through, in an oven preheated to 325°F.

Spinach-Pasta Casserole

If you have a quiet summer afternoon, make this delicious casserole ahead so you can just pop it in the oven on a busy day.

2 large onions, chopped

2 cloves garlic, minced

¼ cup vegetable oil

3 pounds lean ground beef

1 pint canned tomatoes, with juice

½ teaspoon ground cinnamon

⅓ cup plus ¼ cup butter

¼ cup mochiko rice flour*

1 quart low-fat milk

Dash of pepper

Dash of nutmeg

½ cup grated Parmesan cheese

6 cups uncooked elbow macaroni

3 eggs, slightly beaten

2 pounds spinach, cooked

1 pound cheddar cheese, shredded

Sauté the onions and garlic in oil until limp; add the beef and brown. Pour off the excess fat. Add the tomatoes and cinnamon. Set aside. Melt ⅓ cup of the butter, stir in the flour, and cook, stirring constantly, for several minutes. Add the milk, pepper, nutmeg, and Parmesan cheese, and stir until thickened. Set aside.

Cook the macaroni in boiling water. Drain and add the remaining $^1/_4$ cup butter and the eggs. In each of 2 shallow, 9-inch-square baking dishes, layer one-quarter of the macaroni, half of the meat mixture, half of the spinach, one-quarter of the cheddar cheese, one-quarter of the macaroni, half of the sauce, and one-quarter of the cheddar cheese. Bake at 375°F for 30 minutes.

To freeze: Prepare the recipe as directed. Wrap the unbaked casseroles in freezer wrap or foil or place in freezer bags, and freeze. To serve, preheat oven to 375°F. Bake the frozen casseroles for $1^1/_2$ hours, or until hot. Cover with foil after 15 minutes.

Traditional thickeners such as wheat flour, potato flour, and cornstarch will curdle in the freezer. Mochiko rice flour is the exception. It thickens without curdling at freezer temperatures. Look for it in Asian food markets.

Yield: 8 servings per casserole

Summer Vegetable Casserole

You can stock away a flavorful combination of fresh garden vegetables in one easy casserole.

2 tablespoons butter	4 teaspoons fresh parsley
1 cup corn	$^1/_8$ teaspoon pepper
1 cup diced zucchini	$^1/_3$ cup shredded cheddar cheese
1 cup diced fresh tomatoes	
$^1/_2$ cup diced green peppers	$^3/_4$ cup bread crumbs
$^1/_2$ cup diced onions	1 tablespoon grated Parmesan cheese
1 teaspoon dill weed	

Melt the butter in a large frying pan. Add the corn, zucchini, tomatoes, peppers, and onions and sauté for 10 minutes, or until tender. Season with the dill, parsley, and pepper. Mix the cheddar cheese and bread crumbs. Place one-third of the cheese mixture into the bottom of a $1^1/_2$-quart baking dish. Top with half of the vegetables. Repeat. Top with the remaining one-third of the cheese mixture and sprinkle with Parmesan cheese. Bake at 350°F for 30 minutes, or freeze.

To freeze: Prepare the recipe as directed. Wrap the casserole in freezer wrap or foil or place in a freezer bag, and freeze. To serve, thaw the frozen casserole in the refrigerator. Bake at 350°F for 30 minutes, or until the top turns light golden brown and the center is heated through.

Yield: 4 servings

Tomatoes au Gratin

This classic dish is made even better with your vine-ripened tomatoes.

Yield: 4 servings

4 large tomatoes

⅓ cup seasoned dry bread crumbs

2 tablespoons grated Parmesan cheese

2 tablespoons minced fresh parsley

1 tablespoon lemon juice

¼ teaspoon olive oil

¼ teaspoon garlic powder

Cut the tomatoes in half crosswise. Gently squeeze the pieces to remove the seeds and excess juice. Place the tomatoes cut side up in a small baking dish. Bake at 350°F for 10 minutes. In a small bowl, mix the bread crumbs, cheese, parsley, lemon juice, oil, and garlic powder. Carefully spoon the mixture over the tomatoes and into the cavities left by the seeds. Bake for 15 more minutes, or until the tomatoes are softened and the crumbs are lightly browned.

Giant Stuffed Zucchini

Here's an idea for the big zucchini that you forgot to pick while it was still young and tender.

1 egg

1 large clove garlic, crushed

½ cup whole wheat bread crumbs

1 giant zucchini, at least 1 foot long

1 tablespoon wheat germ

1 tablespoon vegetable oil

1 large onion, chopped

½ sweet red or green pepper, chopped

2 small carrots, diced

¼ pound any vegetables on hand—mushrooms, kohlrabi, green beans, or cucumbers

1 very ripe tomato, diced

3 tablespoons tomato paste

1 teaspoon ground oregano

1 teaspoon ground basil

¼ cup chopped walnuts

½ pound cheddar cheese, shredded

Preheat the oven to 350°F. Beat the egg with the garlic. Add the bread crumbs. Cut the zucchini in half lengthwise, scrape out the seed cavity, and sprinkle with wheat germ. Spread the egg mixture over the remaining cut surface. Place zucchini on a rack set over a pan of water and steam in the oven for 10 minutes.

In a large frying pan, heat the oil; sauté the onions, peppers, carrots, and on-hand vegetables until the onions are limp and transparent. Add the tomatoes, tomato paste, oregano, and basil. Drain.

Fill the zucchini shells with the vegetable mixture, top with the chopped walnuts, and cover with the cheese. Preheat the oven to 350°F and bake on a rack over a baking sheet for 35 minutes, or freeze.

To freeze: Prepare the recipe as directed. Freeze the filled zucchini halves on a baking sheet until firm. Wrap them in freezer wrap or foil or place them in freezer bags. To serve, thaw the zucchini in the refrigerator. Preheat the oven to 350°F. Bake thawed zucchini on a rack over a baking sheet for 35 minutes, or until the cheese melts and the zucchini is tender. Cut into thick slices to serve.

Yield: 4 servings as a main dish, or 8 servings as a side dish

Meals in Minutes

When you don't have time to stand over the stove, turn to this assortment of quick and easy dishes. Many can be made ahead and frozen, so they're ready when you need them. Just mix and match to make meals in minutes.

Apple-Cheese Muffins

If you like a slice of cheese on your apple pie, you'll love these moist, fruity muffins for breakfast.

3 medium baking apples	³/₄ cup honey
1 tablespoon lemon juice	1¹/₄ cups buttermilk
2 cups whole wheat flour	2 eggs
1 tablespoon baking powder	¹/₄ cup butter, melted
¹/₄ teaspoon ground cinnamon	
1¹/₂ cups cubed Colby or any medium-sharp cheese	

Peel, core, and cut the apples into chunks. Place them in a large bowl and cover with cold water. Stir in the lemon juice. Preheat the oven to 400°F. Butter a 12-cup muffin tin. Sift the flour, baking powder, and cinnamon into another large bowl. Mix in the cheese.

Drain the apples. Place the honey, buttermilk, eggs, butter, and apples in a food processor. Process with an on/off pulse motion until the apples are in small pieces. Pour into the dry ingredients and mix just until moistened. Fill each muffin cup three-quarters full, and bake for 20 minutes, or until a toothpick inserted into the center of the muffin comes out clean. Serve the muffins warm.

To freeze: Prepare the recipe as directed. Cool, seal the muffins in a freezer bag, and freeze. To serve, thaw the frozen muffins at room temperature for 45 minutes. Or, wrap muffins in foil and reheat in a 350°F oven for 15 minutes. You also can microwave a thawed muffin on high for 20 to 25 seconds or 30 to 60 seconds for 2 muffins. Or, microwave a frozen muffin for 45 to 60 seconds.

Yield: 12 to 15 muffins

Apples and Oat Cereal

Apples give your oatmeal a real lift and give you a healthy way to start the day.

Yield: 4 servings

4 cups water

1⅓ cups oat bran

½ cup raisins

1 apple, shredded

1 tablespoon maple syrup

½ teaspoon ground caraway seeds

½ teaspoon ground cinnamon

1 to 2 cups skim milk

In a 2-quart saucepan, bring the water and oat bran to a vigorous boil, stirring constantly. Reduce the heat to low and cook for 2 minutes, stirring frequently, until thick. Remove from the heat and stir in the raisins, apples, maple syrup, caraway, and cinnamon. Let stand for 5 minutes. Spoon into bowls and pour the milk over the cereal to serve.

Orchard Meat Loaf

Make meat loaf an extra-delicious and nutritious main course by adding your apples.

Yield: 6 servings

1¼ pounds extra-lean ground beef

1 cup rolled oats

1 large onion, diced

1 cup shredded apples

½ cup minced fresh parsley

¼ cup egg substitute

1½ teaspoons Worcestershire sauce

½ teaspoon dried basil

½ teaspoon dried oregano

¼ teaspoon hot pepper sauce

In a large bowl, combine the beef, oats, onions, apples, parsley, egg substitute, Worcestershire, basil, oregano, and hot pepper sauce. Coat a 9 × 5-inch loaf pan with no-stick spray. Add the meat mixture. Bake at 350°F for 1 hour, or freeze.

To freeze: Prepare the recipe as directed. Seal the baked or unbaked meat loaf in a freezer bag. To serve, bake the frozen, uncooked meat loaf uncovered at 350°F for 1½ hours, or until done. To serve cold, thaw the baked meat loaf, packaged, in the refrigerator. To reheat, unwrap and heat the frozen baked meat loaf in a 350°F oven for 1 hour.

NOTE: You also can freeze slices of baked meat loaf. To reheat, microwave a frozen slice on high until hot.

Veal in Apple-Lemon Sauce

Apples make a low-fat sauce for this lean main course.

1½ pounds veal scallops

½ cup whole wheat flour

4 large apples, cut into ½-inch slices

½ cup lemon juice

2 tablespoons olive oil

1 cup thinly sliced mushrooms

1½ cups defatted chicken stock

Pat the veal dry with paper towels. Place between sheets of wax paper and flatten with a mallet until about ⅛ inch thick. Dredge in the flour. Shake off the excess.

In a 2-quart saucepan, cook the apples in the lemon juice for 5 to 7 minutes, or until tender. Puree half of the apples in a blender. Reserve the remaining slices.

In a large no-stick frying pan, heat 1 tablespoon oil. Add the mushrooms and sauté for 5 minutes, or until tender. Remove with a slotted spoon and set aside. Add the remaining 1 tablespoon oil to the pan. Sauté the veal for 1½ minutes on each side. Remove the veal to a platter and keep warm.

Add the stock to the pan and bring to a boil, scraping the bottom of the pan to loosen browned bits. Lower the heat, add the apple puree, and cook for 2 to 3 minutes. Add the veal, mushrooms, and apples. Cook for 5 minutes.

To freeze: You can freeze the apple-lemon sauce. Prepare the sauce as directed. Cool, then pour the sauce into freezer containers, leaving ½-inch headspace, and freeze. To use, thaw the sauce in the refrigerator and add as the recipe directs.

Yield: 6 servings

Grilled Chicken and Artichoke Salad

This super summer salad abounds with the flavor of zesty greens.

2 bunches arugula

1 head radicchio

2½ cups alfalfa sprouts

12 artichoke hearts, halved

8 sun-dried tomatoes, sliced, or fresh cherry tomatoes, halved

1 sweet yellow pepper, thinly sliced

1 pound boneless, skinless chicken breasts

⅓ cup balsamic vinegar

2 tablespoons olive oil

1 tablespoon minced fresh basil or thyme

¼ teaspoon freshly ground black pepper

Divide the arugula, radicchio, sprouts, artichokes, tomatoes, and peppers among 4 serving plates. Set aside.

Grill or broil the chicken for about 5 minutes per side, or until cooked through. Slice as desired and place on the greens. In a small bowl, whisk together the vinegar, oil, basil or thyme, and pepper. Spoon over the salad.

Yield: 4 servings

Banana Pancakes

Use your extra bananas to make pancakes that need no extra syrup.

1⅓ cups whole wheat flour

1½ teaspoons baking powder

¾ cup cooked barley

½ cup skim milk

½ cup mashed bananas

2 egg whites

2 tablespoons maple syrup

1 tablespoon canola oil

2 tablespoons all-fruit preserves

2 bananas, sliced

2 cups orange segments

In a medium bowl, sift together the flour and baking powder. Stir in the barley. In a small bowl, whisk together the milk, mashed bananas, egg whites, and maple syrup. Pour the milk mixture into the flour. Mix until just moistened. Coat a no-stick frying pan with no-stick spray. Heat over medium-high heat. Add half of the oil. Spoon in ¼ cup of the batter for each pancake. Cook until bubbles form on the top, then flip, and cook the other side. Repeat with the remaining oil and batter.

Add the preserves to the frying pan. Stir to melt. Add the bananas and oranges. Heat for 2 to 3 minutes, occasionally flipping the pieces with a spatula. Serve over the pancakes.

Yield: 4 servings

Pesto Turkey

Inside these turkey cutlets, you'll find a pocketful of herbs and vegetables.

1½ cups basil leaves

4 cloves garlic, minced

⅓ cup olive oil

1 pound turkey cutlets

12 mushrooms, sliced

4 small tomatoes, sliced

2 tablespoons grated sapsago or Parmesan cheese

2 tablespoons chopped pine nuts

In a blender or food processor, process the basil and garlic until well chopped. With the machine running, add the oil in a stream. Process until a smooth paste forms.

Cut 4 large squares of foil. Coat one side with no-stick spray. Divide the cutlets among the foil. Spread each with 1 tablespoon of the basil pesto. Top with the mushrooms and tomatoes. Cover with the remaining pesto. Sprinkle with the cheese and pine nuts. Fold the foil to enclose the filling and seal tightly. Place the packets on a baking sheet. Bake at 375°F for 20 minutes.

To freeze: You can freeze the pesto. Prepare it as directed. Put the pesto in ice cube trays, and freeze. When frozen, put the pesto cubes into freezer containers for continued freezer storage. To serve, thaw in the refrigerator.

Yield: 4 servings

Nachos

This is a super-easy way to cook beans into a low-fat meal.

12 corn tortillas

1½ cups cooked pinto beans

1 cup salsa

1 cup minced sweet red peppers

½ cup shredded low-fat Monterey Jack cheese

Cut the tortillas into quarters. Place the pieces on a baking sheet, and bake at 400°F for 5 minutes, or until crisp but not brown. Let cool for a few minutes.

Coarsely mash the beans. Spread the beans on the tortillas and return them to the baking sheet. Dot with the salsa. Sprinkle with the peppers and cheese. Bake for 3 minutes, or until the cheese has melted. Serve warm.

VARIATION: Before the second baking, sprinkle the tortillas with minced jalapeño peppers or minced black olives.

Yield: 4 servings

Rotelle Pasta with Beans and Pecans

This dish is very easy to prepare—just whip up the sauce in a blender or food processor and toss it with the warm pasta and green beans.

1 cup nonfat ricotta cheese

⅓ cup skim milk

¼ cup chopped pecans

1 clove garlic, minced

½ teaspoon freshly ground black pepper

¼ teaspoon dried basil

8 ounces rotelle pasta

2 cups tender, young green beans

2 tablespoons grated Parmesan cheese

In a blender or food processor, process the ricotta, milk, pecans, garlic, pepper, and basil for 2 minutes, or until smooth. Set the sauce aside.

Cook the rotelle in a large pot of boiling water for 10 minutes, or until just tender. Drain and place in a large serving bowl. Meanwhile, steam the beans for 5 minutes, or until just tender. Add to the rotelle and toss lightly. Top with the sauce and toss well. Sprinkle with the Parmesan cheese.

VARIATION: For a richer flavor, toast the pecans before blending them. Watch carefully so they don't burn.

Yield: 4 servings

Berry-Peach Coffee Cake

For a great breakfast, use ripe peaches because they're so sweet. If they're not available, add extra honey to taste in the topping.

Topping

½ cup butter

1 cup whole wheat pastry flour

2 tablespoons honey

3 tablespoons rolled oats

1 teaspoon ground cinnamon

Cake

2 cups blueberries

1 tablespoon whole wheat pastry flour

¾ cup butter, softened

½ cup honey

1¾ cups whole wheat pastry flour

2 teaspoons baking powder

⅛ teaspoon nutmeg

4 eggs

1 cup sliced peaches

To make the topping: In a small saucepan, over medium heat, melt the butter. Remove from heat. Stir in the flour, honey, oats, and cinnamon. Set aside.

To make the cake: Preheat the oven to 325°F. Grease and flour a 13 × 9-inch pan. Clean and dry the blueberries. Toss the blue-berries with 1 tablespoon flour. Set aside. In a large bowl, with mixer set at medium speed, combine the butter and honey until light and fluffy. Reduce the speed to low. Add the flour, baking powder, nutmeg, and eggs. Beat until just blended, scraping the bowl occasionally. Increase the speed to medium and beat until smooth. Fold in 1¾ cups of the blueberries.

Spread the batter evenly in the prepared pan. Drop the topping by teaspoonfuls on top of the batter. Bake the cake for 20 minutes. Meanwhile, cut each peach slice in half. Quickly top the cake with the remaining ¼ cup of the blueberries and the peaches. Bake for 25 to 30 minutes longer, or until a toothpick inserted into the center comes out clean. Serve warm, or cool completely on a wire rack.

To freeze: Prepare the recipe as directed. Cool, wrap the pan with freezer wrap or foil or place in a freezer bag, and freeze. Or, cut the coffee cake into serving portions and wrap them individually. To serve, thaw the whole cake at room temperature for 3 hours or thaw the pieces for 30 minutes. If desired, you can warm the entire cake, covered, in a 350°F oven for about 25 minutes. Or, micro-wave thawed pieces on high for 20 seconds or frozen pieces for 45 to 60 seconds.

Yield: 16 servings

Blueberry Crumb Coffee Cake

This old-fashioned breakfast cake is sometimes called Krum Kuchen and is often baked in a piecrust, similar to shoo-fly pie and funny cake. Try it both ways—you may have a preference.

Yield: 8 servings

2 cups whole wheat pastry flour, sifted

½ cup butter, softened

½ cup plus 2 tablespoons honey

2 eggs, beaten

1 teaspoon baking soda

½ cup buttermilk

1½ cups fresh or thawed frozen blueberries

Preheat oven to 375°F. Butter an 8-inch-square baking pan. In a large bowl, combine the flour and butter, and mix into crumbs with a fork. Then add 2 tablespoons honey and blend. Take out 1 cup of crumbs and reserve. Add the eggs and the remaining honey.

In a small bowl, dissolve the baking soda in the buttermilk and stir into the flour mixture. Pour the batter into the prepared pan. Arrange the fruit on top, and cover with the reserved crumbs. Bake for 30 minutes, or until a toothpick inserted into the center comes out clean.

To freeze: Prepare the recipe as directed. Cool, wrap the pan with freezer wrap or foil or place in a freezer bag, and freeze. Or, cut the coffee cake into serving portions and wrap them individually. To serve, thaw the whole cake at room temperature for 3 hours or thaw the pieces for 30 minutes. If desired, you can warm the entire cake, covered, in a 350°F oven for about 25 minutes. Or, microwave thawed pieces on high for 20 seconds or frozen pieces for 45 to 60 seconds.

Baked Broccoli

Freeze your extra broccoli in this flavorful casserole so it's ready whenever company comes.

Yield: 6 to 8 servings

3 to 4 cups broccoli

1 cup pearl onions

2 eggs, beaten

1 cup ricotta cheese

1 tablespoon minced scallions

Freshly ground black pepper, to taste

1/2 cup grated cheddar cheese

1/2 cup bread crumbs

Butter (optional)

Trim the broccoli, and peel the tough stalks. Parboil the broccoli and onions for 7 minutes, drain, and arrange in a 1½-quart, buttered baking dish. Mix eggs, ricotta cheese, scallions, pepper, and ¼ cup grated cheese. Pour over the broccoli and onions. Sprinkle the bread crumbs and the rest of the grated cheese over the casserole. Bake at 350°F for 45 minutes.

To freeze: Prepare the recipe as directed. Cool, wrap in freezer wrap or foil or place in a freezer bag, and freeze. To serve, preheat oven to 350°F, dot the frozen casserole with butter, if desired, and bake, uncovered, for 1½ hours. Or let thaw overnight in the refrigerator and then bake as above.

Broccoli-Cheese Quiche

Quiches make very good freezer foods. Make several at a time so that you have an easy and convenient meal when you need it.

2 cups broccoli florets

1/2 cup chopped onions

1 cup cottage or ricotta cheese

1/4 cup buttermilk or yogurt

3 eggs, beaten

1/4 cup shredded Swiss cheese

Dash of freshly grated nutmeg

1 unbaked piecrust

Preheat oven to 400° F. Steam the broccoli and onions separately for 3 or 4 minutes, just until crisp-tender. Rinse with cold water, drain, and set aside.

Combine the cottage or ricotta cheese and buttermilk or yogurt in a blender or food processor on low speed. (To make a smooth mixture without a blender, the cheese can be pressed through a sieve.) Place the cheese mixture in a mixing bowl and add the beaten eggs, Swiss cheese, and dash of nutmeg. Place the onions in the bottom of the unbaked piecrust and pour the cheese mixture over them. Arrange the broccoli florets on top, pressing down into the cheese mixture. Bake at 400°F for 20 minutes, then reduce the heat to 350°F, and continue baking for 10 to 15 minutes more. The quiche should be puffed and browned. Serve hot or cold.

To freeze: Prepare the recipe as directed, but bake the quiche about 10 minutes less than the recipe calls for. Cool, then wrap in freezer wrap or foil or place in a freezer bag, and freeze. To serve, thaw the frozen quiche in the refrigerator. Then bake in a 350°F oven for 15 minutes.

Yield: 6 servings

Carrot Muffins

Carrots add moist, sweet flavoring and plenty of vitamin A to these breakfast muffins.

2 cups whole wheat flour

2/3 cup ready-to-eat bran flakes

2 teaspoons baking powder

1 teaspoon ground cinnamon

1/4 teaspoon grated nutmeg

1 1/2 cups skim milk

1 1/2 cups shredded carrots

1/2 cup raisins

1/4 cup egg substitute

1/4 cup honey

2 tablespoons canola oil

2 tablespoons molasses

In a large bowl, combine the flour, bran flakes, baking powder, cinnamon, and nutmeg. In a medium bowl, combine the milk, carrots, raisins, egg substitute, honey, oil, and molasses. Stir the liquid ingredients into the dry ingredients until just moistened. Don't overmix.

Coat 12 muffin cups with no-stick spray. Fill the cups about three-quarters full with the batter. Bake at 375°F for 20 to 25 minutes.

To freeze: Prepare the recipe as directed. Cool, seal the muffins in a freezer bag, and freeze. To serve, thaw the frozen muffins at room temperature for 45 minutes. Or, wrap muffins in foil and reheat in a 350°F oven for 15 minutes. You also can microwave a thawed muffin on high for 20 to 25 seconds or 30 to 60 seconds for 2 thawed muffins. Or, microwave a frozen muffin for 45 to 60 seconds.

Yield: 12 muffins

Sunburgers

Sunburgers are good served with sautéed mushrooms or shredded cheese, which melts when sprinkled over hot burgers.

1 cup ground sunflower seeds

½ cup finely chopped celery

2 tablespoons chopped onions or snipped chives

1 egg, beaten

1 tablespoon chopped green peppers

1 tablespoon chopped fresh parsley

½ cup grated carrots

1 tablespoon vegetable oil

¼ cup tomato juice

Pinch of basil

Preheat the oven to 350°F. Mix together all ingredients well. Add more tomato juice, if necessary, so that the patties hold a good formed shape. Arrange in an oiled, shallow baking dish, and bake for 10 minutes, or until browned. They can also be broiled if coated with oil on both sides before cooking.

To freeze: Prepare the recipe as directed. Cool, place patties in a freezer bag, and freeze. To serve, arrange the frozen patties on a baking sheet. Place in a 350°F oven, and heat for 25 to 30 minutes, or until hot throughout. Or, microwave on high for 3 to 4 minutes for 1 patty.

Yield: 5 patties,
3 inches in diameter

Cranberry Bread

Make a couple of extra loaves to freeze. You'll be glad you did when the winter holiday season approaches.

2 cups unbleached flour

1½ cups whole wheat flour

½ cup cornmeal

1 tablespoon baking powder

½ teaspoon ground cinnamon

½ teaspoon grated nutmeg

¾ cup finely chopped cranberries

1 teaspoon anise seeds

1½ cups nonfat yogurt

¼ cup buttermilk

¼ cup egg substitute

1 tablespoon honey

Sift the unbleached flour, whole wheat flour, cornmeal, baking powder, cinnamon, and nutmeg into a large bowl. Add the cranberries and anise seeds. In a medium bowl, combine the yogurt, buttermilk, egg substitute, and honey. Pour into the flour mixture. Mix well, using a large rubber spatula.

Turn the dough out onto a floured counter. With floured hands, shape into a 7-inch mound, smoothing out any cracks as you go. Coat a baking sheet with no-stick spray. Place the dough on the sheet. Use a sharp knife to slash an X in the top, about $1/2$ inch deep (to help keep the loaf from splitting raggedly as it rises). Sprinkle the top with a bit of unbleached flour. Bake at 450°F for 30 minutes, or until the bottom of the bread sounds hollow when tapped. Remove from the oven and let stand for 20 minutes before slicing. The bread is best served warm.

To freeze: Prepare the recipe as directed. Cool, place in freezer bags, and freeze. To serve, thaw the frozen loaf at room temperature for 2 or 3 hours, or wrap it in foil and heat in a 325°F oven for 15 to 25 minutes.

Yield: 1 loaf

Orange-Cilantro Fettuccine

These oriental flavors make an exciting meal out of spinach fettuccine.

1 cup orange juice

$1/2$ cup vegetable stock

$1/4$ cup chopped fresh cilantro

1 tablespoon grated orange peel

1 tablespoon cornstarch

1 tablespoon low-sodium soy sauce

2 teaspoons Dijon mustard

$1/2$ teaspoon powdered ginger

12 ounces fresh spinach fettuccine

2 tablespoons toasted sesame seeds

In a 2-quart saucepan, whisk together the juice, stock, cilantro, orange peel, cornstarch, soy sauce, mustard, and ginger. Bring to a boil over medium heat. Reduce the heat to low, and cook, stirring often, for 2 to 3 minutes, or until the sauce thickens. Keep warm over low heat.

Meanwhile, in a large pot of boiling water, cook the fettuccine for 3 to 5 minutes, or until tender. Drain and place in a large serving bowl. Toss with the orange sauce and sesame seeds.

Yield: 4 servings

Fava Beans with Tiny Pasta

Make this salad in the morning for a fast meal later.

Yield: 4 servings

3 carrots, thinly sliced

2 cups cooked fava beans

1 cup cooked acini di pepe or other tiny pasta

¼ cup snipped chives

3 tablespoons red wine vinegar

2 tablespoons olive oil

1 teaspoon dried basil

½ teaspoon dry mustard

Blanch the carrots in boiling water for 3 minutes. Drain and place in a large bowl. Add the drained favas, pasta, and chives. In a small bowl, whisk together the vinegar, oil, basil, and mustard. Pour over the salad. Toss well to combine. Allow the salad to marinate at least 2 hours before serving. Serve at room temperature.

Vegetable Lasagna

Eggplant freezes very well in this hearty dish.

½ pound lasagna noodles

1 small eggplant, peeled and sliced into ¼-inch rounds

2 tablespoons olive oil

1 small zucchini, sliced into ¼-inch rounds

3½ cups tomato sauce

2 teaspoons dried oregano

1 teaspoon dried basil

1 clove garlic, minced

1½ cups part-skim ricotta cheese

¼ cup grated Parmesan or dried ricotta cheese

Cook and drain the noodles. Spread them out in single layers so that they will not stick together while you prepare the remainder of the recipe. Preheat the oven to 350°F.

Brush the eggplant slices with oil, and broil until they are light brown and dry. Simmer the zucchini slices in the tomato sauce for 5 minutes, then add the oregano, basil, and garlic.

Oil an 8-inch-square baking dish with 1 tablespoon olive oil, and place a layer of noodles in the bottom. Add a layer of eggplant, then ¾ cup of the ricotta. Pour 1 cup of the tomato sauce over all. Repeat the layers. End with a layer of noodles, then 1½ cups of the tomato sauce. Dribble the remaining 1 tablespoon olive oil over the top, and sprinkle with the grated cheese. Bake for 30 minutes, or until bubbly. Let stand for 10 minutes. Cut into squares.

To freeze: Prepare the recipe as directed, but undercook the noodles slightly and don't sprinkle with grated cheese. Cool, wrap the unbaked casserole with freezer wrap or foil or place in a freezer bag, and freeze. To serve, bake the frozen casserole, covered, at 350°F for 1¼ to 1½ hours. Sprinkle with the cheese halfway through the baking time.

Yield: 6 to 9 servings

Garlic-Roasted Turkey Breast

Flavor turkey breast with the full flavor of roasted garlic.

1 skinless turkey breast (5 pounds)	4 carrots, cut into 3-inch sticks
12 cloves garlic, whole	1 cup defatted stock
1 teaspoon dried thyme	1 teaspoon dried rosemary
1 tablespoon flour	1 bay leaf
8 large mushrooms	

With a sharp knife, make 12 slits in the turkey breast. Fully insert a whole garlic clove into each slit. Rub the breast with the thyme. Place the flour in a large oven cooking bag. Shake to coat the inside of the bag with the flour. Place the turkey breast in the bag.

Arrange the mushrooms and carrots around the breast. Add the stock, rosemary, and bay leaf. Follow the manufacturer's directions for tying the bag and making slits for steam to escape. Place the bag in a roasting pan. Bake at 350°F for 1¼ hours, or to an internal temperature of 175°F. Discard the bay leaf. Serve the turkey breast with the vegetables.

To freeze: Prepare the recipe as directed but seal the turkey breast and vegetables in separate freezer bags. To serve, thaw the turkey breast in the refrigerator. Place it in a roasting pan. Cover with foil and heat in a 350°F oven for 40 to 50 minutes, or until thoroughly heated through. Thaw the vegetables and place them in a saucepan. Cover and warm over low heat until heated through, stirring occasionally.

NOTE: You can strip the turkey from the bones and cut it into large pieces before freezing to save on freezer space. If this is done, package the turkey pieces with the liquid in the cooking bag. Reheat the frozen pieces with the liquid, covered, for 45 to 60 minutes. Heat the vegetables as above. To reheat in a microwave, microwave the frozen pieces on high until hot. Reheat the vegetables separately.

Yield: 10 servings

Fettuccine with Grapes

You can make this aromatic pasta dish in less than 15 minutes.

Yield: 4 servings

8   scallions, julienned

¼   cup defatted chicken stock

2   cups red seedless grapes, halved

¼   teaspoon dried thyme

1¼   cups low-fat cottage cheese

¼   cup skim milk

2   tablespoons grated sapsago or Parmesan cheese

¼   teaspoon grated nutmeg

12   ounces fettuccine

¼   cup minced fresh parsley

In a large no-stick frying pan, sauté the scallions in the stock for 3 minutes. Add the grapes and thyme. Heat for 2 minutes. Set aside. In a food processor or blender, puree the cottage cheese, milk, sapsago or Parmesan, and nutmeg until smooth.

In a large pot of boiling water, cook the fettuccine until tender. Drain and place in a large serving bowl. Add the cheese mixture and grapes. Toss gently to combine. Sprinkle with the parsley.

Enchiladas with Cheese and Kale

Use vitamin-packed kale and scallions from your fall garden.

Yield: 4 servings

2   cups shredded kale

½   cup minced scallions

2   tablespoons olive oil

8   corn tortillas

1   cup shredded low-fat Monterey Jack cheese

1   cup salsa

In a large no-stick frying pan, over medium heat, sauté the kale and scallions in 1 tablespoon of the oil for 5 minutes, or until tender. Divide the mixture among the tortillas. Top with the cheese. Roll up each tortilla to enclose the filling.

Clean the frying pan and warm it over medium heat. Add the remaining oil. Place the enchiladas, seam side down, in the pan. Let brown for several minutes on each side. Add the salsa. Cover the pan, reduce the heat, and simmer for 5 minutes, basting frequently.

Warm Salmon Salad

Try this spicy and aromatic salad when you're in the mood for something different.

2 tablespoons low-sodium soy sauce

2 teaspoons peeled, minced ginger

1 teaspoon honey

2 cloves garlic, minced

1/8 teaspoon red pepper

8 ounces salmon fillet

2 tablespoons olive oil

2 tablespoons balsamic vinegar

2 tablespoons minced shallots

1 tablespoon lemon juice

About 8 cups kale, torn into bite-size pieces

2 sweet green peppers, julienned

1/3 cup defatted stock

In a 9 × 13-inch baking dish, whisk together the soy sauce, ginger, honey, garlic, and red pepper. Cutting on the bias, slice the salmon into 10 to 12 thin pieces. Add to the soy mixture, turning to coat each piece on both sides. Let stand for 15 minutes.

In a small bowl, whisk together the oil, vinegar, shallots, and lemon juice. Divide the kale among salad plates. Top with the peppers.

In a large no-stick frying pan, over medium-high heat, heat the stock. Add the salmon and cook 10 to 15 seconds per side. Add to the salad plates. Drizzle with the oil and vinegar dressing. Serve warm.

Yield: 4 servings

Yogurt Coffee Cake

Here is a moist and flavorful breakfast cake with a topping baked right into it!

Fruit

1½ cups fresh or frozen fruit such as sliced apples, blackberries, blueberries, cherries, cranberries, peaches, pears, raspberries, rhubarb, or strawberries, or 1 cup chopped dried fruit

Topping

2 tablespoons honey, warmed

2 teaspoons ground cinnamon

2 tablespoons whole wheat flour

¾ cup chopped nuts

Cake

½ cup butter, softened

½ cup honey, warmed

2 eggs

1⅓ cups whole wheat flour

1 teaspoon baking soda

1 cup yogurt

1 teaspoon vanilla extract

Preheat oven to 350°F. Butter and flour a 9-inch-square baking pan.

To make the topping: In a small bowl, combine the honey, cinnamon, flour, and nuts.

To make the cake: Cream the butter in a large bowl. Add the honey and eggs, and mix well. Sift together the flour and baking soda, and then fold into the batter along with the yogurt, vanilla, and dried fruit (if you're using it instead of fresh fruit). Pour half of the cake batter into the prepared pan. Cover with half of the topping and all the fresh or frozen fruit (if you're using it instead of dried fruit), then add the remaining batter. Top with the remaining topping. Bake for 45 minutes, or until a toothpick inserted into the center comes out clean. Cool slightly and cut into squares. Serve warm or cold.

To freeze: Prepare the recipe as directed. Cool, wrap the pan with freezer wrap or foil or place in a freezer bag, and freeze. Or, cut the coffee cake into serving portions and wrap them individually. To serve, thaw the whole cake at room temperature for 3 hours or thaw the pieces for 30 minutes. If desired, you can warm the entire cake, covered, in a 350°F oven for 25 minutes. Or, microwave the thawed pieces on high for 20 seconds or the frozen pieces for 45 to 60 seconds.

Yield: 8 servings

Onion-Cheese Turnovers

Buttery onions and cheese stand out in a pastry turnover.

1/4 pound butter

10 medium onions, sliced

2 tablespoons whole wheat flour

Paprika, to taste

Freshly ground black pepper, to taste

1 tablespoon poppy seeds

1/4 pound shredded cheddar cheese

Dough for two 9-inch piecrusts

Melt the butter in a large, heavy saucepan, and add the onions. Sauté until soft and juicy, and sprinkle with the flour. Remove from the heat and season with paprika, pepper, and poppy seeds. Fold in the cheese.

Roll out the pastry to an 1/8-inch-thick rectangle. Cut into ten 5-inch squares. Place 2 or 3 tablespoons of the onion mixture on half of each square. Moisten the edge and fold over the other half. Seal the edges with a fork. Place the turnovers on a baking sheet, and bake them at 425°F for 20 minutes, or until the pastry is browned.

To freeze: Prepare the recipe as directed but don't bake the turnovers. Wrap them with freezer wrap or foil and freeze immediately. When ready to serve, thaw in the refrigerator and bake as described above.

Yield: 10 turnovers

Basic Stir-Fry

This flavorful sauce will turn any combination of ingredients into a delicious stir-fry. Just make the sauce and toss in a selection of ingredients from the lists on the opposite page.

¼ cup water

2 tablespoons low-sodium soy sauce

2 tablespoons rice wine vinegar

2 teaspoons honey

1 teaspoon minced garlic

1 teaspoon sesame oil

1 teaspoon minced fresh ginger

2 teaspoons cornstarch

2 tablespoons water

2 teaspoons oil

Prepare a basic stir-fry sauce. In a 1-quart saucepan, combine water, low-sodium soy sauce, rice wine vinegar, honey, minced garlic, sesame oil, and minced fresh ginger. Bring to a boil, stirring constantly. Stir in the cornstarch that has been dissolved in the water. Cook, stirring, until the sauce is shiny and thick. Remove from the heat and set aside.

Select the ingredients you want to use in your stir-fry from each of the categories on the opposite page. Cut all ingredients into uniform, bite-size pieces. Arrange each category on a separate plate near the stove.

Heat a wok or large frying pan on medium-high heat for 1 minute. Add 1 teaspoon of oil, swirl to distribute, and let heat for 1 minute. Add a basic ingredient and stir-fry for 1 to 5 minutes, or until the food is lightly browned on the outside. Remove with a slotted spoon and set aside. Add 1 teaspoon oil to the pan and your choice of hearty vegetables. Stir-fry for 3 minutes, or until slightly tender. Immediately return the first ingredient to the pan along with your tender vegetables. Stir-fry for 1 minute. Add the reserved sauce and toppings. Toss all ingredients quickly to coat them with the sauce. Serve immediately.

Yield: 4 servings

MIX-AND-MATCH STIR-FRY INGREDIENTS

Of all the dishes we associate with oriental cuisine, stir-fry dishes seem most typical. They permit versatility in the diet and combine a generous amount of vegetables with just a small portion of meat. That gives you a very healthy balance of nutrients. You can take advantage of the speed, nutritiousness, and versatility of stir-fry cooking without having to rely on complicated recipes. Use the following lists to assemble your meal by choosing one ingredient from each section.

Basic Ingredient
(choose 8 ounces or about 1 cup)

Bay scallops

Beef, slivered

Chicken, cubed or slivered

Clams, shucked

Duck, slivered

Firm fish, cubed

Lamb, slivered

Oysters, shucked

Pork, slivered

Sea scallops, halved

Shrimp, peeled and deveined

Tofu, cubed

Turkey, cubed or slivered

Tender Vegetables
(choose 1 to 2 cups)

Bean sprouts

Bok choy leaves, shredded

Lettuce, shredded

Napa cabbage, shredded

Scallions, cut into matchsticks

Spinach or kale, shredded

Watercress, shredded

Hearty Vegetables
(choose 2 to 3 cups)

Asparagus, sliced diagonally

Bamboo shoots, julienned

Bok choy ribs, sliced diagonally

Broccoli, florets or stalks, julienned

Carrots, lightly steamed and julienned

Cauliflower florets

Celery, sliced diagonally

Daikon radish, julienned

Green beans, whole or sliced

Mushrooms, sliced

Onions, slivered

Peas

Snow peas

Sweet peppers, cubed or sliced

Water chestnuts, sliced into coins or quarters

Yellow squash, julienned or cubed

Zucchini, julienned or cubed

Toppings
(choose 2 tablespoons)

Almonds, roasted and slivered

Peanuts, chopped

Pine nuts

Scallions, chopped

Sesame seeds

Easy Peach Coffee Cake

This breakfast coffee cake is so beautiful you might hesitate to eat it!

1 cup whole wheat flour

1 cup unbleached flour

1 tablespoon baking powder

1/3 cup honey

1/4 cup maple syrup

3 tablespoons oil

2 tablespoons butter, softened

1 egg

1 teaspoon vanilla

3/4 cup skim milk

1 1/2 cups sliced peaches

Reserved fruit syrup

Sprinkle of ground cinnamon

Preheat the oven to 350°F. Coat a 9-inch-square pan with no-stick spray. Mix together the flours and baking powder. In a medium bowl, cream together the honey, maple syrup, oil, and butter. Stir in the egg and vanilla. Add the milk alternately with the dry ingredients. Spread half of the batter into the pan with a rubber spatula. Place 1 cup of peach slices in rows over the batter and cover with the remaining batter. Arrange the remaining peach slices in a circle on top of the batter, overlapping the slices. Bake for 40 to 45 minutes, or until a toothpick inserted into the center comes out clean. Immediately sprinkle with cinnamon, then cool on a wire rack. You can warm the reserved peach syrup and pour it over individual pieces of cake. Serve warm.

To freeze: Prepare the recipe as directed. Cool, wrap the pan with freezer wrap or foil or place in a freezer bag, and freeze. Or, cut the coffee cake into serving portions and wrap them individually. To serve, thaw the whole cake at room temperature for 3 hours or thaw the pieces for 30 minutes. If desired, you can warm the entire cake, covered, in a 350°F oven for 25 minutes. Or, microwave the thawed pieces on high for 20 seconds or the frozen pieces for 45 to 60 seconds.

VARIATION: *You can substitute peeled, sliced apples for the peaches. Or, if you'd like, serve the slices topped with apple butter.*

Yield: 12 servings

Fruited French Toast

Use fresh fruits in season to top whole grain French toast.

3 eggs

½ cup milk

½ teaspoon ground cinnamon

½ teaspoon vanilla extract

8 to 10 slices whole wheat bread

2 cups sliced peaches, red or black raspberries, blueberries, or strawberries

¼ cup maple syrup

Mint sprigs or sliced kiwi (garnish)

Place the eggs, milk, cinnamon, and vanilla in a blender. Process on medium speed until smooth. Pour the batter into a shallow bowl. One by one, dip the bread slices in the batter, turning to coat both sides. Cook the dipped bread slices in a frying pan sprayed with no-stick spray until golden brown on both sides. Keep the toast warm until all the pieces are done.

For the topping, combine the fruit with the maple syrup. Spoon it over the French toast when you serve it, or place the fruit topping in a bowl on the table. Garnish with mint sprigs or kiwi.

To freeze: Prepare the recipe as directed but don't add the topping. Cool, wrap the French toast in freezer wrap or foil or place in freezer bags, and freeze. To serve, heat the frozen toast in the toaster oven and serve as above.

Yield: 4 or 5 servings

East Indian-Style Black-Eyed Peas

Serve over cooked brown rice.

3 cups water

1 cup dried black-eyed peas (unsoaked)

1 onion, chopped

2 tablespoons unsweetened shredded coconut

¼ teaspoon turmeric

1 teaspoon honey

¼ teaspoon cumin

Bring the water to a boil. Add the remaining ingredients to the boiling water, and simmer for 1 hour and 10 minutes, or until most of the liquid is absorbed and the beans are tender.

To cook in a slow cooker, combine 2 cups of water and the unsoaked black-eyed peas in a slow-cooker pot. Add the remaining ingredients. Cover. Cook on low for 8 to 10 hours, or until the beans are tender and most of the liquid is absorbed.

Yield: 4 servings

Easy Stuffed Peppers

For a festive dinner, use a combination of colorful peppers, such as red, green, yellow, and orange.

4 large peppers

12 ounces ground turkey

1 cup finely chopped onions

1 teaspoon dried oregano

1½ cups cooked rice

¼ cup grated Parmesan cheese

¼ cup egg substitute

1 cup tomato sauce

Cut the peppers in half lengthwise. Remove and discard the stems and seeds. Blanch the peppers in boiling water for 3 minutes. Drain and set aside.

Crumble the turkey into a 2-quart casserole. Sprinkle with the onions and oregano. Cover with vented plastic wrap and microwave on high for 4 minutes, or until the turkey is cooked through and the onions are translucent. Carefully drain off any accumulated fat. Break up the turkey with a spoon and mix well.

Stir together the rice, Parmesan, egg substitute, and half of the tomato sauce. Divide the mixture among the pepper halves. Arrange the peppers in a 13 × 9-inch baking dish. Top with the remaining tomato sauce. Cover loosely with wax paper. Microwave on high for 6 minutes. Rearrange the peppers and give the dish a half turn. Cover and microwave on high for 6 minutes.of

To freeze: Prepare the recipe as directed. Wrap the baking dish in freezer wrap or foil, or place in a freezer bag, and freeze. To serve, bake the frozen peppers at 350°F, covered, for 1 hour, or until heated through.

VARIATION: This is a good way to use up leftover cooked rice. You may also replace the rice with an equal amount of cooked bulgur, couscous, or millet.

NOTES: If your microwave can't accommodate a 13 × 9-inch baking dish, divide the peppers between two smaller pans. Microwave each pan for a total of 6 minutes.

If you don't have a microwave, brown the turkey and onions in a no-stick frying pan. Mix with the remaining stuffing ingredients and fill the peppers. Arrange in a baking dish, top with the tomato sauce, and cover with foil. Bake at 350° for about 30 minutes.

Yield: 4 servings

Linguine with Sweet Peppers

Let your peppers ripen until they're sweet and red for this recipe.

Yield: 4 servings

1 large onion, sliced
1 bay leaf
1 tablespoon olive oil
2/3 cup defatted chicken stock
3 sweet red peppers, thinly sliced
1 cup sliced mushrooms
4 cloves garlic, minced
1/2 cup minced fresh parsley
1 teaspoon dried basil
1/2 teaspoon dried thyme
1/2 teaspoon dried oregano
4 ounces linguine

In a large no-stick frying pan, sauté the onions and bay leaf in the oil for 5 minutes, or until translucent. Add the stock, peppers, mushrooms, garlic, parsley, basil, thyme, and oregano. Simmer, uncovered, for 5 to 7 minutes, or until the peppers are soft and the liquid has reduced somewhat. Remove the bay leaf.

In a large pot of boiling water, cook the linguine until just tender. Drain and add to the pan with the vegetables. Toss to combine.

Shrimp and Roasted Peppers

Make this festive dish ahead and refrigerate it until you need it.

Yield: 4 servings

1 pound large shrimp
3 sweet red peppers
1 tablespoon snipped chives
1 tablespoon balsamic vinegar
1 tablespoon olive oil
2 cups shredded kale

Steam the shrimp in their shells for 3 minutes, or until they turn bright orange. When cool enough to handle, remove the shells. Slice each shrimp in half lengthwise, removing the vein as you go. Roast the peppers under a broiler until charred on all sides. Set aside until cool enough to handle. Remove the charred skins, seeds, and inner membranes. Slice the peppers into strips.

In a large bowl, combine the shrimp, peppers, chives, vinegar, and oil. Arrange the kale on a serving platter. Place the shrimp mixture on top. Serve chilled.

Snapper with Red-Pepper Salsa

Roasted red peppers have a fabulous, full flavor.

3 sweet red peppers

¼ cup minced fresh parsley

2 tablespoons minced fresh coriander

3 scallions, minced

2 tablespoons lemon juice

1 tablespoon canola oil

½ teaspoon hot pepper sauce

1½ pounds red snapper fillets

Roast the peppers under a broiler until charred on all sides. Set aside until cool enough to handle. Discard the charred skin, seeds, and inner membranes; dice the peppers. Transfer to a bowl.

Add the parsley, coriander, scallions, lemon juice, oil, and hot pepper sauce to the roasted peppers. Set aside. Place the fish in a steamer basket. Steam over boiling water for 7 to 8 minutes, or until the fish flakes easily with a fork. Serve topped with the salsa.

NOTE: *You can freeze the salsa. Put it in a freezer container, leaving ½-inch headspace, and freeze. When ready to use, thaw it in the refrigerator.*

Yield: 4 servings

Broccoli-Potato Frittata

This is a good way to enjoy your frozen broccoli in the middle of winter.

3 tablespoons butter or olive oil

1 cup diced cooked potatoes

10 ounces frozen chopped broccoli, thawed and drained (or 1¾ cups chopped fresh broccoli)

¼ cup chopped scallions

1 small clove garlic, minced

6 eggs

3 tablespoons water

1 tablespoon minced parsley

3 tablespoons grated cheddar or Parmesan cheese

Melt the butter in a large oven-proof frying pan. Add the potatoes, broccoli, scallions, and garlic. Cover and cook for 7 to 10 minutes, stirring occasionally. Preheat the broiler.

Beat the eggs with the water; add the parsley. Pour into the frying pan. Cook over low heat until the bottom is set and lightly browned. Run a spatula around the edge of the frittata to let the uncooked egg run to the bottom. Slip the pan under the broiler and cook until the top is puffed and golden. Sprinkle with the grated cheese and broil to melt.

Yield: 4 servings

Savory Potato Crust

This easy potato-based crust is suitable for almost any entrée filling. It's quicker to make than a standard crust and contains fewer calories.

Yield: 1 crust

3 medium potatoes, finely shredded

¼ cup egg substitute

1 tablespoon canola oil

1 tablespoon flour

Coat a 9-inch pie plate with no-stick spray. Add the potatoes. In a small bowl, combine the egg substitute, oil, and flour. Pour over the potatoes, and pat the mixture in the bottom of the pan and up the sides to form a crust.

Broil about 8 inches from the heating element for 15 minutes, or until browned.

VARIATION: *Add 2 tablespoons minced onion or 2 teaspoons dried herbs—such as oregano, marjoram, or basil—to the potatoes. Or, replace the oil with ¼ cup shredded low-fat cheese.*

Jasmine Chicken with Strawberry Coulis

Use sweet, fully ripe strawberries straight from the garden.

Yield: 4 servings

2 cups water

1 cup defatted chicken stock

3 jasmine-flower tea bags

1 pound boneless, skinless chicken breasts

2 cups strawberries

2 tablespoons evaporated skim milk

In a 2-quart saucepan, bring the water and stock to a boil. Add the tea bags. Cover, remove from the heat, and let steep for 15 minutes. Remove the tea bags.

Cut the chicken into 1-inch strips. Add to the pan and simmer for 10 minutes. Remove the saucepan from the heat, and let the chicken cool in the tea. Remove with a slotted spoon to a serving platter.

In a food processor or blender, puree the strawberries. Stir in the milk. Serve as a sauce with the chicken.

Pecan Waffles in Strawberry Sauce

Here's a special way to use your homemade apricot juice at breakfast time.

Waffles

³/₄ cup whole wheat flour

³/₄ cup unbleached flour

1¹/₂ cups chopped pecans

1¹/₄ cups apricot nectar

¹/₂ cup egg substitute

¹/₄ cup maple syrup

2 tablespoons canola oil

Sauce

2 cups sliced strawberries

¹/₂ cup apricot nectar

2 tablespoons maple syrup

To make the waffles: In a large bowl, sift together the whole wheat flour, unbleached flour, and baking powder. Stir in the pecans. In a medium bowl, whisk together the nectar, egg substitute, maple syrup, and oil. Pour the liquid ingredients over the flour mixture. Mix until just moistened.

Heat a waffle iron, and lightly brush the grids with oil. Pour in enough batter to cover two-thirds of the bottom grids. Bake according to the manufacturer's directions, but start checking for doneness after 3 minutes. Repeat until the batter is used up; occasionally brush the grids with oil to prevent sticking.

To make the sauce: Place the strawberries, nectar, and maple syrup in a food processor. Process with on/off pulses until smooth. Drizzle the sauce over the waffles.

To freeze: Prepare the recipes as directed. Place the waffles into freezer bags, and freeze. Ladle the sauce into freezer containers, leaving ¹/₂-inch headspace, and freeze. To serve the frozen waffles, heat them in a toaster or in a 375°F oven on a baking sheet until hot. Thaw the sauce in the refrigerator, and serve as above.

Yield: 4 to 6 servings

The 20-Minute Pizza

This homemade pizza is more than delicious. It's wholesome, healthy, and ready in less time than it takes to have a pie home-delivered.

½ cup lukewarm water (about 110°F)

1 tablespoon canola oil

1 teaspoon quick-rise active dry yeast

½ teaspoon honey

1¼ cups whole wheat flour

¼ teaspoon garlic powder

¼ teaspoon onion powder

½ cup thick tomato sauce

1 cup shredded part-skim mozzarella cheese

In a large bowl, combine the water, oil, yeast, and honey. Stir to dissolve the yeast. Add the flour, garlic powder, and onion powder. Mix thoroughly. Let the dough rest for 5 minutes. Coat a 12-inch pizza pan with no-stick spray. Place the dough on it and shape into an 11-inch round. Spread on the sauce, leaving a ½-inch border. Sprinkle with the cheese. Bake at 475°F for 12 minutes.

To freeze: Prepare the recipe as directed, but bake the crust separately—without tomato sauce—for 7 minutes. Let it cool. Then spread on the pizza toppings, and cover with wax paper. Wrap in freezer wrap or foil, or place in a freezer bag, and freeze. To serve, unwrap and bake in a 475°F oven for 15 to 20 minutes, or until the cheese is bubbly.

VARIATIONS: *Make a Hawaiian pizza by topping the tomato sauce with unsweetened pineapple (crushed and drained), halved seedless grapes, and raisins.*

Or, replace the tomato sauce in the basic recipe with Mexican salsa. Top with sliced hot peppers and shredded low-fat Monterey Jack cheese.

For a dessert pizza, omit the tomato sauce and top the crust with sliced fruit, chopped nuts, and a mild cheese, such as low-fat Muenster or Havarti.

Yield: 1 pizza, 12 inches in diameter

NOTE: *Don't freeze toppings like raw mushrooms or tofu, or they can lose quality. Wait to add these during the last 10 minutes of baking.*

Broccoli-Tofu Pizza

Here's pizza with an oriental taste.

Yield: 1 pizza, 12 inches in diameter

2 cups fresh chopped broccoli

1 cup pizza sauce

Whole wheat pizza shell (page 271)

1 purple onion, sliced

1 cup tofu, drained and cut into ½-inch chunks

2 cups shredded cheddar cheese

Steam the broccoli for 2 minutes. Drain well and cool. Spread the pizza sauce on the pizza shell. Top with the onion, tofu, cheese, and broccoli. Preheat the oven to 475°F. Place the pizza directly on the oven rack. Place a pan underneath the rack to catch the drippings. Bake for 15 minutes until the cheese is melted and the crust is golden.

Pizza Mexicali

This pizza hails from Mexico.

½ pound lean ground beef

¼ teaspoon ground cumin

½ teaspoon dried oregano

1 clove garlic, minced

5 teaspoons chili powder

1 cup Mexican Tomato Salsa (page 287)

Whole wheat pizza shell (page 271)

1 small onion, sliced

½ cup minced fresh or frozen green peppers

2 cups shredded cheddar cheese

In a medium frying pan, brown the beef and drain well. Add the cumin, oregano, garlic, and chili powder, and cool. Spread the salsa on the shell. Top with the meat mixture, onions, peppers, and cheese. Preheat the oven to 475°F. Place pizza directly on the oven rack. Place a pan underneath the rack to catch the drippings. Bake for 15 minutes until the cheese is melted and the crust is golden.

To freeze: Prepare the recipe as directed, but bake the crust separately—without the salsa—for 7 minutes. Let it cool. Then spread on the pizza toppings, and cover with wax paper. Wrap in freezer wrap or foil or place in a freezer bag, and freeze. To serve, unwrap and bake in a 475°F oven for 15 to 20 minutes, or until the cheese is bubbly.

Yield: 1 pizza, 12 inches in diameter

Pizza Primavera

This pizza calls for an assortment of garden-fresh vegetables.

Yield: 1 pizza, 12 inches in diameter

2 cups shredded zucchini

²/₃ cup sliced carrots

1 cup bite-size pieces cauliflower

1 small clove garlic, minced

2 scallions, including tops, finely chopped

2 teaspoons minced fresh or 1 teaspoon dried mint

1 tablespoon grated Parmesan cheese

³/₄ cup pizza sauce

2 cups shredded mozzarella cheese

Whole wheat pizza shell (page 271)

Blanch the zucchini, carrots, and cauliflower separately for 2 minutes each. Drain well and cool. Lightly toss them with the garlic, scallions, mint, and Parmesan cheese. Spread the sauce on the shell. Top with the vegetable mixture and the mozzarella cheese. Preheat the oven to 475°F. Place the pizza directly on the oven rack. Place a pan underneath the rack to catch the drippings. Bake for 15 minutes until the cheese is melted and the crust is golden.

Sausage-Stuffed Zucchini Wheels

The blend of mellow zucchini and spicy sausage makes a great combination.

Yield: 6 servings

3 medium zucchini

8 ounces lean Italian turkey sausage, casing removed

¹/₂ cup whole wheat bread crumbs

¹/₄ cup shredded low-fat Swiss cheese

2 tablespoons minced fresh parsley

1 tablespoon chopped toasted pine nuts

¹/₄ teaspoon grated nutmeg

Cut off ¹/₂ inch from each end of the zucchini. Using a small spoon or apple corer, remove the pulp and seeds, leaving a ¹/₄-inch-thick shell. Reserve the pulp. Roll paper towels into cylinders and insert one through each zucchini to absorb the moisture. Chill the zucchini with the paper towel in place while preparing the stuffing.

In a large frying pan, crumble the sausage and cook until browned. Drain on paper towels. Transfer the sausage to a food processor. Add the bread crumbs, cheese, parsley, pine nuts, nutmeg, and reserved pulp. Process until well mixed. Remove the paper towels from the zucchini. Stuff with the sausage mixture, packing it in tightly. Chill the zucchini for 1 hour. To serve, cut each zucchini into ¹/₄-inch slices.

Sauces

Applesauce or Pear Sauce

Try some of your homemade applesauce or pear sauce fresh and warm. It's great!

12 medium apples or 16 medium pears

1 cup water

¼ cup lemon juice (optional)

½ cup honey

Ground cinnamon, to taste

Ground cloves, to taste

Ground nutmeg, to taste

Wash and core the apples or pears. Peel, if desired. Cut into chunks or slices. In a large, heavy stainless steel or enamel pot, cook the fruit with the water, lemon juice, honey, cinnamon, cloves, and nutmeg for 20 minutes, or until the fruit is tender. Drain in a colander. Put through a food mill or sieve, if desired.

To can: Pour the sauce into hot, scalded half-pint jars, leaving ½-inch headspace. Seal and process for 15 minutes in a boiling-water bath.

To freeze: Prepare the recipe as directed. Cool the sauce, then ladle into freezer containers, and freeze. To serve cold, thaw the sauce completely in the refrigerator. To serve warm, partially thaw in the refrigerator, then warm in a covered saucepan over medium heat, stirring frequently. Or microwave on high until warm.

Yield: 5 half-pints

Healthy Bean Dips

Beans are low in fat and high in fiber, which helps make a little go a long way when it comes to appeasing your appetite.

Beans Florentine

1 cup cooked Great Northern beans

2 tablespoons chopped cooked spinach (squeezed dry)

½ teaspoon dried thyme

½ teaspoon onion powder

Creole Bean Dip

1 cup cooked red beans

2 tablespoons finely chopped green peppers

2 tablespoons minced tomatoes

5 drops hot pepper sauce

Curried Pea Spread

1 cup cooked split peas

½ to 1 teaspoon curry powder

If cooking your own beans, make sure they're very soft so you can mash them easily. Drain the beans but save at least ½ cup of the cooking liquid. If using canned beans, drain them and reserve all the liquid. Place the beans in a strainer, and rinse under cold water to remove excess sodium. Transfer the beans to a blender or food processor. Process them until smooth, adding only enough liquid to facilitate blending. Stir in the listed condiments and spices. Serve your spreads on toasted pita chips, whole grain crackers, corn tortillas (cut into sixths and toasted), or crudités.

To freeze: Prepare the recipes as directed. Pack into freezer containers, leaving ½-inch headspace, and freeze. To serve, thaw in the refrigerator overnight. Or, microwave on medium until thawed. Correct seasonings.

VARIATION: *If you want to try combinations of your own, use approximately 2 teaspoons of seasonings plus 2 tablespoons of condiments or chopped vegetables for each cup of beans.*

Yield: About 1 cup for each dip

Halifax Blueberry Sauce

Serve over cheese-cake, ice cream, or yogurt.

½ cup currant jelly

2 tablespoons water

2 tablespoons honey

2 teaspoons lemon juice

½ teaspoon ground cinnamon

Freshly grated nutmeg, to taste

2 tablespoons mochiko rice flour*

4 cups blueberries

In a medium saucepan, combine the jelly, water, honey, lemon juice, cinnamon, nutmeg, and flour. Place over medium heat and simmer, stirring constantly, for 5 minutes, or until thick and syrupy. Remove from heat. Add the blueberries and stir until coated.

To freeze: Prepare the recipe as directed. Cool, then pour into freezer containers, and freeze. To serve, partially thaw the frozen sauce in the refrigerator. Place it in a saucepan, and cook over low heat for 15 minutes, or until the mixture is heated through. Or, microwave on medium until thawed, then on high until heated through.

Traditional thickeners such as wheat flour, potato flour, and cornstarch will curdle in the freezer. Mochiko rice flour is the exception; it thickens without curdling at freezer temperatures. Look for it in Asian food markets.

Yield: 4 cups

Carrot Spread

Try this spread on muffins or pumpkin bread.

2 cups shredded carrots

2 cups apple juice

2 tablespoons honey

2 tablespoons lemon juice

1 tablespoon grated lemon rind

In a 2-quart saucepan, combine the carrots, apple juice, honey, lemon juice, and lemon rind. Simmer over medium heat, stirring frequently, for 30 to 45 minutes, or until thick. Store in a tightly closed container in the refrigerator.

Yield: About 1½ cups

Jubilation Sauce

Serve over cheesecake, custard pie, or ice cream.

2 tablespoons cranberry juice concentrate, thawed

2 teaspoons lemon juice

¼ cup honey

¼ teaspoon almond extract

2 tablespoons mochiko rice flour*

4 cups sour cherries

In a medium bowl, whisk together the cranberry juice concentrate, lemon juice, honey, almond extract, and flour. Blend well. Stir in the cherries. Cook over medium heat for 5 to 7 minutes, or until the sauce thickens, stirring occasionally.

To freeze: Combine the ingredients as directed but don't cook. Pour into small freezer containers, leaving ½-inch headspace, and freeze. To serve, partially thaw the frozen cherries and place them in a saucepan. Cook over medium heat, stirring occasionally, for 7 minutes, or until the cherries thaw and the liquid resembles thick syrup. Or, microwave partially thawed cherries on high until warm and thickened, stirring occasionally.

*Traditional thickeners like wheat flour, potato flour, and cornstarch will curdle in the freezer. Mochiko rice flour is the exception; it thickens without curdling at freezer temperatures. Look for it in Asian food markets.

Yield: 3 cups

Dill Butter

Try this on potatoes, cabbage, fish, and pasta.

3 tablespoons finely chopped fresh dill

2 tablespoons finely chopped scallions

1 tablespoon finely chopped fresh parsley

¼ cup butter, softened

1 teaspoon lemon juice

Mix together all the ingredients, and store in the refrigerator until ready to use.

To freeze: Prepare the recipe as directed. Pack into small freezer containers, and freeze. To serve, thaw frozen butter in the refrigerator.

VARIATION: *Make basil butter by mixing 3 cups finely chopped fresh basil leaves with ½ cup softened butter. Add 2 teaspoons lemon juice to keep the basil a bright green.*

Yield: ⅔ cup

Dill Pesto

This is delicious served as a dip for carrot sticks.

3 cloves garlic, halved

1 tablespoon chopped lemon rind

1 3/4 cups chopped parsley

1/3 cup chopped fresh dill

1/4 cup olive oil

2 teaspoons lemon juice

In a food processor or blender, process the garlic and lemon rind until minced. Add the parsley and dill. Process until finely minced, stopping to scrape down the sides of the container as needed.

With the motor running, slowly add the oil and blend until a smooth paste is formed. Blend in the lemon juice. Spoon into a serving dish to serve as a dip for carrots.

To freeze: Prepare the recipe as directed. Put the pesto in ice cube trays, and freeze. When frozen, transfer the pesto cubes into freezer containers for continued freezer storage. Or, freeze in 1/2-cup portions (enough for 4 servings of pasta) in freezer containers, leaving 1/2-inch headspace. To serve, thaw in the refrigerator, allowing about 6 hours. Or, microwave on medium until thawed.

Yield: About 1 cup

Garlic Dill Butter

This spread is lovely when used on garlic bread, as a sauce for fish, or when tossed with steamed vegetables.

6 cloves garlic, whole

1/2 cup butter, softened

1 tablespoon finely chopped fresh dill

Dash of paprika

In a small saucepan, combine the garlic with water to cover. Bring to a boil, reduce heat, and simmer for 10 minutes. Strain, let cool, and slip the skins off the garlic. Crush the garlic through a press. In a food processor or blender, combine the garlic, butter, dill, and paprika. Process until well combined, and store in the refrigerator until ready to use.

To freeze: Prepare the recipe as directed. Pack in small freezer containers, and freeze. To serve, thaw the frozen butter in the refrigerator.

Yield: About 2/3 cup

Tangy Horseradish Dressing

Serve this over fresh greens or on a roast beef sandwich.

Yield: About 1⅓ cups

1 cup low-fat cottage cheese

1 cup nonfat yogurt

3 tablespoons snipped chives

2 tablespoons prepared horseradish

In a blender or food processor, process the cottage cheese until very smooth. Transfer to a medium bowl. Whisk in the yogurt, chives, and horseradish.

Italian Salad Dressing Mix

Blend the herbs now and use them later.

Yield: About 1½ cups

¾ cup dried oregano

6 tablespoons dried basil

3 tablespoons onion powder

1 tablespoon dry mustard

4 teaspoons garlic powder

4 teaspoons paprika

2 teaspoons freshly ground black pepper

Combine the ingredients. Store in an airtight container. Use 1 tablespoon of this mixture for each cup of liquid ingredients in seasonings, sauces, and dressings.

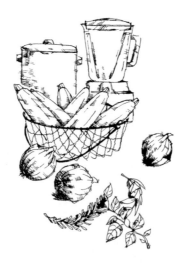

Italian Salad Dressing

This dressing never fails on a salad or submarine sandwich.

Yield: 2 cups

1½ cups unrefined oil, preferably part olive

¼ cup apple cider or wine vinegar

¼ cup lemon juice

2 tablespoons Italian Salad Dressing Mix (page 279)

Combine the ingredients in a 1-quart jar. Cover and shake well to blend. To allow the flavors to further meld, place the dressing in the refrigerator for at least 4 hours, then move to room temperature just before serving.

Lemon Vinaigrette

The refreshing taste of lemon goes well with any salad.

Yield: ½ cup

1 clove garlic, minced

2 tablespoons fresh lemon juice

8 tablespoons olive oil

¼ teaspoon ground cinnamon

¼ teaspoon paprika

Dash of cayenne pepper

Freshly ground black pepper, to taste

In a small bowl, stir together the garlic and lemon juice. Gradually whisk in the oil. Add the cinnamon, paprika, cayenne, and pepper.

THE MANY VERSIONS OF VINAIGRETTE

Vinaigrette is the traditional French salad dressing. A simple combination of olive oil, wine vinegar, mustard, and a dash of freshly ground black pepper, it may be seasoned to suit your taste. Always dress and toss a green lettuce salad at the last minute. Rinse and thoroughly dry the greens so the dressing can cling to the leaves. With salads that improve from marinating—such as bean, cooked-vegetable, or grated-vegetable salads—add the dressing ahead of time, toss, and chill until needed. Store vinaigrette in a tightly sealed glass container in the refrigerator.

Here's a basic vinaigrette and a bowlful of variations.

Basic Vinaigrette

$^1/_2$ cup olive oil

3 to 4 tablespoons red or white wine vinegar

$^1/_2$ teaspoon Dijon mustard

Dash of freshly ground black pepper

Combine all the ingredients and stir well before spooning a small amount over a salad.

VARIATIONS:

For garlic vinaigrette, add 1 garlic clove, minced, to the basic recipe.

For balsamic vinaigrette, substitute balsamic vinegar for the wine vinegar in the basic recipe.

For cider vinaigrette, substitute 2 tablespoons apple cider vinegar for the wine vinegar in the basic recipe (apple cider vinegar is stronger in flavor, so you need less).

For tomato vinaigrette, add 2 or 3 tablespoons tomato juice to the basic recipe.

For shallot vinaigrette, add 1 tablespoon finely minced shallots to the basic recipe.

For three-mustard vinaigrette, reduce the Dijon mustard in the basic recipe to ¼ teaspoon. Add ¼ teaspoon tarragon mustard or green-pepper mustard and ½ teaspoon coarse mustard.

For parsley vinaigrette, add 1 tablespoon minced fresh parsley to the basic recipe. Add garlic, if desired.

For lean vinaigrette, reduce the oil to ⅓ cup and use ¼ cup rice wine vinegar. Season as desired.

Yield: $^1/_2$ to $^2/_3$ cup

Savory Pear Spread

Use this sweet and tangy spread on pancakes, waffles, and muffins.

Yield: About 2 cups

5 ripe pears, chopped

2 tablespoons lemon juice

2 tablespoons honey

1 tablespoon peeled grated ginger

1 tablespoon apple cider vinegar

1/4 teaspoon ground allspice

1/2 teaspoon ground cinnamon

1/4 teaspoon grated nutmeg

In a 2-quart saucepan, combine the pears, lemon juice, honey, ginger, vinegar, allspice, cinnamon, and nutmeg. Cook over low heat for 30 to 40 minutes, or until the pears are very tender. In a food processor or blender, process the mixture until chunky. If the mixture is not thick, return it to the saucepan, and stir over medium heat until the desired thickness is reached. Store in a tightly closed container in the refrigerator.

Green Pepper Pesto

Peppers make a lovely pesto to serve on pasta.

Yield: About 1 1/4 cups

2 green peppers, chopped

1 cup fresh basil

1/2 cup pumpkin seeds

1/4 cup grated Parmesan cheese

1/4 cup olive oil

4 cloves garlic, minced

Blanch the peppers in boiling water for 5 minutes. Drain and transfer to a food processor. Add the basil, pumpkin seeds, cheese, oil, and garlic. Process until smooth.

To freeze: Prepare the recipe as directed. Put the pesto in ice cube trays, and freeze. When frozen, transfer the pesto cubes to freezer containers for continued freezer storage. Or, freeze 1/2-cup portions (enough for 4 servings of pasta) in freezer containers, leaving 1/2-inch headspace. To serve, thaw in the refrigerator, allowing about 6 hours. Or, microwave on medium until thawed.

Herbed Pepper Sauce

Try this Italian sauce on roasted chicken or pork or on pasta.

2 large sweet red peppers, chopped

1 large onion, chopped

1 tablespoon olive oil

1 clove garlic, minced

1 cup defatted chicken stock

1 teaspoon dried oregano

½ teaspoon dried basil

½ teaspoon dried savory

In a large no-stick frying pan, over medium heat, cook the peppers and onions in the oil for 10 minutes, or until soft and lightly browned. Add the garlic, and stir for 1 minute. Add the stock, oregano, basil, and savory. Cover and simmer for 10 minutes. Using a slotted spoon, transfer the vegetables to a blender or food processor. Add enough liquid to facilitate blending. Puree to desired consistency.

To freeze: Prepare the recipe as directed. Cool, then ladle into freezer containers, leaving ½-inch headspace, and freeze. To serve, place the frozen sauce in a saucepan, cover, and simmer over low heat, stirring occasionally. Correct the seasonings. Or, microwave the frozen sauce on high until heated through.

Yield: 2½ cups

Spiced Pineapple Sauce

Spoon over cheesecake or custard, or heat gently and serve over ice cream.

¼ cup honey

½ cup Refrigerator Apricot Jam (page 104)

4 teaspoons lemon juice

½ to 1 teaspoon ground cardamom

¼ teaspoon ground ginger

⅛ teaspoon ground nutmeg

1 fresh pineapple, chopped

In a small bowl, stir together the honey, jam, lemon juice, cardamom, ginger, and nutmeg. Pour the mixture over the pineapple and toss.

To freeze: Prepare the recipe as directed. Pack in freezer containers, leaving ½-inch headspace, and freeze. To serve, thaw completely in the refrigerator, and serve as above. Or, microwave on medium until thawed.

Yield: 5 cups

Creamy Raspberry Dressing

Use this on fruit salads. It's especially good over cantaloupe.

Yield: 2 cups

1 cup nonfat yogurt

1 cup raspberries

¼ teaspoon grated orange rind

¼ teaspoon grated lime rind

¼ teaspoon dried basil

Line a strainer with cheesecloth. Add the yogurt and allow it to drain over a bowl for 30 minutes. Transfer to a medium bowl. Puree the raspberries in a blender or food processor. Fold into the yogurt. Add the orange rind, lime rind, and basil. Combine well.

Rhubarb Sauce

This is a terrific topping for fresh fruit, ice cream, and cakes.

Yield: 4 cups

2 cups orange juice

1 cup honey

½ to 1 teaspoon ground cinnamon

4 cups rhubarb, cut in ½-inch slices

½ cup currants or golden raisins

Bring the orange juice, honey, and cinnamon to boil in a large saucepan. Add the rhubarb and currants. Cook, stirring, for 5 to 10 minutes, or until the rhubarb is tender and liquid is syrupy. Serve warm or cool.

To freeze: Prepare the recipe as directed. Cool, then pour into small freezer containers, and freeze. To serve, partially thaw the frozen sauce in the refrigerator. Transfer to a saucepan, cover, and simmer over low heat until heated through, stirring occasionally. Or, microwave on high until heated through.

Rosemary Pesto

Toss rosemary pesto with angel's hair pasta.

1 clove garlic

1/2 cup fresh oregano leaves

2 tablespoons fresh rosemary leaves

1 tablespoon grated orange rind

1 cup chopped scallions

1/4 teaspoon red-pepper flakes

1/4 cup olive oil

1 tablespoon red wine vinegar

With a food processor running, put the garlic, oregano, rosemary, and orange rind through the feed tube. Stop the processor and scrape down the sides of the container.

With the machine running again, add the scallions and pepper flakes, then the oil and vinegar. Stop and scrape down the sides of the container. Continue processing with on/off turns until the rosemary is well minced and the mixture has formed a paste.

To freeze: Prepare the recipe as directed. Put the pesto in ice cube trays, and freeze. When frozen, transfer the pesto cubes into freezer containers for continued freezer storage. Or, freeze in 1/2-cup portions (enough for 4 servings of pasta) in freezer containers, leaving 1/2-inch headspace. To serve, thaw in the refrigerator. Or, microwave on medium until thawed.

Yield: 1/2 cup

Spinach and Raisin Sauce for Pasta

Spinach and pasta have a great affinity for each other. Raisins and spinach provide an especially good contrast of flavors and textures.

1 medium onion, chopped

2 cloves garlic, minced

1 tablespoon olive oil

8 mushrooms, thickly sliced

4 leaves fresh basil, chopped, or ½ teaspoon dried basil

4 quarts spinach (lightly packed), coarsely chopped

¼ cup golden raisins

2 tablespoons butter, softened

¾ cup shredded mozzarella cheese

Freshly ground black pepper

In a 4- to 6-quart saucepan, over medium heat, cook the onions and garlic in oil. When the onion begins to soften, add the mushrooms and basil. Cook for a few minutes until the mushrooms become limp. Stir in the spinach and raisins. Cover the pan and lower the heat. Simmer for 5 to 7 minutes, or until the spinach is tender. Toss with pasta, adding the butter and the shredded cheese. Grind the pepper over all and serve hot.

To freeze: Prepare the recipe as directed but don't add the butter, cheese, and pepper. Cool, then pack into freezer containers, leaving ½-inch headspace, and freeze. To serve, thaw the frozen sauce in the refrigerator. Place it in a saucepan, cover, and warm over low heat until heated through. Or, microwave on high until warm. Serve as above.

NOTE: *Combine with ½ pound, cooked, whole wheat spaghetti to serve as a first course or main course for a light lunch. But this sauce cooks quickly; you can begin boiling the water for the spaghetti before making the sauce. When the spaghetti is cooked, drain it quickly but thoroughly.*

Yield: About 1 cup

Mexican Tomato Salsa

Keep a container in the freezer to serve with beans and tortillas or Spanish omelets. If you want this sauce hot, leave the seeds in the chili peppers as you mince them.

2 tablespoons olive oil

½ cup finely chopped onions

½ cup minced celery

2 tablespoons minced sweet green or red peppers

2 tablespoons minced hot chili peppers

1 clove garlic, finely chopped

4 medium tomatoes, seeded and chopped

2 tablespoons fresh lime juice

1 teaspoon honey

½ teaspoon dried basil or rosemary

¼ teaspoon dried coriander

¼ teaspoon cumin seeds

¼ teaspoon chili powder, or to taste

In a large frying pan, heat the oil. Add the onions, celery, sweet and hot peppers, and garlic. Cook for 5 minutes, stirring occasionally. Stir in tomatoes, lime juice, honey, basil or rosemary, coriander, cumin seeds, and chili powder. Bring to a boil. Reduce heat to low; cover and simmer for 20 minutes.

To freeze: Prepare the recipe as directed. Cool, then ladle into small freezer containers, and freeze. To serve, place frozen salsa in a saucepan, cover, and simmer over low heat, stirring occasionally. Or, microwave on medium until thawed, then on high until heated through. Correct the seasonings, if needed.

Yield: 5 cups

Spicy Aurora Sauce

This sauce goes well with corn chips and pasta. Or, use it as a gourmet topping for hamburgers.

1 onion, chopped

1 sweet red pepper, chopped

1 tablespoon canola oil

4 cups chopped tomatoes

1 jalapeño pepper, seeded and minced

2 cloves garlic, chopped

1 teaspoon dried oregano

1 cup dry-curd cottage cheese

3 tablespoons grated sapsago or Parmesan cheese

In a large no-stick frying pan, over medium heat, sauté the onions and red peppers in the oil for 5 minutes, or until soft. Add the tomatoes, jalapeño peppers, garlic, and oregano. Cover and cook for 5 minutes, or until the tomatoes are soft and juicy. Remove the cover and cook, stirring occasionally, for 15 minutes.

Transfer to a food processor. Add the cottage cheese and puree for 2 minutes, or until the mixture is pink and no longer looks curdled. Return the mixture to the frying pan, add the sapsago or Parmesan, and reheat briefly. Serve immediately. (To reheat leftovers, use either very low heat or a double boiler.)

Yield: 3 cups

Tomato Paste

Super-condense your tomato harvest into rich, dense tomato paste.

About 42 medium tomatoes

$^3/_4$ cup apple cider vinegar

Wash, peel, and chop the tomatoes. In an 8-quart stainless steel or enamel saucepan, bring the tomatoes to a boil and simmer gently, uncovered, for 1 hour. Remove from heat. Put the tomatoes through a food mill. Discard the seeds, and bring the juice and pulp back to a boil. Boil for 6 hours, or until the tomato mixture is thick and stays on a spoon, stirring occasionally to prevent sticking. Stir in the vinegar and remove from heat.

To freeze: Prepare the recipe as directed. Cool, then spoon the tomato paste into ice cube trays, and freeze. When frozen, transfer the cubes to freezer containers for continued freezer storage. Or, pack the paste in freezer containers, leaving $^1/_2$-inch headspace, and freeze. To serve, thaw in the refrigerator, or microwave on medium until thawed.

Yield: 3 cups

Tomato Sauce

Sweet garden-ripened tomatoes make a fabulous sauce.

About 25 Italian plum tomatoes

1 tablespoon olive oil

1 onion, chopped

1 clove garlic, crushed

1 tablespoon chopped green peppers

2 tablespoons finely chopped carrots

2 tablespoons finely chopped celery

2 tablespoons finely chopped parsley

1 teaspoon oregano

1 bay leaf

Freshly ground black pepper, to taste

1/4 cup lemon juice (if canning)

Loosen the tomato skins by plunging the tomatoes into boiling water for 1 minute, then under cold running water. Remove the skins. Cut the tomatoes into chunks.

Alternatively, you can just wash and core the tomatoes and puree them in a food processor. Although a bit messy, you save yourself the bother of skinning—and you save some of the tomatoes' nutrients. If you like chunky sauce, spare a few tomatoes from the processor, and skin them as above.

Heat the oil in a large, heavy enamel or stainless steel pot, and sauté the onions and garlic. Stir in the green peppers, carrots, celery, and tomatoes; add the parsley, oregano, bay leaf, and black pepper. Simmer, uncovered, for 1 to 2 hours, until thickened, stirring occasionally. Remove the bay leaf.

To can: Add the lemon juice, and pour the sauce into hot, scalded half-pint jars, leaving 1/2-inch headspace. Seal and process in a boiling-water bath for 35 minutes.

To freeze: Prepare the recipe as directed. Cool, then ladle into freezer containers, leaving 1/2-inch headspace, and freeze. To serve, partially thaw the frozen sauce in the refrigerator. Put it in a saucepan, cover, and warm over low heat until thawed, stirring occasionally. Or, microwave on medium until warmed, and then on high until hot, if needed.

Yield: 4 half-pints

Tomato-Zucchini Sauce

This lovely vegetable pasta sauce freezes well.

2 tablespoons olive oil

1 tablespoon butter

3/4 cup chopped onions

1 small sweet red or green pepper, seeded and chopped

1/4 cup chopped carrots

1/4 cup chopped celery

1 clove garlic, minced

2 cups crushed tomatoes

1/2 teaspoon crumbled rosemary

1 teaspoon fresh marjoram

1 bay leaf

3 tablespoons chopped parsley

1/4 cup defatted chicken stock or water

3 medium zucchini, thinly sliced

In a medium stainless steel or enamel saucepan, heat the oil and butter. Add the onions, peppers, carrots, and celery. Sauté for 5 to 8 minutes until soft. Add the garlic and sauté 1 minute. Add the tomatoes, rosemary, marjoram, bay leaf, parsley, and stock or water. Bring to a boil. Reduce heat, cover, and simmer for 25 to 30 minutes. Stir in the zucchini. Cook, covered, for 5 to 7 minutes. Remove the bay leaf before serving.

To freeze: Prepare the recipe as directed. Remove the bay leaf, then cool and ladle the sauce into freezer containers, leaving 1/2-inch headspace, and freeze. To serve, partially thaw the frozen sauce in the refrigerator. Put it in a saucepan, cover, and warm over low heat until heated through, stirring occasionally. Or, microwave on medium until warm, and then on high until hot, if needed.

Yield: About 2 1/2 cups

Jellies, Jams, and Fruit Butters

Apple Butter

Apple butter is a great way to concentrate a large harvest into a few jars of exceptional flavor.

3 cups apple cider

15 medium apples, unpeeled and uncored, sliced thin

Honey (optional)

Ground allspice (optional)

Ground cinnamon (optional)

Ground cloves (optional)

Put the cider in a large enamel or stainless steel pot, and bring to a boil. Add the apples slowly, being careful not to splatter yourself. Allow the apples and cider to come to a boil, then simmer, stirring frequently to prevent sticking.

When the apple butter has begun to thicken considerably, the apple slices will start to fall apart as you stir the butter. When this happens, remove it from the heat, and put everything through a food mill, discarding the peels, seeds, and stems. Put the remaining soupy mixture back into the pot, put the pot back on the heat, and simmer until the apple butter is a thick, dark brown mass. This last part will take 4 to 5 hours. If you want to sweeten the apple butter, use honey and sweeten to taste. You may also want to add spices such as allspice, cinnamon, and cloves to your apple butter. If so, add them to taste.

You can also cook down the butter in the oven or in a slow cooker. After pureeing it, put it in a large roasting pan and cook, uncovered, in the oven at 325°F until thick. Stir occasionally. To use a slow cooker, cook, uncovered, on high for 10 hours, stirring occasionally and pushing the outer edges into the middle.

To can: Once the apple butter is of the desired thickness, bring the mixture to a boil, and pour the apple butter into hot, scalded half-pint jars, leaving a 1/2-inch headspace. Seal and process for 5 minutes in a boiling-water bath.

Yield: 4 half-pints

Apple Jelly

This is the simplest of jellies because apples make their own pectin.

15 medium apples

3 cups honey

Wash the apples. Remove the stems and dark spots. Quarter the apples but do not pare or core. Add just enough water to half cover the apples, and cook in an enamel or stainless steel saucepan until the fruit is soft. Drain, using a jelly bag. You'll get more juice if you squeeze the bag, but it will make the jelly cloudy. Measure 6 cups of the juice. Add ½ cup honey for every cup juice. Boil until a good jelly test is obtained (page 106).

To can: Pour into hot, scalded half-pint jars, leaving ¼-inch headspace. Seal and process for 5 minutes in a boiling-water bath.

VARIATIONS: For apple-mint jelly, add a few mint leaves that have been washed (about ¼ cup mint leaves to 1 quart juice) and a bit of natural green food coloring just before removing the apple jelly from the heat. Stir, remove the leaves, and process as above. This makes an attractive and delicious jelly to serve with lamb.

For apple-cinnamon jelly, drop a stick of cinnamon into each jar before processing.

Yield: 5 half-pints

Black Cherry Conserve

This conserve is good to spread on breakfast breads or to use as a filling for pastries.

4 cups sweet cherries

2 medium navel oranges, peeled, seeded, and chopped (½ cup juice and pieces)

½ cup honey

½ cup lemon juice

2 tablespoons grated orange rind

¾ teaspoon ground cinnamon

6 whole cloves

In a large enamel or stainless steel saucepan, combine the cherries, oranges, honey, lemon juice, rind, and cinnamon. Put the cloves into a cheesecloth bag and add to the saucepan. Bring to a boil, then turn down, and simmer for 20 minutes. Bring back to boil for 4 or 5 minutes, or until thickened.

To can: Pour into hot, scalded half-pint jars, leaving ¼-inch headspace. Seal and process for 15 minutes in a boiling-water bath.

Yield: 3 half-pints

Cherry-Berry Jam

꙰

Raspberries provide the predominant flavor in this multifruit jam, which can be made from all frozen fruits.

Yield: 6 half-pints

3 cups fresh or frozen blueberries, pureed

3 cups fresh or frozen cherries, pureed

2 cups fresh or frozen raspberries, pureed

$^3/_4$ cup apple juice

$4^1/_2$ tablespoons lemon juice

1 cup plus 2 tablespoons honey

Combine the blueberries, cherries, raspberries, apple juice, and lemon juice in an 8-quart enamel or stainless steel saucepan. Place over high heat and stir until the mixture comes to a boil. Add the honey and continue stirring. When the mixture comes to a full boil, begin timing for 25 minutes. The jam is ready when it resembles thick, sticky syrup.

To can: Pour into hot, scalded half-pint jars, leaving $^1/_4$-inch headspace. Seal and process for 5 minutes in a boiling-water bath.

Cranapple Jelly

꙰

The tangy taste of cranberries makes this jelly special.

Yield: 8 half-pints

4 cups cranberries

3 cups water

8 cups diced, unpeeled, and uncored green apples

1 cup cranberry juice

3 cups apple juice

$^1/_2$ cup honey

1 tablespoon lemon juice

Wash the apples and cranberries. Remove the apple stems and dark spots. Cut into quarters but don't peel or core the apples. In 2 enamel or stainless steel saucepans, boil the cranberries in 1 cup of the water for 10 minutes while you boil the apples in the other 2 cups of water for 15 minutes. Strain each through a jelly bag. Combine the strained cranberry and apple juices with the honey and lemon juice in a large enamel or stainless steel pot. Cook for 18 to 20 minutes or until a good jelly test is obtained (page 106).

To can: Ladle into hot, scalded half-pint jars, leaving $^1/_4$-inch headspace. Seal and process for 5 minutes in a boiling-water bath.

Cranberry Butter

Try cranberry butter on muffins or sliced sweet potatoes.

Yield: 3 half-pints

5 cups cranberries

1/3 cup apple juice

1/2 cup maple syrup

1/2 cup sugar

1/4 teaspoon ground cinnamon

In a large enamel or stainless steel pot, combine the cranberries and juice and cook for 20 minutes, or until the cranberries burst and are soft. Puree the cranberries in a blender or food processor. Put the cranberries back into the pot, and add the maple syrup, sugar, and cinnamon. Cook for 10 to 15 minutes, or until thick.

To can: Spoon into hot, scalded half-pint jars, leaving 1/2-inch headspace. Seal and process for 10 minutes in a boiling-water bath.

Concord Grape Conserve

When you're tired of grape jelly, try this interesting conserve.

Yield: 4 half-pints

7 cups grapes, washed and stemmed

1/2 cup honey

1/2 cup pecans, coarsely chopped

1/2 cup raisins

1/4 whole lemon, seeded and very thinly sliced

Freeze the grapes, then dip them into cool water. The skins will slip off the grapes easily. Do not discard the skins. Bring the pulp to a boil in an enamel or stainless steel saucepan, and simmer over low heat until the seeds are loosened. Press the pulp through a colander and/or a strainer to remove the seeds. Combine the pulp, grape skins, honey, pecans, raisins, and lemon in the saucepan. Simmer over low heat to plump the raisins.

To can: Pour into hot, scalded half-pint jars, leaving 1/4-inch headspace. Seal and process for 15 minutes in a boiling-water bath.

Salvation Jam

This jam's name comes from Salvia, the Latin name for sage, which means "salvation."

Yield: 3 half-pints

4 cups peeled, pitted, and finely chopped nectarines

1 package powdered fruit pectin

2 tablespoons lemon juice

1 cup honey

12 large leaves of pineapple sage, torn into small pieces

In a large enamel or stainless steel saucepan, combine the nectarines, pectin, and lemon juice. Heat over medium-high heat until the fruit begins to soften. Mash the fruit. Bring to a rolling boil. Stir in the honey. Tie the pineapple sage leaves in a cheesecloth bag, and put the bag into the fruit mixture. Bring again to a rolling boil. Cook, stirring constantly, for 3 to 5 minutes, or until the mixture resembles a thick syrup. Remove the pineapple sage bag.

To can: Pour the jam into hot, scalded half-pint jars, leaving 1/4-inch headspace. Seal and process for 5 minutes in a boiling-water bath.

Baked Peach Butter

This is an easier way to make great peach butter.

Yield: 3 half-pints

12 cups peeled, pitted, and sliced peaches

4 cups water

3 tablespoons lemon juice

1/4 cup honey or sugar to taste

Place the sliced peaches and water in an 8-quart enamel or stainless steel pot, and cook over medium heat for 20 to 25 minutes, or until the peaches are soft. Stir frequently to prevent the peaches from sticking. When the fruit is tender, add the honey and lemon juice, and stir to combine. Put the peach mixture through a food mill, or put it in a blender or food processor and blend until smooth.

Divide and pour the puree into two shallow 9 × 13-inch baking pans or roasting pans, and bake uncovered for 1 hour at 325°F. Continue baking, stirring every 15 to 20 minutes, until the butter is thick. This will take approximately 1 to 1 1/2 hours. The peach butter will be thick, fine-textured, and a rich reddish amber color.

To can: Ladle into hot, scalded half-pint jars, leaving 1/2-inch headspace. Seal and process for 5 minutes in a boiling-water bath.

Peach Jam

This is faster than Baked Peach Butter (page 295) but tastes sweeter and only slightly less flavorful.

16 medium fully ripened fresh peaches, washed, peeled, and pitted

¼ cup fresh lemon juice

2 packages powdered fruit pectin

2 cups sugar

Chop or coarsely grind the peaches, blending them with the lemon juice. Measure the prepared fruit, packing it down in a cup. You should have 4 full cups. Place the fruit in a 6- to 8-quart enamel or stainless steel saucepan. Add the pectin and mix well.

Bring to a boil over high heat, stirring constantly. When the fruit is boiling, stir while slowly pouring in the sugar. Continue stirring and return to a full rolling boil. When boiling cannot be stirred down, boil for 2 more minutes. Remove from heat. Alternately stir and skim foam off for 5 minutes to cool slightly.

To can: Pour into hot, scalded half-pint jars, leaving ¼-inch headspace. Seal and process for 5 minutes in a boiling-water bath.

To freeze: Prepare the recipe as directed. Ladle into freezer containers, leaving ½-inch headspace, and allow to cool in the refrigerator for 10 hours before freezing. To serve, thaw in the refrigerator.

Yield: 3 half-pints

Persimmon Jelly

This unusual jelly makes a great gift.

68 ripe native persimmons

2 cups water

3 tablespoons lemon juice

1 package powdered fruit pectin

½ cup honey

Wash the persimmons and remove the blossom ends. Place in a 6- to 8-quart enamel or stainless steel saucepan, and add the water. Bring the mixture to a boil. Mash the persimmons. Reduce the heat, and simmer for 10 minutes. Remove from heat. Press the pulp through a strainer to remove the pits. Measure 3 cups of the pulp. Stir in the lemon juice and pectin and return to the saucepan. Bring the mixture to a boil. Stir in the honey all at once. Let the mixture return to a full rolling boil that can't be stirred down. Boil for 1 to 2 minutes, stirring constantly, or until a good jelly test is obtained (page 106). When firm enough, can as for Peach Jam above.

Yield: 3 half-pints

Plum-Honey Preserves

You can use these preserves for spreading on breads or on oriental egg rolls or spare ribs.

Yield: 2 half-pints

16 medium red or purple plums (not prune plums), slightly underripe, or a mixture of underripe and fully ripe plums

1 cup mild-flavored honey

Use a heavy-bottom, 6- to 8-quart enamel or stainless steel pot, preferably one that is wider than deep. Pit the plums, and cut them into large chunks, working over the pot to catch the juices. Stir in the honey. Bring to a boil over low heat, stirring frequently. When the mixture looks soupy, increase the heat and bring to a full rolling boil. Skim off the solid white foam. Continue to stir slowly, but not vigorously, for 15 to 20 minutes, or until the mixture becomes translucent and slightly darker. It will feel thicker when stirred and will thicken further as it cools.

To can: Pour into hot, scalded half-pint jars, leaving $1/4$-inch headspace. Seal and process for 10 minutes in a boiling-water bath.

Quince Marmalade

The name "marmalade" probably is derived from marmelo, the Portuguese word for quince.

Yield: 4 half-pints

4 medium quinces, peeled, cored, and finely chopped in a food processor

1 cup apple juice

1 cup chopped apples

$1/2$ cup honey

In a large pot, combine all the ingredients, and boil gently, covered, for $2^1/2$ hours. Uncover and simmer for 30 more minutes.

To can: Pour into hot, scalded half-pint jars, leaving $1/4$-inch headspace. Seal and process for 10 minutes in a boiling-water bath.

Raspberry Jelly with Homemade Pectin

Apples add flavor and pectin to this jelly.

Yield: 6 half-pints

5 cups homemade apple pectin (page 101)

1½ cups honey

1 cup raspberry juice

In a large enamel or stainless steel saucepan, stir together the apple pectin, honey, and raspberry juice. Bring to a boil over high heat for 18 minutes, stirring constantly, until syrupy and a good jelly test is obtained (page 106).

To can: When firm enough, ladle into hot, scalded half-pint jars, leaving ¼-inch headspace. Seal and process for 5 minutes in a boiling-water bath.

Honey-Strawberry Jam

This jam is not as stiff as those made with sugar. Its loose texture is a delightful change, and it's really good over ice cream!

Yield: 4 half-pints

4 cups stemmed and thoroughly crushed strawberries

2 tablespoons lemon juice

1 package powdered fruit pectin

1¾ cups honey

Combine the berries and lemon juice in a 6- to 8-quart enamel or stainless steel saucepan. Mix the pectin into the fruit. Place over high heat, and stir until the mixture comes to a boil. Immediately add the honey, and stir until the mixture comes to a full rolling boil that cannot be stirred down. Start timing for about 10 to 12 minutes. Continue to stir slowly.

The jam will foam at first, then it will subside, and when ready, it will feel thick and sticky when stirred. The color will be a deep garnet red.

To can: Ladle into hot, scalded half-pint jars, leaving ¼-inch head-space. Seal and process for 5 minutes in a boiling-water bath.

Strawberry-Rhubarb Preserves

This preserve has the famous tangy-sweet flavor of strawberry-rhubarb pie.

Yield: 4 half-pints

1¹⁄₃ cup honey

4 cups strawberries, washed, stemmed, and thickly sliced

4 cups washed and diced unpeeled rhubarb

3 tablespoons lemon juice

Drizzle ¹⁄₃ cup of the honey over the strawberries. Leave at room temperature for 3 to 4 hours. Combine the strawberries, their juice, rhubarb, lemon juice, and the remaining honey in a medium enamel or stainless steel saucepan. Bring slowly to a boil, stirring occasionally. Cook rapidly for 15 to 20 minutes, or until the berries are clear and the syrup is thickened. Stir frequently to prevent sticking. (If the fruit is clear and tender but the syrup is too thin, remove the fruit with a slotted spoon and boil the syrup rapidly almost to a jellying point.) Remove from the heat and skim off the foam.

To can: Pour into hot, scalded half-pint jars, leaving ¹⁄₄-inch headspace. Seal and process for 10 minutes in a boiling-water bath.

Pickles, Condiments, and Relishes

Apricot Chutney

Serve as a condiment with Indian meals or with roast meats and poultry.

Yield: 4 half-pints

½ cup honey

½ cup apple cider vinegar

½ cup coarsely chopped onions

½ teaspoon ground allspice

1 tablespoon chopped raisins

1 tablespoon crushed and minced peeled ginger

5 cups fresh apricots, pitted and quartered

In a large enamel or stainless steel pot, combine the honey, vinegar, onions, allspice, raisins, and ginger. Simmer for 10 minutes. Add the apricots and simmer for 30 minutes, or until thick, stirring occasionally.

To can: Pour into hot, scalded half-pint jars, leaving ½-inch headspace. Seal and process for 10 minutes in a boiling-water bath.

Pickled Beets

The Rodale Food Center rated these pickled beets "excellent."

1 gallon small beets with roots and 2-inch stems

2 tablespoons whole allspice

2 sticks cinnamon, 2 inches long

1 1/2 quarts vinegar

1/2 cup honey

Cook the beets in water to cover or in a microwave. When tender, dip the beets in cold water, and slip off the skins. If the beets are very small, keep whole; if not, slice thickly or cut in quarters.

Put the beets in a large enamel or stainless steel pot. Combine the allspice, cinnamon, and vinegar in a medium bowl, pour over the beets, and bring to a boil. Then add the honey.

To can: Pack into hot, scalded pint jars. Cover the beets with boiling syrup, leaving 1/2-inch headspace. Seal and process for 30 minutes in a boiling-water bath.

Yield: 9 pints

Dilled Brussels Sprouts

Pickling is one of the best ways to preserve extra brussels sprouts.

2 quarts brussels sprouts, cleaned and trimmed

2 cups water

2 cups vinegar

1 cup lemon juice

1/2 to 1 teaspoon cayenne pepper

9 sprigs fresh dill

4 cloves garlic

1 teaspoon mustard seeds

Steam the brussels sprouts for 15 minutes, or until just tender. Combine water, vinegar, lemon juice, cayenne, and 5 sprigs of dill in an enamel or stainless steel pot, and boil for 5 minutes.

To can: Pack the brussels sprouts into hot, scalded pint jars. Place 1 clove garlic, 1 sprig dill, and 1/4 teaspoon mustard seeds in each jar. Pour the hot vinegar solution over the brussels sprouts, leaving 1/4-inch headspace. Seal and process for 15 minutes in a boiling-water bath.

Yield: 4 pints

Pickled Cauliflower

Pickle your cauliflower overnight and serve as a salad tomorrow.

1 head cauliflower

1 small red onion, thinly sliced

½ cup olive oil

⅓ cup tarragon vinegar

2 teaspoons minced fresh dill or 1 teaspoon dried dill weed

½ teaspoon honey

½ teaspoon Dijon mustard

¼ teaspoon dry mustard

Minced fresh parsley (garnish)

Separate the cauliflower into florets, cutting the larger florets in half or into quarters. Steam the cauliflower for 10 minutes, or until crisp-tender. While the cauliflower steams, separate the onion slices into rings and arrange these on the bottom of a large serving bowl.

Combine the oil, vinegar, dill, honey, Dijon mustard, and dry mustard in a small jar or bowl and shake or stir until well combined. Place the steamed cauliflower in the serving bowl on top of the onion rings. Slowly pour the dill dressing over the hot cauliflower until all of the cauliflower is lightly coated with dressing. Without stirring, allow the cauliflower to cool, then refrigerate for 6 to 8 hours or overnight.

Before serving, toss the onions and cauliflower in the dressing, then drain well. Arrange on serving dishes and garnish with minced parsley, if desired.

Yield: 8 servings

Spiced Crabapples

Here's an old-fashioned favorite that's great for home-grown crabapples.

4 quarts crabapples

1 cup honey

6 cups vinegar

1 stick cinnamon, about 3½ inches long

1 tablespoon whole cloves

1 teaspoon whole allspice

1 teaspoon whole mace

Wash the crabapples well; be sure to remove the blossom ends. Combine the vinegar and honey in a medium saucepan. Place the cinnamon, cloves, allspice, and mace in a cheesecloth bag and add it to the vinegar and honey. Bring the mixture to a boil. When this syrup is cool, add the crabapples and heat slowly so that the fruit won't burst. It helps to prick each apple to avoid bursting. Bring to a boil. Allow to cool overnight.

To can: Remove the spice bag. Heat slowly to the boiling point. Pack the crabapples in hot, scalded pint jars. Fill with the hot syrup, leaving ¼-inch headspace. Seal and process for 20 minutes in a boiling-water bath.

Yield: 6 to 8 pints

Crisp Lime Pickles

These salt-free pickles are extra crisp.

About 9 small cucumbers, sliced ½ inch thick

1 cup pickling lime*

1 gallon water

6 cups white vinegar

3 cups honey

6 teaspoons Rodale's Whole Pickling Spice (page 116)

In a large enamel, stainless steel, or glass bowl, soak the cucumbers in the lime and water overnight. Stir occasionally to disperse the lime. Wash the cucumbers thoroughly in cold running water.

Soak for 4 hours in ice water, then drain completely. In a medium enamel or stainless steel saucepan, bring the vinegar and honey to a boil.

To can: Pack the cucumbers into hot, scalded pint jars, and place 1 teaspoon of the pickling spice in each jar. Pour the hot vinegar mixture over the cucumbers, leaving ½-inch headspace. Seal and process for 10 minutes in a boiling-water bath.

Yield: 6 pints

*Pickling lime is a fine white powder otherwise known as calcium hydroxide and is used in commercial pickles to keep them crisp without salt. It's available in season where you normally buy canning supplies.

Freezer Pickles

Try these super-fast freezer pickles.

Yield: 2 quarts

About 5 small cucumbers, washed and thinly sliced

1 large onion, thinly sliced

½ cup vegetable oil

1½ cups white vinegar

½ cup honey

½ cup water

2 cloves garlic, crushed

8 sprigs fresh dill

Layer the cucumbers and onions in two 1-quart freezer containers. In a medium bowl, whisk together the oil, vinegar, honey, water, and garlic. Blend well. Place the dill on top of the cucumbers. Pour the liquid mixture into the freezer containers, leaving 2-inch headspace. Cover and freeze.

Kosher Dills

This is a zesty-flavored pickle!

4½ cups white vinegar

4½ cups water

14 cloves garlic

7 grape leaves

7 spears horseradish root, 3 × 1½ inches

20 small cucumbers, washed, dried, and cut in half lengthwise

14 sprigs fresh dill

7 teaspoons mustard seeds

21 peppercorns

7 whole cloves

In a medium enamel or stainless steel saucepan, boil together the vinegar, water, and garlic. Reserve the garlic.

Meanwhile, place 1 grape leaf and 1 horseradish spear into each hot, scalded pint jar. Place the cucumbers into the jars. (Cutting the cucumbers in half instead of into spears insures a crisp pickle. If you want spears, cut them further at serving time.) To each jar, add 2 sprigs dill, 1 teaspoon mustard seeds, 3 peppercorns, and 1 clove. Pour the boiling liquid into the jars, allowing ¼-inch headspace. Add 2 of the reserved garlic cloves to each jar. Cover and turn once to disperse spices. Seal and process for 15 minutes in a boiling-water bath.

Yield: 7 pints

VARIATION: *Use all vinegar instead of a vinegar-water mixture for liquid and you can cut the processing time to 10 minutes.*

Old-Fashioned Cucumber Chunks

These pickles shouldn't be canned but are best kept in the refrigerator for up to two months.

13 small cucumbers, washed, dried, and cut into 1-inch pieces

1½ cups pickling salt

4 quarts water

5 cups vinegar

3 cups water

2 tablespoons Rodale's Whole Pickling Spice (page 116)

1 cup honey

Put the cucumbers into a crock or large enamel or stainless steel container. Dissolve the salt in the 4 quarts of water, and pour over the cucumbers. Cover with a plate to weight down the cucumbers so that they remain submerged in the brine. Let stand overnight.

Drain and rinse. Place cucumbers in large enamel or stainless steel pot. Pour the vinegar and 3 cups of water over the cucumbers. Add a cheesecloth bag containing the pickling spices and bring to a boil. Simmer for 10 minutes. Remove the spice bag. Add the honey and stir well. Bring to a boil.

Pack the pickles into hot, scalded jars and pour the hot syrup over them. If there is not enough liquid to cover, add more vinegar.

Yield: 7 pints

Salt-Free Bread-and-Butter Pickles

Now you can have pickles without disrupting a low-salt diet.

15 medium cucumbers

5 medium onions

5 cups vinegar

½ cup honey

2 teaspoons celery seeds

2 teaspoons ground ginger

2 teaspoons mustard seeds

1 teaspoon turmeric

Thinly slice the cucumbers and onions. Combine the vinegar, honey, celery seeds, ginger, mustard seeds, and turmeric in an enamel or stainless steel saucepan, and bring to a boil. Add the cucumbers and onions, and bring to the boiling point.

To can: Pack the cucumbers and onions in hot, scalded pint jars. Then pour the hot vinegar over them, leaving ¼-inch headspace. Seal and process for 10 minutes in a boiling-water bath.

Yield: 11 pints

Sweet Gherkins

Use extra-fresh cucumbers for extra-crispy gherkins.

About 30 to 45 immature cucumbers, 1½ to 3 inches long

6 cups apple cider vinegar

¾ teaspoon turmeric

2 teaspoons celery seeds

2 teaspoons Rodale's Whole Pickling Spice (page 116)

8 sticks cinnamon, 1 inch long

½ teaspoon fennel seeds

2 cups honey

Wash the cucumbers, place in a large container, and cover with cold water and ice cubes. Refrigerate for 5 hours. Drain.

Place the cucumbers in a large enamel or stainless steel pot. Add the vinegar, turmeric, and a cheesecloth bag containing the celery seeds, pickling spices, cinnamon, and fennel seeds. Bring to a boil. Add the honey. Bring to a boil again.

To can: Pack the cucumbers into hot, scalded pint jars. Cover with the boiling liquid, leaving ¼-inch headspace. Seal and process for 10 minutes in a boiling-water bath.

Yield: 10 or 11 pints

Pickled Eggplant

This is a great salad and antipasto addition.

6 eggplant, peeled and cut into thick sticks, 2 inches long

2 medium or 1 large onion, coarsely chopped

3½ cups red wine vinegar

½ cup honey

1 cup water

½ teaspoon whole allspice

½ teaspoon white peppercorns

1 stick cinnamon, 1 inch long

Boil the eggplant and onions in water for 5 minutes. Drain and cover with cold water; drain again. Place the vinegar, honey, and water in an enamel or stainless steel saucepan. Add a cheesecloth bag containing the allspice, peppercorns, and cinnamon, and bring the mixture to a boil. Simmer until the syrup is thick. Add the eggplant and onions. Heat through.

To can: Remove the spice bag. Pour into hot, scalded pint jars, leaving ¼-inch headspace. Seal and process for 15 minutes in a boiling-water bath.

Yield: 4 or 5 pints

Penang Pickled Garlic

Pickled garlic adds character to many Southeast Asian recipes.

Yield: 2 half-pints

1 cup garlic cloves

1½ cups rice vinegar

2 tablespoons Rodale's Whole Pickling Spice (page 116)

Peel the garlic and blanch for 30 seconds. Drain.

In a small enamel or stainless steel saucepan, combine the vinegar and pickling spices, and bring to a boil.

To can: Pack the garlic in 2 hot, scalded half-pint jars. Pour the hot liquid over the garlic, leaving ½-inch headspace. Seal and process for 10 minutes in a boiling-water bath.

NOTE: *Use pickled garlic in other recipes as you would use plain garlic, or stuff it between chicken meat and skin before roasting. Strain the liquid to make a wonderfully fragrant vinegar for marinades and salad dressings.*

Mango Chutney

Serve on tea sandwiches with cheese or on roasted meat.

Yield: 6 pints

6 large ripe mangoes, peeled and sliced

3 cups apple cider vinegar

1½ cups chopped green peppers

1 cup and 2 tablespoons raisins

1 cup currants

1 cup slivered almonds

¾ cup lime juice

¾ cup minced onions

5 tablespoons honey

1 piece ginger, 3 inches long, peeled and finely chopped

1½ tablespoons crushed mustard seeds

1½ tablespoons minced hot chili pepper, or 1 dried chili pepper, ground

Combine all the ingredients in a large saucepan. Bring to a boil, then simmer for 30 minutes. Drain off the juice and boil it down to half of its volume. Add it to the chutney, and reheat.

To can: Pour the mixture into hot, scalded pint jars, leaving ¼-inch headspace. Seal and process for 5 minutes in a boiling-water bath.

Brine-Cured Vegetables with Dill

This is the old-fashioned way to make pickles.

4 handfuls fresh dill

3 cloves garlic, peeled

3 hot chili peppers, washed, slit, and seeds removed

3 cups Jerusalem artichokes, sliced into ¹/₂-inch rounds

6 scallions, including tops, cut in half

¹/₂ head cauliflower, broken into florets

1¹/₂ cups green beans, whole

3 medium carrots, cut in diagonal slices

3 stalks celery, cut in diagonal slices

10 small pickling onions

¹/₂ cup pickling salt

8 cups white vinegar

Place a handful of the dill on the bottom of a 1-gallon glass jar or crock. Add the garlic and peppers. Top with the Jerusalem artichokes. Add a layer of dill. Place the scallions on the dill. On top of them, place a layer of cauliflower. Next, add a layer of beans and then a layer of dill. The carrots are the next layer, followed by the celery, topped with the whole small onions. Top all with the remaining dill.

Combine the salt with 2 cups of the vinegar. Mix to dissolve the salt. Pour into the jar or crock. Add the remaining 6 cups of vinegar to cover the ingredients. Be sure all the vegetables are covered with the vinegar solution. Crunch up enough clear plastic wrap to push the vegetables down, then cover the jar or crock with a weight.

Let stand on the kitchen counter for 4 to 6 days, then refrigerate. Drain before serving.

Yield: 1 gallon

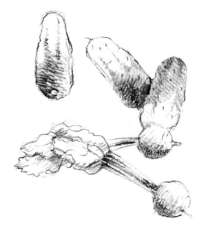

Honey Mustard

Serve with sandwiches, in salad dressings, or as a glaze on meats and poultry. It's also wonderful with cold shrimp and fish.

Yield: 2 half-pints

1 cup apple cider vinegar
³/₄ cup dry mustard

¹/₃ cup honey
3 eggs

In the top of a double boiler, combine all the ingredients, and simmer, stirring until smooth. Continue to simmer for 8 to 10 minutes, or until thick and smooth.

To can: Pour into hot, scalded half-pint jars, leaving ¹/₄-inch headspace. Seal and process in a boiling-water bath for 10 minutes.

Hot Mustard

Try this on egg rolls.

Yield: About ²/₃ cup

¹/₂ cup dry mustard
2 teaspoons vinegar

¹/₄ cup boiling water

Combine the mustard and vinegar. Gradually stir in the water. Allow to stand at room temperature for at least 15 minutes before using.

Prepared Mustard

This fine-flavored recipe rivals Dijon mustard.

Yield: 1/2 cup

1/4 cup dry mustard

1/4 cup hot water

3 tablespoons white wine vinegar

1/8 teaspoon garlic powder

Pinch of dried tarragon

1/4 teaspoon molasses

Soak the mustard in the water and 1 tablespoon of the vinegar for at least 2 hours.

Combine the remaining vinegar, garlic, and tarragon in a separate bowl, and let stand for 30 minutes. Strain the tarragon from the liquid, and add the liquid to the mustard mixture. Stir in the molasses. Pour the mustard into the top of a double boiler over simmering water. Cook for 15 minutes, or until thickened. (The mustard will thicken a bit more when chilled.) Remove the mustard from the heat and pour into a jar. Let cool, uncovered. Then replace the lid and store in the refrigerator.

Okra Pickles

These pickles are spicy and smooth.

Yield: 6 pints

5 cups water

3 cups white vinegar

3 teaspoons celery seeds

6 quarts small okra pods, washed, with stems removed

24 baby onions, peeled

6 cloves garlic

6 small hot chili peppers (optional)

6 pieces green pepper, 1-inch square

Combine the water, vinegar, and celery seeds in an enamel or stainless steel pot, and bring to a boil.

To can: Pack the okra firmly in hot, scalded pint jars. In each jar, put 4 onions, 1 clove garlic, 1 chili pepper, and 1 square of green pepper. Pour the boiling brine over the okra, leaving 1/4-inch headspace. Seal and process for 15 minutes in a boiling-water bath. Let ripen for several weeks before using.

No-Cook Scallion and Chili Chutney

If it's too hot to cook, you can still make this chutney.

Yield: 1 cup

6 scallions

2 chili peppers

1 cup cilantro leaves

1 tablespoon lemon juice

1 teaspoon salt

1 teaspoon sugar

1/2 teaspoon curry powder

1/2 teaspoon ground cumin

In a food processor or blender, combine all the ingredients. Process for about 1 minute, or until the ingredients are well blended.

To freeze: Prepare the recipe as directed. Place in a freezer container, and freeze.

Onion Pickles

These pungent cocktail onions are great in salads, casseroles, and stir-fries.

Yield: 4 pints

28 small white onions

6 cups white vinegar

2 tablespoons celery seeds

2 tablespoons mustard seeds

4 spears horseradish root, 3 × 1 1/2 inches

6 teaspoons honey

4 small hot chili peppers (fresh or dried)

To make peeling easier, drop the onions in boiling water. After about 2 minutes, remove the onions and plunge them into cold water. Then drain and peel.

In an enamel or stainless steel pot, combine the vinegar, celery seeds, mustard seeds, and horseradish. Simmer for 15 minutes. Add the honey. Remove and reserve the horseradish root.

To can: Pack the onions into hot, scalded pint jars. Pour the liquid over the onions, leaving 1/4-inch headspace. Add 1 chili pepper and 1 piece of reserved horseradish root to each jar. Seal and process for 10 minutes in a boiling-water bath.

Pepper-Onion Relish

This relish will make a plain hamburger great.

4 cups finely chopped onions

4 cups vinegar

2 cups finely chopped green peppers

2 cups finely chopped sweet red peppers

1/2 cup honey

Combine all the ingredients in a large enamel or stainless steel pot, and bring to a boil. Cook for 45 minutes, or until slightly thickened, stirring occasionally.

Pack the hot relish into hot, scalded pint jars, filling to the top of the jar. Seal tightly. Cool and store in the refrigerator.

To can: Pack the hot relish into hot, scalded pint jars, leaving 1/4-inch headspace. Seal and process in a boiling-water bath for 5 minutes.

Yield: 4 pints

Pickled Green Peppers

Here's another no-salt pickle you'll enjoy.

3 pounds green peppers, cleaned and sliced lengthwise

1 quart apple cider vinegar

1/4 cup honey

Steam the pepper strips for 2 minutes. Drain. Combine the vinegar and honey in an enamel or stainless steel saucepan. Bring to a boil.

To can: Pack the pepper strips in hot, scalded pint jars. Cover with the hot vinegar mixture, leaving 1/4-inch headspace. Seal and process for 10 minutes in a boiling-water bath.

Yield: 4 or 5 pints

Red Pepper Relish

This relish is extra flavorful if you use fresh, garden-ripened red peppers.

12 medium sweet red peppers, stems and seeds removed

2 cups chopped onions

2 cups white vinegar

3 cups honey

4 teaspoons salt

1 lemon, sliced

4 teaspoons whole allspice

½ teaspoon ground ginger

Cover the peppers with boiling water and let stand for 5 minutes; drain. Repeat and drain well. Chop coarsely in a food processor. The mixture should measure about 4 cups.

In an enamel or stainless steel saucepan, combine the onions, vinegar, honey, salt, and lemon with a cheesecloth bag containing the allspice and ginger. Boil for 30 minutes, stirring occasionally. Let stand overnight. The next day, bring the mixture to a boil in a large saucepan and simmer for 10 minutes.

To can: Pour the hot mixture into hot, scalded half-pint jars. Seal and process for 10 minutes in a boiling-water bath.

Yield: 6 half-pints

Quince Chutney

Serve this as a relish with roasted meats or poultry.

4 medium quinces, peeled, cored, and quartered

1½ cups apple juice

½ cup apple cider vinegar

½ cup coarsely chopped onions

½ cup honey

½ cup raisins

1 tablespoon crushed, minced, and peeled ginger

½ teaspoon ground coriander

½ teaspoon ground cardamom

In a medium enamel or stainless steel saucepan, combine all the ingredients. Bring to a boil and simmer for 45 minutes.

To can: Pour into hot, scalded pint jars, leaving ½-inch headspace. Seal and process for 10 minutes in a boiling-water bath.

Yield: 3 pints

Green Tomato Chutney

This recipe can be used as green tomato mince-meat pie filling. Just put tomatoes and apples through a meat grinder.

Yield: 6 pints

4 ½ cups finely chopped green tomatoes

4 ½ cups peeled and chopped tart apples

3 cups currants

2 cups minced onions

1 cup vinegar

1 cup water

½ cup honey

2 tablespoons mustard seeds

2 teaspoons ground ginger

½ teaspoon cayenne pepper

2 lemons, seeded, quartered, and thinly sliced

2 cloves garlic

In a large enamel or stainless steel pot, combine all the ingredients. Simmer for 20 minutes or until the fruit is soft.

To can: Pack into hot, scalded pint jars, leaving ¼-inch headspace. Seal and process for 5 minutes in a boiling-water bath.

VARIATION: *You can also substitute raisins for the currants.*

Green Tomato Pickles

This is a country favorite, great for using when frost threatens in the fall.

Yield: 5 quarts

9 cups white vinegar

1 ¼ cups honey

15 medium green tomatoes, cut into ½-inch slices

10 medium onions, cut into ½-inch slices

10 teaspoons celery seeds

5 teaspoons mustard seeds

5 teaspoons dill seeds

15 peppercorns

5 cloves garlic

In an enamel or stainless steel pot, bring the vinegar and honey to a boil. Meanwhile, layer the tomatoes and onions in 5 hot, scalded quart jars. To each jar, add 2 teaspoons celery seeds, 1 teaspoon mustard seeds, 1 teaspoon dill seeds, 3 peppercorns, and 1 clove garlic.

To can: Pour the boiling vinegar mixture into quart jars, allowing ¼-inch headspace. Seal, then turn the jars once to disperse the spices. Process for 15 minutes in a boiling-water bath.

Refrigerator Zucchini Pickles

Here's something different to do with zucchini.

Yield: 4 pints

16 to 20 small zucchini	2 teaspoons celery seeds
7 or 8 small white onions	2 teaspoons dry mustard
1 quart apple cider vinegar	2 teaspoons mustard seeds
1 cup honey	2 teaspoons turmeric

Cut the unpeeled zucchini into thin slices. Peel the onions, and slice thinly. In an enamel or stainless steel saucepan, combine the remaining ingredients. Bring to a boil, and pour over the vegetables. Let stand for 1 hour.

Return to the heat, bring to a boil, and cook for 3 minutes. Pour into hot, scalded pint jars. Cover tightly and refrigerate.

Zucchini and Carrot Pickles

These pickles have a delicious oriental flavor.

Yield: 2 cups

3 tablespoons rice vinegar	1 clove garlic
1 tablespoon tamari or low-sodium soy sauce	2 or 3 small zucchini, julienned
1 teaspoon mustard seeds	2 or 3 medium carrots, julienned
1 dried red chili pepper	
1 1/4-inch-thick slice ginger	

Combine the vinegar, tamari, mustard seeds, chili pepper, ginger, and garlic in a small bowl. Place the zucchini and carrots in a shallow dish or bowl and pour the marinade over them. Cover and chill at least overnight, stirring occasionally.

Seasonings

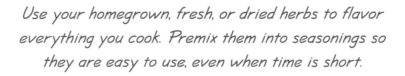

Use your homegrown, fresh, or dried herbs to flavor everything you cook. Premix them into seasonings so they are easy to use, even when time is short.

Herb Salt

Blend your own!

1 teaspoon garlic salt

2 teaspoons onion salt

1 teaspoon dried parsley

½ teaspoon dried basil

½ teaspoon dried marjoram

Combine all the ingredients in a small bowl, and mix well. Store sealed in an airtight glass jar in a cool, dry place.

NOTES: Basil and marjoram are mild; you could also add a small pinch of thyme or mint. (Careful, don't overdo it!) This way you will soon learn the strength of each herb and see for yourself what you like and how much of each to use. It can be great fun.

To release the flavors of the herbs, grind them in a mortar with the salt or herb salt. This blends them before they go into the mixture.

Yield: 5 teaspoons

Herb Seasoning

This spicy seasoning perks up any food.

Yield: About ⅓ cup

¼ teaspoon garlic powder

½ teaspoon onion powder

1 tablespoon dried parsley

½ teaspoon paprika

⅛ teaspoon ground red pepper

½ teaspoon dried thyme

½ teaspoon dried marjoram

1 teaspoon ground toasted sesame seeds

Combine all the ingredients in a small bowl, and mix well. Use in a shaker as a seasoning in place of salt. Store sealed in an airtight glass jar in the refrigerator.

FLAVORED VINEGAR COMBINATIONS

Use herb vinegars for extra flavorful soups, sauces, marinades, and dressings. Combine some sprigs of fresh herbs or sprinklings of dried herbs with vinegar to give it a gourmet flavor.

Let the herbs steep in the vinegar for a couple of weeks until the vinegar takes on their fragrance, then strain the herbs out. Place in glass jars, seal with nonmetal tops, and store in a cool, dark place. (Also see the herb vinegar discussion on page 124.) Here are some good combinations.

- Borage, dill, shallots, and white wine vinegar

- Chili peppers, garlic, oregano, and apple cider vinegar

- Cilantro, garlic, and rice vinegar

- Dill, nasturtiums, garlic, and apple cider vinegar

- Fennel leaf, garlic, parsley, and white wine vinegar

- Mint, honey, cardamom seed, and white vinegar

- Rosemary, raisins, orange peel, garlic, and white wine vinegar

- Rose petals, violet petals, and rice vinegar

- Sage, parsley, shallots, and red wine vinegar

- Savory, chive blossoms, and apple cider vinegar

Basic Coating Mix

Use this blend to coat foods before baking. The flavors subtly enhance almost any food.

Yield: About 2¹/₄ cups

2 cups whole wheat pastry flour

1 tablespoon paprika

1 tablespoon dry mustard

1 teaspoon dried basil

1 teaspoon dried marjoram

1 teaspoon dried thyme

1 teaspoon freshly ground black pepper

1 teaspoon ground celery seed

Combine all the ingredients in a small bowl, and mix well. Store sealed in an airtight glass jar in the refrigerator.

FLAVORED OIL COMBINATIONS

Use herb-flavored oils for extra flavorful cooking, marinades, salad dressings, or vinaigrettes.

Combine some sprigs of fresh herbs or a bit of dried herbs with healthful oils in combinations such as the following. Place in scalded glass jars, seal, and store in the refrigerator.

- Basil, chili powder, garlic, and olive oil
- Chervil, tarragon, shallots, and peanut oil
- Dill, garlic, and sunflower oil
- Fresh ginger, cardamom seed, cilantro, and safflower oil
- Lemon verbena, lemon thyme, and walnut oil
- Lovage, garlic, celery leaf, and olive oil
- Oregano, thyme, garlic, and olive oil
- Saffron, garlic, and olive oil

Classic Fines Herbes

Chop these herbs finely and add to dishes in the final minutes of cooking to release all the herbal flavor.

Yield: 3 tablespoons

1 tablespoon chopped fresh basil, marjoram, rosemary, tarragon, or thyme (or a combination of 2 or more of these herbs)

1 tablespoon chopped fresh chervil

1 tablespoon chopped fresh chives

Combine all the ingredients in a small bowl, and mix well. Store the bowl tightly covered with plastic wrap in the refrigerator. Add the entire mixture to appropriate sauces, soups, and egg dishes made to serve 6.

All-Purpose Blend

This is a mild but full-flavored blend.

Yield: About 2½ tablespoons

1 teaspoon dried basil

1 teaspoon celery flakes

1 teaspoon dried chervil

1 teaspoon dried chives

1 teaspoon dried marjoram

1 teaspoon dried parsley

¼ teaspoon dried savory

¼ teaspoon dried thyme

Combine all the ingredients in a small bowl, and mix well. Store sealed in an airtight glass jar in a cool, dry place.

Chili Powder

Fresh chili powder tastes better than many store-bought types.

Yield: About ¹/₄ cup

2 tablespoons cumin seeds or 2 tablespoons ground cumin

4 dried hot chili peppers, ground,* or 2 teaspoons crushed red pepper flakes

2 teaspoons dried oregano

2 teaspoons garlic powder

2 teaspoons onion powder

1 teaspoon ground allspice

¹/₈ teaspoon ground cloves

Combine all the ingredients in a blender or electric grinder, and grind until the mixture is a coarse powder. Store sealed in an airtight glass jar in the refrigerator. Use in recipes as directed.

If using dried hot chili peppers, remove the seeds before grinding or the mixture will be too hot.

Homemade Chili Seasoning

Here's your ticket to award-winning chili.

Yield: ¹/₄ cup

3 tablespoons chili powder

1¹/₂ tablespoons ground cumin

1 teaspoon dried oregano

¹/₂ teaspoon rubbed sage

¹/₂ teaspoon allspice

¹/₄ teaspoon ground red pepper

Combine all the ingredients in a small bowl, and mix well. Store sealed in an airtight glass jar in the refrigerator.

Pizza Seasoning

This seasoning will make any pizza great.

Yield: ⅓ cup

¼ cup dried oregano

2 tablespoons dried basil

2 teaspoons onion powder

1½ teaspoons garlic powder

¼ teaspoon crushed red pepper flakes

Combine all the ingredients in a small bowl, and mix well. Store sealed in an airtight glass jar in a cool, dry place. Sprinkle on top of pizza before baking or add 1 tablespoon to every quart of tomato sauce as a seasoning.

Taco Mix

You can use this seasoning in many Mexican dishes.

Yield: About 1½ cups

½ cup instant minced onion

5 tablespoons chili powder

3 tablespoons cornstarch

3 tablespoons dried oregano

2 tablespoons dried basil

2 tablespoons crushed red pepper flakes

2 tablespoons garlic powder

Combine all the ingredients in a small bowl, and mix well. Store sealed in an airtight glass jar in a cool, dry place. Use 1½ tablespoons of this mix for each pound of meat in any recipe in which you would find these flavors pleasing. For meatless grain and bean dishes, start with 1½ tablespoons for every 2 cups bulk, and adjust the seasoning to taste.

Curry Powder

Use this to make curried vegetables, rice, and meats.

Yield: About 1¾ cups

½ cup ground coriander

¼ cup chili powder

¼ cup dry mustard

¼ cup ground cardamom

¼ cup ground cloves

4 teaspoons cinnamon

1 tablespoon ground fennel seeds

1 tablespoon turmeric

Combine all the ingredients in a small bowl, and mix well. Store sealed in an airtight glass jar in a cool, dry place. Add to curried foods as needed.

Bouquet Garni

The bouquet garni is a traditional combination of herbs that is added to soups, stews, or sauces to enhance their flavor.

Yield: 1 bouquet garni

1 bay leaf

2 sprigs fresh or 1½ teaspoons dried parsley

1 sprig fresh or 1 teaspoon dried thyme

Gather the herbs together and tie with string. Place them in a piece of cheesecloth, tied closed, or in a metal tea ball. For even more flavor, tie herbs between 2 stalks of celery. When desired flavor has been obtained in the soup, stew, or sauce, remove and discard the bouquet garni.

Fish Blend I

Flavor fish without a lot of butter and salt.

Yield: 2 tablespoons

2 teaspoons dried basil

2 teaspoons freshly ground black pepper

2 teaspoons onion powder

Combine all the ingredients in a small bowl, and mix well. Store sealed in an airtight glass jar in a cool, dry place. Use to season fish before cooking.

Fish Blend II

This is a warm, aromatic blend.

Yield: About 2 tablespoons

1 teaspoon dried basil

1 teaspoon dried chervil

1 teaspoon dried marjoram

1 teaspoon dried parsley

1 teaspoon dried tarragon

Combine all the ingredients in a blender or grinder, and pulse until the herbs are small flakes. Store sealed in an airtight glass jar in a cool, dry place. Use as a seasoning to taste.

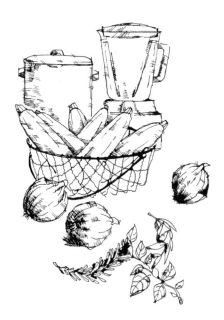

Seafood Coating Mix

Although originally designed to complement fish, this seasoning mixture works equally well for most nonmeat bean- and grain-based patties.

Yield: About 5½ cups

5 ⅓ cups whole wheat pastry flour

5 tablespoons dried parsley flakes

2 tablespoons dried marjoram

2 tablespoons dried thyme

2 tablespoons ground celery seed

1 tablespoon onion powder

1 teaspoon freshly ground black pepper

2 bay leaves, powdered

Combine all the ingredients in a small bowl, and mix well. Store sealed in an airtight glass jar in the refrigerator.

Poultry Seasoning

Poultry comes to life with this seasoning.

Yield: About ¼ cup

4 teaspoons dried marjoram

4 teaspoons onion powder

2 teaspoons dried sage

2 teaspoons dried savory

2 teaspoons dried thyme

1 teaspoon celery seeds

1 teaspoon white pepper

Combine all the ingredients in a blender or electric grinder, and grind until the mixture is a powder. Store sealed in an airtight glass jar in a cool, dry place. Sprinkle on poultry before cooking, or add 2 teaspoons to poultry, soups, stews, or casseroles made to serve 4 to 6.

Curry Coating Mix

~❧~

The taste of chicken takes on a nice twist with this simple but uniquely flavored mix.

Yield: About 2½ cups

2 cups whole wheat pastry flour

3 tablespoons curry powder

1½ teaspoons freshly ground black pepper

Combine all the ingredients in a bowl. Use what you need to coat your poultry before baking. Store the rest in a sealed glass jar in the refrigerator.

MARINADE MAGIC FOR POULTRY

Tasty, low-fat marinades impart great flavor to poultry.

Use marinades before you cook or to baste the meat as it cooks to help keep it juicy. For best results, simply skin the poultry and place it in a large bowl or shallow baking dish with the marinade. Cover the meat and let stand at room temperature for no longer than one hour. Flip the pieces often to ensure even coverage. Then cook immediately. For longer marinating, place the poultry in the refrigerator.

Here are five tasty marinades suitable for any type of poultry. Vary the proportions to suit your taste.

- Buttermilk, curry powder, and minced fresh cilantro or parsley
- Chicken stock, minced fresh thyme, freshly ground black pepper, dried mustard, and freshly ground red pepper
- Chicken stock, minced garlic, minced fresh ginger, low-sodium soy sauce, and grated orange rind
- Chicken stock, lemon juice, minced onions, minced garlic, minced fresh oregano, and crushed celery seeds
- Tomato juice, minced garlic, minced fresh oregano, ground cumin, and ground coriander

Beef Blend

This blend will give classic flavor.

Yield: About 3 tablespoons

2 teaspoons dried parsley

2 teaspoons garlic powder

2 teaspoons freshly ground black pepper

2 teaspoons onion powder

Combine all the ingredients in a small bowl, and mix well. Store sealed in an airtight glass jar in a cool, dry place. Sprinkle on beef before cooking.

Barbecue Spice

This blend offers bolder flavor.

Yield: About ¼ cup

2 tablespoons chili powder

2 tablespoons dry mustard

1 tablespoon garlic powder

1 tablespoon ground cumin

1 tablespoon paprika

½ teaspoon ground red pepper

½ teaspoon ground cloves (optional)

Combine all the ingredients in a small bowl, and mix well. Store sealed in an airtight glass jar in the refrigerator. To use, sprinkle on meats before baking or broiling, or add to flour or breading mixtures for chicken or fish.

MARINADE MAGIC FOR MEAT

Low-fat meats can be tenderized by a good marinade. Marinades also add flavor as the meat absorbs the liquids and spices.

Marinades work best on small pieces of meat. For maximum effect, marinate the meat overnight and turn the pieces frequently to expose as much surface as possible to the marinade's flavorful ingredients.

Since most marinades are acid-based, always use a nonreactive container, such as glass, ceramic, or stainless steel. Don't use aluminum or plastic. And remember that although acidic ingredients help protect the food from bacterial growth, refrigerating the meat during marination is the safest course.

Here are some savory citrus marinades suitable for any type of meat. Vary the proportions to suit your taste.

- Lemon juice and pulp, coarse mustard, and dried sage

- Lemon juice and pulp and cranberry sauce

- Lemon juice and pulp, crushed fennel seeds, and minced garlic

- Lemon juice and pulp, dried tarragon, and minced shallots

- Lemon juice and pulp, tomato puree, dried oregano, and dried basil

- Lime juice and pulp, grated nutmeg, and ground allspice

- Lime juice and pulp and minced ginger

- Lime juice and pulp, nonfat yogurt, and curry powder

- Lime juice and pulp, peanut oil, and hot pepper sauce

- Orange juice and pulp, low-sodium soy sauce, minced ginger, and sesame oil

Egg Blend

These herbs do wonderful things for egg dishes.

Yield: About 3 tablespoons

1 tablespoon dried parsley

1 teaspoon dried basil

1 teaspoon dried chervil

1 teaspoon dried chives

1 teaspoon dried marjoram

1 teaspoon dried tarragon

Combine all the ingredients in a small bowl, and mix well. Store sealed in an airtight glass jar in a cool, dry place.

Seasoning Blends for Soups

~

Here's how to add life to homemade soups.

The dominant taste of the soup before herbs are added dictates which ones will season best. In general, cream soups take well to delicately flavored herbs, poultry-based soups can make use of ones a little stronger, and beef and lamb foundations can sustain a still stronger accent of herbs. Most vegetable, grain, and bean soups made with a vegetable rather than a meat stock also can support herbs in this latter category.

Cream Soup Seasoning Blend

¼ cup dried basil

¼ cup dried celery pieces

¼ cup dried marjoram

¼ cup dried parsley

4 teaspoons freeze-dried chives

4 teaspoons dried thyme

Poultry Soup Seasoning Blend

¼ cup dried basil

¼ cup freeze-dried chives

¼ cup dried marjoram

¼ cup dried savory

¼ cup dried tarragon

4 teaspoons dried sage

Beef and Lamb Soup Seasoning Blend

¼ cup dried savory

¼ cup dried celery pieces

¼ cup dried parsley

¼ cup dried basil

¼ cup dried marjoram

¼ cup dried thyme

¼ cup freeze-dried chives

Yield: 1 to 1½ cups for each blend

Combine all the ingredients in a small bowl, and mix well. Store them in an airtight glass jar in a cool, dry place. Fifteen minutes before the completion of any soup, grind 1 or 2 teaspoons of any of the following blends for each cup of liquid in the recipe, and add the herbs to the soup. Further adjust seasonings to taste.

Chiffonade of Fresh Herbs

Use the most tender leaves so they'll melt into the dish you're making.

Yield: About ⅓ cup

3 tablespoons chopped fresh parsley

1 teaspoon chopped fresh basil

1 teaspoon chopped fresh chervil

2 teaspoons chopped fresh chives

1 teaspoon chopped fresh thyme

Combine all the ingredients in a small bowl, and mix well. Use the entire amount to flavor a stew, a soup, or a fresh green salad made to serve 4.

Desserts

Apple Squares

Here's a different and healthy way to serve apples.

4 apples, coarsely shredded	1 teaspoon ground cinnamon
2 cups cold cooked rice	1/4 cup raisins
1/2 cup unbleached flour	1/2 cup egg substitute
1/4 cup whole wheat flour	2 tablespoons maple syrup
1 tablespoon baking powder	1 tablespoon vanilla extract

Put the apples into a strainer. Press with a spoon to extract excess liquid. Set the apples aside. In a large bowl, mix the rice, unbleached flour, whole wheat flour, baking powder, and cinnamon. Stir in the raisins.

In a medium bowl, combine the egg substitute, maple syrup, and vanilla. Pour the liquid ingredients over the flour mixture. Add the apples. Mix well.

Coat a 9-inch-square baking dish with no-stick spray. Spread the apple mixture evenly in the pan. Bake at 325°F for 40 to 45 minutes.

To freeze: Prepare the recipe as directed. Cool, then wrap the dish in freezer wrap or foil or place in a freezer bag, and freeze. To serve, thaw in the refrigerator overnight. If desired, warm in a 350°F oven for 20 to 25 minutes. Or, microwave thawed individual squares for 45 seconds on high.

Yield: 6 servings

Apples Stuffed with Prunes

This recipe tastes rich but doesn't include a bit of fat.

4   large McIntosh apples

1   teaspoon lemon juice

¼   cup finely chopped prunes

1   tablespoon ground walnuts

1   teaspoon honey

¼   teaspoon ground cinnamon

¼   cup orange or apple juice

Core the apples, and remove about 1 inch of the peel from around the tops. Rub the exposed surfaces with the lemon juice. Prick the skins in several places with a fork to keep the apples from bursting.

In a small bowl, combine the prunes, walnuts, honey, and cinnamon. Divide the mixture among the apples, stuffing it into the cored areas. Arrange the apples in a 3-quart baking dish. Add the orange or apple juice to the bottom of the dish. Cover with vented plastic wrap. Microwave on high for 4 minutes. Give the dish a half turn and microwave on high for 3 minutes, or until the apples are tender and easily pierced with a sharp knife.

To freeze: Prepare the recipe as directed. Cool, then wrap the dish in freezer wrap or foil or place in a freezer bag, and freeze. To serve, thaw in the refrigerator. If desired, cover and warm in a 350°F oven for 15 to 20 minutes, or microwave on high for 3 to 4 minutes.

NOTE: If you don't have a microwave, core the apples, then slice them in half through the cored areas for quicker cooking. Stuff with the prune mixture (you might want to double the amount) and place, cut side up, in a 7 × 11-inch baking dish. Add ½ cup orange or apple juice to the bottom of the dish, cover the dish tightly with foil, and bake at 375° for 30 minutes, or until tender but not collapsed.

Yield: 4 servings

Apricot-Nut Bars

Keep some of these around all the time for lunch or snacks.

²/₃ cup dried apricots

1¹/₃ cups whole wheat pastry flour

³/₄ cup honey

¹/₂ cup butter, softened

¹/₂ teaspoon baking powder

2 eggs, well beaten

¹/₂ teaspoon vanilla extract

¹/₂ cup chopped walnuts

Preheat the oven to 350°F. Rinse the apricots, cover with water, and boil for 10 minutes. Drain, cool, and chop.

Coat an 8-inch-square pan with no-stick spray. Mix 1 cup of the flour, ¹/₄ cup of the honey, and the butter. Press into the prepared pan and bake for 20 to 25 minutes.

Meanwhile, sift the remaining flour and baking powder together. In a large bowl, with a mixer at low speed, gradually beat the remaining honey into the eggs; mix in the flour mixture and vanilla. Stir in the walnuts and apricots. Spread over the baked layer. Bake for 30 minutes, or until a toothpick inserted into the center comes out clean; cool in the pan. Cut into bars.

To freeze: Prepare the recipe as directed. Wrap the bars in freezer wrap or foil or place in freezer bags, and freeze. To serve, thaw in the refrigerator.

Yield: 32 bars

Yogurt-Fruit Freeze

This recipe requires an ice cream maker.

2 cups yogurt

1 cup unsweetened pineapple or orange juice

¹/₂ cup stewed dried apricots or peaches

3 tablespoons honey

2 tablespoons lemon juice

Mix together the yogurt, pineapple or orange juice, stewed fruit, honey, and lemon juice until blended. Process in an ice cream maker for 25 minutes, following the manufacturer's directions, or until the fruit mixture appears frozen.

Yield: 4 to 6 servings

Apricot, Peach, or Nectarine Leather

These have more flavor than most commercial fruit leathers.

1 gallon pitted apricots, peaches, or nectarines

1½ cups unsweetened pineapple juice

¼ cup mild-flavored honey (or more to taste)

3 teaspoons almond extract (optional)

Place the pitted fruit and pineapple juice in a large, heavy pot. Cover the pot and set it over low heat. Cook the fruit until soft. Using a strainer, drain off the juice, lifting the fruit from the sides of the strainer to allow all the juice to run out freely. The more juice that is strained out, the quicker the process of leather making will be. The juice is too good to discard. Can or freeze it or drink it fresh.

Run the fruit through a blender, food processor, or food mill, removing the skins if you prefer a smooth product, or use the skins as part of the pulp for the leather. A food processor will puree the skins right along with the pulp. Sweeten the pulp to taste with honey, and add the almond extract, if you wish. The pulp should be as thick as a very thick applesauce. Spread the pulp ¼ inch thick on baking sheets that have been lightly oiled or covered with freezer paper or plastic wrap.

Place the baking sheets in a warm oven or food dryer. If using an oven, turn it on to 120°F and leave the oven door slightly open to allow moisture to escape. The leather will dry in 12 hours.

When the leather is dry enough to be lifted or gently pulled from the baking sheets, put it on cake racks so it can dry on both sides. Dust the leather lightly with cornstarch to absorb any stickiness. Then stack the leather in layers with wax paper, freezer paper, or plastic wrap between each sheet. Cover the stack with freezer paper or plastic wrap, and store in a cool, dry place.

Yield: 4 sheets, each about 10 x 5 inches

Banana-Berry Shakes

You can serve luscious low-fat shakes—just take advantage of the rich flavor and creamy texture of tropical fruits.

Yield: 8 servings

4 cups sliced strawberries

2 large bananas, peeled and sliced

1 cup orange juice

1 cup nonfat vanilla yogurt

8 ice cubes

In a blender, combine half of the strawberries, half of the bananas, half of the juice, half of the yogurt, and half of the ice cubes. Puree until thick and smooth. Repeat with the remaining strawberries, bananas, juice, yogurt, and ice cubes.

Frozen Blueberry Yogurt

Hardly anything is simpler to make, tastier, or more nutritious than home-made frozen yogurt.

Yield: 4 to 6 servings

2 cups blueberries

1/3 cup mild-flavored honey

2 cups nonfat yogurt

Cook blueberries and honey together for about 4 minutes. Let cool completely. Put the blueberry mixture in a food processor, and process for a few seconds, or until thoroughly blended. Fold in the yogurt. Put into freezer containers, leaving 1/2-inch headspace, and freeze. Process again if a smoother texture is desired and refreeze. To serve, put the yogurt in the refrigerator 1/2 hour before serving. Or, reprocess until fluffy but not thawed.

Cantaloupe Ice

This light, refreshing ice could be used as a palate cleanser before the entrée in the French and Italian manner.

Yield: 3 or 4 servings

2 cups cantaloupe puree

1 cup water

¼ cup mild-flavored honey

1 tablespoon lime juice

⅛ teaspoon ground cinnamon

Place the cantaloupe, water, honey, lime juice, and cinnamon in a blender, and process until thoroughly combined. Pour the mixture into 2 ice cube trays. Place in the freezer and freeze for at least 4 hours. When ready to serve, pop the cantaloupe cubes out of the trays and place them in a food processor or blender. Process until smooth and serve immediately.

Cherry-Maple Crunch

It's hard to believe this dessert is so easy to make because it tastes so good.

Yield: 6 servings

3 cups pitted sour cherries

1 teaspoon cornstarch

⅓ cup maple syrup

½ cup rolled oats

2 tablespoons canola oil

Coat a 9-inch pie plate with no-stick spray. Add the cherries. In a cup, dissolve the cornstarch in the maple syrup. Pour over the cherries.

In a small bowl, combine the oats and oil. Sprinkle over the cherries. Bake at 350°F for about 40 minutes, or until lightly browned.

To freeze: Prepare the recipe as directed. Cool, then wrap the plate with freezer wrap or foil or place in a freezer bag, and freeze. To serve, bake unthawed and uncovered at 350°F for 30 to 40 minutes, or until warm. Or, microwave on high until warm. You can also thaw this dessert at room temperature for about 3 hours, and serve it cool.

Sour Cherry Compote with Vanilla Sauce

Enjoy apricots and cherries in a creamy but fat-free vanilla sauce.

Sour Cherry Compote

2 cups sliced apricots in juice

2 cups pitted sour cherries

2 tablespoons honey

1 tablespoon lemon juice

½ teaspoon grated lemon rind

Vanilla Sauce

2 tablespoons cornstarch

2 cups skim milk

2 tablespoons honey

¼ cup egg substitute

2 teaspoons vanilla extract

To make the compote: Drain the apricots, reserving ¼ cup juice. Place the apricots and remaining juice in a 2-quart saucepan. Add the cherries, honey, lemon juice, and lemon rind. Bring to a boil over medium heat. Cover and simmer for 5 minutes. Set aside.

To make the sauce: Place the cornstarch in a 1-quart saucepan. Whisk in a little of the milk to dissolve the cornstarch. Whisk in the honey and remaining milk. Cook over medium heat, stirring constantly, for 5 to 10 minutes, or until the mixture comes to a boil and thickens. Remove from the heat, and whisk in the egg substitute and vanilla. Return to the heat and cook, stirring constantly, for 1 minute. Serve warm or chilled over the compote.

VARIATION: *You may also serve the compote as a low-fat topping for waffles, pancakes, cooked cereal, and yogurt.*

NOTE: *You may use fresh, frozen, canned, or dried sour cherries for this quick compote. If you're using dried cherries, reduce the amount to 1 cup, and simmer them in water to cover until plumped. Drain and proceed with the recipe.*

Yield: 6 servings

Kiwi Freeze

This creamy ice fruit is extra easy.

2 kiwis, peeled and sliced

½ cup nonfat vanilla yogurt

Peel, slice, and freeze the kiwis. When you're ready for something special, let the fruit soften for a few minutes at room temperature. Process in a food processor or blender until smooth and creamy. Then fold in the vanilla yogurt.

Yield: 1 serving

Frozen Fruit Bars

Make delicious frozen bars from your own garden-fresh fruit.

Fill containers such as ice cube trays or small dixie cups two-thirds full with fruit pieces such as banana slices, crushed pineapple, kiwi slices, seedless grape halves, strawberries, or sweet cherries. Finish filling the container with fruit juice such as apple, grape (white, pink, or red), orange, pineapple, or any mixed fruit juice. Cover the containers and start to freeze. When partially frozen, insert a stick in each, then freeze thoroughly, and serve.

If you don't know where to start, try the following excellent combination.

½ cup chopped fresh pineapple

½ cup chopped strawberries

½ cup mashed bananas

½ cup orange juice

In a small bowl, stir together the pineapple, strawberries, bananas, and orange juice. Spoon the mixture into an ice cube tray. Cover with plastic wrap and start to freeze. When partially frozen, insert sticks, and freeze thoroughly before serving.

VARIATIONS: For a creamy flavor, mix an equal proportion of heavy cream or yogurt with fruit juice or fruit puree before pouring over the fruit pieces. Or, puree overripe bananas with the fruit juice for a creamier bar.

NOTES: Keep these pointers in mind to ensure successful frozen fruit bars every time.

- *Use small pieces of fruit; large ones freeze too hard.*

- *Do not use water to bind fruit pieces; it freezes too hard.*

- *Remove bars from the freezer about 5 minutes before serving for easier eating, unless the weather is really hot.*

Yield: 14 bars

Fruit-Nut Bars

These easy-to-make bars pack a lot of nutrition into a small space.

2 cups nuts

1 cup dates, pitted prunes, raisins, or dried apricots

2 eggs, beaten

⅓ cup honey

Preheat oven to 375°F. Grind the nuts and fruit together. Blend with the eggs and honey. Place in a lightly oiled 9-inch-square pan. Bake for 20 minutes, or until firm. Cut and serve.

To freeze: Prepare the recipe as directed. Wrap the bars in freezer wrap or foil, or place in freezer bags, and freeze. To serve, thaw in the refrigerator.

Yield: 24 bars

Golden Aura Compote

Serve on shortbread, as a cake topping, or on ice cream.

¾ cup dried apricots, chopped

¾ cup dried pears, chopped

½ cup water

¼ cup maple syrup

½ teaspoon ground nutmeg

½ cup yogurt

1 cup heavy cream

¼ teaspoon almond extract

Whole almonds (optional)

Whipped cream (optional)

In a small saucepan, combine the apricots, pears, water, maple syrup, and nutmeg. Cook over low heat for 5 minutes, or until the fruit softens.

In a blender or food processor, puree the fruit blend until smooth, then cool completely. Gently fold the yogurt into the fruit puree. In a medium bowl, combine the cream and almond extract. Whip the heavy cream for 3 minutes, or until soft peaks form. Carefully fold the whipped cream into the fruit mixture. Chill completely and garnish with whole almonds and whipped cream, if desired.

To freeze: Prepare the recipe as directed. Ladle into freezer containers, leaving 1-inch headspace, and freeze. To serve, thaw in the refrigerator overnight.

VARIATION: *Substitute dried apples and peaches for dried pears and apricots.*

Yield: 4 servings

Nectarine Sorbet

It's easy to make your own sorbets, ice milks, and frozen yogurt from summer-fresh fruit.

Yield: 4 servings

4 cups chopped nectarines

2 cups apple juice concentrate

Puree the nectarines in a blender or food processor. Transfer to a large nonmetallic bowl. Stir in the apple juice concentrate.

Freeze the mixture in an ice cream maker, following the manufacturer's directions. If you don't have an ice cream maker, freeze the mixture in a shallow bowl. For the first 2 hours, stir or beat the mixture every 15 to 20 minutes to break up ice crystals and to prevent it from freezing solid too fast. Then allow the mixture to freeze to the desired texture.

Peach Paradise

This is a quick, tasty, and delicate cobbler that freezes well. You can substitute fresh cherries, plums, or berries for the peaches.

Yield: 8 or 9 servings

1/3 cup buttermilk

1/4 cup honey

1 egg, slightly beaten

3 tablespoons butter, melted

1/2 cup whole wheat pastry flour

2 teaspoons baking powder

3 cups peeled, sliced peaches

1 teaspoon cornstarch

1/2 teaspoon ground cinnamon

1/8 teaspoon ground nutmeg

Preheat oven to 375°F. In a medium bowl, beat together the buttermilk, honey, egg, and butter. Stir together the flour and baking powder. Stir the dry ingredients into the egg mixture. Combine the peaches, cornstarch, cinnamon, and nutmeg in a medium bowl. Spread into an 8-inch-square pan coated with no-stick spray. Top the fruit with the batter, spreading to cover. Bake for 18 to 20 minutes until crisp and golden.

To freeze: Prepare the recipe as directed. Cool, then wrap the pan in freezer wrap or foil, or place in a freezer bag, and freeze. To serve, thaw the frozen cobbler, covered, in a 350°F oven for 20 to 25 minutes.

Seared Pineapples and Peaches

Grill the fruit and serve with a creamy raspberry sauce.

Yield: 8 servings

2 cups nonfat yogurt

½ cup skim milk

4 cups raspberries

2 ripe pineapples

4 peaches

2 cups blueberries

Combine the yogurt, milk, and 2 cups of the raspberries in a blender or food processor. Puree on medium speed. Transfer to a bowl and chill.

Slice the tops and bottoms off the pineapples. With a sharp knife, remove the outer peel and the inner core of each. Slice the flesh crosswise into 1-inch-thick pieces. Halve the peaches and remove the pits.

Prepare an outdoor grill, and place the pineapples and peaches directly on the rack. When the coals are hot, grill for about 4 minutes per side, or until golden brown. Use a metal spatula to transfer the fruit to dessert plates. Sprinkle with the blueberries and the remaining raspberries. Top with the sauce.

Lemon Pumpkin Pie

This is a great way to preserve pumpkins that you can't store any longer.

Yield: 8 servings

1½ cups pumpkin puree

¾ cup egg substitute

¾ cup evaporated skim milk

⅓ cup maple syrup

½ teaspoon ground cinnamon

½ teaspoon ground ginger

¼ teaspoon grated nutmeg

1 cup nonfat vanilla yogurt

1 tablespoon lemon juice

2 teaspoons grated lemon rind

Coat a 9-inch pie plate with no-stick spray. In a large bowl, beat together the pumpkin, egg substitute, milk, maple syrup, cinnamon, ginger, and nutmeg. Pour into the pie plate. Bake at 350°F for 55 minutes, or until a knife inserted in the center comes out clean. Cool.

In a small bowl, whisk together the yogurt, lemon juice, and lemon rind. Spread on top of the pie. Chill.

To freeze: Prepare the recipe as directed, but don't bake. Wrap the pie in freezer wrap or foil, or place in a freezer bag, and freeze. To serve, bake the frozen pies for 10 minutes at 400°F. Then lower the oven temperature to 350°F and bake for 60 to 70 minutes, or until a knife inserted in the center comes out clean. If you do bake the pie before freezing, thaw for 2 to 3 hours at room temperature.

Pumpkin Bread

Here's a classic recipe for pumpkin bread.

4 eggs, beaten

2 cups honey

2 cups cooked pumpkin, fresh or canned

1 cup vegetable oil

⅔ cup water

3½ cups whole wheat flour

2 teaspoons baking soda

1 teaspoon ground cinnamon

1 teaspoon ground nutmeg

Preheat the oven to 350°F. Beat the eggs, honey, pumpkin, oil, and water together well. In a separate bowl, mix the flour, baking soda, cinnamon, and nutmeg. Then pour the dry mixture into the wet mixture, and mix thoroughly. Pour the mixture into two 9 × 5-inch loaf pans coated with no-stick spray. Bake for 1 hour and 10 minutes.

To freeze: Prepare the recipe as directed. Wrap in freezer wrap or foil, or place in freezer bags, and freeze. To serve, thaw in the refrigerator.

Yield: 2 loaves

Berry Ice

Use vine-ripened raspberries for this recipe.

4 cups raspberries

1 cup water or unsweetened orange juice

¼ to ½ cup mild-flavored honey

Mint leaves (garnish)

Puree the berries, then blend with the water or orange juice and honey in a blender or food processor. Pour into a metal bowl and freeze until mushy. Return to the blender or food processor, and process again until completely smooth. Pour into a covered mold or a freezer container, and freeze until firm (4 hours or more, depending on the shape of the container).

Remove the ice from the freezer 15 minutes before serving to soften slightly. Serve garnished with fresh mint.

Yield: 4 servings

Black Raspberry Pie

Black raspberries star in this pie.

Yield: 8 servings

1 envelope unflavored gelatin

⅓ cup white grape juice

4 cups black raspberries

⅓ cup honey

1 baked piecrust, 9 inches in diameter

In a cup, sprinkle the gelatin over the grape juice. Set aside to soften for 5 minutes. In a 2-quart saucepan, lightly crush the raspberries with a potato masher. Add the gelatin and honey. Over medium-high heat, bring the mixture to a boil, stirring constantly. Remove from the heat and cool for about 5 minutes. Spoon the filling into the piecrust. Cool completely before slicing.

To freeze: Prepare the recipe as directed. Wrap the pie in freezer wrap or foil, or place in freezer bags, and freeze. To serve, thaw the pie for 2 to 3 hours at room temperature.

Strawberries with Two Melons

This colorful fruit salad is simple to make.

Yield: 4 servings

2 cups halved strawberries

1½ cups cantaloupe chunks

1½ cups honeydew chunks

1 lime, thinly sliced

1 cup nonfat vanilla yogurt

1 tablespoon lime juice

¼ teaspoon ground cardamom

In a large bowl, combine the strawberries, cantaloupe, honeydew, and lime. In a small bowl, combine the yogurt, lime juice, and cardamom. Pour over the fruit and toss to combine.

Strawberry Sundaes

These fruity sundaes will satisfy your sweet tooth.

Yield: 4 servings

¼ cup apple juice

1 tablespoon unflavored gelatin

3 cups sliced strawberries

2 cups nonfat plain or vanilla yogurt

¼ cup orange juice

Place the apple juice in a custard cup. Sprinkle with the gelatin and let it stand for a few minutes to soften. Stir well, then microwave on high for 30 seconds, or until the gelatin has dissolved.

Puree 2 cups of the strawberries in a food processor. With the motor running, pour in the gelatin. Mix well. Transfer to a bowl, and fold in the yogurt. Process in an ice cream maker, following the manufacturer's directions.

While the yogurt is freezing, puree the orange juice and remaining strawberries in a food processor. Cook over low heat, or microwave on high for 2 minutes, until the color is bright and the sauce is bubbly. Serve warm or at room temperature over the frozen yogurt.

Strawberry-Yogurt Ice Cream

This ice cream is delicious when you whip yogurt into it. It's also more nutritious and less fattening.

Yield: 6 servings

1 cup heavy cream

2 cups sliced strawberries

1 cup nonfat yogurt

⅓ cup mild-flavored honey

Whip the cream and set aside. Puree the strawberries, yogurt, and honey in a blender or food processor until smooth. Fold the strawberry mixture into the whipped cream, pour into an 8-inch-square pan, cover, and freeze until firm. Reprocess (without thawing) for a smoother texture and to recombine ingredients that may have separated.

Beverages

Hot Mulled Apple Punch

This is a great drink on cold days.

3 quarts apple juice or cider

1 large apple, cored and very thinly sliced

6 whole cloves

6 allspice berries

1 cinnamon stick

4 Red Zinger tea bags

12 thin lemon slices

Pour the apple juice or cider into a 4-quart saucepan. Stick the apple slices with the cloves and add to the pan. Add the allspice and cinnamon stick. Cover and bring to a simmer over medium heat. Remove from the heat, and add the tea bags. Cover and steep for 15 minutes.

Remove the bags before serving. Ladle into mugs, and garnish each with a lemon slice and an apple slice.

Yield: 12 servings

Banana-Fruit Shake

Drink this shake for a nutritious snack.

2 cups cranberry juice

2 cups nonfat vanilla yogurt

1 cup coarsely chopped peaches

1 cup frozen banana slices

1 tablespoon honey

1/4 teaspoon ground cinnamon

2 ice cubes

In a blender, combine all the ingredients. Blend on high speed until smooth and creamy.

Yield: 4 servings

Tropical Breakfast Shake

These fruits give this shake a tropical flavor.

2 cups drained canned crushed pineapple

1½ cups ice cubes

1⅓ cups nonfat yogurt

2 medium bananas, coarsely chopped

½ cup apricot nectar

¼ cup toasted wheat germ

1 kiwi, peeled and sliced

In a blender, combine the pineapple, ice cubes, yogurt, bananas, apricot nectar, and wheat germ. Blend until smooth. Serve in tall glasses; garnish with the kiwi slices.

Yield: 4 servings

Cinnamon-Berry Nectar

You can make this nectar with either fresh or frozen berries. Warmed up, it becomes a sauce to serve over pancakes, waffles, ice cream, or yogurt.

8 cups blackberries or raspberries

1 cup water

½ to ¾ cup honey

¼ cup orange juice

2 teaspoons vanilla extract

1 to 1½ teaspoons ground cinnamon

In an 8-quart saucepan, combine the berries and water. Bring to a boil over medium heat, and cook the berries until they release their juices and are soft, about 5 to 10 minutes for frozen and 6 to 8 minutes for fresh. Lower the heat, and add the honey, orange juice, vanilla, and cinnamon. Cook 1 minute more. Remove from the heat, and puree in a food processor or blender. Cool. If there are too many seeds for your taste, strain the nectar through a fine mesh sieve.

To freeze: Prepare the recipe as directed, but don't cool. Pour the juice into freezer containers, leaving ½-inch headspace, and freeze right away. To serve, thaw in the refrigerator.

VARIATIONS: To make a cool summer party drink, place the nectar in a glass, and add 4 ounces of mineral water or sparkling water. Or, use 6 tablespoons of nectar per one 23-ounce bottle of sparkling or mineral water, and serve in wine glasses.

Yield: 4 ⅔ cups

HERB TEAS FROM THE WESTERN RESERVE

Try some of the following delightful herb tea blends developed by the Western Reserve Herb Society of northeastern Ohio. The society shares these and many other delicious herb recipes in the 311-page cookbook *Cooking with Herb Scents*. You can get a copy for $16.95 plus $2.00 shipping and handling. Send your check to the Western Reserve Herb Society, 11030 East Boulevard, Cleveland, OH 44106.

Good Bee Tea Blend

The scarlet petals of bergamot make this tea a rosy red.

Yield: 4 cups

2 cups dried red bergamot flower petals

2 cups crushed, dried lemon verbena leaves

Combine the dried ingredients. Store in an airtight container.

Place 3 tablespoons of the tea blend in a paper coffee filter. Tie the filter with a string to form a bag. Place in a prewarmed teapot. Add 6 cups of boiling water. Cover the pot with a tea cozy, and let steep for 20 minutes.

Love of Lemon Tea Blend

This delicately scented tea is an Herb Society favorite.

Yield: 4¹/₂ cups

1 cup crushed lemon verbena leaves

1 cup crushed lemon balm leaves

1 cup crushed lemon-scented geranium leaves (such as Rober's Lemon Rose)

1 cup crushed lemon thyme leaves

3 tablespoons dried lemon rind pieces

1 generous tablespoon dried calendula petals

Combine the dried ingredients. Store in an airtight container.

Brew the tea as described in Good Bee Tea Blend above.

Apple-Cinnamint Tea Blend

Save apple peel from unwaxed red apples to dry for tea blends.

Yield: 4 cups

3 cups crushed, dried apple mint leaves

¹⁄₂ cup dried apple peel, broken into small pieces

¹⁄₂ cup coarsely cracked cinnamon sticks (about 4-inch sticks)

Combine the dried ingredients. Store in an airtight container.

Brew the tea as described in Good Bee Tea Blend on the opposite page.

Apple-Dazzle Cooler

This recipe makes herb tea extra festive.

Yield: 6 servings

4 cups brewed Apple-Cinnamint Tea Blend (above), cooled

1 cup apple cider or apple juice

1 cup sparkling water

Combine the ingredients and serve over ice.

Une Tisane Française Blend

The Western Reserve Herb Society has been creating this classic French blend since 1981.

Yield: 3¹⁄₂ cups

2 cups crushed, dried lemon balm leaves

1 cup crushed, dried mint leaves

¹⁄₂ cup dried lavender blossoms

Combine the dried ingredients. Store in an airtight container.

Brew the tea as described in Good Bee Tea Blend on the opposite page.

Cherry Juice

Sweet cherries make a rather bland juice, so add some sour cherry juice to this, if possible.

2 quarts cherries

Lemon juice

Honey

Extract the juice in a juicer or do it by hand as follows. Do not add any water unless the berries threaten to scorch. Just crush the berries in an enamel or stainless steel pot, and simmer them in their own juice, stirring occasionally, until they are soft. Strain by letting the liquid drip through a jelly bag or several thicknesses of cheesecloth for several hours, until the pulp releases no more liquid. Heat liquid to a simmer and add lemon juice and honey to taste.

To can: Pour the hot juice into hot, scalded jars, leaving ¼-inch headspace for half-pints and pints and ½-inch headspace for quarts. Seal and process pints and quarts in a boiling water bath for 5 minutes.

To freeze: Prepare the recipe as directed. Pour the juice into freezer containers, leaving ½-inch headspace, and freeze right away. To serve, thaw in the refrigerator.

Yield: 1 quart

Cranberry Juice

Cranberries make a delicious juice that doesn't need processing.

1 quart cranberries

4 cups water

Honey (optional)

In an enamel or stainless steel pot, combine the berries and water. Bring to a boil and cook until the berries burst. Strain through a jelly bag or several thicknesses of cheesecloth. Boil for 1 minute, and add honey, if desired.

To can: Pour the boiling juice into hot, scalded pint or quart jars, leaving ¼-inch headspace for pints and ½-inch headspace for quarts, and seal. No further processing is necessary.

To freeze: Prepare the recipe as directed. Pour the juice into freezer containers, leaving ½-inch headspace, and freeze right away. To serve, thaw in the refrigerator.

Yield: 1½ quarts

Grape Juice

You can use white or blue grapes, but blue grapes produce about twice as much juice as white grapes do.

7 cups seeded grapes

½ cup water

Honey (optional)

Extract the juice with a juicer or by hand as follows. Place the grapes in an enamel or stainless steel pot, and cover them with ½ cup boiling water (1 cup water for every 7 pounds grapes). Heat slowly to simmer and continue to simmer for 10 minutes, or until the fruit is very soft. Do not boil. Strain through a jelly bag or several thicknesses of cheesecloth. Refrigerate for 24 to 48 hours and then strain once more to remove any sediment that remains. (Tartaric acid in the grape juice gives the sediment a sharp, unpleasant taste.) Heat to a simmer, and add honey to taste, if desired.

To can: Pour the hot juice into hot, scalded jars, leaving ¼-inch headspace for pints and ½-inch headspace for quarts. Seal and process pints and quarts in a boiling-water bath for 5 minutes.

To freeze: Prepare the recipe as directed. Pour the juice into freezer containers, leaving ½-inch headspace, and freeze right away. To serve, thaw in the refrigerator.

Yield: 1½ quarts

Sparkling Honeydew Cooler

Serve in tall, chilled glasses garnished with mint as an after-dinner cooler.

2½ cups frozen honeydew melon chunks

¼ cup egg substitute

2 tablespoons heavy cream

2 cups sparkling water (or to taste)

1 tablespoon frozen orange juice concentrate

1 tablespoon honey

½ to 1 teaspoon ground nutmeg, to taste

Place the melon, egg substitute, cream, ½ cup of the water, orange juice concentrate, honey, and nutmeg in a blender or food processor. Process until smooth, stopping to scrape the sides of the container as necessary. Add the remaining sparkling water to taste.

VARIATION: Substitute 2½ cups frozen kiwi slices or cantaloupe chunks for the honeydew.

Yield: 4 servings

Kiwi Coolers

*Kiwis give this drink
an interesting
chartreuse color.*

Yield: 8 servings

9 kiwis

4 cups pineapple juice

8 ice cubes

2 cups sparkling water

8 large strawberries

Peel the kiwis and cut them into small pieces. Place half in a blender with half of the juice and half of the ice cubes. Blend until smooth. Stir in half of the sparkling water. Repeat with the remaining kiwis, juice, ice cubes, and sparkling water. Pour into tall glasses, and garnish each serving with a strawberry.

Tropical Eye-Opener

*You can make this
drink while you're
waiting for your toast
to pop up.*

Yield: 2 servings

1 large ripe mango

1 large, ripe banana, peeled
and sliced

Juice of 1 large pink
grapefruit

½ cup skim milk

1 tablespoon rolled oats

1 dried fig, chopped

Freshly grated nutmeg

Peel the mango over a bowl to catch the juices. Then use a paring knife to slice the flesh away from the stone. Transfer the flesh to a blender. Add the banana, grapefruit juice, skim milk, oats, and fig. Blend until smooth.

Pour into chilled glasses for breakfast or a refreshing snack. Dust with freshly grated nutmeg before serving.

Berry and Currant Juice

Use any berry except cranberries to combine with currants for a zesty fruit juice.

4 1/2 quarts fruit (the ratio of berries to currants depends on taste)

Lemon juice (optional)

Honey (optional)

Extract the juice with a juicer or do it by hand as follows. Crush the berries in an enamel or stainless steel pot, and simmer them in their own juice, stirring occasionally, until the berries are soft. Add a small amount of water only if the berries threaten to scorch. Strain by letting the liquid drip through a jelly bag or several thicknesses of cheesecloth for several hours, until the pulp releases no more liquid. Heat the liquid to a simmer, and add the lemon juice and honey to taste.

To can: Pour the hot juice into hot, scalded jars, leaving 1/4-inch headspace for half-pints and pints and 1/2-inch headspace for quarts. Seal and process the pints and quarts in a boiling-water bath for 30 minutes.

To freeze: Prepare the recipe as directed. Pour the juice into freezer containers, leaving 1/2-inch headspace, and freeze right away. To serve, thaw in the refrigerator.

Yield: 1 1/2 quarts

Fruit-Flavored Herb Teas

These herb teas, served hot or cold, are a healthful alternative to coffee and black tea. Try them all to find your favorite.

1/4 cup mashed bananas
1 drop mint extract
1 cup brewed aniseed tea

1/4 cup papaya juice
2 drops mint extract
1 cup brewed chamomile flower tea

1 teaspoon apricot syrup
1 drop almond extract
1 cup brewed fennel seed tea

2 tablespoons grape juice
1 thin slice lemon
1 cup brewed linden blossom tea

1/4 cup pineapple juice
Dash of ground nutmeg
1 cup brewed peppermint leaf tea

1 tablespoon lime juice
1 teaspoon honey
1 cup brewed sage leaf tea

1/4 cup apple juice
Dash of ground cinnamon
1 cup brewed spearmint leaf tea

Combine the fruit or juice with the flavoring, and add to the hot herb tea. Serve immediately, or cool and add ice.

Yield: 1 serving

Fruit Punch

This full-flavored punch is great for any get-together.

8 cups frozen strawberries, partially thawed

4 cups Peach-Berry Nectar (page 354), thawed

1¼ cups orange juice

½ cup lemon juice

1 cup diced pineapple, thawed if frozen

1⅓ cups water

⅔ cup honey

2 quarts sparkling water

In a blender, puree 6 cups of the strawberries until smooth. In a large bowl, stir together the strawberry puree, remaining strawberries, nectar, orange juice, lemon juice, and pineapple.

In a 1-quart saucepan, stir together the water and honey, and bring to a boil. Pour the honey water over the fruit mixture and stir. Just before serving, gently stir in the sparkling water.

Yield: 24 servings

Fruit Spritzers

A variety of fruit juices and berries make this a healthful way to quench your thirst.

1 cup frozen strawberries, raspberries, or sliced peaches, partially thawed

½ cup apple juice

½ cup orange or pineapple juice

2 ice cubes, cracked

½ to 1½ cups cold sparkling water

Thin lemon or orange slices

Place the fruit, apple juice, orange juice, and ice in a blender. Process on medium speed until smooth. Pour into a serving pitcher, and stir in the sparkling water, using as much as you wish to thin the drink. Serve in chilled glasses. Cut a slit halfway through each slice of lemon or orange, and slip it over the rim of the glass to garnish.

Yield: 4 servings

Anise-Spearmint Tea

Anise seeds give old-fashioned spearmint tea a new perspective.

Yield: 24 servings

1½ cups dried spearmint leaves

¼ cup anise seed

¼ cup coarsely chopped, dried lemon peel

Combine the herbs in a bowl and blend well. Store in an airtight container. To serve, put a tablespoon of the mix into a tea ball, and steep in 1 to 2 cups hot water until fragrant and flavorful.

Spiced Spearmint Tea

Spice up spearmint with cloves and cinnamon.

Yield: 24 servings

2 cups dried spearmint leaves

1 heaping tablespoon whole cloves

1 tablespoon cinnamon

Combine the herbs in a bowl and blend well. Store in an airtight container. To serve, put a tablespoon of the mix into a tea ball, and steep in 1 to 2 cups hot water until fragrant and flavorful.

Peach, Apricot, or Nectarine Nectar

This is a juicy puree instead of a clear juice.

3½ quarts fruit

3½ cups water

Extract juice with a juicer or by hand as follows. In an enamel or stainless steel pot, add 1 cup boiling water to each quart ripe, pitted peaches, apricots, or nectarines. Cook until the fruit is soft, and press it through a sieve or food mill. Reheat and add honey to taste, remembering that the juice can be diluted to taste later.

To can: Pour the hot nectar into hot, scalded jars, leaving ¼-inch headspace for half-pints and pints and ½-inch headspace for quarts. Seal and process half-pints and pints for 15 minutes in a boiling-water bath.

To freeze: Prepare the recipe as directed. Pour the nectar into freezer containers, leaving ½-inch headspace, and freeze right away. To serve, thaw in the refrigerator.

NOTE: *Although the nectar can be thinned with water to make juice, it's more convenient to can it as is and then thin it with ice water when you serve it.*

Yield: 4½ quarts

Peach-Berry Nectar

Eat this partially frozen on a hot day.

2 cups peaches

2¾ cups apple juice

1 cup strawberries or raspberries

Puree the peaches and ½ cup of the apple juice in a food processor or blender. Pour into a large bowl. Puree the strawberries and ¾ cup of the apple juice in the food processor or blender, strain the mixture to remove the seeds, and add to the peach puree. Stir the remaining apple juice into the fruit puree.

To freeze: Prepare the recipe as directed. Pour the nectar into freezer containers, leaving ½-inch headspace, and freeze right away. To serve, thaw in the refrigerator. The nectar is delicious while still partially frozen.

VARIATIONS: *Substitute apricots for the peaches and add another ½ cup apple juice.*
Use red- or golden-fleshed plums in place of peaches (other varieties will be unattractive).

Yield: 4 to 6 servings

Plum Juice

If you have a prolific plum tree, preserve some of your harvest as juice.

2 to 2½ quarts plums

Water

Honey (optional)

Extract the juice with a juicer or by hand as follows. In an enamel or stainless steel pot, put 1 cup of water for every cup of cut-up plums. Simmer for 10 to 15 minutes, or until the fruit is soft. Strain through a jelly bag or several thicknesses of cheesecloth. Heat to a simmer, and add honey to taste, if desired.

To can: Pour the hot juice into hot, scalded jars, leaving ¼-inch headspace for pints and ½-inch headspace for quarts. Process the pints and quarts for 5 minutes in a boiling-water bath.

To freeze: Prepare the recipe as directed. Pour the juice into freezer containers, leaving ½-inch headspace, and freeze right away. To serve, thaw in the refrigerator.

Yield: 1 quart

Raspberry Juleps

Raspberries and orange juice make a healthy julep.

¼ cup fresh mint leaves

¼ cup lemon juice

2 tablespoons honey

6 cups orange juice

1⅓ cups raspberry puree

In a blender, combine the mint, lemon juice, and honey. Puree until the mint is very finely chopped. Pour into a large pitcher. Stir in the orange juice and raspberry puree. Serve over ice.

NOTE: *When preparing these juleps, don't be tempted to blend the orange juice and raspberry puree in the blender, or the mixture will separate.*

Yield: 8 servings

Summer Drink on the Green

Try this on St. Patrick's Day.

Yield: 2 servings

½ cup apple juice

½ cup (packed) spinach leaves

1 banana

1 tablespoon sesame tahini

1 ice cube

Place all the ingredients in a blender and whip until frothy.

Tomato Juice Cocktail

For safety, this must be pressure-canned or frozen.

24 to 36 large, ripe tomatoes

4 medium carrots

2 large sweet green or red peppers

4 stalks celery, diced, leaves included

2 onions, diced

1 clove garlic, minced

¼ cup lemon juice

2 tablespoons honey (or to taste)

½ teaspoon freshly ground black pepper

2 bay leaves

2 sprigs fresh basil, dill, or thyme (optional)

Wash the tomatoes, cut out the ends, and chop into small pieces. Scrub and grate the carrots. Core, seed, and mince the peppers.

Combine all the ingredients in large enamel or stainless steel pot, and simmer over low heat for 45 to 50 minutes, stirring occasionally, until the vegetables are soft. Pick out the herbs. Strain the vegetables from the juice.

To can: Return the strained juice to the pot, and bring to a boil. Pour into hot, scalded quart jars, leaving ½-inch headspace. Seal and process for 30 minutes at 10 pounds pressure.

To freeze: Prepare the recipe as directed. Pour the juice into freezer containers, leaving ½-inch headspace, and freeze right away. To serve, thaw in the refrigerator.

Yield: 4 quarts

Tomato Juice

Sweet, ripe tomatoes will give your juice a delicious flavor. Add Italian plum tomatoes for a thicker juice.

Many people prefer the taste of juice made from tomatoes that are first pureed (raw) then strained, as in Method 1. The yield is a little less, but for small quantities, this method is practical. For large amounts of tomatoes, the second method is preferable even though it involves 2 heatings.

Method 1

15 to 20 medium tomatoes
8 teaspoons lemon juice

Wash the tomatoes and cut out the ends. Cut into chunks and puree in a food processor or blender, then strain through a fine sieve or food mill. Bring the juice to a boil. Add 4 teaspoons of the lemon juice to each quart and half that amount to each pint to raise the acid content.

To can: Pour the hot juice into hot, scalded jars, leaving $1/4$-inch headspace for pints and $1/2$-inch headspace for quarts. Seal and process the pints for 35 minutes and the quarts for 40 minutes in a boiling-water bath.

To freeze: Prepare the recipe as directed. Pour the juice into freezer containers, leaving $1/2$-inch headspace, and freeze right away. To serve, thaw in the refrigerator.

Method 2

15 to 20 medium tomatoes   8 teaspoons lemon juice
Spices or honey (optional)

Wash the tomatoes, cut out the ends, and chop. In an enamel or stainless steel pot, simmer slowly for 15 minutes, or until soft. Press through a fine sieve or food mill. Add spices (sprigs of parsley, dill, or basil, or $1/2$ teaspoon cinnamon and $1/4$ teaspoon nutmeg) or honey to taste, if desired. Add 4 teaspoons of the lemon juice to each quart and half that amount to each pint to raise the acid content.

To can: Reheat the juice to just below boiling and pour into hot, scalded jars, leaving $1/4$-inch headspace for pints and $1/2$-inch headspace for quarts. Seal and process the pints for 35 minutes and the quarts for 40 minutes in a boiling-water bath.

Yield: 2 quarts

To freeze: Prepare the recipe as directed. Freeze as for Method 1.

Spiced Tomato Juice

Give your tomato juice extra zip with this recipe.

12 to 16 medium tomatoes	1 stick of cinnamon
3/4 cup chopped onions	3 teaspoons honey
3 whole cloves	6 teaspoons lemon juice

Cook the tomatoes, onions, cloves, and cinnamon by Method 2 for Tomato Juice (page 357), and add 2 teaspoons of the honey and 4 teaspoons of the lemon juice to each quart and half those amounts to each pint before canning.

To can: Reheat the juice to just below boiling and pour into hot, scalded jars, leaving 1/4-inch headspace for pints and 1/2-inch headspace for quarts. Seal and process the pints for 35 minutes and the quarts for 40 minutes in a boiling-water bath.

To freeze: Prepare the recipe as directed. Pour the juice into freezer containers, leaving 1/2-inch headspace, and freeze right away. To serve, thaw in the refrigerator.

Yield: 3 pints

Spicy Hot Tomato Juice

This juice is particularly good if you add a dash of Worcestershire sauce and a spoonful of horseradish when serving.

12 to 16 medium tomatoes	2 fresh chili peppers, split and seeded
1 green pepper, chopped	6 teaspoons lemon juice
1 small onion, chopped	
3 cloves garlic, halved	

Cook the tomatoes, peppers, onions, garlic, and chili peppers by Method 2 for Tomato Juice (page 357). Add 4 teaspoons of the lemon juice to each quart and half that amount to each pint.

To can: Reheat the juice to just below boiling and pour into hot, scalded jars, leaving 1/4-inch headspace for pints and 1/2-inch headspace for quarts. Seal and process the pints for 35 minutes and the quarts for 40 minutes in a boiling-water bath.

To freeze: Prepare the recipe as directed. Pour the juice into freezer containers, leaving 1/2-inch headspace, and freeze right away. To serve, thaw in the refrigerator.

Yield: 3 pints

Recommended Reading

Ball Corporation. *Ball Blue Book.* 32nd ed. Muncie, Ind.: Ball Corporation, 1991.

Chioffi, Nancy, and Gretchen Mead. *Keeping the Harvest.* Rev. ed. Pownal, Vt.: Garden Way Publishing, 1991.

Greene, Janet, Ruth Hertzberg, and Beatrice Vaughan. *Putting Food By.* New York: NAL/Dutton, 1993.

Hupping, Carol, et al. *Stocking Up III.* Emmaus, Pa.: Rodale Press, 1986.

Hurley, Judith Benn. *Rodale's Garden-Fresh Cooking.* Emmaus, Pa.: Rodale Press, 1987.

Pennington, Jean A. T. *Food Values of Portions Commonly Used.* 15th ed. New York: HarperCollins Publishers, 1989.

Prevention magazine editors. *The Healing Foods Cookbook.* Emmaus, Pa.: Rodale Press, 1991.

Reynolds, Susan, and Paulette Williams Ybarra. *So Easy to Preserve.* Athens, Ga.: Cooperative Extension Service, University of Georgia, 1986.

Rogers, Jean, ed. *Prevention's Quick and Healthy Low-Fat Cooking.* Emmaus, Pa.: Rodale Press, 1993.

Rosensweig, Linda, et al. *New Vegetarian Cuisine.* Emmaus, Pa.: Rodale Press, 1994.

Shepherd, Renee, and Fran Raboff. *Recipes from a Kitchen Garden.* Vol. II. Felton, Calif.: Shepherd's Garden Publishers, 1990.

United States Department of Agriculture Staff. *Complete Guide to Home Canning, Preserving, and Freezing.* Rev. ed. New York: Dover Publications, 1994.

Western Reserve Herb Society Staff. *Cooking with Herb Scents.* Donna D. Agan, ed. Cleveland, Ohio: Western Reserve Herb Society, 1991.

Whealy, Kent, ed. *Garden Seed Inventory.* 3rd ed. Decorah, Iowa: Seed Saver Publications, 1992.

Whealy, Kent, and Steve Demuth, eds. *Fruit, Berry and Nut Inventory.* 2nd ed. Decorah, Iowa: Seed Saver Publications, 1993.

Wolf, Ray, ed. *Managing Your Personal Food Supply.* Emmaus, Pa.: Rodale Press, 1977.

Index